CW00431471

A Taste *of* Scotland 2002

**THE GUIDE TO THE BEST PLACES TO EAT
AND STAY IN SCOTLAND**

welcome
to the guide

A very warm welcome to the 2002 Taste of Scotland Guide.

Each year, life at Taste of Scotland just gets more and more interesting and the past 12 months have certainly been no exception.

Most significantly, Taste of Scotland has been appointed to implement the new VisitScotland Food Quality Assurance Scheme – watch out for more details in late summer 2002.

In the meantime, our research confirmed a resounding 'thumbs up' from readers to the changes we introduced in the 2001 Guide – such as more colour – and prompted useful new suggestions, many of which we have implemented this year.

We are proud to have forged new partnerships with the organisers of many of the Food Festivals and Farmers Markets which are run across the country.

We re-launched the Natural Cooking of Scotland initiative, for which we have been appointed Co-ordinators, at the Skye and Lochalsh Food Festival. You can read more about the initiative on the VisitScotland pages.

It is a pleasure to work with so many excellent Scottish companies who continue to support Taste of Scotland and our commitment to good food.

As ever please do keep us informed of your views – by e-mail, postcard or letter – because they are immensely valuable to us.

Finally a big thank you to all our Taste of Scotland quality advisors who literally eat their way round Scotland – all in a good cause – to ensure the rest of us enjoy good food and a warm welcome when we follow in their footsteps.

Amanda J Clark
Chief Executive

Credits

Editorial
Amanda Clark, Angela Nealon, Tracey Brown, Wendy Barrie,
Emma Macdonald, Julie Hill

Published by
Taste of Scotland Limited, 33 Melville Street, Edinburgh EH3 7JF
Telephone 0131 220 1900   Fax 0131 220 6102
www.taste-of-scotland.com   e-mail tastescotland@sol.co.uk
A non-profit making company limited by guarantee trading as Taste of Scotland

Design, Illustration and Typesetting
Frame Creative, Edinburgh
Jim Middleton (Editorial), David Healy (Senior Designer),
Euan Davidson (Production Manager)

Printed by
Scotprint, Haddington, East Lothian

Corporate Sales and Marketing, Sponsorship
Classic Concepts, Edinburgh
Susan Ireland, Kareen Lee, Mike Marley

Trade Board Members
Laurie Black, Chairman Taste of Scotland Board, Fouters Bistro, Ayr
Annie Paul, Taychreggan Hotel   David Wilson, The Peat Inn
Nick Nairn, Nairns   Brian Simpson, Scottish Quality
                        Salmon

Taste of Scotland is grateful for the continued support of
VisitScotland   Scottish Quality Salmon
Scottish Tourism Forum   Scottish Enterprise
Scotland the Brand   Highlands & Islands Enterprise
Dorling Kindersley

And all our corporate partners
Alexander Wines, Anta, Baxters of Speyside, Brodies, Highlands &
Islands Enterprise, Historic Scotland, McLelland Cheese, The
Macallan, Mackie's, National Trust for Scotland, Skye & Lochalsh
Enterprise, Walkers Shortbread, Lloyds TSB and Virgin

Cover photography
Glendale Herbs   Isle of Skye Black Face Lamb
Wendy Barrie   Graham Lees Photography

With thanks to photographers
Renzo Mazzolini   White House Studios

Thanks also to   Express Media
                        Carole Inglis

Contents

the macallan
awards

The 2001 Winners of the Macallan Taste of Scotland Awards are:

COMMENDED ESTABLISHMENTS SHORTLISTED

BED AND BREAKFAST

- Kilmeny Country Guest House, Isle of Islay
- East Lochhead, Lochwinnoch, Glasgow (Outskirts)

LIGHT BITE

- Storehouse of Foulis, Evanton
- Pollok House, Glasgow

OUT OF TOWN RESTAURANT

- Ivy House, Ayr
- Old Bakehouse, West Linton

COUNTRY HOUSE

- Airds Hotel, Appin
- Shieldhill, Biggar

RESTAURANT

- 11 Park Avenue, Carnoustie
- 63 Tay Street, Perth

BEST NEWCOMER

- Airds Hotel, Appin
- Ivy House, Ayr
- Old Bakehouse, West Linton
- Storehouse of Foulis, Evanton

OVERALL EXCELLENCE AWARD

- Kinloch House, Blairgowrie
  listed on page 42

BED AND BREAKFAST AWARD

- Craigadam, Castle Douglas
  listed on page 48

LIGHT BITE AWARD

- Coach House, Luss, Loch Lomond
  listed on page 158

OUT OF TOWN RESTAURANT AWARD

- Monachyle Mhor, Balquhidder
  listed on page 35

COUNTRY HOUSE AWARD

- Kinloch House, Blairgowrie
  listed on page 42

RESTAURANT AWARD

- The Witchery by the Castle, Edinburgh listed on page 79

BEST NEWCOMER AWARD

- 63 Tay Street, Perth
  listed on page 180

NOW IN THEIR 14TH YEAR, these Awards were set up to encourage the pursuit of excellence and, by so doing, encourage others to emulate the winners. This ethos remains unchanged – with public nominations being the starting point, inspectors' nominations follow and then each shortlisted establishment is further judged by an expert panel. All the establishments listed here have consistently demonstrated their commitment to excellence.

The Macallan Single Malt is renowned for its unique character and unrivalled quality and as such makes a perfect partner for these Awards. This partnership certainly captures the imagination of the public as every year a record number of nominations are received.

The Awards are restricted to establishments which are listed in the previous Taste of Scotland Guide and thus are already highlighted as leaders in their specific category.

This year, once again, the judging for the Awards was an exceptionally difficult task with nominations coming in from all areas and for all types of establishments. It is particularly heartening that the standards encountered across Scotland are continually rising, resulting in a growing number of eligible contenders.

We again invite Taste of Scotland customers to nominate establishments in which you have received outstanding experiences this year. In addition, Taste of Scotland Quality Advisors are being asked to nominate their favourite places throughout the inspection season. Please use the feedback forms towards the back of this Guide to forward your nominations for The Macallan Taste of Scotland Awards 2002. Letters and postcards are also welcome and taken into consideration.

Simply nominate an establishment which has impressed you greatly, tell us why and leave the rest to us. Closing date for entries – 30 June 2002.

The 2001 Winners are highlighted in the listings with this symbol:

The taste
of success

THE ENTERTAINMENT world can drool as much as it likes over its Oscars, Emmys and Grammies – winning a 'Tasty' is really something to shout about!

Over the years, a Taste of Scotland Award has come to be regarded as one of the most prestigious prizes in the country's hospitality industry.

As you will read over the next few pages, becoming a member of the Taste of Scotland Scheme is quite an achievement in itself. Membership is granted only after rigorous inspection by our Quality Advisors.

To take one of our category awards singles out an establishment as something rather exceptional.

Keith and Nicola Braidwood, winners of the 2000 Overall Excellence Award.

Our Overall Excellence Award only finds its way to those whose establishments combine all the qualities we look for in a dining experience – and then some.

As you can see from the list of previous winners, it's not just a question of size, although several of our large hotels have rightly taken the top honours over the years.

Last year, the Overall Excellence Award went to one of our smaller establishments, Braidwoods in Dalry.

Keith and Nicola Braidwood had already made their mark by winning a Special Merit for Newcomers Award in 1995, shortly after they opened their two-roomed restaurant, a converted miller's cottage deep in the heart of the Ayrshire countryside.

Having already won an enviable reputation for quality among their customers, it would have been difficult for them to get any busier.

But the Taste of Scotland Award for Overall Excellence was a validation of all the hard work they had done to build their business and justified their insistence on the highest standards of service and quality.

The previous year's award had gone to Shirley and Eddie Spear who run the Three Chimneys Restaurant in Skye.

When they joined the Taste of Scotland Scheme in 1985, there were those who doubted the wisdom of setting up their kind of business in such a remote corner of the country.

But, as Shirley says: 'We're not trying to recreate a London restaurant

THE MACALLAN TASTE OF SCOTLAND AWARDS – ROLL OF HONOUR
Past winners of these prestigious awards:

- Auchendean Lodge Hotel, Dulnain Bridge
- Auchterarder House, Auchterarder
- Ballathie Country House Hotel, Kinclaven, nr Perth
- Braidwoods, Dalry
- Cosses Country House, Ballantrae
- Creel Restaurant with Rooms, Isle of Orkney
- Crinan Hotel, Crinan
- East Haugh Country House Hotel, Pitlochry
- Gordon's Restaurant, Inverkeilor
- Greywalls, Gullane
- Kilmichael Country House Hotel, Isle of Arran
- Kind Kyttocks Tearoom, Falkland
- Kinloch Lodge, Isle of Skye
- Knockinaam Lodge, Portpatrick
- Let's Eat, Perth
- Livingston's Restaurant, Glasgow
- No.1 Princes Street, The Balmoral Hotel, Edinburgh
- Old Pines Restaurant with Rooms, Spean Bridge
- Stravaigin, Glasgow
- The Albannach, Lochinver
- The Old Smiddy Guest House, Laide
- The Wheatsheaf Hotel, Swinton
- Three Chimneys Restaurant and the House Over-By, Isle of Skye
- Turnberry Hotel, Turnberry
- Ubiquitous Chip, Glasgow

Skye's The Three Chimneys, run by Shirley and Eddie Spear.

in the middle of the Scottish Highlands. What we have here is a traditional crofters cottage and there's no point in trying to turn it into something it was never meant to be.

'At first it could be difficult to get supplies locally but there's so much more now. One of the nicest things is being able to use fresh seafood that is fished in these waters – this is where it's best and this is where it's best eaten.'

At the time of winning the award, the Three Chimneys had just been expanded to become a restaurant with rooms by taking in the House Overby. The press coverage of the awards couldn't have come at a better time for the Spears.

All Taste of Scotland establishments are special. Once you have visited a few, you'll begin to appreciate what a difficult job the awards judges have.

Of course, you can help them in their deliberations by telling us about your dining experiences and where you think the next awards should go.

'To travel hopefully is a better thing than to arrive …'
Robert Louis Stevenson

star grading
by VisitScotland

WHEN ROBERT LOUIS Stevenson penned that memorable aphorism towards the end of the 19th century, he probably had a fair point.

If he were travelling today, however, at the dawn of the 21st century, he would almost certainly be more enthusiastic about arriving because he would have a much clearer idea of what to expect at the end of his day's journey.

And the reason is that he would be able to make full use of the unique star grading system operated by VisitScotland.

Whether, like old RLS, you're travelling by donkey or by some more comfortable method of transportation,

How grading works

The VisitScotland star grading scheme is based on quality. Whether you're looking at a remote bed & breakfast with only a couple of rooms or a huge city centre hotel, the same criteria apply:

★★★★★ Exceptional, world class
★★★★ Excellent
★★★ Very good
★★ Good
★ Fair and acceptable

Natural Cooking of Scotland

Think fresh, think simple, think Scottish – the message behind the Natural Cooking of Scotland initiative couldn't be more straightforward.

It's one of the most heartening and ambitious projects ever devised to improve the quality of eating out in Scotland. Given that cooking is an intrinsic part of Scottish culture, the experience of eating should be wholesome and memorable.

The Natural Cooking of Scotland awareness roadshow is spreading the word that, by using fresh local produce, caterers can provide what the customer really wants at an economical price.

To help caterers source good quality local produce, the initiative also sets up links to local suppliers.

It's all part of a national commitment to raising the standard of the Scottish visitor experience.

Natural Cooking of Scotland initiative is supported by Scottish Tourist Board/visitscotland, Scottish Enterprise and Highlands and Islands Enterprise.

the scheme provides a fast, accurate guide to what you can expect from an establishment.

The whole system is based on quality – it's not just a checklist of facilities – and has been devised by taking the customer's point of view.

Each establishment is rigorously assessed on quality: the quality of the welcome, the service, the food, the hospitality, ambience and the comfort and condition of the property.

These are the factors which are taken into account, not the size of the accommodation or the range of facilities it has, when VisitScotland determines how many stars are to be allocated.

The scheme is supported by a team of trained quality advisors whose task it is to grade each property each year.

To help make your choices even more informed, the VisitScotland

FOOD MATTERS – TO ALL OF US

Your interest in food – what you eat, how you eat it and where you eat it – may range from keen interest to mild obsession.

The fact that you're reading this Guide, however, puts you among the growing ranks of people who really care about food.

system also gives you information about the type of accommodation you'll find when you arrive.

The range of accommodation types included in this Guide are: Guest House, Bed & Breakfast, Hotel, Small Hotel, International Resort Hotel, Inn, Restaurant with Rooms.

All the current star ratings are included in each Taste of Scotland entry, where applicable.

When the star grading system was being drawn up, one of the prime motivations was to make the scheme as user-friendly as possible for the traveller.

User-friendly is not a term you're likely to find in any of Robert Louis Stevenson's books but it's a concept we can be fairly sure he'd approve of!

As you wander through these pages – and through the doors of the establishments themselves – you'll encounter dazzling varieties of food and diverse styles of cooking.

But wherever you choose to dine, you can be sure that the establishment has met the high standards required by Taste of Scotland, and that those standards have been thoroughly checked and approved by our team of inspectors.

Each member of the team has a qualification relating to food and cooking and they use this specialist expertise in their incognito assessments of current and prospective members of the Taste of Scotland Scheme.

What the inspectors do, in effect, is put themselves in your shoes. They are just like any other customers, only qualified!

They also play a part, together with you the customer, in choosing who wins the coveted Taste of Scotland Awards each year.

How to use this guide

All establishments listed in this Guide have exceeded an inspection conducted by a fully qualified Taste of Scotland Inspector. They are listed in alphabetical order under the nearest town or village. Island entries are shown under I for Isle. A full list of members is in the alphabetical index at the rear of the Guide or look at the fold-out map to see the locations of all Taste of Scotland establishments.

All the information included in the entry is accurate at time of printing – however we do urge customers to call and verify prices and opening times prior to setting off on a journey. Often seasonal variations may result in information included in the entry changing at short notice and a call will avoid disappointment.

Prices for accommodation are per person sharing a room and a guideline only. For single rates and special rates please call the establishment and verify these in advance.

At time of going to press the most up to date Scottish Tourist Board star ratings information available is included in the entry.

Visitor attractions are also graded by stars for the standard of customer care they provide – welcome, hospitality, service, and how the attraction itself is presented. Establishments with a concern for the environment take part in the Board's Green Tourism Business Scheme and their efforts are graded either Bronze, Silver or Gold.

We always welcome feedback on Taste of Scotland, both in using this Guide and the dining experience – please keep us informed.

MEAL PRICES

£ symbols indicate the price category which the establishment has told us they fall into. They are:

£	=	up to £10 per person
££	=	£11–£20 per person
£££	=	£21–£30 per person
££££	=	over £30 per person

◗	*Opening arrangements*
🏠	*Number of rooms*
🛏	*Accommodation rates*
SP	*Special rates available*
★	*Scottish Tourist Board star rating*
♟	*Licensing information*
UL	*Unlicensed*
✕	*Information on meals*
P	*Parking arrangements*
V	*Vegetarians welcome*
⚹	*Children welcome*
♿	*Facilities for disabled visitors*
✂	*Restrictions on smoking*
🐾	*Information on pets*
💳	*Credit cards accepted*
🍴	*Owner/Proprietor/Manager/ Chef*

THE TASTE OF SCOTLAND
2002

This is to certify that

Chirnside Hall Country House Hotel

has been selected for membership of

The Taste of Scotland Scheme

in recognition of its commitment to the pursuit of excellence in food preparation and service

Taste of Scotland current members are identified by the 2002 Certificate of Membership (above) which should be prominently displayed.

Town or Village

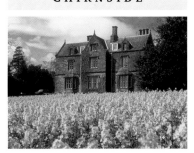

CHIRNSIDE

Establishment   **Chirnside Hall Country House Hotel**

Inspector's 2002 comment
- *"The Dutch owners' love of all things Scottish is very apparent on a visit to Chirnside Hall. Warm hospitality and good food awaits you."*

Style of cooking
- *Modern Scottish.*

Description

CHIRNSIDE HALL is a delightful country house full of original features which has been sensitively refurbished in recent years. The proprietors, Christian and Tessa Korsten, are very helpful and friendly. Cooking here is of a very high standard with interesting menus – only the best of locally sourced ingredients is used.

Menu specialities

Warm tartlet of smoked salmon and leeks, with a grain mustard sauce. Roast loin of lamb with skirlie and black pudding. Iced chocolate parfait with orange compote.

STB Rating   **STB ★★★★ Small Hotel**

Facilities and services

◗ *Open all year* 🏨 *Rooms: 10 en suite* 🛏 *DB&B £62.50–£80 B&B £50–£70* 🆂🅿 *Special rates available* ✗ *Light snack lunch – for residents Dinner £££* Ⓥ *Vegetarians welcome* ⚥ *Children welcome* ✌ *No smoking in dining room* 🐕 *Dogs welcome* 🆔 *Mastercard/Eurocard, Visa, Switch* 🅜 *Proprietors: Christian & Tessa Korsten*

Address
Contact details

Chirnside nr Duns Berwickshire TD11 3LD
Tel: 01890 818219 Fax: 01890 818231
E-mail: chirnsidehall@globalnet.co.uk
Web: www.chirnsidehallhotel.com

How to get there

Between Chirnside and Foulden on the A6105, 1 mile east of Chirnside.

Map reference

[D6]

ABERDEEN

The Allan

- *"A friendly guest house where nothing is too much trouble for hosts Liz and Brian."*
- *Modern Scottish cooking.*

THIS IS a homely guest house, run by Liz and Brian Taylor, where guests are warmly welcomed. It is very well-appointed and food is freshly prepared to order. Menus are a blend of the best of traditional with a modern twist, offering guests a varied choice. A suitable venue for families, holidaymakers or business guests.

Finnan Haddie tartlet. Grampian chicken, combined with chorizo sausage, pan-fried new potatoes and wilted wild rocket – continuing the East meets West theme. Clootie dumpling with boozy raisins and whisky cream custard with home-made tablet.

STB ★★★★ Guest House

◐ *Open all year* 🏠 *Rooms: 7 (6 en-suite, 1 private bathroom)* 🍴 *DB&B £38.50–£58.50 B&B £28–£48* ✖ *Residents only Packed lunches by arrangement £ Dinner by arrangement ££* Ⓥ *Vegetarians welcome Gluten-free and dairy-free diets catered for* ☽ *Children welcome* 🖰 *Mastercard/Eurocard, Visa, Delta* 🅽 *Owners: Brian & Liz Taylor*

56 Polmuir Road Aberdeen AB11 7RT
Tel: 01224 584484 Fax: 01224 595988
E-mail: allaninfo@camtay.co.uk
Web: www.camtay.co.uk
Polmuir Road is a T junction to Murray Terrace which is off Great Southern Road. [D4]

ABERDEEN

Ardoe House Hotel

- *"Enjoy life in the grand style. Good food, excellent accommodation and leisure facilities – spoil yourself!"*
- *Modern and traditional Scottish cuisine.*

ARDOE HOUSE is a classic Scots baronial granite mansion with full leisure facilities. Dining is à la carte, from an extensive menu of unusually treated dishes and imaginative combinations, or table d'hôte. Chef Ivor Clark draws inspiration from classic French cooking, whilst using fresh Scottish produce. Full leisure facilities.

Marinated fillet of sea bass with pickled vegetables, served with a seed mustard and herb dressing. Roast loin of lamb, with black pudding and leek cake, served with a port and rosemary jus. Warm oat and orange tart with a butterscotch sauce and cinnamon ice cream.

STB ★★★★ Hotel

◐ *Open all year* 🏠 *Rooms: 112 en suite* 🍴 *DB&B from £70 B&B from £47.50* 🆂 *Special rates available* ✖ *Food available all day £££ Lunch ££ Dinner £££* Ⓥ *Vegetarians welcome* ☽ *Children welcome* ♿ *Facilities for disabled* ✖ *No smoking in dining room* 🖰 *Mastercard/Eurocard, American Express, Visa, Diners Club, Switch* 🅽 *General Manager: Andy Burgess*

South Deeside Road Aberdeen AB12 5YP
Tel: 01224 860600 Fax: 01224 861283
E-mail: ardoe@macdonald-hotels.co.uk
Web: www.macdonald-hotels.co.uk
B9077, 3 miles west of Aberdeen. Turn left at hotel sign and up driveway.[D4]

ABERDEEN

Atholl Hotel

- *"One can always rely on the Atholl for good food and great service whether on business, on holiday or just meeting friends."*
- *Traditional Scottish cooking.*

THE ATHOLL HOTEL is under the personal supervision of Gordon Sinclair. The hotel has a comfortable and warm atmosphere. The cooking is simple and straightforward with high quality ingredients and there is much evidence of local quality produce. Menus change monthly with specials changing nightly depending upon availability.

Queen scallop pâté with chive scented jus. Halibut en croute: fresh halibut fillet with spring onion and soft cheese baked in puff pastry, with a lemon and lime sauce. Raspberry royale: fresh raspberries, cream topped with toasted oatmeal.

STB ★★★★ Hotel

◐ *Open all year except New Year's Day* 🏨 *Rooms: 35 en suite* 🛏 *B&B £72–£95* 🆘 *Special rates available* ✗ *Lunch ££ Dinner ££* Ⓥ *Vegetarians welcome* ✸ *Children welcome* 🎫 *Mastercard/Eurocard, American Express, Visa, Diners Club, Switch* 🅽 *Managing Partner: Gordon Sinclair*

54 Kings Gate Aberdeen AB15 4YN
Tel: 01224 323505 Fax: 01224 321555
E-mail: info@atholl-aberdeen.co.uk
Web: www.atholl-aberdeen.com
Follow signs for A96 north. Turn right at King's Gate roundabout, the hotel is situated ½ mile along King's Gate in the heart of the city's West End. [D4]

ABERDEEN

Craiglynn Hotel

- *"A most genteel place, warm and welcoming with good home cooking."*
- *Lovingly prepared Scottish cooking.*

CRAIGLYNN HOTEL is an impressive house, with many of its original features preserved. Service is friendly and attentive, where guests are welcomed like part of the family. The dining room menus are short, since everything is prepared from fresh local produce. Bedrooms are very comfortable and have unique en suite facilities.

Cream of watercress soup. Thinly sliced medallions of pork finished in white wine, shallots and cream. Apple and bramble crumble.

STB ★★★★ Small Hotel

◐ *Open all year except Christmas Day and Boxing Day* 🏨 *Rooms: 8 en suite* 🛏 *B&B £30–£40 per person sharing double/twin room* 🍷 *Restricted licence* ✗ *Non-residents – by reservation Dinner ££* Ⓥ *Vegetarians welcome* ✂ *No smoking in dining room and bedrooms* 🎫 *Mastercard/Eurocard, American Express, Visa, Diners Club, Switch, JCB, Solo* 🅽 *Partners: Hazel & Chris Mann*

36 Fonthill Road Aberdeen AB11 6UJ
Tel: 01224 584050 Fax: 01224 212225
E-mail: info@craiglynn.co.uk
Web: www.craiglynn.co.uk
On corner of Fonthill Road and Bon Accord Street, midway between Union Street and King George VI Bridge. Car park access from Bon Accord Street.[D4]

ABERDEEN

Lairhillock Inn & Crynoch Restaurant at Lairhillock

- *"History, atmosphere and good food combine to make a memorable meal."*
- *Modern cooking with continental influences.*

ROGER THORNE is maintaining the Lairhillock's tradition of good food and lively atmosphere. The award-winning Crynoch Restaurant offers fine dining using only the best local ingredients and is surrounded by some wonderful antique furnishings. In the original inn meals are both substantial and enjoyable.

Inn: Chunky seafood chowder. Braised lamb shank set on mashed potatoes, red wine, rosemary and root vegetable sauce. Clootie dumpling.

❶ *Open all year except Christmas Day, Boxing Day, and 1, 2 Jan Crynoch Restaurant closed Tue* ✗ *Lunch (Inn) £ (Crynoch Rest) Sun ££ Dinner (Inn) ££ (Crynoch Rest) except Tue £££* 🅥 *Vegetarians welcome* ✹ *Children welcome* ♿ *Facilities for disabled visitors* ✽ *No smoking in the Conservatory* 🐕 *Dogs welcome in Snug Bar* 💳 *Mastercard/Eurocard, American Express, Visa, Diners Club, Switch, Delta* 🔲 *Proprietors: Roger Thorne & Angela Maddox*

Netherley, by Stonehaven Aberdeenshire AB39 3QS
Tel: 01569 730001 Fax: 01569 731175
E-mail: lairhillock@breathemail.net
Web: www.lairhillock.co.uk
From Aberdeen take A90 to Stonehaven. After 6 miles take the Durris road – second right after Portleithen. Drive for 4 miles along this road. From the south, once on straight after Cammachmore, turn left at the Durris junction. [D4]

ABERDEEN

The Marcliffe at Pitfodels

- *"A stunning place to stay with good food and lovely staff to look after you."*
- *Modern classic cooking with French influence.*

THE MARCLIFFE AT PITFODELS' atmosphere is luxurious, and enhances modern design with antiques and baronial detailing. The attention given to guests is superb. In the Conservatory the dining experience is well-balanced and extensive; and the cooking is accomplished.

Fresh lobster is available all year round. 100 malt whiskies and 300 wines available. Wild mushroom risotto with medallions of lobster and monkfish. Seared venison with cauliflower purée, gratin potatoes, spinach parcels. Whisky ice cream with figs in balsamic.

STB ★★★★★ Hotel

❶ *Open all year* 🛏 *Rooms: 34 en suite, 4 suites* 🛏 *DB&B £82.50–£150 B&B £52.50–£125* 🆂🅿 *Special rates available* ✗ *Lunch £££ Dinner £££* 🅥 *Vegetarians welcome* ✹ *Children welcome* ♿ *Facilities for disabled visitors* 💳 *Mastercard/Eurocard, American Express, Visa, Diners Club, Switch* 🔲 *Proprietor: Stewart Spence*

North Deeside Road Aberdeen AB15 9YA
Tel: 01224 861000 Fax: 01224 868860
E-mail: reservations@marcliffe.com
Web: www.marcliffe.com
On A93 to Braemar. 1 mile from A92. 3 miles from city centre.[D4]

ABERDEEN

Norwood Hall Hotel

- *"Enjoy the baronial-style for a wedding, a business meeting or simply fine dinning – Norwood has it all!"*
- *Modern Scottish with international influences.*

THIS VICTORIAN mansion house hotel has been sympathetically restored to its former glory. It is run by a professional and dedicated team who offer true Scottish hospitality, together with the best of local produce. Food is attractively presented in the Victorian dining room and flavours do not disappoint. Less formal bar meals also available.

Woodland mushrooms cooked in Madeira and served in a warm brioche bun topped with poached egg. Noisette of lamb topped with a maize-fed chicken mousseline, set on a carrot dauphinoise with a tarragon sauce. Strawberry and green peppercorn mousse served with warm peppered strawberries.

STB ★★★★ Hotel

◗ *Open all year* 🏠 *Rooms: 21 en suite* 🛏 *DB&B £70–£102 B&B £50–£82* 💷 *Special rates available* ✗ *Lunch from ££ Dinner £££* Ⓥ *Vegetarians welcome* ⚘ *Children welcome* ♿ *Facilities for disabled visitors* ✄ *No smoking in dining room* 💳 *Mastercard/Eurocard, American Express, Visa, Diners Club, Switch, Delta* 🔪 *General Manager: Morag MacIndoe*

Garthdee Road Cults Aberdeen AB15 9FX Tel: 01224 868951 Fax: 01224 869868 E-mail: info@norwood-hall.co.uk Web: www.norwood-hall.co.uk 1 mile from the Bridge of Dee roundabout off the A90 and the A96.[D4]

ABERDEEN

Simpson's Hotel Bar/Brasserie

- *"Simpson's is a touch of the Mediterranean in the granite city – where you can enjoy good food and comfortable surroundings."*
- *Modern Scottish cuisine with international influences.*

MUCH OF Simpson's designer furniture and tiles come from Spain. The rich colour schemes of the vaulted ceiling restaurant extend to the sophisticated hotel; even the courtyard has a Mediterranean feel. Head chef Graham Mutch mixes traditional and original in innovative recipes using the best of Aberdeenshire products.

Highland haggis and Orkney smoked cheese croquettes with a beetroot and red onion chutney. Half rack of lamb with Dornoch black pudding mash and red wine jus. Sherry trifle crème brûlée.

STB ★★★★ Hotel

◗ *Open all year* 🏠 *Rooms: 50 en suite* 🛏 *B&B £105–£140* 💷 *Special rates available* ✗ *Lunch ££ Dinner £££* Ⓥ *Vegetarians welcome* ⚘ *Children welcome* ♿ *Facilities for disabled visitors* ✄ *Rooms non smoking. Smoking area in Restaurant* 💳 *Mastercard/Eurocard, American Express, Visa, Switch, Delta* 🔪 *General Manager: Shona Stewart*

59 Queens Road Aberdeen AB15 4YP Tel: 01224 327777 Fax: 01224 327700 E-mail: address@simpsonshotel.co.uk Follow signs for A96 North. Turn right at Queens Road Roundabout, hotel is 500 yards down the road on right-hand side. [D4]

ABERDEEN

The Victoria Restaurant

- *"A friendly tea room well worth a visit for a snack lunch or delicious coffee and home bakes."*
- *Quality home baking, snacks and light lunches.*

THE VICTORIA has been a restaurant for over 50 years and is now owned by Gillian and Gordon Harold. Gillian is head chef and Gordon is in charge of the front of house. There is an evident commitment to quality with highly visible sourcing of Scottish produce and skilful cooking.

Home-made bread topped with Scottish Brie, baked in the oven and served with Gillian's apple chutney. Baked apple crêpe with butterscotch sauce and local ice cream. Traditional afternoon tea with fresh cream scones, cakes and cookies.

◑ *Open all year except 2 weeks Jan Closed local holidays, Christmas and New Year Closed Sun* ✗ *Food available all day except Sun £ Lunch except Sun £* Ⓥ *Vegetarians welcome* ✳ *Children welcome* ✦ *No smoking in restaurant* 🕮 *Mastercard/Eurocard, Visa, Switch, Delta* 🕅 *Proprietors: Gillian & Gordon Harold*

140 Union Street Aberdeen AB10 1JD
Tel: 01224 621381
In the middle of the main street, on the first floor above Jamieson and Carry the Jewellers.[D4]

ACHILTIBUIE

Summer Isles Hotel

- *"Creative and wholesome fresh dishes appear on the daily changing restaurant menu."*
- *Innovative modern Scottish cooking.*

THE SUMMER ISLES HOTEL commands spectacular views out to the Summer Isles. The award-winning chef Chris Firth-Bernard creates wonderful dishes from the freshest of seafood and Highland beef and game. All this and a wine list of over 400 bins. A must for the traveller who likes to relax within comfortable surroundings.

Warm mousse of Tanera Bay scallops with mussels and saffron. Pan-fried fillet of Black Isle lamb served on a courgette and potato rösti with lemon thyme. Summer fruit meringue roulade with treacle and Drambuie ice box pudding.

STB ★★★★ Small Hotel

◑ *Open Easter to mid Oct* 🏠 *Rooms: 13, 12 with en suite facilities (plus log cabins adjacent to hotel)* 🛏 *DB&B £79–£110 B&B £44–£75* ✗ *Food available all day £ Lunch £££ Dinner ££££* Ⓥ *Vegetarians welcome* ✳ *Children welcome* ✦ *No smoking in restaurant and bedrooms* 🕮 *Mastercard/Eurocard, Visa, Switch* 🕅 *Proprietors: Mark & Gerry Irvine*

Achiltibuie Ross-shire IV26 2YG
Tel: 01854 622282 Fax: 01854 622251
E-mail: summerisleshotel@aol.com
Web: www.summerisleshotel.co.uk
A835 to Ullapool and beyond – 10 miles north of Ullapool turn left onto single track road to Achiltibuie. Village is 15 miles on (i.e. 25 miles from Ullapool).[B3]

AIRTH, BY FALKIRK

Radisson SAS Airth Castle Hotel

- *"Airth Castle is ideally situated for business needs, conferences, and romantic breaks."*
- *Modern Scottish cooking.*

AIRTH CASTLE HOTEL offers dining in two different styles. The castle provides formal dining in elegant surroundings. The conservatory restaurant, within a large glass pyramid, offers brasserie-style dining to the same high standards. The leisure facilities here are excellent and children are well-catered for.

Hot oak smoked trout with braised chicory and tomato dressing. Noisettes of Ayrshire lamb baked in a herb crust, garlic and sautéed artichokes with cognac jus. Cinnamon poached pear with butterscotch ice cream and Drambuie sabayon.

STB ★★★★ Hotel

◗ *Open all year Castle Restaurant closed Sun* ⌂ *Rooms: 122 en suite (23 in castle)* ⊨ *DB&B £70–£95 B&B £55–£65* ⓈⓅ *Special rates available* ✕ *Food available all day Stables Bar £ Lunch Conservatory Restaurant ££ Dinner Conservatory Restaurant ££ Castle Restaurant ££££* Ⓥ *Vegetarians welcome* ☀ *Children welcome* ♿ *Facilities for disabled visitors* ☂ *Dogs welcome* ⊞ *Mastercard/Eurocard, American Express, Visa, Diners Club, Switch* Ⓝ *General Manager: Stuart Grant*

Airth, by Falkirk Stirlingshire FK2 8JF Tel: 01324 831411 Fax: 01324 831419 E-mail: stuart.grant@radissonsas.com Web: www.radissonsas.com M9, follow signs to Kincardine Bridge. Castle on A905 on left-hand side.[C5]

ALYTH

Drumnacree House Hotel and The Oven Bistro

- *"A pleasant and relaxing stay here is combined with friendly service and good food."*
- *Scottish and international.*

DRUMNACREE HOUSE has Tayside's only wood-burning oven at which new owner Gail McFadden supervises, using much of the produce from the hotel's own baby vegetable and herb garden. Menus are well-thought out and the results are a success. Gail is assisted by her husband Derek who is front of house.

Melted Camembert on home-made sour dough bread, with Cumberland sauce. Twin steaks of venison and beef fillet served with a wine and redcurrant jus. Hot Drumnacree pudding served with crème anglaise and raisin and Glenturret sauce.

STB ★★★★ Small Hotel

◗ *Open all year Closed Mon – residents only* ⌂ *Rooms: 6 en suite* ⊨ *DB&B £50–£65 B&B £35–£40* ⓈⓅ *Special rates available* ✕ *Lunch except Mon £ Dinner except Mon ££* Ⓥ *Vegetarians welcome* ☀ *Children welcome* ♿ *Facilities for disabled visitors* ☂ *Dogs welcome* ⊞ *Mastercard/Eurocard, Visa, Switch, Delta* Ⓝ *Owners: Derek & Gail McFadden*

St Ninians Road Alyth Perthshire PH11 8AP Tel: 01828 632194 Fax: 01828 632194 E-mail: derek@drumnacreehouse.co.uk Web: www.drumnacreehouse.co.uk Turn off A926 Blairgowrie-Kirriemuir to Alyth. Take first turning on left after Clydesdale Bank. Hotel 300 yards on right.[D5]

ARDNAMURCHAN

Dalilea House

- *"A welcoming, friendly home with delicious food is what makes Dalilea House special."*
- *Scottish farmhouse cooking.*

DALILEA HOUSE is set in its own grounds and surrounded by farmland and farm animals. Mairi's cooking is best described as traditional farmhouse at its best – a most enjoyable experience. Vegetables and herbs come from Dalilea's own garden – free-range hens provide the eggs! Fishing/rowing boats on Loch Shiel are available.

Nettle tip and nutmeg soup. Fillet of whiting with orange and chive butter. Rhubarb and ginger crumble.

STB ★★★ Guest House

◑ Open 1 Apr to 30 Oct 🏠 Rooms: 5 (4 en suite, 1 private facilities) 🛏 DB&B £45–£50 B&B £25–£30 💷 Special rates available 🍷 Restricted hotel licence ✗ Food available all day £ Packed lunches £ Dinner ££ Non residents welcome at evening meals only – reservations necessary Ⓥ Vegetarians welcome – prior notice appreciated 🐾 Children welcome 🚭 No smoking in dining room 🐕 Dogs welcome 💳 Mastercard/Eurocard, Visa, Delta 🔪 Proprietor/Chef: Mairi Macaulay

Dalilea Acharacle Argyll PH36 4JX
Tel: 01967 431253 Fax: 01967 431364
E-mail: stay@dalilea.co.uk
Web: www.dalilea.co.uk
From Fort William on A830 towards Mallaig, take A861 at Lochailort or from Glencoe or Oban on the A82 cross the Corran/Ardgour ferry onto A861, through Strontian and Acharacle.[B4]

ARDNAMURCHAN

Feorag House

- *"A highland gem – stunning views, comfortable surroundings and exquisite food."*
- *Skilful home cooking.*

PETER AND HELEN STOCKDALE have created a wonderful 'home from home' atmosphere here. From delightful afternoon tea on arrival, to delicious food and helpful advice – your every need is catered for. Add to this breathtaking views, wild birds and animals and a plethora of wild flowers – this is truly a holiday made in heaven!

Seared monkfish on Thai noodles with sweet chilli dressing. Roast rack of Scottish lamb with fresh ratatouille, new potatoes with red onion and red wine jus. Feorag House apple crumble.

STB ★★★★★ Guest House

◑ Open all year 🏠 Rooms: 3 en suite 🛏 DB&B £59–£69 💷 Special rates available Ⓤ Unlicensed – guests welcome to take own wine ✗ Dinner ££ Residents only Ⓥ Vegetarians welcome – by arrangement 🐾 Children over 10 years welcome 🚭 No smoking throughout 💳 Mastercard/ Eurocard, Visa, Switch, Delta, JCB 🔪 Proprietors: Peter & Helen Stockdale

Glenborrodale Acharacle Argyll PH36 4JP
Tel: 01972 500248 Fax: 01972 500285
E-mail: admin@feorag.demon.co.uk
Web: www.feorag.co.uk
36 miles or 1 hour's drive from Corran Ferry. Take A861 then B8007 to Glenborrodale. 200 yards beyond school on left.[B5]

ARDNAMURCHAN

Water's Edge

- *"Outstanding hospitality, delicious food and breathtaking scenery – an all-round exceptional experience."*
- *Homely Scottish cooking.*

THE 'JUST FOR TWO' room at Water's Edge is a very special experience. Joan's dinners are exquisite while husband Rob cooks up a great breakfast. However, it is the little things like the unusual dinner call and a unique 'good night' that make this place really special – why not find out for yourself!

A light pea, apple and mint soup, thickened with courgette. Local salmon cooked in foil with fresh dill served with a gentle basil and spinach sauce, new potatoes topped with sautéed leeks. Fresh local strawberries served with an almond tart.

STB ★★★★ B&B

◗ *Open from mid Feb to mid Nov* 🏠 *Rooms: 1 en suite* 🛏 *DB&B £46–£51* 🍷 *Unlicensed – guests welcome to take own wine* 🅥 *Vegetarians welcome* ✄ *No smoking throughout* 🐕 *Dogs welcome by arrangement* 💳 *No credit cards* 🔑 *Proprietors: Rob & Joan Thompson*

Kilchoan Ardnamurchan Argyll PH36 4LL
Tel: 01972 510261
E-mail: rob@ardnamurchan75.freeserve.co.uk
Web: www.ardnamurchan.com/watersedge
From Corran Ferry (8 miles south of Fort William) take A861 to Salen, then B8007 to Kilchoan. In village, pass school on left, follow road round bay to Ferry Stores: take cul-de-sac straight ahead. Water's Edge is bungalow with flagpole. [B5]

ARDRISHAIG

Bridge House Hotel

- *"Informal friendly hospitality matched by excellent Scottish cooking."*
- *Traditional Scottish with flair.*

WATTY AND MICHAELA Dewar are friendly, welcoming hosts, who go out of their way for their guests. There are six bedrooms that have been refurbished to a high standard. The food is extremely wholesome, created with imaginative flair. There is a traditional dining room, and also a relaxing beer garden overlooking Loch Fyne.

Warm salad of avocado, smoked bacon and fresh langoustines. Rack of West Highland lamb on a bed of minted spinach with Drambuie and port wine sauce. Chocolate and almond torte with frozen vanilla mousse and seasonal berries.

STB ★★★ Small Hotel

◗ *Open all year* 🏠 *Rooms: 6 en suite* 🛏 *DB&B £55–£75 B&B £35–£55* 💷 *Special rates available* ✗ *Lunch ££ Dinner £££* 🅥 *Vegetarians welcome* 🧒 *Children welcome* ♿ *Facilities for disabled visitors* ✄ *No smoking in dining room* 🐕 *Dogs welcome* 💳 *Mastercard/Eurocard, Visa, Switch, Delta, Solo* 🔑 *Owners: Watty & Michaela Dewar*

St Claire Road Ardrishaig By Lochgilphead PA30 8EW
Tel: 01546 606379 Fax: 01546 606593
E-mail: bridge-house@lineone.net
Web: www.smoothhound.co.uk/
From Lochgilphead take A83 Campbeltown road for 2 miles, next to Ardrishaig Boat Basin and Crinan Canal.[B5]

ARISAIG

Old Library Lodge & Restaurant

- *"A bright welcoming restaurant which gives efficient service and interesting choice of menu."*
- *Good, fresh food, seafood a speciality.*

THE OLD LIBRARY LODGE and Restaurant enjoys an attractive situation on the waterfront in Arisaig. Guests may choose from an à la carte menu with a choice of five of everything – starters, main courses and puddings. Alan does most of the cooking, and everything possible is sourced locally. Breakfast is something to really look forward to.

Pan-fried cous-cous coated goats cheese. Grilled local scallops on a celeriac purée. Caramelised lemon tart with home-made elderflower ice cream.

STB ★★★ Restaurant with Rooms

◗ *Open 24 Mar to end Oct Closed Tue lunch* ⊞ *Rooms: 6 en suite* ⇔ *DB&B from £60 B&B from £38* ⓢ *Special rates available* ▮ *Refreshment licence* ✕ *Lunch except Tue £–££ Dinner £££* Ⓥ *Vegetarians welcome – prior notice required* ⊞ *Mastercard/Eurocard, American Express, Visa, Switch, Delta* ⦿ *Proprietors: Alan & Angela Broadhurst*

Arisaig Inverness-shire PH39 4NH
Tel: 01687 450651 Fax: 01687 450219
E-mail: reception@oldlibrary.co.uk
Web: www.oldlibrary.co.uk
In centre of village on waterfront, next to Post Office.[B4]

AUCHENCAIRN

Balcary Bay Hotel

- *"Dishes are prepared and served with precision and skill in idyllic setting overlooking Balcary Bay."*
- *Modern Scottish cooking.*

THIS SUPERB HOUSE dates back to 1625 and is set in a splendid position. Enjoy lunch in the delightful conservatory overlooking the bay or take afternoon tea in the lounge. Evening meals are a special occasion with menus carefully chosen and prepared by Chef Charlie Kelly, under the careful management of Graeme Lamb.

Roasted Kirkcudbright scallops with sun blushed tomatoes and fresh pea sauce. Best end Scottish lamb served with white bean purée, sweet roast garlic and lavender jus. Crème brûlée flavoured with Glayva and served with oatmeal tuile.

STB ★★★★ Hotel

◗ *Open Mar to end Nov* ⊞ *Rooms: 20 en suite* ⇔ *DB&B £56–£80 B&B £56–£63* ⓢ *Special rates available* ✕ *Lunch Sun – booking advisable ££ Lunch Mon to Sat – by prior reservation only ££ Bar Lunches daily Dinner £££* Ⓥ *Vegetarians welcome* ✻ *Children welcome* ♿ *Facilities for disabled visitors* ⌇ *Smoking discouraged in dining areas* ⊞ *Mastercard/ Eurocard, American Express, Visa, Switch, Delta* ⦿ *General Manager: Graeme Lamb*

Auchencairn, nr Castle Douglas Dumfries & Galloway DG7 1QZ
Tel: 01556 640217 Fax: 01556 640272
E-mail: reservations@balcary-bay-hotel.co.uk
Web: www.balcary-bay-hotel.co.uk
A711 Dalbeattie-Kirkcudbright to Auchencairn. Then take 'no through road' signposted Balcary (single track) for 2 miles. [C7]

AUCHTERARDER

Auchterarder House

- *"Sumptuous surrounds, exquisite hospitality and some of the finest food to be found in Scotland."*
- *Outstanding country house cooking with modern influences.*

LUXURIATE IN STYLE in one of Scotland's finest Jacobean homes. Each exquisite bedroom is individually designed and public rooms are breathtaking. However, the highlight of the Auchterarder experience is the food. Masterchef Willie Deans leads an award-winning team that create true culinary masterpieces. Winner of The Macallan Taste of Scotland Award 2000.

Bresse pigeon grilled with truffled noodles, sweet 'n' sour swede, vermouth sauce. Steamed coriander and cumin fused fillet of turbot, warm salad of mushrooms and lobster, cèpe dressing, leek and bacon crumble. Smoked banana soufflé, spiced tropical fruits in a briar rosehip syrup, rum and golden raisin water ice.

STB ★★★★ Hotel

◗ Open all year 🏠 Rooms: 15 en suite 🛏 B&B £135–£295 🆒 Special rates available ✕ Food available all day £ Lunch ££ Dinner ££££ Ⓥ Vegetarians welcome ⅍ No smoking in dining room 🆒 Mastercard/Eurocard, American Express, Visa, Diners Club, Switch, Delta 🆒 Owned by The Wrens Hotel Group

Auchterarder Perthshire PH3 1DZ
Tel: 01764 663646 Fax: 01764 662939
E-mail: auchterarder@wrensgroup.com
Web: www.wrensgroup.com
B8062 from Auchterarder to Crieff. Hotel is 1 mile from village.[C5]

AUCHTERARDER

Denfield House

- *"Excellent food and accommodation with every home comfort."*
- *Creative modern Scottish.*

DENFIELD HOUSE is a charming house set in the most beautiful part of Perthshire. Owner, Ailsa Reynolds is a skilled and committed cook and the meals are highly accomplished with interesting and innovative menus. On arrival guests are offered afternoon tea with home baking, cakes and biscuits. A delightful, relaxing and very hospitable place.

Siamese prawn soup with coriander dumplings. Fillet of Gask venison served on pumpkin and rosemary barley risotto. Strawberries with white pepper and mint ice cream.

◗ Open 7 Jan to 23 Dec Closed Christmas Day and Boxing Day 🏠 Rooms: 5, 2 en suite 🛏 DB&B £65 B&B £35 🆒 Special rates available 🍷 Table licence ✕ Picnic hampers on request £ Dinner £££ Ⓥ Vegetarians welcome – by prior arrangement ✹ Children welcome ⅍ No smoking in dining room 🐕 Dogs welcome 🆒 Mastercard, Visa, Delta 🆒 Owners: Ailsa & Jamie Reynolds

Trinity Gask Auchterarder Perthshire PH3 1LH
Tel: 01764 683474 Fax: 01764 683776
E-mail: ailsa@denfieldhouse.com
Web: www.denfieldhouse.com
Take B8062 from Auchterarder towards Crieff. Take a right turn immediately after Kinkell Bridge. Denfield House approx 1½ miles on left.[C5]

AUCHTERARDER

The Dormy Clubhouse

- *"A relaxed, informal dining experience with breathtaking views of world famous golf courses and surrounding countryside."*
- *Classic British using finest Scottish ingredients.*

RELAX AND ENJOY good food, comfortable surroundings and some of the golf world's most famous views – the last greens of both the Kings and Queens Courses at Gleneagles. The Dormy Clubhouse isn't just for golfers! Indeed the flexible menus make this an attractive option for families and non-golfers looking for 'food with a view'.

Array of buffet starters including Scottish smoked salmon. Roast duckling with red cabbage and black cherry sauce. Classic Scottish puddings and farmhouse cheese.

◑ *Open all year Closed Oct 17 to Mar 15 (dinner) Closed Christmas Day (dinner) and New Year's Eve (dinner) Open 7 days a week all day (summer)* ✗ *Food available all day ££ Lunch ££ Dinner ££* Ⓥ *Vegetarians welcome* ✶ *Children welcome* ♿ *Facilities for disabled visitors* 🖃 *Mastercard/Eurocard, American Express, Visa, Diners Club, Switch, Delta* 🔏 *Restaurant Manager: Gavin Paisley*

The Gleneagles Hotel Auchterarder Perthshire PH3 1NF
Tel: 01764 662231 (ext 4359)
Web: www.gleneagles.com
By Auchterarder, follow signs to Gleneagles. The Dormy Clubhouse is on the left on main driveway to hotel.[C5]

AUCHTERHOUSE

East Mains House & The Music Room Restaurant

- *"Warm hospitality and good food."*
- *Good Scottish cooking with classic influences.*

EAST MAINS has been tastefully upgraded to a high standard. On arrival guests are offered tea and home baking in the lounge. The Music Room Restaurant offers only good fresh local ingredients prepared and presented by Sharon Russell who cares passionately about the food. Themed food and music evenings are particularly enjoyable.

Cream of mushroom soup with home-made walnut and sunflower seed bread. Fillet of Tay salmon, with fennel and lemon cous-cous. East Mains gooseberry and elderflower fool with orange fork biscuits.

STB ★★★★ B&B

◑ *Open all year except Christmas Day, Boxing Day, New Year's Eve and New Year's Day Restaurant closed Sun Mon Tue – non residents* 🛏 *Rooms: 3 with private facilities* 🛏 *DB&B £45–£55 B&B £27–£40* ✗ *Dinner available all week for residents* Ⓥ *Vegetarians welcome* ✶ *Children welcome* ♿ *Facilities for disabled visitors* ✺ *No smoking in restaurant* 🐕 *Guide dogs only* 🖃 *Mastercard/Eurocard, Visa, Delta* 🔏 *Chef/Proprietor: Sharon Russell*

Auchterhouse, by Dundee Angus DD3 0QN
Tel: 01382 320206 Fax: 01382 320206
E-mail: dfrangus@aol.com
North-west of Dundee, – 7 miles. Take A923 Coupar Angus road from Dundee, through Birkhill and Muirhead villages and join B954 road to Auchterhouse. Left at crossroads in village, 500 yards on right. [D5]

AVIEMORE

Corrour House Hotel

- *"Guests are so well looked after – they return each year."*
- *Imaginative country house cooking.*

THIS IS a charming family-run hotel which offers true Highland hospitality from accomplished hosts, David and Sheana Catto. This elegant house stands in four acres of garden and woodland and enjoys fine views of the Cairngorm Mountains. The cooking is excellent making best use of local produce whatever the meal.

Gratin of Hebridean prawns with chilli and Cheddar. Fillet of Aberdeen Angus beef with port mushrooms. Decadent chocolate parfait with Drambuie oranges.

STB ★★★★ Small Hotel

◐ *Open 27 Dec to 31 Oct* ⌂ *Rooms: 8 en suite* ⊨ *DB&B £70 B&B £45* ▣ *Winter rates available* ✗ *Dinner 4 course menu ££* Ⓥ *Vegetarians welcome* ⚱ *Children welcome* ✄ *No smoking in dining room and some bedrooms* ⊞ *Mastercard/Eurocard, Visa* ▨ *Proprietors: Mr & Mrs Catto*

Rothiemurchus, by Aviemore PH22 1QH Tel: 01479 810220 Fax: 01479 811500 Web: www.corrourhousehotel.co.uk Rothiemurchus is a ½ mile from Aviemore, on road to Glenmore and Cairngorms.[C4]

AVIEMORE

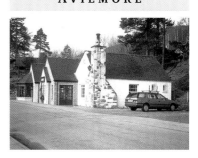

The Old Bridge Inn

- *"A warm welcome and good food awaits the visitor to this traditional inn."*
- *Hearty pub food.*

THE OLD BRIDGE INN offers pub food as it should be – freshly prepared and cooked. Innkeeper Iain MacRury and chef Norma Hutton concentrate on fresh local produce for their extensive and imaginative menu. There is a special children's menu. In the evenings, the menu is based on food cooked on a large chargrill. Live music.

Highland game terrine with cranberry sauce. Baked loin of Strathspey venison with mushroom purée wrapped in filo pastry set on a pool of port and thyme. Chocolate brandy mousse with a mandarin orange sauce.

◐ *Open all year* ✗ *Lunch £ Dinner ££* Ⓥ *Vegetarians welcome* ⚱ *Children welcome* ♿ *Facilities for disabled visitors* ⊞ *Mastercard/ Eurocard, Visa, Switch* ▨ *Owner: Dr William J Cox; Restaurant Manager: Mairhi Bremner; Head Chef: Denis Lyons*

23 Dalfaber Road Aviemore PH22 1PU Tel: 01479 811137 Fax: 01479 811372 At south end of Aviemore, take B970 ski road (Cairngorms) for 300 yards then take turning on left for another 300 yards.[C4]

AYR

Enterkine House

- *"Finest Scottish food served in elegant surroundings".*
- *Classic Scottish.*

RECENTLY RENOVATED and restored to its former glory, Enterkine sits amidst 310 acres of green fields, rivers and woodlands. Guests can enjoy a plethora of pursuits either outdoors or indoors. This is a great place in which to relax in luxurious surroundings and delight in Scottish fare and exquisite wines.

Assiette of West Coast seafood, sauce vierge. Scotch beef fillet, hot-pot potatoes, roast roots, oxtail red wine sauce. Warm poached pear, malted chocolate mousse, praline parfait, caramel sauce.

STB ★★★★★ Small Hotel

◗ *Open all year* ⌂ *Rooms: 6 en suite* ⇔ *DB&B from £150 B&B from £115* ⑤⑨ *Special rates available* ✕ *Food available all day £ Lunch except Mon Tue ££ Dinner ££££* Ⓥ *Vegetarians welcome* ☀ *Children over 11 years welcome* ♿ *Facilities for disabled visitors* ✂ *No smoking in restaurant* ⌘*Dogs welcome* ⊞ *Mastercard/ Eurocard, American Express, Visa, Switch, Delta* ⋈ *General Manager: Jon Cann*

Annbank By Ayr KA6 5AL
Tel: 01292 521608/520580 Fax: 01292 521582
E-mail: mail@enterkine.com
Web: www.enterkine.com
From A77 follow signs from Annbank/Mossblown. Follow road through Mossblown. Enterkine first left past right turn for Annbank. [C6]

AYR

Fouters Bistro

- *"An eclectic menu offering excellent food that is skilfully prepared and simply presented."*
- *Modern Scottish cooking.*

FOUTERS' CONSISTENTLY good food, fine wines and relaxed atmosphere have long ensured the bistro's place on Scotland's culinary map. Much effort goes into sourcing only the freshest Scottish ingredients which are sympathetically and skilfully prepared by Fouter's talented and creative team. This year Fouters enjoys a fresh new Mediterranean look with bright new menu formats.

Steamed scallops, chilli ginger dressing. Loin of hill lamb, rösti and glazed shallots, wild garlic jus. Chocolate mousse tart.

◗ *Open all year except 25 to 27 Dec and 1 to 3 Jan Closed Sun* ✕ *Lunch except Sun £ Dinner except Sun £££* Ⓥ *Vegetarians welcome Special diets catered for* ☀ *Children welcome* ⊞ *Mastercard/Eurocard, American Express, Visa, Diners Club, Switch, Solo* ⋈ *Owners: Laurie & Fran Black*

2A Academy Street Ayr KA7 1HS
Tel: 01292 261391 Fax: 01292 619323
E-mail: qualityfood@fouters.co.uk
Web: www.fouters.co.uk
Town centre, opposite Town Hall. [C6]

AYR

AYR

Horizon Hotel

- *"Good food cooked simply and well-presented."*
- *A marriage of traditional and modern.*

THIS IS AYR'S only seafront hotel and enjoys panoramic views over to Arran. Owners Alan and Elizabeth Meikle are charming hosts and offer informal dining in the Glasshouse Restaurant which serves good food simply prepared and well-presented. New for summer 2001, The Gallery Fine Dining Restaurant serving contemporary Scottish food.

Glasshouse: Deep-fried mushrooms filled with haggis, with a whisky mayonnaise. Salmon and spring onion fish cake with a lemon and herb sauce served with vegetables and potatoes. Baked apple and plum crumble with a vanilla anglaise.

STB ★★★ Hotel
Green Tourism Two Leaf Silver Award

◗ Open all year ▥ Rooms: 22, 17 en suite ⑲ Special rates available ✗ Food available all day £ Lunch £ Dinner ££ Ⓥ Vegetarians welcome ⚘ Children welcome ♿ Facilities for disabled visitors ✔ Smoking permitted in certain areas ⌢Dogs welcome
⊞ Mastercard/Eurocard, Visa, Switch, Delta
Ⓜ Proprietors: Alan & Elizabeth Meikle

Esplanade Ayr KA7 1DT
Tel: 01292 264384 Fax: 01292 264011
E-mail: mail@horizonhotel.com
Web: www.horizonhotel.com
Follow seafront signs through Ayr town onto Esplanade. Hotel situated at North end of Esplanade next to coach/car park. [C6]

The Ivy House: Finalist The Macallan Taste of Scotland Awards 2001

- *"Excellent hospitality and breathtaking food prepared by an award-winning team of chefs."*
- *Classic Scottish with modern twist.*

BE PAMPERED at this recently refurbished country house and delight in the fine food prepared by chef Joe Queen and his accomplished team. Great care is taken selecting only the finest raw materials which are then sympathetically prepared and served by friendly staff.

Pressed terrine of foie gras and duck confit. Roast rack of lamb, black pudding and sage mousse, basil-flavoured gnocchi, aubergine gâteau, rosemary essence. Individual baked banana toffee crumble.

STB ★★★★ Small Hotel

◗ Open all year ▥ Rooms: 5 en suite ⊨ DB&B £120–£210 B&B £85–£130 ⑲ Special rates available ✗ Food available all day £ Lunch ££ Dinner £££ Ⓥ Vegetarians welcome ⚘ Children welcome ♿ Facilities for disabled visitors ✔ No smoking in restaurant ⌢ Guide dogs only
⊞ Mastercard/Eurocard, American Express, Visa, Switch, Delta, Solo Ⓜ Operations Director/Chef: Mr Joe Queen

2 Alloway Ayr KA7 4NL
Tel: 01292 442336 Fax: 01292 445572
E-mail: theivyhousealloway@hotmail.com/
enquiries@theivyhouse.uk.com
Web: www.theivyhouse.uk.com
From Glasgow, follow A77 to Ayr. Left at Monkton roundabout, continue towards Ayr – pick up sign for Alloway-Doonfoot. Right through Doonholm Road to the T junction. Right past Burns Cottage on the left – The Ivy House is 300m. further on. [C6]

AYR

Visitor Centre Restaurant, Culzean Castle & Country Park, The National Trust for Scotland

- *"Generous helpings of good, traditional home cooking and baking."*
- *Traditional Scottish.*

SITUATED IN THE GRAND, converted stables of Culzean Castle, this is no ordinary self-service restaurant. Choose from a choice of sandwiches and salads or a mouth-watering selection of home-baked cakes and scones. Ingredients are locally sourced and, wherever possible, organic. Fresh fruit and vegetables from Culzean's own garden available when in season.

Poached local salmon with lime mayo and seasonal leaves. Breast of chicken stuffed with haggis and wild mushroom sauce served with seasonal vegetables from the castle's walled garden. Summer pudding with berries from the Castle Garden.

STB ★★★★ Visitor Attraction

◐ *Open 1 Apr to 31 Oct Weekends from Nov to 31 Mar* ♥ *Licensed* Ⓥ *Vegetarians welcome* ☀ *Children welcome* ♿ *Facilities for disabled* ⊁ *No smoking throughout* 🐕*Dogs welcome in grounds only* 💳 *Mastercard, Visa, Switch* 👤 *Catering Manager: Bill Hudson*

Maybole Ayrshire KA19 8LE
Tel: 01655 884502 Fax: 01655 884521
E-mail: whudson@nts.org.uk
Web: www.nts.org.uk
12 miles south of Ayr off the A719, 4 miles west of Maybole. [C6]

BALLACHULISH

Ballachulish House

- *"Superb food and a warm welcome greets you when you stay at Ballachulish House."*
- *Innovative Scottish dishes.*

MARIE MCLAUGHLIN welcomes you into this 17th century Laird's house. To quote the 5th Duke of Argyll in 1760, "The best hospitality I ever had on my travels was at Ballachulish House." Steeped in history every traveller would feel relaxed here. Seafood, game and Scottish meats are evident on the menu.

House-smoked Gressingham duck with an orange and elderflower dressing. Pine nut encrusted rack of Skye lamb. Iced parfait cranachan tower with fresh local raspberries.

STB ★★★★★ Small Hotel

◐ *Open all year* 🛏 *Rooms: 8 en suite* 🛌 *DB&B £70–£100 B&B £40–£70* 💷 *Special rates available* ✘ *Food available all day £ Lunch ££ Dinner £££* Ⓥ *Vegetarians welcome* ⊁ *No smoking throughout* 💳 *Mastercard/Eurocard, American Express, Visa, Switch, Delta, JCB* 👤 *Proprietor: Marie McLaughlin*

Ballachulish Argyll PH49 4JX
Tel: 01855 811266 Fax: 01855 811498
E-mail: mclaughlins@btconnect.com
Web: www.ballachulishhouse.com
Follow the A82 until it intersects the A828 (Oban road). Follow the A828 under the Ballachulish Bridge. Continue for approx 200 metres then turn left at the Dragons Tooth Golf Course and follow the signs to Ballachulish House. [B5]

BALLANTRAE

BALLATER ROYAL DEESIDE

Cosses Country House

- *"As it says in the room directory -'YOU are the important people here' and a stay at Cosses makes you feel like royalty!"*
- *Gourmet country house cooking.*

COSSES IS LOCATED in a beautiful rural location and is a treasury of good food. Susan, who is a Cordon Bleu Chef, creates menus that are unique and moreover quite delicious. Everything here is home-grown or home-made. There are endless special touches. Winner of The Macallan Taste of Scotland Award 2000.

Sautéed Ballantrae prawns in a light saffron cream sauce with leek risotto. Breast of Gressingham duckling with Czar plum sauce, clapshot and Cosses seasonal vegetables. Brandy snap cones filled with Cosses rhubarb fool, with poached rhubarb and rhubarb and ginger sauce.

◐ Open all year except occasionally Christmas and New Year 🏠 Rooms: 3 en suite 🛏 DB&B £57–£80 B&B £32–£48 🅂🄿 Special rates available ✕ Dinner £££ Dinner for non-residents – by reservation only Ⓥ Vegetarians welcome ✵ Children over 12 years only welcome in the dining room ✄ No smoking in dining room 🖭 Mastercard, Visa ⛊ Proprietors: Susan & Robin Crosthwaite

Cosses Ballantrae Ayrshire KA26 0LR Tel: 01465 831363 Fax: 01465 831598 E-mail: cosses@compuserve.com Web: www.cossescountryhouse.com From A77 at southern end of Ballantrae, take inland road at Caravan sign. Cosses is c. 2 miles on right. [B6]

Auld Kirk Hotel

- *"An exciting menu offering the best of Scottish produce."*
- *Imaginative modern Scottish.*

THE AULD KIRK HOTEL is the place where you can really relax and recharge your batteries. Built in 1869, this fine former church has been tastefully converted, enabling retention of many of the original features into a family-run hotel. The food here is exciting and imaginative and presented with flair.

Loch Fyne herrings/mackerel pan-fried, black pudding, Orkney cheese champ and Chianti. Rump of hillside lamb, rosemary Puy lentils, Arran mustard, red wine vinegar. Marmalade bread and butter pudding, crème anglaise.

◐ Open all year except 25 26 Dec Closed Sun Mon from 1 Nov to 18 Mar 🏠 Rooms: 7 en suite 🛏 DB&B £45–£55 B&B from £30 🅂🄿 Special rates available off season ✕ Food available all day £–££ Lunch ££ Dinner ££ – closed Mon Tue during winter months Ⓥ Vegetarians welcome ✵ Children welcome ♿ Facilities for disabled visitors ✄ No smoking in restaurant ⛾ Dogs welcome by prior arrangement and at proprietors' discretion 🖭 Mastercard/Eurocard, Visa, Switch, Delta ⛊ Director/Chef: James A Johnson

Braemar Road Ballater AB35 5RX Tel: 013397 55762 Fax: 013397 55707 E-mail: auldkirkhotel@aol.com Web: www.auldkirkhotel.com 46 miles west of Aberdeen on A93. 67 miles north of Perth on A93. [D4]

BALLATER ROYAL DEESIDE

Balgonie Country House Hotel

- *"A lovely hotel offering superb food."*
- *Traditional and innovative recipes using fresh local produce.*

BALGONIE's proprietors, John and Priscilla Finnie, pride themselves on maintaining a friendly but unobtrusive service. The dining room is the heart of Balgonie providing excellent cuisine using locally sourced fish and game. When in season, herbs and soft fruits from the garden are always found on the menu.

Terrine of pheasant and wild mushrooms with Cumberland sauce. Roast loin of lamb set on spinach with roasted shallots and rosemary jus. Vanilla yoghurt terrine with poached pear.

STB ★★★★ Hotel

◐ Open 12 Feb to 5 Jan 🏨 Rooms: 9 en suite 🛏 DB&B £85–£95 B&B £55–£70 💷 Special rates available ✕ Lunch – by reservation only ££ Dinner 4 course menu – non-residents by reservation £££ Ⓥ Vegetarians welcome – prior notice required ⚘ Children over 5 years welcome at dinner ✍ No smoking in dining room 💳 Mastercard/Eurocard, American Express, Visa, Switch, Delta 🍴 Proprietor: John G Finnie

Braemar Place Ballater AB35 5NQ
Tel: 013397 55582 Fax: 013397 55482
E-mail: balgoniech@aol.com
Web: www.royaldeesidehotels.com
Off A93 Aberdeen-Perth, on outskirts of village of Ballater. [D4]

BALLATER ROYAL DEESIDE

Darroch Learg Hotel

- *"An inspiring food experience."*
- *Modern Scottish cooking.*

THE HOTEL sits high up on a rocky hillside, with excellent views across Royal Deeside. The dining room and spacious conservatory allow diners to enjoy the wonderful outlook of the hills of Glen Muick. The menu offers top quality local meat, confidently and expertly prepared in interesting combinations and sauces.

Poached fillet of smoked haddock with an etuvee of asparagus and hollandaise sauce. Loin of Deeside venison with wild mushrooms, Savoy cabbage, celeriac purée and a venison jus. Classic lemon tart with raspberry sauce.

STB ★★★★ Hotel

◐ Open Feb to Dec closed Christmas 🏨 Rooms: 18 en suite 🛏 DB&B £60–£105 B&B £42–£77 ✕ Food available all day £££ Lunch £££ Dinner ££££ Ⓥ Vegetarians welcome ⚘ Children welcome ♿ Facilities for disabled visitors ✍ No smoking in dining room or bedrooms 💳 Mastercard/ Eurocard, American Express, Visa, Diners Club, Switch 🍴 Proprietors: Nigel & Fiona Franks

Braemar Road Ballater Aberdeenshire
AB35 5UX
Tel: 013397 55443 Fax: 013397 55252
E-mail: nigel@darrochlearg.co.uk
Web: www.darrochlearg.co.uk
½ mile from centre of village of Ballater, on A93 at Western edge of village. [D4]

BALLATER ROYAL DEESIDE

Deeside Hotel

- *"This hotel lives up to it's reputation – good food, served well."*
- *Traditional Scottish cooking with modern twist.*

THE DEESIDE is a family-run establishment. In the evening, meals are available in both the restaurant and bar where you can also sample a good selection of Scottish real ales and malt whiskies. The dining room also has a spacious sunny conservatory which extends the appeal of this well-run friendly hotel.

Creamy seafood and dill chowder. Baked fillet of hake and queen scallops with a spicy tomato compote. Clootie dumpling.

STB ★★★ Small Hotel

◗ *Open mid Feb to mid Dec* 🏨 *Rooms: 9 en suite* 🛏 *DB&B £39–£44 B&B £23–£28* 🆂🅿 *Special rates available* ✕ *Dinner ££* Ⓥ *Vegetarians welcome by arrangement* ✳ *Children welcome* ♿ *Facilities for disabled visitors* 🚭 *No smoking in restaurant* 💳 *Mastercard/ Eurocard, Visa, Switch* ⚐ *Directors: Donald & Alison Brooker*

Braemar Road Ballater AB35 5RQ
Tel: 013397 55420 Fax: 013397 55357
E-mail: deesidehotel@btconnect.com
Web: www.deesidehotel.co.uk
On west side of Ballater, set back from A93 Braemar road. [D4]

BALLATER ROYAL DEESIDE

Glen Lui Hotel

- *"Friendly staff, lovely atmosphere and skilled cooking all add to the charm of this hotel."*
- *Modern Scottish cooking, with distinct French influences.*

AT THE GLEN LUI, service is friendly and menus are well-presented and varied. The wrap-around conservatory/ restaurant offers an extensive à la carte menu with a distinct French influence compiled by new French Chef Olivier Denis. There is a comprehensive wine list. Member of the Certified Aberdeen Angus Scheme. Investor in People Award.

Grampian chicken and pistachio nut terrine with pear chutney. Papillote of North Sea smoked haddock and leeks. Cinnamon poached pear in a meringue nest with ginger sauce and cream.

STB ★★★★ Hotel
Green Tourism Three Leaf Gold Award

◗ *Open all year* 🏨 *Rooms: 19 en suite* 🛏 *DB&B £46–£62 B&B £30–£46* 🆂🅿 *Special rates available* ✕ *Lunch £ Dinner £-££* Ⓥ *Vegetarians welcome* ✳ *Children welcome* ♿ *Facilities for disabled visitors* 🚭 *No smoking in restaurant and bedrooms* 💳 *Mastercard/Eurocard, American Express, Visa, Switch, Delta* ⚐ *Proprietors: Serge & Lorraine Geraud*

Invercauld Road Ballater Aberdeenshire AB35 5RP
Tel: 013397 55402 Fax: 013397 55545
E-mail: infos@glen-lui-hotel.co.uk
Web: www.glen-lui-hotel.co.uk
Off A93 at western end of Ballater at end of Invercauld Road. [D4]

BALLATER ROYAL DEESIDE

The Green Inn Restaurant With Rooms

- *"Outstanding cuisine – a real find!"*
- *Modern regional Scottish cooking, with good use of international influences.*

JEFF PURVES' cooking is innovative and imaginative, and he applies this to the excellent local produce available on Deeside and combining flavours with assured confidence. Jeff uses cream only when necessary, replacing sugar with honey. The Green Inn is a real gem and well worth the visit. Winner of The Macallan Taste of Scotland Award 1995.

Cheesecake of oak-smoked haddock and Highland Cheddar with a tarragon cream. Escalope of wild salmon and Loch Fyne langoustine tails with a tomato and basil butter sauce. Warm syrup tart with liquorice ice cream.

STB ★★★★ Restaurant with Rooms

◑ *Open all year except 2 weeks Oct, Christmas Day and 26 to 28 Dec Closed Sun Oct to Mar* ⌂ *Rooms: 3 en suite* 🛏 *DB&B £54.50–£59.50* 💷 *Special rates available* ✗ *Dinner £££* Ⅴ *Vegetarians welcome* ✶ *Children welcome* ♿ *Facilities for disabled visitors* ✍ *Smoking permitted at coffee stage only* 💳 *Mastercard/ Eurocard, American Express, Visa, Diners Club, Switch* ⋈ *Proprietors: J J & C A Purves*

9 Victoria Road Ballater AB35 5QQ
Tel: 013397 55701 Fax: 013397 55701
E-mail: info@green-inn.com
Web: www.green-inn.com
In centre of Ballater on village green. [D4]

BALLATER ROYAL DEESIDE

Station Restaurant

- *"A popular venue with a choice of divine experiences in a relaxed atmosphere with excellent cooking and value for money."*
- *Modern British.*

THE SETTING IS UNIQUE – it is set in the station's original wooden panelled dining room now converted into a stylish bistro blending the best of the old and new. It offers food all day from full Scottish breakfast through to dinner, including blackboard specials, all using Scottish produce.

Scottish salmon fish cake with red pepper and coriander sauce. Pan-fried sirloin of Scottish beef with garlic butter, thick-cut chips and spinach. Bread and butter pudding with home-made custard.

◑ *Open all year (Thu to Sun during Nov to Mar)* ✗ *Food available all day £ Lunch £ Dinner except Mon Tue ££* Ⅴ *Vegetarians welcome* ✶ *Children welcome* ♿ *Facilities for disabled visitors* ✍ *No smoking throughout* 💳 *Mastercard/ Eurocard, American Express, Visa, Diners Club, Switch, Delta* ⋈ *Proprietors: Nigel & Fiona Franks*

Station Square Ballater AB35 5QB
Tel: 013397 55050
In Station Square, in the centre of Ballater. [D4]

BALQUHIDDER

Monachyle Mhor: Winner 2001 – Out of Town Award

- *"Peace, tranquility and wonderful food at this retreat deep in the heart of Rob Roy country."*
- *Modern Scottish cooking.*

THE LEWIS' fully deserve their reputation for hospitality and comfort. Both the restaurant and cosy bar serve imaginative, good food offering game from the estate, fish from the West Coast and the finest Scottish meat cooked with a French influence by highly skilled Chef Tom Lewis. Interesting, discerning wine list.

Scallops on charred asparagus and balsamic pink grapefruit; Champagne and caviar beurre blanc. Pan-fried breast of grouse and loin of rabbit with cabbage, bacon and pinhead oatmeal, chanterelles, sage and game jus. White chocolate bavarois with Grand Marnier fruit salad.

STB ★★★ Small Hotel

◑ Open all year 🏠 Rooms: 10 en suite 🛏 B&B £40–£50 ✕ Food available all day £–£££ Lunch ££ Dinner £££ Ⓥ Vegetarians welcome ✖ No smoking in restaurant 💳 Mastercard/Eurocard, Visa, Switch 🍴 Proprietors: Jean Lewis & Tom Lewis

Balquhidder Lochearnhead Perthshire FK19 8PQ
Tel: 01877 384 622 Fax: 01877 384 305
E-mail: info@monachylemhor.com
Web: www.monachylemhor.com
11 miles north of Callander on A84. Turn right at Kingshouse Hotel – 6 miles straight along glen road. [C5]

BANAVIE

Glen Loy Lodge Hotel

- *"A charming Highland retreat with hospitable, well-informed hosts."*
- *Skilled Scottish cooking.*

ORIGINALLY BUILT in the 1920s, Glenloy has been refurbished into a charming country house hotel. The cooking adds innovative modern twists to traditional items, from dinner menus to interesting choices for breakfast. Savour the inspirational wine list of over 100 bins ranging from quality house wines to mature classed growth clarets from the 80s and 90s.

Seared monkfish and scallops in Parmesan and vermouth cream sauce, flavoured with smoked salmon flakes. Breast of Gressingham duck with a fresh apricot and cherry sauce served with saffron rice. Melting chocolate pudding with crème fraîche.

STB ★★★ Small Hotel

◑ Open all year except Nov 🏠 Rooms: 8 en suite 🛏 DB&B £54–£69 B&B £30–£45 🆂 Special rates available ✕ Lunch ££ Dinner £££ Ⓥ Vegetarians welcome ✖ Children welcome ✖ No smoking throughout 🐕Dogs welcome 💳 Mastercard/Eurocard, Visa, Switch, Delta 🍴 Proprietors: Pat & Gordon Haynes

Banavie, Nr Fort William Inverness-shire PH33 7PD
Tel: 01397 712 700 Fax: 01397 712 700
E-mail: glenloy.lodge@virgin.net
Web: www.smoothhound.co.uk/hotels/glenloyl.html
4 miles north of Banavie on the B8004. [B4]

BANCHORY

The Horsemill Restaurant, Crathes Castle, The National Trust for Scotland

- *"No visit to Crathes Castle is complete without popping into the restaurant to enjoy fine food."*
- *Quality meals, snacks and home baking.*

THE ORIGINAL 'horse mill' has been tastefully converted into a very fresh and sunny tea-room and restaurant. Food is served in a modern and imaginative way and everything is made on the premises. Staff are delightful.

Tomato and red pepper soup served with a cheese and herb scone. Smoked haddock fish cakes with spicy tomato chutney. Selection of home baking.

STB ★★★★ Castle

◐ *Open all year except 25 Dec to 9 Jan* ♟ *Licensed* ✕ *Food available all day from £ Lunch £* Ⓥ *Vegetarians welcome* ✲ *Children welcome* ♿ *Facilities for disabled visitors* ✕ *No smoking throughout* 💳 *Mastercard, Visa, Switch* 🍴 *Catering Manager: Alison Mitchell*

Banchory AB31 3QJ
Tel: 01330 844525 Fax: 01330 844797
E-mail: amartin@nts.org.uk
Web: www.nts.org.uk
On A93, 3 miles east of Banchory and 15 miles west of Aberdeen. [D4]

BANCHORY

The Old West Manse

- *"A wonderful establishment, excellent food, delightfully comfortable with lovely people."*
- *Superior home cooking.*

A VERY HIGH LEVEL of comfort awaits guests at the Old West Manse. Jayne and John Taylor have established themselves as offering exceptional quality. Skill and dedication is evident in the cooking – food is fresh and the Taylor's anticipate their guests' every need. All public rooms are immaculate and bedrooms are exceptionally comfortable.

Herb crêpes with smoked salmon and cucumber, served with warm savoury scones. Fillet of Scottish beef with roasted shallots, herbs and tarragon sauce with a horseradish mash. Rich chocolate mousse with a raspberry and vodka coulis.

STB ★★★★★ B&B

◐ *Open all year* 🛏 *Rooms: 3 (2 en suite, 1 private facilities)* 🍽 *DB&B from £46 B&B from £27.50* ✕ *Residents only Packed lunch on request £ Dinner ££* Ⓥ *Vegetarians welcome* ✲ *Children welcome* ✕ *No smoking in bedrooms or dining room* 🐕 *Dogs by prior arrangement* 💳 *Mastercard/Eurocard, Visa, Switch, Delta* 🍴 *Owners: Jayne & John Taylor*

71 Station Road Banchory Aberdeenshire AB31 5UD
Tel: 01330 822202 Fax: 01330 822202
Situated on the A93 Aberdeen to Braemar road. Car park entrance is approx 60 metres past A980 junction on right (travelling from Aberdeen). [D4]

BANCHORY

Raemoir House Hotel

- *"Treat yourself to a delightful lunch amidst the splendour of Raemoir."*
- *Imaginative Scottish Cooking.*

SET IN 3500 ACRES of beautiful grounds Raemoir is a stunning building furnished to the highest standard. Chef John Barbour prepares food to a very high standard with skill and imagination. Lunch can be taken in the comfortable bar or sumptuous dining room – all food is freshly prepared. Staff are attentive, yet inconspicuous.

Pressed confit of duck with artichoke terrine, roasted shallots and candied kumquats. Halibut fillet with lobster mousseline and leek parcel, celeriac fricadelle and shellfish bisque. Layered white and dark chocolate parfait with Jaconde biscuits and Grand Marnier syrup.

STB ★★★★ Hotel

◗ *Open all year* 🏨 *Rooms: 21 en suite* 🛏 *DB&B £65–£85 B&B £40–£60* 💷 *Special rates available* ✕ *Lunch ££ Dinner £££* 🅅 *Vegetarians welcome* 🧒 *Children welcome* ♿ *Facilities for disabled visitors* 🚭 *No smoking in dining room* 🐕 *Dogs welcome* 💳 *Mastercard/Eurocard, American Express, Visa, Diners Club, Switch, Delta* 🎩 *Directors: Lesley & Roy Bishop-Milnes*

Banchory Royal Deeside B31 4ED Tel: 01330 824884 Fax: 01330 822171 At the junction of B977 and A980 – 17 miles west of Aberdeen. [D4]

BANFF

Banff Springs Hotel

- *"A warm welcome and friendly staff await the guests."*
- *Traditional Scottish cooking.*

WITH WONDERFUL VIEWS of the Buchan coastline, Banff Springs is in a superb location. The restaurant is a particularly good place to enjoy the views. The cooking uses only good local fresh ingredients, presented and prepared by a chef who cares and understands his subject. In this pleasant atmosphere, staff are keen to ensure guests enjoy their stay.

Arbroath smokies, mayonnaise and cream laced with malt whisky, served with yoghurt dill dressing and oatcakes. Medallions of beef fillet topped with a Stilton soufflé surrounded by Madeira essence and roasted shallots. Baileys and cinnamon brûlée with vanilla shortbread.

STB ★★★ Hotel

◗ *Open all year except Christmas Day* 🏨 *Rooms: 31 en suite* 🛏 *DB&B £51–£64.50 B&B £31.50–£45* 💷 *Special rates available* ✕ *Lunch £ Dinner £££* 🅅 *Vegetarians welcome* 🧒 *Children welcome* ♿ *Facilities for disabled visitors* 🚭 *No smoking in restaurant* 💳 *Mastercard/ Eurocard, American Express, Visa, Switch, Delta* 🎩 *Proprietor: Nicola Antliff*

Golden Knowes Road Banff AB45 2JE Tel: 01261 812881 Fax: 01261 815546 E-mail: info@banffspringshotel.co.uk Web: www.banffspringshotel.co.uk On the western outskirts of Banff on the A98 Fraserburgh to Elgin road. [D3]

BANKFOOT

Perthshire Visitor Centre

- *"Well worth stopping off on a long journey. Good food and lots of interesting things to see."*
- *Home cooking.*

THE MACBETH EXPERIENCE is the focus of this visitor centre which includes a friendly restaurant with a conservatory, waitress service and a varied selection of meals, desserts and home baking. Sunday lunches and high teas served. Good, fresh coffee also available here! Shop includes a food hall, gifts and leisure wear.

Chicken liver pâté with chutney and oatcakes. Macsweens haggis. Salmon fish cakes. Venison pie. Bankfoot cheesecake. Orkney ice cream.

STB ★★★★ Visitor Attraction

◑ *Open all year except Christmas Day and New Year's Day* ♟ *Table licence* ✘ *Food available all day £* Ⓥ *Vegetarians welcome* ☆ *Children's play area* ♿ *Facilities for disabled visitors* 💳 *Mastercard/Eurocard, Visa* 🗡 *Proprietors: Wilson & Catriona Girvan and Calum MacLellan*

Bankfoot Perth PH1 4EB
Tel: 01738 787696 Fax: 01738 787120
E-mail: wilson@macbeth.co.uk
Web: www.macbeth.co.uk
8 miles north of Perth on A9. Follow signs for Bankfoot. [D5]

BEAULY

Lovat Arms Hotel

- *"Enjoy the friendliness, the tartans and quality beef from the family farm at Torachilty."*
- *Modern Scottish cooking.*

THE LOVAT ARMS is a stylish family-owned hotel in the centre of a picturesque small market town. The food is very well-cooked and presented by head chef Donald Munro who uses his skills to present local produce in innovative ways for good value for money. Afternoon Tea and High Tea available.

Hot smoked salmon flaked on to salad leaves sprinkled with lime and dill dressing. Noisette of lamb from Torachilty (the Fraser family's farm) presented on a bed of Highland stovies with an onion sauce. Strupag ice cream served with a malt whisky sauce.

◑ *Open all year* 🛏 *Rooms: 22 en suite* 🍴 *DB&B £50–£80 B&B £35–£60* 💷 *Special rates available* ✘ *Food available all day £–££ Lunch £–££ Dinner £–£££* Ⓥ *Vegetarians welcome* ☆ *Children welcome* ♿ *Facilities for disabled visitors* 🚭 *No smoking in dining room* 💳 *Mastercard/ Eurocard, Visa, Switch, JCB* 🗡 *Proprietor: William Fraser*

Beauly Inverness-shire IV4 7BS
Tel: 01463 782313 Fax: 01463 782862
E-mail: lovat.arms@cali.co.uk
On A862, 11 miles from Inverness in Beauly centre. [C4]

BEAULY

Made In Scotland

- *"You can feast your eyes on the wonderful Scottish Giftware then enjoy freshly prepared produce in the restaurant."*
- *Scottish cooking.*

MADE IN SCOTLAND is located in a well-designed, modern restaurant with daily blackboard specials. It is a welcoming place to enjoy a range of home baking and meals all freshly prepared on the premises, combined with the widest range of high quality Scottish crafts and gifts you will find in Scotland.

Traditional Cullen skink with a tattie and herb scone. Local breast of barn chicken stuffed with Stornoway black pudding, served with a malt and mustard sauce. Ecclefechan tart served with crème fraîche.

STB ★★★★ Tourist Shop

◐ *Open all year except Christmas Day, Boxing Day, 1 and 2 Jan ✘ Food available all day £ Lunch £ Ⓥ Vegetarians welcome ☀ Children welcome ⅏ Facilities for disabled visitors ✄ No smoking throughout ▣ Mastercard/Eurocard, American Express, Visa, Switch ▨ Retail Manager: Anne Boyd*

Station Road Beauly IV4 7EH
Tel: 01463 782578 Fax: 01463 782409
E-mail: mis@enterprise.net
Web: www.made-in-scotland.co.uk
Only ¼ hour by road from Inverness, on the south edge of Beauly on the A862. [C4]

BIGGAR

Shieldhill Castle: Finalist The Macallan Taste of Scotland Awards 2001

- *"Shieldhill combines sumptuous surroundings, excellent service and wonderful gourmet dining."*
- *Modern Scottish.*

SHIELDHILL is a true country house hotel. The cooking here is completely in keeping with the surroundings, with a team of highly skilled chefs making best use of local produce in an imaginative way. Shieldhill also has a highly acclaimed wine list to complement the à la carte dinner menu.

Smoked trout soufflé with a mussel and leek butter sauce. Niçoise of lamb with rösti potatoes and a thyme jus. Caramelised lemon tart with a plum chutney.

STB ★★★★ Hotel

◐ *Open all year ▦ Rooms: 16 en suite ⨳ B&B £59–£248 ▩ Special rates available ✘ Food available all day £ Lunch ££ Dinner £££ Ⓥ Vegetarians welcome ☀ Children welcome ⅏ Facilities for disabled visitors ✄ Dogs welcome ▣ Mastercard/Eurocard, Visa, Switch, Delta ▨ Proprietors: Bob & Christina Lamb; Head Chef: Ashley Gallant*

Quothquan Biggar ML12 6NA
Tel: 01899 220035 Fax: 01899 221092
E-mail: enquiries@shieldhill.co.uk
Web: www.shieldhillcastle.com
Turn off A702 on to B7016 Biggar to Carnwath road in middle of Biggar. After 2 miles turn left into Shieldhill Road, castle is on right. [C6]

BIGGAR

Skirling House

- *"The perfect stopover, and over, and over!"*
- *Skilled Scottish cooking.*

THIS FASCINATING house is the home of Bob and Isobel Hunter. Bob presents a four course set menu each evening cooked with a light, well executed touch and served in the new conservatory extension. The house cellar is well stocked. A gem of an architectural find where hospitality is warm and genuine.

Quails eggs in a Parma ham nest. Tenderloin of pork with a fig and thyme stuffing. Goats cheese baked in a filo basket with red onion confit. Gooseberry and elderflower fool with shortbread biscuit.

STB ★★★★★ B&B

◗ *Open 1 Mar to 31 Dec* 🏨 *Rooms: 5 en suite* 🛏 *DB&B £57–£67 B&B £35–£45* 🍷 *Restricted hotel licence* ✗ *Dinner 4 course menu ££* Ⅴ *Vegetarians welcome* ⅋ *Facilities for disabled visitors* ⊁ *No smoking throughout* 💳 *Mastercard, Visa, Switch, Delta* Ⅺ *Proprietors: Bob & Isobel Hunter*

Skirling Biggar Lanarkshire ML12 6HD Tel: 01899 860274 Fax: 01899 860255 E-mail: enquiry@skirlinghouse.com Web: www.skirlinghouse.com In Skirling village overlooking the village green. 2 miles from Biggar on A72. [C6]

BLAIR ATHOLL

The House of Bruar

- *"Self-service restaurant offering a variety of dishes to suit all tastes."*
- *A good selection of popular dishes.*

THE HOUSE OF BRUAR is a large, splendidly designed 'emporium' selling the best of Scottish country products – cashmere, cloth, wildflowers, country wear – with a golf shop, mail order, food hall and 400-seater restaurant. The lengthy blackboard menus offer snacks and full meals, with many classic Scottish dishes; the cooking is fresh and accomplished.

Grilled salmon with lemon and parsley butter. Pan-fried strips of pork fillet in a creamy mushroom sauce. Treacle tart and fresh whipped cream.

◗ *Open all year except Christmas Day, Boxing Day and New Year's Day* ✗ *Food available all day* Ⅴ *Vegetarians welcome* ⅋ *Children welcome* ⅋ *Facilities for disabled visitors* ⊁ *No smoking throughout* 💳 *Mastercard/Eurocard, American Express, Visa, Switch, Delta*

Bruar Falls by Blair Atholl Perthshire PH18 5TW Tel: 01796 483236 Fax: 01796 483218 E-mail: office@houseofbruar.demon.co.uk Web: www.houseofbruar.com 7 miles north of Pitlochry on the side of A9 at Bruar. Restaurant services A9.[C4]

BLAIR ATHOLL

The Loft Restaurant

- *"The Loft offers delicious food served by friendly attentive staff."*
- *Scottish with an international influence.*

WITH ITS twisted old beams, stone walls and oak flooring this is a great setting to sample the excellent cuisine of Head Chef Paul Collins. Menus are refreshing and appealing to suit all. The Loft has a conservatory bar and roof terrace. Booking advisable.

Salad of West Coast scallops, shallot purée. Best end of Dunkeld lamb, Anna potatoes, tomato and basil sauce. Sablé of Scottish berries.

◐ *Open all year* ✖ *(Morning coffee to late dinner available) Lunch £ Dinner ££* Ⓥ *Vegetarians welcome* ✸ *Children welcome* ⅍ *No smoking in restaurant* ⊞ *Mastercard/ Eurocard, American Express, Visa, Diners Club, Switch, Delta, JCB* ⋈ *Partner: Mrs P M Richardson*

Golf Course Road Blair Atholl by Pitlochry PH18 5TE
Tel: 01796 481377 Fax: 01796 481511
Web: www.theloftrestaurant.co.uk
Take B8079 off A9, 5 miles north of Pitlochry. In village take golf course road by Tilt Hotel, the Loft is 50 yards on right. [C4]

BLAIRGOWRIE

Cargills Restaurant & Bistro

- *"Enjoy a memorable meal with good service in lively surroundings."*
- *Modern Scottish cooking with some European influence.*

CHEF/PROPRIETOR Willie Little creates an impressive selection of high quality dishes all very reasonably priced. A blackboard shows daily specials in addition to the menu. A carefully chosen wine list complements the food. Ideal for a relaxed lunch or dinner. Sunday brunch has also become a firm favourite.

Cargills venison and haggis terrine with red onion marmalade. Hand-dived scallops with noodles and lime coriander dressing. Apple and Swiss chard pie with ice cream and mint syrup.

◐ *Open all year except 1 and 2 Jan Closed Tue* ✖ *Lunch except Tue £–££ Dinner except Tue ££* Ⓥ *Vegetarians welcome* ✸ *Children welcome* ♿ *Facilities for disabled visitors* ⊞ *Mastercard/ Eurocard, Visa, Switch, Delta* ⋈ *Chef/Proprietor: Willie Little*

Lower Mill Street Blairgowrie Perthshire PH10 6AQ
Tel: 01250 876735 Fax: 01250 876735
E-mail: exceed@btconnect.com
Web: www.exceed.co.uk
At the Square in the centre of Blairgowrie, turn left off A93 Perth-Braemar road into Mill Street. Cargills is behind the car park, 200 yards down on the left. [D5]

BLAIRGOWRIE

Kinloch House: Winner 2001 – Overall Excellence & Country House Award

- *"First-class cuisine and hospitality."*
- *Outstanding Scottish cuisine.*

SET IN 25 ACRES, Kinloch House Hotel is a fine example of a Scottish country house. Service is impeccable yet unobtrusive in an elegant dining room. Menus offer the finest Scottish produce, carefully prepared by head chef Bill McNicoll who also runs cookery courses. The hotel has a health and fitness centre.

Ravioli of game placed on red cabbage with woodland mushrooms. Fillet of Angus beef with an oxtail mousse, glazed vegetables, fondant potatoes and a Madeira reduction. Spiced apple tart with creamed almond topping and lemon crème fraîche.

STB ★★★★★ Hotel

◗ *Open 29 Dec to 18 Dec* 🏠 *Rooms: 20 en suite* 🛏 *B&B £74.45–£81.25* ✗ *Lunch ££ Dinner £££* Ⓥ *Vegetarians welcome* ✻ *Children welcome – over 7 years only at dinner* ♿ *Facilities for disabled visitors* ✰ *No smoking in dining room* 💳 *Mastercard/ Eurocard, American Express, Visa, Diners Club, Switch, Delta* Ⓜ *Proprietors: The Shentall Family*

By Blairgowrie Perthshire PH10 6SG Tel: 01250 884 237 Fax: 01250 884 333 E-mail: reception@kinlochhouse.com Web: www.kinlochhouse.com On A923, 3 miles west of Blairgowrie. [D5]

BLAIRGOWRIE

Rosemount Golf Hotel Ltd

- *"An ideal base for many outdoor activity holidays complemented with good quality freshly prepared food."*
- *Traditional Scottish cooking with a modern flair.*

THE ROSEMOUNT is situated on the south side of Blairgowrie in a quiet location amongst its award-winning gardens. The restaurant has an extensive menu to suit every palate. A popular place with golfers and locals and boasts a lively bar/19th hole with golfers from the nearby course. Two self-contained chalets within grounds.

Oak-smoked fillets of trout with mixed leaves and horseradish dressing. Medallions of Highland venison with fondant potatoes, braised red cabbage and parsnip purée surrounded with a redcurrant jus. Poached pear coated with caramel sauce and vanilla ice cream.

STB ★★★ Small Hotel

◗ *Open all year* 🏠 *Rooms: 12 en suite* 🛏 *DB&B £50–£60 B&B £37.50–£42.50* 🅂 *Special rates available* ✗ *Lunch £ Dinner ££* Ⓥ *Vegetarians welcome* ✻ *Children welcome* ✰ *Smoking and non smoking dining rooms* 🐕 *Dogs welcome in chalets only* 💳 *Mastercard/Eurocard, Visa, Diners Club, Switch, Delta* Ⓜ *Director: Alistair C Gibb*

Golf Course Road Blairgowrie Perthshire PH10 6LJ Tel: 01250 872604 Fax: 01250 874496 E-mail: info@rosemountgolf.co.uk Web: www.rosemountgolf.co.uk The hotel is situated in Golf Course Road within walking distance of Blairgowrie Golf Club and directly accessible of the A93 Perth-Braemar road. [D5]

BOAT OF GARTEN

The Boat

- *"Lovely food, atmosphere and comfortable elegant decor makes this a great place when touring the area."*
- *Modern/traditional Scottish cuisine.*

IAN AND SHONA Tatchell are committed and welcoming hosts. They have upgraded the hotel to a high standard and this same commitment to customer care is evident. Chef Tony Alcott prepares meals combining traditional and modern techniques using only the very best ingredients.

Baked parcel of monkfish with garlic, spinach, and bacon with a red wine and olive dressing. Caramelised suprême of Guinea fowl with honey and lemon glaze on wild mushroom and rosemary risotto. Warm orange toffee pudding on an apricot brandy sabayon.

STB ★★★★ Hotel

❶ *Open all year* ♨ *Rooms: 32 en suite* ⬌ *DB&B £80–£95 B&B £50–£65* ▦ *Special rates available* ✘ *Lunch ££ Dinner £££* Ⓥ *Vegetarians welcome* ✱ *Children over 12 years welcome* ✌ *No smoking in restaurant and most bedrooms* 🐕*Dogs welcome (not in public areas)* ▣ *Mastercard/Eurocard, Visa, Switch, Delta* ⚑ *Owners: Ian & Shona Tatchell*

Boat of Garten Inverness-shire PH24 3BH
Tel: 01479 831258 Fax: 01479 831414
E-mail: holidays@boathotel.co.uk
Web: www.boathotel.co.uk
From Aviemore take A95 to Grantown-on-Spey and turning left Boat of Garten. After 1 mile turn right into Boat of Garten. The hotel is adjacent to the Strathspey Steam Railway. [C4]

BRIDGE OF ORCHY

Bridge of Orchy Hotel

- *"A popular spot for walkers where the food is freshly prepared and well-presented."*
- *Modern and stylishly presented Scottish fare.*

THIS COMFORTABLE hotel, with warm log fires and delightful candlelit dining room, makes a very enjoyable place from which to explore this stunning part of the Highlands and to relax after a long day. Equally this is a good spot to stop and enjoy good Scottish cooking with a modern twist.

Ravioli of langoustine in a shellfish bisque. Best end of lamb with fondant potato, roast garlic, baby vegetables and rosemary jus. Caramelised lemon tart.

STB ★★★★ Small Hotel

❶ *Open all year except Dec* ♨ *Rooms: 10 en suite* ⬌ *B&B £30–£55* ▦ *Special rates available* ✘ *Food available all day ££ Lunch – by arrangement in dining room: Bar lunches served daily ££ Dinner £££* Ⓥ *Vegetarians welcome* ✱ *Children welcome* ✌ *No smoking in dining room* ▣ *Mastercard/Eurocard, American Express, Visa, Diners Club, Switch, Delta*

Bridge of Orchy Argyll PA36 4AD
Tel: 01838 400208 Fax: 01838 400313
E-mail: info@bridgeoforchy.co.uk
Web: www.scottish-selection.co.uk
On main A82 road to Fort William. 6 miles north of Tyndrum. [C5]

BRIDGE OF WEIR

The Lochnagar

- *"Delightful coffee shop and restaurant with wonderful home baking – don't miss the craft shop!"*
- *Modern Scottish cooking.*

VERY HIGH STANDARD of home cooking here, especially the baking. The atmosphere is friendly which is obvious by its popularity. Preparation of the compact lunch menu, made with quality ingredients, is careful and sensitive. A small indoor children's play area includes tables for parents to enjoy coffee or lunch. Very impressive coffee shop. Booking advisable.

Smoked Fencebay salmon pâté with rye toast. Chicken, leek and smoked bacon en croustade. Lochnagar chocolate fudge cake with Orkney creamery ice cream.

◑ *Open 8 Jan to 29 Dec Closed Sun* ♆ *Licensed* ✕ *Food available all day £ Lunch except Sun ££* Ⓥ *Vegetarians welcome* ⚘ *Children welcome* ♿ *Facilities for disabled visitors* ✄ *No smoking throughout* 💳 *Mastercard/Eurocard, Visa, Switch, Delta, Solo, Visa Electron, JCB* ⚑ *John & Mary-Ann Rankin and Hamish & Kate Rankin*

Main Street Bridge of Weir Renfrewshire PA11 3LA
Tel: 01505 613410 Fax: 01505 613410
E-mail: johnrankin_1@excite.co.uk
In centre of village of Bridge of Weir. Car parking to rear of building. 5 miles from Glasgow Airport. [C5]

BRORA

Royal Marine Hotel

- *"Traditional Edwardian house hotel with leisure facilities located next to coastline and mouth of the River Brora."*
- *Good Scottish cooking with modern influences.*

THE ROYAL MARINE HOTEL is a popular choice for anglers, golfers and families. Dark Edwardian woodwork and tartan fabrics create a homely atmosphere. Guests may choose from bar lunches, all-day casual meals in the Garden Restaurant or set and à la carte menus with daily specialities in the dining room.

Salad of Brora lobster, hotel's cured salmon and queen scallops served with extra virgin olive oil dressing. Seared fillet of heather-reared loth lamb carved over a fine ratatouille, pomme dauphinoise and thyme-scented jus. Caramelised cherries with Drambuie and natural yoghurt.

STB ★★★★ Hotel

◑ *Open all year* 🏠 *Rooms: 22 en suite* 🛏 *DB&B £50–£80 B&B £40–£65* 🆂 *Special rates available* ✕ *Food available all day ££ Lunch £ Dinner £££* Ⓥ *Vegetarians welcome* ⚘ *Children welcome* ♿ *Facilities for disabled visitors* ✄ *No smoking in restaurant* 💳 *Mastercard/Eurocard, American Express, Visa, Diners Club, Switch* ⚑ *Managing Director: Robert Powell*

Golf Road Brora Sutherland KW9 6QS
Tel: 01408 621252 Fax: 01408 621181
E-mail: info@highlandescape.com
Web: www.highlandescape.com
On the A9 from Golspie to Helmsdale. At Brora cross bridge over River Brora and take Golf Road on right. Hotel is on left. [C3]

BUCKIE

CAIRNBAAN

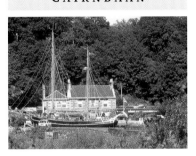

The Old Monastery Restaurant

- *"The best of local produce is used here to create inspirational food."*
- *Classical European in a modern style.*

UNDER THE CARING ownership of Val and Calum Buchanan the Old Monastery has developed its own reputation for quality. Menus change regularly and feature locally-sourced Scottish produce. Calum is a great wine enthusiast and has compiled an eclectic wine list to complement the menus.

Salmon and celeriac terrine wrapped in smoked salmon, Puy lentil vinaigrette. Saddle of Scottish hill lamb, sweet garlic croquette, Provençal olives, basil-infused tomatoes, lamb sauce. Coconut bavarois with bananas in warm orange and lime sauce, caramel ice cream.

◑ *Open all year except 3 weeks Jan – Phone for festive hours Closed Sun Mon except first Sun of each month when open for lunch and music (musical evenings throughout year)* ✕ *Lunch except Mon ££ Dinner except Sun Mon £££* Ⓥ *Vegetarians welcome* ♣ *Children welcome (over 8 years in evening is preferred)* ✄ *No smoking in restaurant* ⊞ *Mastercard/Eurocard, American Express, Visa, Switch, Delta* ⚄ *Proprietors: Calum & Valerie Buchanan*

Drybridge Buckie Moray AB56 5JB
Tel: 01542 832660 Fax: 01542 839437
E-mail: calum or val @oldmonastery.com
Web: www.oldmonastery.com
Turn off A98 opposite main Buckie Junction onto Drybridge road. Continue up hill for 2½ miles. [D3]

Cairnbaan Hotel

- *"Well-prepared seafood and bread making skills are evident at this smart, friendly location."*
- *Imaginative Scottish.*

THE CAIRNBAAN HOTEL has recently changed hands and is now run by Darren Dobson who is very much 'at the helm'. The restaurant has been very tastefully refurbished resembling that of a ship's deck. This is a busy and lively hotel offering good home-made food using fresh local produce.

Sweet-marinated herring with a pear, watercress and walnut salad. Roast breast of pheasant on skirlie toast with rowan jelly. Compote of sweet oranges topped with fresh cream flavoured with home-made marmalade and Drambuie.

STB ★★★★ Hotel

◑ *Open all year* ⌂ *Rooms: 11 en suite* ⇔ *DB&B £50–£75 B&B £45–£55* ⊠ *Special rates available* ✕ *Lunch ££ Dinner ££* Ⓥ *Vegetarians welcome* ♣ *Children welcome* ♿ *Facilities for disabled visitors* ✄ *No smoking in the dining room* ⊞ *Mastercard/Eurocard, Visa, Switch, Delta* ⚄ *Owner: Darren Dobson*

Cairnbaan By Lochgilphead Argyll PA31 8SJ
Tel: 01546 603668 Fax: 01546 606045
E-mail: cairnbaan.hotel@virgin.net
Web: www.cairnbaan.com
Two miles north of Lochgilphead on the Oban road. [B5]

CAIRNDOW

Loch Fyne Oyster Bar

- *"Informal restaurant offering skilfully cooked seafood all day and evening – excellent food shop attached!"*
- *Fresh seafood.*

THE RESTAURANT here eschews 'haute cuisine'; dishes are very simply prepared, so the fresh natural flavour of the seafood can be enjoyed. The adjacent shop features an extensive chilled cabinet displaying all their products in an attractive layout. Permits 'carry-outs'. Winner of The Macallan Taste of Scotland Award 1995.

Fresh rock oysters from Loch Fyne. Queen scallops roasted with bacon. Bradan roast (salmon smoked in a hot kiln) served hot with a whisky sauce. Shellfish platter – fresh oysters, langoustines, queen scallops, brown crab and clams.

◗ *Open all year except Christmas Day and New Year's Day* ✖ *Food served all day* ££ Ⓥ *Vegetarians welcome* ▦ *Mastercard/Eurocard, Visa, Diners Club, Switch, Delta* 𝕄 *Proprietors: Loch Fyne Oysters Ltd*

Clachan Cairndow Argyll PA26 8BL
Tel: 01499 600 236 Fax: 01499 600 234
E-mail: info@loch-fyne.com
Web: www.lochfyne.com
At head of Loch Fyne on A83 Arrochar to Inveraray road. Well signposted on right-hand side 10 miles before Inveraray. [C5]

CALLANDER

Roman Camp Country House Hotel

- *"Award-winning food in one of Scotland's best country house hotels."*
- *Modern Scottish cuisine.*

ROMAN CAMP offers the peace of the past alongside every possible modern convenience. In the dining room, the best of fresh local produce is imaginatively used to create the finest Scottish cuisine, complemented by an excellent wine list. Service is unhurried and impeccable, the food is first class.

Ravioli of scallops with shellfish velouté and morels. Roe deer loin with basil mousseline, confit tomato and aubergine purée. Lemon savarin with apricot sorbet.

STB ★★★★ Small Hotel

◗ *Open all year* 🏠 *Rooms: 14 en suite* 🛏 *DB&B £90–£125 B&B £55–£90* ▣ *Special rates available* ✖ *Lunch* ££ *Dinner 4 course menu* ££££ Ⓥ *Vegetarians welcome* ♣ *Children welcome* ♿ *Facilities for disabled visitors* ✎ *No smoking in dining room* ▦ *Mastercard/Eurocard, American Express, Visa, Diners Club, Switch, Delta* 𝕄 *Proprietors: Eric & Marion Brown*

Callander FK17 8BG
Tel: 01877 330003 Fax: 01877 331533
E-mail: mail@roman-camp-hotel.co.uk
Web: www.roman-camp-hotel.co.uk
At the east end of Callander main street from Stirling, turn left down 300 yard drive to hotel. [C5]

CARNOUSTIE

11 Park Avenue: Finalist The Macallan Taste of Scotland Awards 2001

- *"The enthusiastic welcome was truly matched by the delicious food."*
- *Modern Scottish cooking.*

11 PARK AVENUE's simple exterior does not reflect the warmth and extent of hospitality to be found within. Staff are delightful and most efficient. Decor is tasteful and of extremely high standard. A stunning eating experience is guaranteed. Food is sophisticated, well-executed and of top quality, offering good value for money.

Warm salad of roast red pepper with goats cheese, tapenade, pine nuts, with rocket and pesto. Crispy Gressingham duck with blueberries and port wine sauce. Warm almond and apricot tart with crème anglaise and vanilla ice cream.

◗ *Open all year except first 2 weeks Jan Closed Sun Mon* ✕ *Lunch – by arrangement ££ Dinner except Sun Mon ££–£££* Ⓥ *Vegetarians welcome* ✷ *Children welcome* & *Facilities for disabled visitors* ✰ *No smoking in dining room* ▣ *Mastercard/Eurocard, American Express, Visa, Diners Club, Switch, Delta, JCB* ▨ *Chef/Proprietor: Stephen Collinson*

11 Park Avenue Carnoustie Angus DD7 7JA
Tel: 01241 853336 Fax: 01241 859333
E-mail: parkavenue@genie.co.uk
Web: www.11parkavenue.co.uk
Park Avenue runs from the main street in Carnoustie towards the railway and beach. [D5]

CARNOUSTIE

Carnoustie Hotel, Golf Resort & Spa

- *"Exceptionally good food, in comfortable surroundings, whilst watching golf on an internationally famous course."*
- *Modern Scottish cooking.*

CARNOUSTIE is a modern spacious hotel which is privately owned and run to a very high standard. Superbly situated, most public rooms overlook the golf course as do many bedrooms. Food here is excellent and presented by a skilled team. Menus are sophisticated and expertly executed.

Chilled fettucine of smoked Orkney salmon with seared scallops, mango salsa and basil oil. Prime fillet of Angus beef Rossini, maxim potatoes, wild local mushrooms and truffle infused jus. Hot Perthshire strawberry and star anise soufflé.

STB ★★★★ Leisure Centre

◗ *Open all year* ⌂ *Rooms: 85, 75 en suite and 10 suites* ⊨ *DB&B £95–£137.50 B&B £57.50– £110* ▧ *Special rates available* ✕ *Food available all day from £££ Lunch ££ Dinner £££* Ⓥ *Vegetarians welcome* ✷ *Children welcome* & *Facilities for disabled visitors* ✰ *No smoking in dining room* ⚲ *Dogs welcome* ▣ *Mastercard/Eurocard, American Express, Visa, Diners Club, Switch, Delta* ▨ *General Manager: Mr Jerry Foster*

The Links Carnoustie Angus DD7 7JE
Tel: 01241 411999 Fax: 01241 411998
E-mail: enquiries@carnoustie-hotel.com
Web: www.carnoustie-hotel.com
From Dundee, east on A92 towards Arbroath, after 7 miles turn right at first signpost for Carnoustie. Follow road for 1½ miles to main street. Left for 500m, right at signpost for beach and golf course. [D5]

CARRADALE

Dunvalanree

- *"A popular, friendly family-run establishment offering excellent food."*
- *Scottish home cooking.*

DUNVALANREE IS PERCHED on the cliff above Port Righ Bay. Bedrooms are furnished to a high standard and retain original 1930s features. Many thoughtful touches can be found here. Owner Alyson Milstead is very keen on sourcing local ingredients whenever possible. Quails and hens supply the house. Very friendly atmosphere.

Smoked mussels 'Dunvalanree' (cooked in garlic butter with bacon lardons). Locally-landed scallops with cherry tomatoes, chilli and coriander. Hot chocolate gâteau with Drambuie sauce.

STB ★★★★ Small Hotel
Green Tourism Two Leaf Silver Award

◗ *Open all year* 🏬 *Rooms 7, 5 en suite* 🛏 *DB&B £37–£50 B&B £22–£36* 💷 *Special rates available* ✗ *Dinner ££* Ⓥ *Vegetarians welcome* ✱ *Children welcome* ♿ *Facilities for disabled visitors* ✔ *No smoking throughout* 🐾 *Dogs welcome* 💳 *Mastercard/Eurocard, Visa, Delta* Ⓜ *Owners: Alyson & Alan Milstead*

Port Righ Bay Carradale, Kintyre Argyll PA28 6SE
Tel: 01583 431226 Fax: 01583 431339
E-mail: eat@dunvalanree.com
Web: www.dunvalanree.com
At the crossroads in the centre of Carradale (just past the bus stop) turn right and continue to the very end of the road, about ½ a mile.
[B6]

CASTLE DOUGLAS

Craigadam: Winner 2001 – Bed and Breakfast Award

- *"With its beautiful setting and panoramic views this working farm maintains its exceptional standards for hospitality and fine food."*
- *Delightful home cooking.*

CRAIGADAM IS A LARGE and elegant farmhouse. The dining room and drawing room are filled with family treasures and the cooking is carefully balanced, presented with great attention to detail and the flavours are delightful. Dinner is enjoyed in the oak-panelled dining room, drinks and coffee served in the drawing room.

Smoked haddock mousseline with prawn and hollandaise sauce, and home-made bread. Noisettes of Galloway lamb on a bed of spinach with a mint sauce. Lemon meringue roulade with mango and passion fruit sauce.

STB ★★★★ B&B

◗ *Open all year except Christmas Eve to 2 Jan* 🏬 *Rooms: 6 en suite* 🛏 *DB&B £45 B&B £30* ⚗ *Licensed* ✗ *Dinner ££* Ⓥ *Vegetarians welcome* ✱ *Children welcome* ✔ *No smoking in bedrooms* 💳 *Mastercard/ Eurocard, Visa, Switch, Delta, JCB, Solo, Visa Electron* Ⓜ *Partner: Celia Pickup*

Craigadam Castle Douglas DG7 3HU
Tel: 0155 665 0233 Fax: 0155 665 0233
E-mail: inquiry@craigadam.com
Web: www.craigadam.com
2 miles north of Crocketford on the A712.
[C7]

CASTLE DOUGLAS

Longacre Manor

- *"Individual attention in a relaxing and pleasant atmosphere."*
- *Creative Scottish cooking.*

LONGACRE MANOR offers elegance and charm in a relaxing and comfortable atmosphere, in Edwardian style. Every attention is given by hosts Elma and Charles Ball to ensure that guests enjoy a memorable stay. Elma prepares innovative dishes using fresh local produce whilst Charles offers first-class service of food and wine.

Watercress soup. Gigot of Galloway lamb in redcurrant jus. Chocolate and brandy mousse.

STB ★★★★ Small Hotel

◗ *Open all year* ⌂ *Rooms: 4 en suite* ⋈ *DB&B £47.50–£62.50 B&B £30–£45* ✕ *Dinner ££ – prior reservation for non residents* Ⓥ *Vegetarians welcome* ♦ *Children over 10 years welcome* ✲ *No smoking in dining room* 🐕*Dogs welcome* 🎫 *Mastercard/Eurocard, Visa, Switch, Delta* ▨ *Partner: Mrs E M Ball*

Ernespie Road Castle Douglas
Dumfries & Galloway DG7 1LE
Tel: 01556 503576 Fax: 01556 503886
E-mail: ball.longacre@btinternet.com
Web:
www.aboutscotland.co.uk/south/longacre.html
A75 Dumfries–Stranraer, approx 17 miles from Dumfries. Follow sign at roundabout to Castle Douglas. Longacre on left-hand side of road.
[C7]

CASTLE DOUGLAS

Threave Garden, The National Trust for Scotland

- *"A peaceful haven set in beautiful countryside with good home cooking."*
- *Skilful home cooking with local produce.*

THE RESTAURANT at Threave Garden is at the entrance to some 26 hectares of one of the finest gardens in the country. Kate Henderson and her team prepare innovative dishes using local game, fish, vegetables and fruit, all served by enthusiastic staff. Some excellent examples of home baking and Scottish food.

Venison pâté with orange and redcurrant marmalade. Haggis and neep lasagne with whisky and leek sauce. Meringue roulade with seasonal fruits.

STB ★★★★ Garden

◗ *Open 1 Mar to 23 Dec* ▧ *Special rates available* ✕ *Food available all day £ Lunch £* Ⓥ *Vegetarians welcome* ♦ *Children welcome* ♿ *Facilities for disabled visitors* ✲ *No smoking throughout* 🐕*Dogs welcome in the grounds but not in the restaurant* 🎫 *Mastercard/ Eurocard, Visa, Switch* ▨ *Catering Manager: Kate Henderson*

Threave Castle Douglas Kirkcudbrightshire DG7 1RX
Tel: 01556 502575 Fax: 01556 502683
Web: www.nts.org.uk
Off A75, 1 mile west of Castle Douglas, follow signs to Threave Garden. [C7]

CHIRNSIDE

Chirnside Hall Country House Hotel

- *"The Dutch owners' love of all things Scottish is very apparent on a visit to Chirnside Hall. Warm hospitality and good food awaits you."*
- *Modern Scottish.*

CHIRNSIDE HALL is a delightful country house full of original features which has been sensitively refurbished in recent years. The proprietors, Christian and Tessa Korsten, are very helpful and friendly. Cooking here is of a very high standard with interesting menus – only the best of locally sourced ingredients is used.

Warm tartlet of smoked salmon and leeks, with a grain mustard sauce. Roast loin of lamb with skirlie and black pudding. Iced chocolate parfait with orange compote.

STB ★★★★ Small Hotel

◖ *Open all year* ▦ *Rooms: 10 en suite* ⇔ *DB&B £62.50–£80 B&B £50–£70* ⑤ *Special rates available* ✖ *Light snack lunch – for residents Dinner £££* Ⓥ *Vegetarians welcome* ⚘ *Children welcome* ✽ *No smoking in dining room* 🐕*Dogs welcome* ▣ *Mastercard/Eurocard, Visa, Switch* ⋈ *Proprietors: Christian & Tessa Korsten*

Chirnside nr Duns Berwickshire TD11 3LD
Tel: 01890 818219 Fax: 01890 818231
E-mail: chirnsidehall@globalnet.co.uk
Web: www.chirnsidehallhotel.com
Between Chirnside and Foulden on the A6105, 1 mile east of Chirnside. [D6]

CLACHAN BY TARBERT

Balinakill Country House Hotel

- *"A good combination of Victorian opulence and modern comfort."*
- *Fresh local produce skilfully prepared.*

BALINAKILL is a grand mansion house set in parkland grounds which benefits from the caring owners' attentions. All bedrooms are en suite, offering modern conveniences in traditional surroundings. Menus are prepared by Angus, focusing greatly on using only the freshest and best local produce – particularly local game, seafood and cheeses.

Sound of Gigha crab and prawn salad. Medallions of Kintyre venison with home-made venison sausage and a mustard mash. Meringue nest filled with a trio of home-made ice creams served with fresh seasonal fruits.

STB ★★★ Hotel

◖ *Open all year* ▦ *Rooms: 11 en suite* ⇔ *DB&B £49–£54 B&B £35–£40* ⑤ *Special rates available* ✖ *Food available all day £ Lunch £ Dinner ££* Ⓥ *Vegetarians welcome* ⚘ *Children welcome* ♿ *Facilities for disabled visitors* ✽ *No smoking in dining room* 🐕*Dogs welcome* ▣ *Mastercard, Visa, Switch, Delta* ⋈ *Proprietors: Angus & Susan Macdiarmid*

Clachan By Tarbert Argyll PA29 6XL
Tel: 01880 740206 Fax: 01880 740298
E-mail: info@balinakill.com
Web: www.balinakill.com
Heading south: on A83 between Tarbert and Campbeltown. As you approach the village of Clachan, Balinakill is on the left. [B6]

COMRIE	CRAIGELLACHIE

The Royal Hotel

- *"A comfortable stay in a delightful small village."*
- *Modern traditional.*

THE FRONTAGE of the Royal Hotel belies the size and hidden treasures within. The hotel has eleven individually designed en suite bedrooms with every facility. Guests can enjoy a meal chosen from the Grill or dinner menu in either the conservatory-style brasserie or the more formal restaurant.

Pan-fried king scallops rested on buttered spinach surrounded by a tomato, butter sauce. Baby fillets of beef coated with a duo of sauces topped with shallots. Zabaglione profiteroles: choux buns filled with ice cream, glazed with a hot chocolate sauce.

STB ★★★★ Small Hotel

◗ *Open all year* ♠ *Rooms: 11 en suite* ⊨ *DB&B £75–£95 B&B £55–£75* ⓢⱣ *Special rates available* ✗ *Lunch ££ Dinner £££* Ⓥ *Vegetarians welcome* ⚘ *Children welcome* ♿ *Facilities for disabled visitors* ✔ *No smoking in dining room* ♞ *Dogs welcome* ⊞ *Mastercard/Eurocard, American Express, Visa, Diners Club, Switch, Delta* ⚑ *General Managers: Jerry & Teresa Milsom*

Melville Square Comrie Crieff Perthshire PH6 2DN
Tel: 01764 679200 Fax: 01764 679219
E-mail: reception@royalhotel.co.uk
Web: www.royalhotel.co.uk
Comrie is situated on the A85, the hotel is located on the main square of the village. [C5]

Craigellachie Hotel

- *"A most sophisticated meal in elegant country house surroundings."*
- *Sophisticated Scottish with international flair.*

LOCATED AT THE HEART of whisky country, within the attractive Speyside village of Craigellachie, new chef Brian Gollan has introduced some real sophistication to this country house/sporting hotel. The hotel has three dining areas each unique in style but all with a warm, welcoming atmosphere and professional, yet unobtrusive service.

Delice of Loch Duart salmon, lobster and leeks with soy bean salad and lemon brioche. Medallion of venison with foie gras, pomme gratin, honeyed parsnips and a ginseng sauce. Ginger bread and white chocolate parfait with malted Agen prunes.

STB ★★★★ Hotel

♠ *Rooms: 25 en suite* ⊨ *B&B £57.50–£72.50* ⓢⱣ *Special seasonal rates available* ✗ *Lunch £–£££ Dinner 4 course menu £–££££* Ⓥ *Vegetarians welcome* ⚘ *Children welcome* ✔ *No smoking in restaurants* ⊞ *Mastercard/ Eurocard, American Express, Visa, Diners Club, Switch, Delta, JCB* ⚑ *General Manager: Duncan Elphick*

Craigellachie Speyside Banffshire AB38 9SR
Tel: 01340 881 204 Fax: 01340 881 253
E-mail: sales@craigellachie.com
Web: www.craigellachie.com
On A941/A95, 12 miles south of Elgin. [D4]

CRIEFF

CRIEFF

The Bank Restaurant

- *"Comfortable surroundings and excellent food."*
- *Modern Scottish cooking.*

THE BANK RESTAURANT is a restaurant within a converted banking hall. Oak panelling covers the walls and quite eclectic objets d'art add to the ambience. Chef/Proprietor Bill McGuigan is passionate about the food he produces and endeavours to source all ingredients locally, his wife Lilias is very hospitable front of house.

Pittenween crab and spring onion salad with chilli oil dressing. Fillet of 'Buccleuch Estate' beef with spinach and garlic potatoes, and a truffle-infused jus. Lemon tart with honey ice cream.

◗ *Open all year except 2 weeks Jan Closed Sun evening and Mon – winter* ✖ *Lunch £ Dinner ££–£££* Ⓥ *Vegetarians welcome – prior notice preferred* ✻ *Children welcome* ⊞ *Mastercard/ Eurocard, American Express, Visa, Switch, Delta* ▨ *Proprietors: Bill & Lilias McGuigan*

*32 High Street Crieff Perthshire PH7 3BS
Tel: 01764 656575 Fax: 01764 656575
E-mail: info@thebankrestaurant.co.uk
Web: www.thebankrestaurant.co.uk
In Crieff town centre opposite tourist office and town clock. [C5]*

Crieff Hydro

- *"An excellent choice of dining options for holiday or corporate guests."*
- *Scottish produce with modern influences.*

THE PROFESSIONAL STAFF and excellent facilities at Crieff Hydro make it a popular venue for short breaks, family holidays and corporate events. In meeting this diverse customer base the hotel offers three dining options – a delightfully grand Victorian dining room, an informal Mediterranean-style brasserie and light snacks in the Winter Garden coffee shop.

A layered gâteau of cured Scottish salmon, avocado and tomato concasse topped with sesame seeds. Medallions of venison wrapped in smoked bacon placed onto a loganberry sauce. Raspberry and Drambuie teardrop encased in tuille biscuit and a pool of coulis.

STB ★★★★ Hotel

◗ *Open all year* 🏠 *Rooms: 216 en suite (and 28 self-catering units)* 🛏 *DB&B £59–£212 B&B £55–£108* 🖬 *Special rates available* ✖ *Lunch £–££ Dinner ££* Ⓥ *Vegetarians welcome* ✻ *Children welcome* ♿ *Facilities for disabled visitors* ✯ *No smoking in brasserie* 🐕 *Kennels available for dogs of hotel guests* ⊞ *Mastercard/ Eurocard, American Express, Visa, Switch, Delta* ▨ *Executive Chef: Alec Summers*

*Crieff Perthshire PH7 3LQ
Tel: 01764 655555 Fax: 01764 653087
E-mail: enquiries@crieffhydro.com
Web: www.crieffhydro.com
1 hour from either Edinburgh or Glasgow. Follow A85 from Perth to Crieff (signposted Crianlarich) for 20 minutes. From Crieff town centre – up on the hill overlooking the town. [C5]*

CRIEFF

Glenturret Distillery

- *"A popular venue offering a choice of dining experiences and very good self service food!"*
- *Traditional Scottish fare.*

THE SMUGGLERS RESTAURANT, situated on first floor of the converted warehouse, is self-service with high standards of cooking. The Pagoda Room offers a more formal setting. The menus feature Highland venison, beef, lamb and salmon. Coffee, afternoon tea and home baking are also available during the day. **N.B. Exciting new development opening summer 2002 'Home of The Famous Grouse'.**

Hot salmon smoked over barley woodchips and the 'Glenturret 12 Years', coated with honey and brown sugar. Local venison served with a pickled walnut sauce. Chocolate cup and saucer filled with fruits of the forest and whisky cream.

STB ★★★★★ Visitor Attraction

◗ Open all year except 25, 26 Dec, 1, 2 Jan (and Apr 2002 only) ✕ Food available all day £ Lunch ££ Dinner – by private arrangement only ££££ Ⓥ Vegetarians welcome ✵ Children welcome ♿ Facilities for disabled visitors ✄ Facilities are non smoking but smoking area provided in Smugglers Restaurant ▦ Mastercard/Eurocard, American Express, Visa, Switch ▮ Executive Chef: Steve Craik

The Hosh Crieff Perthshire PH7 4HA
Tel: 01764 656565 Fax: 01764 654366
E-mail: glenturret@highlanddistillers.co.uk
Web: www.glenturret.com
Approx 1 mile outside Crieff on A85 Crieff to Comrie road. Just over 1 hour from Edinburgh (M9) and Glasgow (M8). [C5]

CRINAN

Crinan Hotel

- *"A vintage location – enjoy views onto the canal and loch."*
- *Fresh imaginative fine cooking.*

LOCATED by the famous Crinan canal the main restaurant, the Westward, offers a delicious table d'hôte menu and an à la carte lunch is available in the bar. The exclusive and celebrated Lock 16 Restaurant is on the top storey of the hotel. Winner of The Macallan Taste of Scotland Award 1998.

Duck, foie gras and Puy lentil terrine with winter truffle and sweet shallot dressing. Pan-fried tranche of halibut with shellfish risotto, roasted salsify and saffron velouté. Baked fig tarte tatin with vanilla ice cream and marsala wine syrup.

STB ★★★★ Hotel

◗ Open all year ▦ Rooms: 22 en suite ⬌ DB&B £105–£120 B&B £75–£90 ▦ Special winter rates available ✕ Lunch £ Dinner (Westward Restaurant) ££££ Dinner (Lock 16 mid Apr to end Sep only) except Sun Mon booking essential ££££ Ⓥ Vegetarians welcome ✵ Children welcome ♿ Facilities for disabled visitors ▦ Mastercard/Eurocard, American Express, Visa, Switch ▮ Proprietors: Nick & Frances Ryan

Crinan Lochgilphead Argyll PA31 8SR
Tel: 01546 830261 Fax: 01546 830292
E-mail: nryan@crinanhotel.com
Web: www.crinanhotel.com
A82 Glasgow-Inveraray, then A83 to Lochgilphead. Follow A816 (Oban) for c.5 miles, then B841 to Crinan. [B5]

CUMBERNAULD

Westerwood Hotel, Golf & Country Club

- *"An attractive modern hotel, offering good quality food and superb facilities."*
- *Modern Scottish.*

WESTERWOOD is now under the ownership of Morton Hotels and boasts a superb championship golf course set on the edge of the Kilsyth Hills. The hotel offers a high standard of accommodation within easy reach of major cities and a high level of service and cuisine to appeal to the most discerning of customers.

West coast lobster bisque with poached scallop quenelles. Roast loin of blackface lamb with chicken and leek farci. Dark chocolate mousse with toasted coconut cream.

STB ★★★ Hotel

🏨 *Rooms: 100 en suite* 🛏 *Prices on application* 🆂 *Special rates available* ✗ *Lunch £–££ Dinner ££–£££* Ⓥ *Vegetarians welcome* ✚ *Children welcome* 💳 *Mastercard/Eurocard, American Express, Visa, Switch* 🔪 *General Manager: Paul Russell*

St Andrews Drive Cumbernauld G68 0EW Tel: 01236 457171 Fax: 01236 738478 E-mail: westerwood@morton-hotels.com Web: www.morton-hotels.com Situated just off A80 Cumbernauld. From the North take slip road marked services. From South take turning Wardpark/Castlecary. Go past Dobbies Garden Centre and follow hotel signs. [C6]

CUPAR

Ostlers Close Restaurant

- *"The very best of quality food with hospitality to match."*
- *Elegant Scottish cuisine.*

THE FOOD AT OSTLERS is of the highest standard. Jimmy and Amanda Graham deserve the excellent reputation which they have earned over the years. Jimmy is passionate about Scottish meat, seafood, game and wild mushrooms, and Amanda is equally passionate about the wines and home-made desserts – a perfect combination.

Seared West Coast scallops on a bed of potato mash with a Glamis asparagus butter sauce. Roast breast of free-range duck on oriental flavoured Puy lentils with a plum sauce. A plate of chocolate desserts.

◗ *Open all year except Christmas Day, Boxing Day, 1 Jan and first 2 weeks early summer Closed Sun Mon* ✗ *Lunch Fri, Sat only – booking essential Dinner except Sun Mon £££* Ⓥ *Vegetarians welcome – please mention at booking* ✚ *Children welcome* ⚬ *Smoking restricted until all diners at coffee stage* 💳 *Mastercard/Eurocard, American Express, Visa, Switch, Delta* 🔪 *Proprietors: Jimmy & Amanda Graham*

Bonnygate Cupar KY15 4BU Tel: 01334 655574 Web: www.ostlersclose.co.uk Small lane, near the cross, directly off A91 main road through town. [D5]

DALRY

Braidwoods

- *"This unpretentious country restaurant is serving some of the very best food to be found in Scotland today."*
- *Innovative modern Scottish cooking.*

THE HIGHEST STANDARDS are set here and are continuously exceeded. Nothing is needed to aid the cooking – it is remarkably skilled and of exceptional quality. Booking is essential – table is yours for the duration of your meal. Winner of The Macallan Taste of Scotland Award 1995 and 2000, and Overall Excellence Award 2000.

Whole roast boneless quail stuffed with black pudding on braised Puy lentils. Baked fillet of West Coast turbot with pea purée, boulangere potatoes and roast chicken juices. Trio of apple, brûlée, strudel and Calvados ice cream.

❶ *Open last week Jan to first week Sep and third week Sep to 31 Dec except Christmas Day Closed Sun pm, Mon and Tue lunch* ❦ *Table licence* ✗ *Lunch except Mon Tue ££ Dinner except Sun Mon £££* Ⓥ *Vegetarians welcome – prior notice required* ♣ *Children over 12 years welcome* ✬ *No smoking throughout* 🏧 *Mastercard/Eurocard, American Express, Visa, Switch, Delta* 🅜 *Owners: Keith & Nicola Braidwood*

Drumastle Mill Cottage By Dalry KA24 4LN Tel: 01294 833544 Fax: 01294 833553 E-mail: keithbraidwood@bt.connect.com Web: www.braidwoods.co.uk A737 Kilwinning-Dalry. On southern outskirts of Dalry, take road to Saltcoats for 1 mile and follow signs. [C6]

DAVIOT NR INVERNESS

The Lodge at Daviot Mains

- *"Margaret Hutcheson continually endeavours to find the best produce to tempt her guests."*
- *Creative home cooking.*

DAVIOT MAINS is built in the traditional style of a Highland lodge and is the warm and welcoming home of Margaret, Alex and Rachel Hutcheson. Margaret's excellent home cooking uses ingredients which are meticulously sourced to provide only the very best of Highland produce and served in generous portions.

According to season: home-made soups, fresh local salmon and trout, Aberdeen Angus beef, Scotch lamb, vegetables and cheeses. Local fruits and delicious home-made puddings.

STB ★★★★ B&B

❶ *Open all year Note: Dinner served Mon to Fri Apr to Sep incl, thereafter Mon to Sat incl ££ – booking essential* 🛏 *Rooms: 7 en suite* 🛏 *DB&B £40–£47 B&B £25–£32* 🅢 *Special rates available – Nov to Mar* ❦ *Licensed* Ⓥ *Vegetarians welcome – prior notice required Special diets on request* ♣ *Children welcome* ♿ *Facilities for disabled visitors* ✬ *No smoking throughout* 🏧 *Mastercard/ Eurocard, Visa* 🅜 *Owners: Alex & Margaret Hutcheson*

Inverness IV2 5ER Tel: 01463 772215 Fax: 01463 772099 E-mail: taste@daviotmainsfarm.co.uk Web: www.daviotmainsfarm.co.uk On B851 (B9006) to Culloden/Croy, 5 miles south of Inverness. Ignore signs for Daviot East and Daviot West. [C4]

DINGWALL

Kinkell House

- *"A homely and cosy small hotel with first-class cooking."*
- *Country house cooking with modern influences.*

KINKELL HOUSE is situated in a peaceful location on the Black Isle and commands unhampered and striking views across the Firth to Ben Wyvis. Ronnie and Fiona MacDonald extend a welcome to guests who will enjoy Chef Douglas Hamilton's very assured cooking making best use of the excellent local produce.

Platter of various West Coast shellfish. 8 oz fillet of prime local beef served with a rich red wine jus. Soft poached summer berries with tutti-frutti ice cream.

STB ★★★★ Small Hotel

● Open all year ⌂ Rooms: 9 en suite ⋈ B&B £45–£55 ♛ Restricted licence ✕ Lunch booking required £££ Dinner booking required £££ Ⓥ Vegetarians welcome ⚘ Children welcome ⚒ Facilities for disabled visitors ⚭ Smoking permitted in sitting room only ⚘ Dogs welcome ⊞ Mastercard/Eurocard, Visa, Switch, Solo, JCB, Maestro Ⓝ Proprietor: Ronnie MacDonald

Easter Kinkell by Conon Bridge Dingwall Ross-shire IV7 8HY
Tel: 01349 861270 Fax: 01349 865902
E-mail: kinkell@aol.com
Web: www.kinkell-house.co.uk
10 miles from Inverness on A9. Take the B9169 from there. Kinkell House 1 mile. [C3]

DIRLETON

The Open Arms Hotel

- *"A good quality hotel and bistro, set in a delightful East Coast village."*
- *Modern Scottish.*

THE OPEN ARMS has long been established for offering a high quality experience and now under the ownership of Chris and Lyn Hansen this reputation is sure to grow. Originally a farmhouse the atmosphere is warm and friendly and the cooking is assured using best produce skilfully prepared and presented.

Filo parcels filled with black pudding and chilli. Grilled hot smoked salmon with a crab and avocado beurre blanc and finished with a mango and dill vinaigrette.

STB ★★★★ Small Hotel

● Open all year ⌂ Rooms: 10 en suite ⓢ Special rates available ✕ Lunch ££ Dinner £££ Ⓥ Vegetarians welcome ⚘ Children welcome ⚒ Facilities for disabled visitors ⚭ No smoking in dining areas ⚘ Dogs welcome ⊞ Mastercard/ Eurocard, Visa, Switch Ⓝ Owner: Chris Hansen

Dirleton East Lothian EH39 5EG
Tel: 01620 850241 Fax: 01620 850570
E-mail: openarms@clara.co.uk
Web: www.openarmshotel.com
From Edinburgh take coast road to Gullane and North Berwick, Dirleton lies halfway between Gullane and North Berwick. [D5]

DORNOCH

Mallin House Hotel

- *"A casual and friendly seaside hotel."*
- *Scottish cooking with seafood a speciality.*

MALLIN HOUSE with its unique peach-coloured exterior is conveniently located within the town and close by the Royal Dornoch Golf Club. Owner and Chef Malcolm Holden's skilled cooking produces excellent satisfying meals chosen from a varied menu offering fresh quality seafood and meat, and popular dishes with a twist.

Oak smoked salmon served on a bed of leaves. Breast of pheasant stuffed with cranberry and orange stuffing, wrapped in bacon, oven-roasted and served in a pool of onion marmalade gravy. Crème caramel with cream.

STB ★★ Small Hotel

◗ *Open all year* 🏨 *Rooms: 10 en suite* 🛏 *DB&B £48–£55 B&B £30–£35* ✕ *Lunch ££ Dinner £–££* Ⓥ *Vegetarians welcome* ☀ *Children welcome* ♿ *Facilities for disabled visitors* 💳 *Mastercard/ Eurocard, American Express, Visa, Switch, Delta* 🍴 *Proprietors: Malcolm & Linda Holden*

Church Street Dornoch IV25 3LP
Tel: 01862 810335 Fax: 01862 810810
E-mail: mallin.house.hotel@zetnet.co.uk
Web: www.users.zetnet.co.uk/mallin-house
Down to centre of town, turn right. [C3]

DORNOCH

The Royal Golf Hotel

- *"Recently refurbished to provide contemporary elegance and comfort."*
- *Innovative Scottish cooking.*

THE ROYAL GOLF HOTEL is a traditional Scottish hotel which has been completely and sumptuously refurbished and overlooks the golf course and the sandy beaches of the Dornoch Firth beyond. Head Chef Jeanette Weatheritt creates wonderful dishes using the fresh local produce available: fine dining in the dining room, more informal meals in the Conservatory.

Fresh asparagus wrapped in filo pastry, glazed with a hollandaise sauce. Roulade of salmon filled with a langoustine and queen scallop mousse, served with a saffron and chive sauce. Crisp brandy snap basket, filled with bananas, flamed in brandy and served with a butterscotch sauce and whipped cream.

STB ★★★★ Hotel
Green Tourism Two Leaf Silver Award

◗ *Open all year* 🏨 *Rooms: 25 en suite* 🛏 *DB&B £65–£130 B&B £55–£120* 🆂🅿 *Special rates available* ✕ *Lunch £ Dinner 4 course menu £££* Ⓥ *Vegetarians welcome* ☀ *Children welcome* 🚭 *No smoking in restaurant* 💳 *Mastercard/ Eurocard, Visa, Diners Club, Switch* 🍴 *General Manager: Andrew Wescott*

The First Tee Dornoch Sutherland IV25 3LG
Tel: 01862 810283 Fax: 01862 810923
E-mail: royalgolf@morton-hotels.com
Web: www.morton-hotels.com
From A9, 2 miles into Dornoch town square, straight across crossroads, 200 yards on right. [C3]

DUFFTOWN

A Taste of Speyside Restaurant

- *"This is a little restaurant with a 'big heart' and great food."*
- *Excellent wholesome Scottish food.*

AT TASTE OF SPEYSIDE the commitment to fresh local produce is as strong as ever. Value for money is to the fore and food is wholesome. The menu makes the most of local ingredients and is enhanced by a well-chosen wine list. A superb selection of Speyside malt whiskies are available.

Whisky chicken liver pâté. Rabbit and mutton casserole with cheese and oatmeal crust. Speyside stottie – treacle biscuit and Brazil nut base topped with home-made chocolate ice cream, whipped liqueur cream and chopped nuts.

❶ *Open 1 Mar to 1 Nov and Christmas Closed Sun* ✘ *Food available all day except Sun ££ Lunch except Sun ££ Dinner except Sun ££* Ⓥ *Vegetarians welcome* ✱ *Children welcome* ✄ *Smoking permitted in dining room* 🈺 *Mastercard/Eurocard, American Express, Visa, Switch, Delta* ✗ *Partners: Raymond McLean & Peter Thompson*

10 Balvenie Street Dufftown Banffshire AB55 4AB
Tel: 01340 820860 Fax: 01340 820860
E-mail: taste.speyside@nest.org.uk
Web:
www.scottish-info.com/scotland/speyside.htm
Half mile past the Glenfiddich Distillery in centre of village, 50 yards short of clock tower.
[D4]

DULNAIN BRIDGE

Auchendean Lodge Hotel

- *"It's unique! Great food, wonderful views and Edwardian charm."*
- *Original, talented, eclectic cooking.*

OWNERS Eric Hart and Ian Kirk, are convivial professionals who give their guests a memorable dining experience. The hotel's garden provides many vegetables along with many local specialities, complemented by an excellent wine list. The relaxing atmosphere here – quirky and individual – is a delight. Winner of The Macallan Taste of Scotland Award 2000.

Wild cèp mushroom soufflé. Apple-stuffed wild pheasant breast with calvados and apple sauce. Liquorice and blackcurrant ripple ice cream.

STB ★★★★ Small Hotel

❶ *Open most of the year* 🛏 *Rooms: 5 en suite* 🛌 *DB&B £46–£84 B&B £26–£59* 🆂 *Special rates available* ✘ *Pre-booked packed lunch £ Dinner £££* Ⓥ *Vegetarians welcome – advise on booking* ✱ *Children welcome* ♿ *Facilities for disabled visitors* ✄ *No smoking in dining room and one lounge* 🈺 *Mastercard/Eurocard, Visa* ✗ *Proprietors: Eric Hart & Ian Kirk*

Dulnain Bridge Grantown-on-Spey Inverness-shire PH26 3LU
Tel: 01479 851 347 Fax: 01479 851 347
E-mail: hotel@auchendean.com
Web: www.auchendean.com
On A95, 1 mile south of Dulnain Bridge. [C4]

DUNBLANE

Cromlix House

- *"Stunning country house for fine dining, with sensational views over the grounds."*
- *Outstanding modern Scottish cuisine.*

DAVID AND AILSA ASSENTI exemplify the true traditions of country house hospitality – each guest is cherished. Everything here is of the highest standard. Head chef Paul Devonshire produces imaginative meals for the discriminating palate. Menus change daily using seasonally available produce. The wine list is discerning and extensive.

Cherry tomato clafoutis, mixed leaves, toasted pine kernels and pesto dressing. Roast wild venison, potato and carrot rösti, confit of baby onions and spiced jus. Caramel panna cotta, pastry cream filled tortellini, blood orange compote and Tia Maria syrup.

STB ★★★★★ Small Hotel

◗ *Open all year* ⌂ *Rooms: 14 en suite (incl 8 suites)* ⇄ *DB&B from £130 B&B £100–£170* ⁇ *Special rates available – Oct to mid May* ♟ *Residents and diners licence only* ✘ *Lunch Mon to Fri – Oct to mid May pre-booked only; Sat Sun ££–£££ Dinner ££££* Ⓥ *Vegetarians welcome* ✞ *No smoking in dining room* 🐕 *Dogs in bedrooms only* ▣ *Mastercard/Eurocard, American Express, Visa, Diners Club, Switch* ▨ *Proprietors: David & Ailsa Assenti*

Kinbuck Nr Dunblane Perthshire FK15 9JT Tel: 01786 822125 Fax: 01786 825450 E-mail: reservations@cromlixhouse.com Web: www.cromlixhouse.com 5 minutes off the A9. North of Dunblane Exit A9 to Kinbuck (B8033). Through Kinbuck village, cross narrow bridge and drive is 2nd on left. [C5]

DUNBLANE

Rokeby House

- *"A delightful combination of fresh local produce, warm hospitality and gracious surroundings."*
- *Modern Scottish/home cooking.*

ROKEBY HOUSE was built in 1907 and has been restored to its former glory by Proprietors Richard Beatts and Peter Corkill. Rokeby has a combination of gracious surroundings and warm hospitality making an ideal place to rest. Guests can enjoy relaxing in the lovely gardens which include a secret garden and Italian garden.

Oven-roasted fillet of Orkney salmon with herb crust. Roasted breast of duck with a port and Seville orange glaze, herb roasties, vegetables in season. Apples and mixed fruits in a whisky cream.

STB ★★★★★ B&B

◗ *Open all year* ⌂ *Rooms: 3 en suite* ⇄ *DB&B £70–£100 B&B £45–£75* ⁇ *Special rates available* ✘ *Dinner £££* Ⓥ *Vegetarians welcome* ♿ *Facilities for disabled visitors* ✞ *No smoking throughout* ▣ *Mastercard/Eurocard, Visa, Switch, Delta* ▨ *Owner/Proprietor: Richard Beatts*

Doune Road Dunblane FK15 9AT Tel: 01786 824447 Fax: 01786 821399 E-mail: rokeby.house@btconnect.com Web: www.aboutscotland.com/stirling/rokeby.html M9, pass Stirling travelling north. At Keir Mains roundabout take B8033 to Dunblane. Then follow A820 to Doune. Rokeby is approx ¾ miles along Doune road on left. [C5]

DUNFERMLINE

Davaar House Hotel and Restaurant

- *"Family-run hotel offering Scottish hospitality and good home cooking."*
- *Good home cooking.*

DAVAAR HOUSE is centrally situated in a residential area of Dunfermline and stands in lovely gardens. The food is cooked by Doreen Jarvis and her daughter Karen who create traditional dishes with intuitive flair and enthusiasm whilst Jim Jarvis looks after the front of house in a relaxed and hospitable style.

West Coast scallops seared in sesame oil on a lemon zest sauce. Roast saddle of Spring Perthshire lamb encased in garden herbs, with a redcurrant infused jus. White chocolate truffle mousse with a coulis of fresh raspberries and tuille wafers.

STB ★★★ Small Hotel

❶ *Open all year except 23 Dec to 6 Jan Closed Sun* 🏨 *Rooms: 10 en suite* 🛏 *DB&B £54–£68 B&B £35–£50* 💲 *Special rates available* 🍷 *Restricted licence* ✕ *Lunch (Dec only) except Sun ££ Dinner except Sun £££* Ⓥ *Vegetarians welcome* ✻ *Children welcome* ♿ *Facilities for disabled visitors* ⌇ *No smoking in restaurant and first floor bedrooms* 💳 *Mastercard/ Eurocard, Visa, Switch, Delta* 🍴 *Proprietors: Doreen & Jim Jarvis*

126 Grieve Street Dunfermline KY12 8DW Tel: 01383 721886 Fax: 01383 623633 From M90, junction 3, A907 Dunfermline. Straight on through town, over Sinclair Gardens roundabout. At 4th set of traffic lights turn right into Chalmers Street, Grieve Street 2nd left. [D5]

DUNFERMLINE

Garvock House Hotel

- *"Good use is made of fresh local produce which can be savoured in the peaceful surroundings and relaxed atmosphere."*
- *Modern Scottish cooking.*

GARVOCK HOUSE is an elegant house dating back over 200 years and retaining many original features, lovingly restored by its present owners. The cooking is excellent – a blend of innovative Scottish modern with traditional and, more recently available, Scottish ingredients. Much attention to detail – from turndown service to the care given to the presentation of your meal.

Smoked haddock and sweetcorn soup with seared scallops, crispy pancetta and truffle oil. Saddle of rabbit stuffed with wild mushrooms and apricot mousse, on carrot and potato rösti with smoked shallots and tomato and tarragon jus. Mosaic of fresh fruits with lemon chiboust.

STB ★★★★ Small Hotel

❶ *Open all year* 🏨 *Rooms: 11 en suite* 🛏 *B&B from £47.50* 💲 *Special rates available* ✕ *Lunch ££ Dinner £££* Ⓥ *Vegetarians welcome* ✻ *Children welcome* ♿ *Facilities for disabled visitors* ⌇ *No smoking in dining room* 🐕 *Small dogs welcome* 💳 *Mastercard/Eurocard, Visa, Switch, Delta* 🍴 *Proprietors: Rui & Pamela Fernandes*

St John's Drive Transy Dunfermline KY12 7TU Tel: 01383 621067 Fax: 01383 621168 E-mail: sales@garvock.co.uk Web: www.garvock.co.uk Exit junction 3, M90 and follow A907 into Dunfermline. After football stadium turn left into Garvock Hill and first right into St John's Drive. Hotel is 500m on right-hand side. [D5]

DUNKELD

The Pend

- *"Personal and friendly service combined with good home cooking."*
- *Scottish home cooking.*

THE PEND is a delightful house with plenty of character and tasteful decoration. Owner/chef Marina Braney is eager to provide guests with an optimum level of service and an award-winning wine list. Dinner is served at a set time, special diets and requests are catered for, and everyone is seated around one table.

West Coast scallops with bacon and broad bean salad. Scottish leg of lamb steaks with blackcurrant jus and home-grown vegetables. Coffee and almond meringue dessert.

STB ★★★★ B&B

◗ *Open all year* 🏨 *Rooms: 3* 🛏 *DB&B £50–£60 B&B £30–£35* 💷 *Special rates available* ✗ *Dinner ££ Residents only* Ⓥ *Vegetarians welcome* 🧒 *Children welcome* 🐕*Dogs welcome* 💳 *Mastercard/Eurocard, American Express, Visa, Diners Club, Switch, Delta, JCB* 🍴 *Owner/Chef: Marina Braney*

5 Brae Street Dunkeld Perthshire PH8 OBA Tel: 01350 727586 Fax: 01350 727173 E-mail: molly@thepend.sol.co.uk Web: www.thepend.com In the town centre, on Brae Street, off the High Street. Opposite the turning to the cathedral. [C5]

DUNKELD

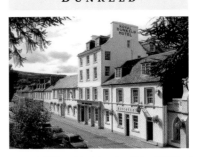

The Royal Dunkeld Hotel

- *"A friendly hotel in the centre of Dunkeld."*
- *Scottish cooking.*

THE ROYAL DUNKELD HOTEL is a former coaching inn now fully modernised with all modern amenities and offering a friendly welcome. There is a choice of dining here – informally in the Gargoyles Lounge Bar, in the more formal restaurant, or the beer garden. Food here is traditional, freshly prepared and well-presented.

Asparagus, haddock and smoked salmon terrine glazed with hollandaise sauce. Breast of duck with an apple curry and cinnamon sauce, with potatoes and fresh vegetables. Individual rhubarb trifle mousse with whipped cream and raspberry coulis.

STB ★★★ Hotel

◗ *Open all year* 🏨 *Rooms: 35 en suite* 🛏 *DB&B £45–£55 B&B £30–£37.50* 💷 *Special rates available* ✗ *Lunch ££ Dinner £££* Ⓥ *Vegetarians welcome* 🧒 *Children welcome* ♿ *Facilities for disabled visitors* 🚭 *No smoking in dining room* 🐕 *Dogs welcome* 💳 *Mastercard/Eurocard, American Express, Visa, Switch, Delta* 🍴 *Proprietor: Neil Menzies*

Atholl Street Dunkeld Perthshire PH8 0AR Tel: 01350 727322 Fax: 01350 728989 E-mail: reservations@royaldunkeld.co.uk Web: www.royaldunkeld.co.uk Just off A9, on the main street of Dunkeld. 15 miles north of Perth. [C5]

DUNOON

Chatters Restaurant

- *"Exceptional food in warm, friendly surrounds – a great reason to plan a trip to Dunoon."*
- *Traditional French-influenced Scottish cooking.*

SUCH IS THE QUALITY of the ambience and food at Chatters that this busy restaurant attracts regular visitors from all over Scotland and beyond. Owner Rosemary MacInnes is one of Scotland's warmest hosts and her passion for fine Scottish produce is clearly evident in Chatter's mouth-watering menus. Winner of The Macallan Taste of Scotland Award 1994.

Warm roulade of spinach filled with woodland mushrooms on a red pepper and tomato coulis. Loin of local venison with a confit of carrot and celery and a rowan jelly reduction. Chocolate and whisky torte on an elderflower sabayon with a quenelle of Belgian chocolate mousse.

◐ *Open Mar to mid Jan except Christmas Day, Boxing Day and New Year's Day Closed Sun Mon Tue* ♟ *Table licence* ✘ *Lunch except Sun Mon Tue £–££ Dinner except Sun Mon Tue ££–£££* ✌ *Smoking in lounge only* 💳 *Mastercard/ Eurocard, Visa* 🛂 *Proprietor: Rosemary Anne MacInnes*

58 John Street Dunoon Argyll PA23 8BJ
Tel: 01369 706402
E-mail: oldmill@cwcom.net
Web: www.oldmill.mcmail.com/chatters
Approach John Street from mini-roundabout on the sea front road. Restaurant opposite the cinema. [B5]

DUNOON

Enmore Hotel

- *"Right on the seafront, this hotel offers good food and exceptional hospitality."*
- *Modern Scottish cooking.*

ENMORE HAS BEEN LOVINGLY restored to its former glory by owners Angela and David Wilson. Angela is genuinely warm and friendly and ensures guests every need is met, meanwhile David is an accomplished chef, producing excellent menus using the finest Scottish produce together with herbs and vegetables from Enmore's own garden.

Hot smoked salmon with lemon and butter sauce. Local venison fillet served with a spiced fruit sauce. Garden-produced rhubarb fool with hot chocolate sauce with chocolate tuile biscuit.

STB ★★★★ Hotel

◐ *Open all year except 20 Dec to 20 Jan* 🏨 *Rooms: 9 en suite* 🛏 *B&B £39–£75* 🆖 *Special rates available* ✘ *Snack food available all day £–£££ Lunch – booking essential ££–£££ Dinner – booking essential £££* Ⓥ *Vegetarians welcome* ⚹ *Children welcome* ♿ *Facilities for disabled visitors – dining only* 💳 *Mastercard/ Eurocard, American Express, Visa, Switch, Delta* 🛂 *Proprietors: Angela & David Wilson*

Dunoon PA23 8HH
Tel: 01369 702230 Fax: 01369 702148
E-mail: enmorehotel@btinternet.com
Web: www.enmorehotel.co.uk
On seafront near Hunters Quay Ferry, approx 1 mile from town centre. Situated between the 2 ferries serving Dunoon. [B5]

EDINBURGH

EDINBURGH

A Room In The Town

- *"A lively and informal city bistro serving the best of Scottish produce."*
- *Modern Scottish cooking.*

THIS BUSY BISTRO RESTAURANT offers a unique atmosphere with its simple, yet effective decor. Blackboard menus adorn the walls describing the daily dishes which are creative with unusual combinations, prepared by Head Chef Gillian Reid. Diners are also welcome to take their own wine (corkage charged), although the restaurant is licensed.

Scottish cap mushrooms topped with white pudding, sun-dried tomatoes and Orkney smoked Cheddar. Seared West Coast scallops with crab, saffron and Ayrshire bacon mash, lime butter sauce. Chilled apricot and Mascarpone rice pudding with shortbread.

◑ Open all year except Christmas Day, Boxing Day, and 1, 2 Jan ✖ Lunch £ Dinner £££ Ⓥ Vegetarians welcome ⊞ Mastercard/Eurocard, Visa, Switch, Delta, JCB, Solo ⋈ Proprietors: John Tindal & Peter Knight; Head Chef: Gillian Reid

18 Howe Street Edinburgh EH3 6TG Tel: 0131 225 8204 Fax: 0131 225 8204 Web: www.aroomin.co.uk/thetown Turn off Princes Street up Frederick Street – Howe Street is a continuation of Frederick Street – over the hill, down towards Stockbridge. [D5]

Atrium

- *"Striking modern restaurant offering excellent dining experience and service."*
- *Outstanding modern Scottish cooking.*

THE IMAGINATIVE cooking is as distinctive as the restaurant it serves. Neil Forbes, Head Chef, offers an à la carte menu based on fresh local produce. Menus are inspired, creative and well-balanced, as befits one of Edinburgh's foremost restaurants. Andrew Radford was winner of The Macallan Taste of Scotland Award 1994.

Sautéed scallops, globe artichoke and crab salad, dill hollandaise. Breast of Gressingham duck, bok choi, sticky belly pork, lentil and coriander sauce. Nougat glace with cherry syrup, almond tuille.

◑ Open all year except few days Christmas and few days New Year Closed Sun ✖ Lunch Mon to Fri ££ (also during Edinburgh Festival and International Rugby Home Games) Dinner Mon to Fri £££ Ⓥ Vegetarians welcome ⚹ Children welcome ⊞ Mastercard/Eurocard, American Express, Visa, Diners Club, Switch, Delta ⋈ Proprietors: Andrew & Lisa Radford

10 Cambridge Street Edinburgh EH1 2ED Tel: 0131 228 8882 Fax: 0131 228 8808 Web: www.atriumrestaurant.com Within Saltire Court, sharing entrance with Traverse Theatre, adjacent to Usher Hall. [D5]

EDINBURGH

The Balmoral Hotel

- *"A world class hotel with exceptional comfort and dining."*
- *Outstanding skilled Scottish cooking.*

THE BALMORAL has it all – No. 1 for outstanding classically orientated cooking; less formal meals at Hadrian's; not to mention NB's Bar and Palm Court. Winner of The Macallan Taste of Scotland Award 1995 and 1999. Executive Chef Jeff Bland is a highly skilled craftsman making dining here a truly memorable experience.

Isle of Skye crab with avocado and caviar. Fillet of Aberdeen Angus beef with Lie de Vin. Iced Macallan whisky parfait served with fruit soup.

STB ★★★★★ Hotel

◐ *Open all year* ⌂ *Rooms: 188 en suite* ⇔ *DB&B £120–£1120 B&B £90–£1000* ⊞ *Special rates available* ✕ *Food available all day £££ Lunch £££–££££ Dinner £££–££££* Ⓥ *Vegetarians welcome* ✻ *Children welcome* ⚇ *Facilities for disabled visitors* ✖ *No smoking area in restaurants* ⊞ *Mastercard/Eurocard, American Express, Visa, Diners Club, Switch, Delta* ⋈ *Hotel Manager: Stephen J Wright*

1 Princes Street Edinburgh EH2 2EQ
Tel: 0131 556 2414 Fax: 0131 557 3747
Web: www.rfhotels.com
Princes Street at the corner of North Bridge at East End of Princes Street. [D5]

EDINBURGH

blue bar cafe

- *"Modern Bistro in centre of theatre/business development using fresh local produce."*
- *Modern bistro style.*

blue, owned by Andrew and Lisa Radford, is perfect for the discerning diner looking for a more informal, yet exceptionally high quality, experience. David Haetzman, Head Chef, is highly skilled and innovative and his menus offer great choice, from light snacks to main meals. Staff are friendly and efficient under the guidance of Liza Robinson.

Seared scallops, cauliflower purée, shitake mushrooms. Rump of lamb, pea purée, bubble and squeak. Apple and rhubarb tart, calvados parfait.

◐ *Open all year except 1 week Christmas* ✕ *Food available 12 noon–3 pm, 6 pm–11 pm* £ *Lunch* ££ *Dinner* ££ Ⓥ *Vegetarians welcome* ✻ *Children welcome* ⚇ *Facilities for disabled visitors* ⊞ *Mastercard/Eurocard, American Express, Visa, Diners Club, Switch* ⋈ *Proprietors: Andrew & Lisa Radford*

10 Cambridge Street Edinburgh EH1 2ED
Tel: 0131 221 1222 Fax: 0131 228 8808
Web: www.bluebarcafe.com
Adjacent to the Usher Hall. On the first floor of Saltire Court, above the Atrium and Traverse Theatre box office. [D5]

EDINBURGH

Bouzy Rouge

- *"A city restaurant offering contemporary Scottish cuisine in a unique atmosphere."*
- *Modern Scottish.*

B OUZY ROUGE has its own particular style which remains uniquely contemporary with this restaurant which also offers an attractive conservatory restaurant to the rear. The cooking is modern Scottish and menus are compiled by both Alan Brown, proprietor, and the chef. Great value for money – from business lunches and casual dining to a gourmet menu.

Trio of Scottish puddings, buttered shallots, Orkney cheese sabayon. Suprême of Perthshire Pheasant, apricot and pistachio stuffing, rich forrester jus. Sticky toffee pudding, rich butterscotch sauce.

◗ *Open all year except New Year's Day* ✖ *Food available all day £–££ Lunch £ Dinner £–££* Ⓥ *Vegetarians welcome* ✳ *Children welcome* 🆑 *Mastercard/Eurocard, American Express, Visa, Diners Club, Switch, Delta, Solo, Electron* 🅽 *Proprietors: Alan & Audrey Brown; Manager: Allison Beattie*

1 Alva Street Edinburgh EH2 4PH
Tel: 0131 225 9594 Fax: 0131 225 9593
E-mail: reservations@bouzy-rouge.com
Web: www.bouzy-rouge.com
Corner of Queensferry Street and Alva Street. Located on basement level. [D5]

EDINBURGH

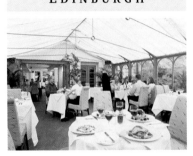

Bruntsfield Hotel – The Potting Shed

- *"Relaxing, pleasant atmosphere."*
- *Innovative Scottish cooking.*

T HE BRUNTSFIELD HOTEL is a town house hotel overlooking the famous Bruntsfield Golf Links. The Potting Shed Restaurant offers good food in a friendly, relaxed atmosphere prepared by Head Chef Martyn Dixon. Excellent range of value for money wines. One, two and three course lunch and dinner menus are available.

Mediterranean char-grilled vegetable roulade with chilli and tomato coulis. Breast of Barbary duck stuffed with apples and prunes and served with orange cous cous and blackcurrant jus. Red wine poached pear with cassis jelly and clotted cream ice cream.

STB ★★★★ Hotel

◗ *Open all year* 🛏 *Rooms: 75 en suite* 🛏 *DB&B £45–£77.50 B&B £42.50–£75* 🅿 *Special rates available* ✖ *Food available all day (Kings Bar) £ Lunch £ Dinner (Kings Bar) £ Lunch Sun (Potting Shed) Dinner (Potting Shed) ££* Ⓥ *Vegetarians welcome* ✳ *Children welcome* ♿ *Facilities for disabled visitors* ✖ *Smoking in bar area of restaurant only* 🆑 *Mastercard/ Eurocard, American Express, Visa, Diners Club, Switch, Delta* 🅽 *Hotel Manager: Andrea Whigham*

69 Bruntsfield Place Edinburgh EH10 4HH
Tel: 0131 229 1393 Fax: 0131 229 5634
E-mail: bruntsfield@queensferry-hotels.co.uk
Web: www.thebruntsfield.co.uk
1 mile south of Edinburgh city centre on A702, overlooking Bruntsfield Links. [D5]

EDINBURGH

Cafe Hub

- *"Informal casual modern dining from brunch to dinner."*
- *Light, innovative and above all fresh.*

THE HUB is one of Edinburgh's hidden jewels. On the ground floor, Cafe Hub continues to play host to cafe concerts, culinary evenings and many art and craft exhibitions. Hub Chef, Nick Bryan creates food which is both stylish and imaginative. Private dining areas are also available for those extra special occasions.

Basil and lemon risotto, Parma ham, prawns. Sea bass, bacon, chervil and mushrooms. Honey wafer, pecan butter parfait, honey sauce.

Open all year except Christmas Day Food available all day £ Lunch ££ Dinner ££ Vegetarians welcome Children welcome Facilities for disabled visitors Facilities for smoking on terrace area Mastercard/ Eurocard, American Express, Visa, Diners Club, Switch, Delta Cafe Manager: Craig Winning; Chef: Nick Bryan

Castlehill Royal Mile Edinburgh EH1 2NE
Tel: 0131 473 2067 Fax: 0131 473 2016
E-mail: thehub@eif.co.uk
Web: www.eif.co.uk/thehub
A landmark church at the top of the Royal Mile, where Castlehill meets the Lawnmarket and Johnston Terrace. [D5]

EDINBURGH

Caledonian Hilton Hotel

- *"A world famous jewel in Edinburgh's crown."*
- *Fresh, lively and world class.*

THE 'CALEY' is an Edinburgh institution. The Pompadour Restaurant offers creative, modern French cuisine and some of the best views in the city – Castle view and Princes Street. The food is complex, intricate and deftly handled. Service is state-of-the-art; the wine list exceptional. Downstairs there is Chisholm's – a modern brasserie-style restaurant.

Compote of Western Isle seafood with fine leaves, saffron vinaigrette and basil oil. Pan-fried medallions of Aberdeen Angus beef with quails eggs, celeriac purée and red wine mushroom jus. Chocolate and pink grapefruit parfait, caramelised citrus fruits and Glenkinchie syrup.

STB ★★★★★ Hotel

Open all year Rooms: 249 en suite B&B £100–200 Special rates available Lunch (Chisholm's) ££ Dinner (Chisholm's) ££ Lunch (The Pompadour) Tue to Fri ££ Dinner (The Pompadour) Tue to Sat £££ Vegetarians welcome Children welcome in Chisholm's Facilities for disabled visitors Smoking area in Chisholm's Mastercard/Eurocard, American Express, Visa, Diners Club, Switch, Delta General Manager: Dagmar Mühle

Princes Street Edinburgh EH1 2AB
Tel: 0131 222 8888 Fax: 0131 222 8889
E-mail: ednchhirm@hilton.com
Web: www.hilton.com
West end of Princes Street at junction with Lothian Road. [D5]

EDINBURGH

EDINBURGH

Channings Restaurant

- *"Excellent example of contemporary French cooking in a relaxed friendly atmosphere within walking distance from the West End of Edinburgh."*
- *Distinctive and contemporary cooking.*

CHANNINGS OFFERS a choice of dining from the bar, conservatory or restaurant. All areas offer tempting menus which are well-balanced and innovative and the dishes are prepared and presented by Head Chef, Richard Glennie and his highly skilled team. Dining at Channings is a unique experience in one of Edinburgh's sought after residential areas.

Spiced diver scallops, avocado, tomato and white crab salad. Herb crusted cutlets and braised shin of lamb served on a white bean and bacon cassoulet, gratin dauphinoise and young spring vegetables. Tasting of three chocolate desserts.

STB ★★★★ Hotel

◗ *Open all year except 23 to 27 Dec incl* 🏠 *Rooms: 46 en suite* 🛏 *B&B £125–£240* 💷 *Special rates available* ✗ *Food served all day £ Lunch ££ Dinner £££* 🅥 *Vegetarians welcome* ✶ *Children welcome* ✽ *No smoking in restaurant* 💳 *Mastercard/ Eurocard, American Express, Visa, Diners Club, Switch, Delta* 🍴 *Head Chef: Richard Glennie*

15 South Learmonth Gardens Edinburgh EH4 1EZ
Tel: 0131 315 2225 Fax: 0131 332 9631
E-mail: restaurant@channings.co.uk
Web: www.channings.co.uk
From West End, cross Dean Bridge into Queensferry Road, then right, just after pedestrian lights, into South Learmonth Avenue and then right at the bottom. [D5]

Daniel's Bistro

- *"A relaxed French bistro offering authentic Alsation dishes alongside the best modern Scottish cooking."*
- *Modern Scottish and French Provincial.*

DANIEL'S is an old converted bonded warehouse and is a feat of architectural design blended with simple furnishings. All this makes for a relaxed and friendly atmosphere created and pursued by Patron Daniel. Menus range from classic Scottish dishes to more continental choices – all skilfully prepared and presented – there is something to suit everyone here.

Tarte Flambee: milk bread dough with a topping of crème fraîche, fromage frais, onions and bacon lardons. Slow cooked duck confit served with paysanne sautéed potatoes. Daniel's special bread and butter pudding.

◗ *Open all year except Christmas Day, Boxing Day, 1 and 2 Jan* ✗ *Lunch £–££ Dinner ££* 🅥 *Vegetarians welcome* ✶ *Children welcome* ♿ *Facilities for disabled visitors* ✽ *Separate smoking dining area* 💳 *Mastercard/Eurocard, American Express, Visa, Switch, Delta* 🍴 *Owner: Daniel J. Vencker*

88 Commercial Street Edinburgh EH3 6SF
Tel: 0131 553 5933 Fax: 0131 553 3966
Web: www.edinburghrestaurants.co.uk
Located in Leith near the harbour. The building is opposite the new Scottish Executive and near HMS Britannia. [D5]

EDINBURGH

EDINBURGH

Dubh Prais Restaurant

- *"A popular haunt with delicious local cuisine."*
- *Contemporary Scottish cooking.*

DUBH PRAIS (Gaelic for black cooking pot) is easily recognised by the sign of the black pot on the Royal Mile. Chef/Proprietor James McWilliams presents a menu which offers traditional Scottish dishes using seasonal produce. The restaurant is popular with tourists and locals for its fine examples of Scottish flavour and consistent quality.

West Coast broth: salmon, squid, mussels, smoked haddock steamed in a creamy fish stock. Breast of chicken stuffed with smoked Argyll ham, Isle of Mull Cheddar, roasted and served with sage and sherry sauce. Atholl brose parfait: home-made ice cream with honey, Drambuie and toasted oatmeal served with a bramble sauce.

❶ *Open all year except 2 weeks Christmas and 2 weeks Easter Closed Sun Mon* ✘ *Lunch except Sun Mon £ Dinner except Sun Mon £££* Ⓥ *Vegetarians welcome* ✱ *Children welcome* ✹ *Guests are asked not to smoke cigars or pipes* 🎫 *Mastercard/Eurocard, American Express, Visa, Switch, Delta, JCB* ▮ *Chef/Proprietor: James McWilliams; Proprietor: Heather McWilliams*

123b High Street Edinburgh EH1 1SG Tel: 0131 557 5732 Fax: 0131 557 5263 Web: www.bencraighouse.co.uk Edinburgh Royal Mile, opposite Crowne Plaza hotel. [D5]

Duck's at Le Marché Noir

- *"Contemporary Scottish food with an International influence. Relaxing and welcoming atmosphere."*
- *Excellent modern French/Scottish cuisine.*

IN THIS STYLISH New Town restaurant, award-winning international chefs produce imaginative contemporary cuisine using fresh Scottish ingredients. The exceptional menus are well-presented, changing monthly. Malcolm Duck takes justifiable pride in his extensive and spectacular wine list. A private dining room and special menus also available.

Pan-fried haggis on roast carrot and turnip with sautéed wild mushrooms and whisky jus. Sesame coated salmon fillet on a pak choy, baby corn and chilli butter with pickled cucumber ribbons and soy dressing. Baileys bavarois with toasted marshmallow and Cointreau sabayon.

❶ *Open all year except 25 and 26 Dec* ✘ *Lunch ££ Dinner £££* Ⓥ *Vegetarians welcome* ✱ *Children welcome* ♿ *Disabled access* ✹ *No smoking room in restaurant* 🎫 *Mastercard/ Eurocard, American Express, Visa, Diners Club, Switch, Delta, JCB* ▮ *Proprietor: Malcolm Duck*

2/4 Eyre Place Edinburgh EH3 5EP Tel: 0131 558 1608 Fax: 0131 556 0798 E-mail: bookings@ducks.co.uk Web: www.ducks.co.uk At the northern end of Dundas Street lies Eyre Place. Duck's lies near the junction of the two. [D5]

EDINBURGH

Grain Store Restaurant

- *"Cooking of a real ability shines through in superbly flavoured contemporary dishes."*
- *Modern Scottish.*

A MODERN STAIRCASE opens into a series of chambers, with attractive bare stone walls, superb arched windows, wood floors, with wood furniture and fittings. The cooking is accomplished, innovative and delicious, with a menu that changes with the seasons, all complemented by excellent service. Look out for the cheeseboard as Ian Mellis' famous shop is right next door.

Loch Fyne oysters grilled with spinach and hollandaise. Whole roasted grouse, braised plums and rosemary. White chocolate crème brûlée with dark chocolate ice cream.

❶ *Open all year except Boxing Day* ✕ *Lunch £–££ Dinner ££–£££* Ⓥ *Vegetarians welcome* ✶ *Children welcome* ▣ *Mastercard/Eurocard, American Express, Visa, Switch, Delta, JCB, Solo* Ⓜ *Partner/Manager: Paul MacPhail; Partner/ Chef: Carlo Coxon*

30 Victoria Street Edinburgh EH1 2JN Tel: 0131 225 7635 Fax: 0131 622 7313 E-mail: contact@grainstore-restaurant.co.uk Web: www. grainstore-restaurant.co.uk 2 minutes walk from the castle. Victoria Street is between the Grassmarket and George IV Bridge. [D5]

EDINBURGH

Haldanes Restaurant

- *"Basement restaurant with a warm comfortable atmosphere – an excellent example of Scottish cuisine."*
- *Innovative Scottish cuisine.*

H ALDANES HAS ESTABLISHED itself as one of the foremost Edinburgh restaurants. Proprietor George Kelso creates Scottish cuisine in his own unique style while his wife Michelle, as front of house, gives excellent service to diners – a truly professional combination. In summer, diners may also enjoy the terraced garden to the rear.

Warm salad of Highland venison with a balsamic dressing. Filo basket of West Coast king scallops and Scottish salmon fillets with a lemon butter sauce. Fresh warm crêpes filled with vanilla pod ice cream, orange and Grand Marnier Syrup.

❶ *Open all year except Christmas Day and Boxing Day* ✕ *Lunch except Sun Sat ££ Dinner £££* Ⓥ *Vegetarians welcome* ✶ *Children welcome* ✲ *No smoking in restaurant* ▣ *Mastercard/Eurocard, American Express, Visa, Switch, Delta* Ⓜ *Proprietor/Chef: George Kelso*

39a Albany Street Edinburgh EH1 3QY Tel: 0131 556 8407 Fax: 0131 556 2662 E-mail: dinehaldanes@aol.com Web: www.haldanesrestaurant.com Edinburgh New Town – off Broughton Street on the corner of Albany Street and York Lane. [D5]

EDINBURGH

Henderson's Salad Table

- *"A vibrant and contemporary restaurant that has been successfully satisfying the needs of its huge local following for many years."*
- *Innovative and interesting vegetarian cuisine.*

HENDERSON'S, still actively run by the family, appeals to all ages proving that wholefoods can be fun, especially Monday to Saturday nights when 'real' musicians enliven the wine bar. Vegetarian salads, savouries, quiches and puddings are freshly prepared and eagerly consumed throughout the day with an unusual selection of real ales and wines.

Roasted red pepper and tomato soup with home-made nutty malt bread. Broccoli and Brie crumble with choice of freshly prepared salads. Orange and ginger vacherin. Wide selection of herbal teas, coffee and fresh pressed juices.

◑ *Open all year except Christmas Day, Boxing Day, 1 and 2 Jan Closed Sun except during Edinburgh Festival* ✘ *Food available all day except Sun £ Lunch except Sun £ Dinner except Sun £–££* Ⓥ *Vegans welcome* ✶ *Children welcome* ✔ *No smoking in main restaurant and wine bar areas* ⊞ *Mastercard/Eurocard, American Express, Visa, Switch, Delta, JCB* ⋈ *Proprietors: The Henderson Family*

94 Hanover Street Edinburgh EH2 1DR
Tel: 0131 225 2131 Fax: 0131 220 3542
E-mail: mail@hendersonsofedinburgh.co.uk
Web: www.hendersonsofedinburgh.co.uk
2 minutes from Princes Street under Henderson's wholefood shop, at the junction with Thistle Street. [D5]

EDINBURGH

Howies Restaurant

- *"A fun and friendly bistro restaurant serving exciting, fashionable Scottish food."*
- *Modern Scottish with international influences.*

THIS IS A SIMPLE bistro-style restaurant where the atmosphere is fun, young and informal. Food is unpretentious, focusing on good quality, freshly prepared produce. Great care is taken over the regularly changing menus to create appealing choices. Bring your own bottle still operating (£3 corkage) or use the contemporary wine list.

Grilled black pudding, frisee salad, roast apple and ginger dressing. Char-grilled chicken suprême, mango and leek stuffing and wilted greens. Chocolate and orange ganache with raspberry coulis.

◑ *Open all year except 25, 26 Dec and 1, 2 Jan Closed Mon lunch only* ✘ *Lunch except Mon £ Dinner ££* Ⓥ *Vegetarians welcome* ✶ *Children welcome* ⅋ *Facilities for disabled visitors* ⋔ *Guide dogs only* ⊞ *Mastercard/Eurocard, American Express, Visa, Diners Club, Switch, Delta, JCB*

63 Dalry Road Edinburgh EH11 2BZ
Tel: 0131 313 3334 Fax: 0131 313 3334
E-mail: howiesuk@hotmail.com
Web: www.howies.uk.com
On the south side of Dalry Road, between Richmond Terrace and Caledonian Road, 2 minutes from Haymarket. [D5]

EDINBURGH

EDINBURGH

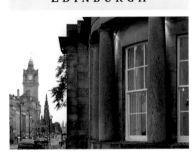

Howies Stockbridge

- *"Relaxed, informal dining in an energetic Stockbridge bistro."*
- *Modern Scottish with international influences.*

HOWIES STOCKBRIDGE is a lively, buzzing bistro where great attention has been given to design. The two or three course menus represent excellent value for money as do the house wines. The food here is exciting and delicious with the best of Scottish produce being used innovatively. £3 corkage charge.

Warm crab and ginger flan with lemon and dill dressing. Pan-fried lamb chops with butter bean, garlic and rosemary stem and red wine reduction. Iced pear parfait with Kirsch cherries.

◑ *Open all year except 25, 26 Dec and New Year's Day* ✗ *Lunch £ Dinner ££* Ⓥ *Vegetarians welcome* ✻ *Children welcome* ♿ *Facilities for disabled visitors* ⚬ *No smoking room in restaurant* ✦ *Guide dogs only* ▩ *Mastercard/ Eurocard, American Express, Visa, Diners Club, Switch, Delta, JCB*

4-6 Glanville Place Edinburgh EH3 6SZ
Tel: 0131 225 5553 Fax: 0131 225 5553
E-mail: howiesuk@hotmail.com
Web: www.howies.uk.com
Located by the Stockbridge, on the corner of Hamilton Place. [D5]

Howies Waterloo Place

- *"The latest Edinburgh Howies is fun, sleek and trendy yet with the same high quality fresh cooking as all the others."*
- *Contemporary Scottish cooking.*

THIS LATEST ADDITION to the Howies 'family' of restaurants is centrally located in the East End of the capital within traditional surroundings which have been sensitively renovated. Cooking here is skilled and contemporary and may be enjoyed either in the restaurant area or in the bar where food is served all day. £3 corkage charge.

Gravadlax of Scotch salmon with a wholegrain mustard and dill dressing. Sweet skinned salmon fillet with sauce vierge and fine herb salad. Roast pear with Mascarpone and red wine syrup.

◑ *Open all year except Christmas Day and New Year's Day* ✗ *Food available all day in Bar £ Lunch £ Dinner ££* Ⓥ *Vegetarians welcome* ✻ *Children welcome* ⚬ *No smoking in restaurant* ▩ *Mastercard/Eurocard, American Express, Visa, Diners, Club, Switch, Delta, JCB*

29 Waterloo Place Edinburgh
Tel: 0131 556 5766 Fax: 0131 556 5766
E-mail: howiesuk@hotmail.com
Web: www.howies.uk.com
Centre of Edinburgh. An extension of the East End of Princes Street. Two minute walk from Princes Street. [D5]

EDINBURGH

Igg's Restaurant

- *"A restaurant that brings Spanish sunshine to Edinburgh – many authentic dishes prepared with the best Scottish ingredients."*
- *Spanish dishes with Scottish produce.*

IGG'S IS A SMALL, FRIENDLY, owner-run restaurant in the heart of Edinburgh's Old Town which has been extended into the premises next door and has been elegantly refurbished. At lunchtime and evenings a tapas menu is available as well as a good priced three/four course table d'hôte and à la carte evening menu.

Warm tart tatin of beetroot topped with a quenelle of Mascarpone and a tomato chive dressing. Fillet of Stobo Estate beef topped with a blue cheese crust on a rösti potato with a whisky sauce. Hot chocolate pudding with a warm chocolate sauce and vanilla ice cream.

◗ *Open all year except 1 to 3 Jan Closed Sun* ✗ *Lunch except Sun ££ Dinner except Sun £££* Ⓥ *Vegetarians welcome* ✳ *Children welcome* ♿ *Facilities for disabled visitors* ▣ *Mastercard/ Eurocard, American Express, Visa, Diners Club, Switch, Delta, JCB* Ⓜ *Owner: Iggy Campos*

15 Jeffrey Street Edinburgh EH1 1DR Tel: 0131 557 8184 Fax: 0131 652 3774 Jeffrey Street lies between the Royal Mile and Market Street, behind Waverley Station. [D5]

EDINBURGH

Keepers Restaurant

- *"Unpretentious city restaurant offering excellent value."*
- *Traditional and contemporary Scottish cooking.*

KEEPERS SPECIALISES IN GAME – supported by fish, shellfish and prime meat. The restaurant serves lunch and dinner on a table d'hôte (five starters, five main courses) and à la carte basis. Individual rooms (or, indeed, the entire place) can be reserved. A true modern Scottish experience with cosy intimate atmosphere.

Baked asparagus in filo pastry with tomato chutney. Pan-fried partridge with a garlic and whisky sauce on horseradish mash. Drambuie crème Brûlée with fresh berries.

◗ *Open all year Closed Sun Mon and Sat lunch unless by prior arrangement* ✗ *Lunch except Sun Mon Sat £ Dinner except Sun Mon ££* Ⓥ *Vegetarians welcome* ✳ *Children welcome* ✍ *No smoking area by request* ▣ *Mastercard/ Eurocard, American Express, Visa, Switch* Ⓜ *Proprietors: Keith & Mairi Cowie*

13B Dundas Street Edinburgh EH3 6QG Tel: 0131 556 5707 Fax: 0131 556 5707 E-mail: keithcowie@keepers.sagehost.co.uk Web: www.keepers.sagehost.co.uk At the southern end of Dundas Street, near the junction with Abercromby Place. [D5]

EDINBURGH

Lafayette

- *"Elegant dining in Tudor building."*
- *Fresh Scottish produce cooked in French style.*

SET IN A BEAUTIFUL Tudor building, proprietors Thierry Menard and Sebastien Leparoux have created a welcoming and elegant restaurant. Scottish produce is prepared and presented with French style and complemented by a comprehensive wine list. A memorable and enjoyable experience.

Marbled terrine of quail and foie gras served with a grape chutney and brioche. Pan-fried fillet of Aberdeen Angus beef with a red wine and shallot jus, and gratin dauphinoise. Banana parfait with rhubarb ice cream.

◗ *Open all year except Christmas Day, Boxing Day, 1 and 2 Jan Closed Sun* ✗ *Lunch except Sun ££ Dinner except Sun £££* Ⓥ *Vegetarians welcome* ✱ *Children welcome* ▣ *Mastercard/ Eurocard, American Express, Visa, Switch, Delta* Ⓜ *Partners: Thierry Menard and Sebastien Leparoux*

9 Randolph Place Edinburgh EH3 7TE
Tel: 0131 225 8678 Fax: 0131 225 6477
Web: www.lafayette-restaurant.co.uk
From West End – first right into Randolph Place. Lafayette on left-hand side at corner of Randolph Lane. [D5]

EDINBURGH

La Garrigue

- *"A welcome return to Edinburgh, where Jean-Michel portrays the classic tastes of his homeland."*
- *Regional French cuisine.*

LA GARRIGUE is the brainchild of Jean-Michel Gauffre renowned Masterchef who has gone back to his roots eloquently portraying the dishes of 'Doc, in particular La Garrigue. Jean-Michel has set out his stall using his enviable skills and unique style. It is entirely French in style – but don't worry as the menu is also translated to English!

Home-made salted cod purée with garlic croutons and rocket leaf salad. Leg of rabbit filled with a cevennes ham and juniper berries farce. Ewe milk cheesecake with blueberries.

◗ *Open all year Closed Sun evening and all day Mon* ✗ *Lunch except Mon ££ Dinner except Sun Mon ££* Ⓥ *Vegetarians welcome* ✱ *Children welcome* ▣ *Mastercard/Eurocard, American Express, Visa, Diners Club, Switch, Delta* Ⓜ *Chef-Patron: Jean Michel Gauffre*

31 Jeffrey Street Edinburgh EH1 1DH
Tel: 0131 557 3032 Fax: 0131 557 3032
Off The Royal Mile, 5 minutes from Waverley Station (rail). [D5]

EDINBURGH

Le Café Saint-Honoré

- *"Relaxed friendly atmosphere – an excellent example of fresh produce cooked and served in French-style."*
- *Scottish produce with French influence.*

CAFÉ ST-HONORÉ has a Gallic charm although Chef/Proprietor Chris Colverson favours a more Scottish style of cooking with French influences in the preparation. Menus change daily and are à la carte, and very reasonably priced. The cooking is adventurous and highly professional; interesting combinations and fresh, innovative sauces appear regularly.

Home-made noodles, with braised squid and olives. Shank of lamb, garlic confit, spinach, boudinnoir. Crème brûlée.

◗ Open all year except Christmas Day, Boxing Day, and 2 days over New Year Closed Sun (except during Edinburgh Festival) and Sat Lunch ✗ Lunch ££ Pre and Après Theatre Suppers Dinner £££ Ⓥ Vegetarians welcome ✱ Children welcome ✌ 2 non-smoking dining areas and 1 smoking dining area 🅿 No parking ⊞ Mastercard/Eurocard, American Express, Visa, Diners Club, Switch, Delta, JCB ⚄ Chef/Proprietors: Chris Colverson; Gill Colverson

*34 North West Thistle Street Lane Edinburgh EH2 1EA
Tel: 0131 226 2211
Web: www.icscotland.co.uk/cafe-sthonore
Centre of Edinburgh, just off Frederick Street, 3 minutes from Princes Street. At Frederick Street end of lane. [D5]*

EDINBURGH

No 3 Royal Terrace

- *"An elegant bistro restaurant beautifully situated overlooking the town to the Firth. Both staff and exciting cooking are exemplary."*
- *Modern Scottish.*

NO 3 ROYAL TERRACE is elegant and comfortable with a welcoming ambience. The eating experience here is second to none with Scottish produce served in an innovative style. Choice of dining (same menu) in downstairs bistro or upstairs restaurant. Also open for Sunday brunch. Private parties in 'special room' – no extra charge.

Steamed West Coast mussels with chilli, tomato and coriander. Char-grilled fillet of Borders ostrich with pak choy and pave potatoes veiled with an oriental sauce. Sticky toffee crème Brûlée with home-made honeycomb ice cream.

◗ Open all year except Christmas Day, Boxing Day and 1, 2 Jan ✗ Lunch ££ Dinner £££ Ⓥ Vegetarians welcome ✱ Children welcome ⊞ Mastercard/Eurocard, American Express, Visa, Diners Club, Switch ⚄ Head Chef: Steven Worth

*3 Royal Terrace Edinburgh EH7 5AB
Tel: 0131 477 4747 Fax: 0131 477 4747
E-mail: nigel@howgate.f9.co.uk
Web: www.howgate.f9.co.uk
From east end of Princes Street travel down Leith Walk. At first roundabout after the Playhouse Theatre take 2nd left onto London Road then sharp right onto Blenheim Place/Royal Terrace, restaurant just after Greenside Parish Church. [D5]*

EDINBURGH

No 27 Charlotte Square
The National Trust For Scotland

- *"An elegant classical setting with Scotland's finest produce complementing the dining experience."*
- *Modern and traditional Scottish cooking served in style.*

GRACIOUS DINING by night yet an excellent place for lunches and coffees too. A jewel in The National Trust for Scotland's crown. A beautiful venue – not only for its fine food but also for the lovely gift and book shop and gallery area. Function facilities available.

Roulade of monkfish wrapped in smoked salmon, served with chilli mayonnaise. Saddle of venison sliced around a spinach timbale, set on a tayberry salsa. Brandy basket filled with cranachan cream, set on an orange Drambuie syrup.

❶ *Open all year except 25, 26 Dec and 1, 2 Jan* ❣ *Licensed* ✗ *Food available all day £–££ Lunch £ Dinner ££* Ⓥ *Vegetarians welcome* ❋ *Children welcome* ♿ *Facilities for disabled visitors* ✵ *No smoking throughout* ❸ *Mastercard, Visa, Diners Club, Switch, Delta* 🅺 *Restaurant Manager: Lesley Fair*

27 Charlotte Square Edinburgh EH2 4ET
Tel: 0131 243 9339 Fax: 0131 243 9595
E-mail: catering@nts.org.uk
Web: www.nts.org.uk
In Edinburgh city centre, 2 minutes from West End of Princes Street. [D5]

EDINBURGH

Restaurant At The Bonham

- *"A stylish comfortable venue in Edinburgh's West End with contemporary cooking."*
- *Creative yet simple, contemporary European-influenced dishes.*

A UNIQUE COMBINATION of modern decor and lighting set in a traditional Victorian building. The Bonham is a spacious and chic hotel using the highest standards of fabric and furnishings which is complemented by an evident commitment to professionalism and training. Head Chef Michel Bouyer combines great produce with European-influenced dishes which are light and most enjoyable.

Pressed terrine of duck confit and wild mushroom with pear chutney. Prosciutto wrapped chicken suprême spiced barley risotto and lime leave sauce. Elderflower panacotta with exotic fruit salad.

STB ★★★★ Hotel

❶ *Open all year except 3 to 6 Jan incl* 🛏 *Rooms: 48 en suite* 🛌 *B&B £135–£295* 🆂 *Special rates available* ✗ *Lunch ££ Dinner £££* Ⓥ *Vegetarians welcome* ❋ *Children welcome* ♿ *Facilities for disabled visitors* ✵ *Smoking area in restaurant* ❸ *Mastercard/Eurocard, American Express, Visa, Diners Club, Switch, Delta* 🅺 *General Manager: Fiona Vernon; Head Chef: Michel Bouyer*

35 Drumsheugh Gardens Edinburgh EH3 7RN
Tel: 0131 623 9319 Fax: 0131 226 6080
E-mail: restaurant@thebonham.com
Web: www.thebonham.com
Drumsheugh Gardens is in the heart of the West End. The Bonham lies at the junction with Rothesay Place. [D5]

EDINBURGH

The Scotch Whisky Heritage Centre

- *"A unique venue with fine fresh fare."*
- *Fresh, simple and Scottish.*

LOCATED ON the lower ground level of the Heritage Centre the bistro is open to the public even if they do not partake in the highly interesting and educational tour. The bistro has counter and staff service and offers light snacks and dishes of the day all using well-sourced produce. Private function room also available.

Home-made soup with crusty bread. Wild mushroom terrine with thyme dressing. Prawn and smoked salmon mousse. Scottish salmon roasted with leeks. Smoked trout fillet with raspberry dressing. Baked tomato filled with root vegetables. Apple and whisky tart. Bread and butter pudding. Sticky toffee pudding.

STB ★★★★★ Visitor Attraction

◗ *Open all year except Christmas Day*
♥ *Licensed* ✗ *Food available all day £ Lunch £*
Ⓥ *Vegetarians welcome* ⚹ *Children welcome*
♿ *Facilities for disabled visitors* 🔳 *Mastercard/ Eurocard, American Express, Visa, Diners Club, Switch, Delta* ⚑ *General Manager: Susan Morrison*

354 Castlehill The Royal Mile Edinburgh EH1 2NE
Tel: 0131 220 0441 Fax: 0131 220 6288
E-mail: s.morrison@whisky-heritage.co.uk
Web: www.whisky-heritage.co.uk
30 metres from Edinburgh Castle Esplanade at the top of the Royal Mile. [D5]

EDINBURGH

Sheraton Grand Hotel

- *"The Grill Room with its superb atmosphere and view of the castle offers excellent cuisine."*
- *Scottish/international.*

THE SHERATON GRAND hotel has two restaurants: The Grill Room and The Terrace. The latter overlooks Festival Square and offers a sophisticated brasserie style menu. The former is formal and intimate: Executive Chef Nicolas Laurent offers innovative dishes with international flavours.

Emincé of Eyemouth lobster with crab tian, orange and cardamom dressing. Rosace of spring lamb with shallot and garlic confit. Hot caramelised apple, blackberry parfait.

STB ★★★★★ Hotel
Green Tourism Two Leaf Silver Award

◗ *Open all year* 🛏 *Rooms: 260 en suite* 🛏 *DB&B £114.50–£182 B&B £82.50–£150* ✗ *Lunch (The Terrace) ££ (The Grill Room) £££ Dinner (The Terrace) ££ (The Grill Room) ££££*
Ⓥ *Vegetarian menus available in both restaurants* ⚹ *Children welcome with special menu available* ♿ *Facilities for disabled visitors* ✂ *Pipes and cigars after 9 pm in The Grill Room No smoking area in both restaurants* 🔳 *Mastercard/Eurocard, American Express, Visa, Diners Club, Switch* ⚑ *Executive Assistant Manager: Jorgen Rasmussen; Executive Chef: Nicolas Laurent; Food & Beverage Services Manager: Jean-Philippe Maurer*

1 Festival Square Edinburgh EH3 9SR
Tel: 0131 221 6422 Fax: 0131 229 6254
E-mail: GrandEdinburgh.sheraton@sheraton.com
Web: www.starwood.com
Vehicle access adjacent from western approach road. Pedestrian entrance off Festival Square. [D5]

EDINBURGH

EDINBURGH

Skerries Seafood Restaurant

- *"Superb selection of dishes, full of flavour and style."*
- *Fish and modern Scottish cooking.*

AT SKERRIES, award-winning chef Paul Temple presents an interesting menu using excellent produce mainly from the Orkney and Shetland Isles. Although the emphasis is on seafood, there is also a variety of dishes using Orkney beef and lamb. Vegetarians are well-catered for. Less formal meals are available in the Stane Bar.

Tartare of monkfish with avocado mousse served with a crème fraîche and lemon dressing. Baked fillet of halibut set on a cabbage and potato cake topped with crispy ham, served with a light tarragon essence. Caramelised pear tart served with a vanilla and tarragon sauce anglaise.

STB ★★★★ Small Hotel

◗ *Open all year except New Year's Day Closed Sun* 🏠 *Rooms: 16 en suite* 🛏 *B&B £35–£55* 🆂🅿 *Special rates available* ✕ *Food available all day £ Lunch £ Dinner except Sun £££* Ⓥ *Vegetarians welcome* ✹ *Children welcome* ✹ *No smoking in restaurant* 💳 *Mastercard/ Eurocard, American Express, Visa, Diners Club, Switch, Delta* ⊠ *Proprietor: Mrs Shirley Mowat*

Dunstane House 4 West Coates Haymarket Edinburgh EH12 5JQ
Tel: 0131 337 6169 Fax: 0131 337 6060
E-mail: reservations@dunstanehousehotel.co.uk
Web: www.dunstanehousehotel.co.uk
Located on the A8 road going west from city centre towards the airport. 10 minutes walk from Princes Street, past Haymarket Railway Station. [D5]

Stac Polly

- *"An intimate and elegant cellar restaurant serving excellent contemporary cuisine."*
- *Modern/Scottish cuisine.*

DESCEND FROM STREET LEVEL to cosy cellar restaurant – elegantly decorated, stylishly Scottish. Candles add to the intimate atmosphere complemented by good linen, china and glassware. Service here is first-class. The menu is interesting and varied offering the best of fresh local produce cooked in exciting ways. Quality is a passion here.

Baked filo pastry parcels of haggis, served on a sweet plum sauce. Oven-roasted loin of lamb on a horseradish mash with a cider and honey glaze. Chocolate Marquise with coffee bean sauce and cinnamon ice cream.

◗ *Open all year incl Sun* ✕ *Lunch £ Dinner ££* Ⓥ *Vegetarians welcome* ✹ *Smoking area in restaurant* 💳 *Mastercard/Eurocard, American Express, Switch, Visa, Diners Club* ⊠ *Proprietor: Roger Coulthard*

29-33 Dublin Street Edinburgh EH3 6NL
Tel: 0131 556 2231 Fax: 0131 557 9779
Web: www.stacpolly.co.uk
At the east end of Queen Street, Dublin Street runs down hill off Queen Street. [D5]

EDINBURGH

The Stockbridge Restaurant

- *"Elegant modern basement restaurant."*
- *Modern Scottish cooking.*

STOCKBRIDGE RESTAURANT is located in fashionable St Stephen Street in Stockbridge. Dining is in elegant surroundings of gold and black decor. The black walls are enhanced with a selection of prints from Scottish artists. Juliet Wilson takes great attention in preparing the Scottish produce in innovative modern style. Stockbridge Restaurant is easily recognised by fairy lights on stairs to entrance. Small room for private function.

Carrot, orange and coriander soup. Mussels in white wine, shallots and garlic. Lemon baked Alaska with white chocolate, orange and Cointreau sauce.

◑ Closed Sun, Mon ✘ £–£££ Ⅴ Vegetarians welcome ⊞ Mastercard/Eurocard, American Express, Visa, Switch ⋈ Owner/Head Chef: Juliet Wilson

54 St Stephen Street Edinburgh EH3 5AL Tel: 0131 226 6766 Fax: 0131 226 6766 From Princes Street to Frederick Street, to Howie Street, turn left at traffic lights, St Stephen Street 2nd on right. [D5]

EDINBURGH

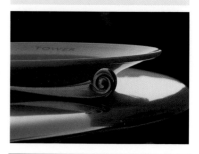

Tower Restaurant and Terrace

- *"An exceptional contemporary restaurant in a stunning city setting."*
- *Stylish cuisine.*

THIS MODERN STYLISH restaurant looks out over the rooftops of Old Edinburgh (come at night to see the floodlit castle – spectacular!) The food here is of the highest quality, cooked with deft simplicity and elegantly presented. Accomplished and friendly staff offer excellent service. An enthusiastic wine team have created an inspirational wine list.

Buckie shell crab with citrus mayonnaise and potato salad. Scottish lamb shank, cutlet and loin, with roasted root vegetables and buttered mash. Individual hot sticky ginger pudding with stem ginger syrup and bitter lime sorbet.

◑ Open all year except Christmas Day and Boxing Day ✘ Food available all day ££ Lunch ££ Dinner £££ Ⅴ Vegetarians welcome ✱ Children welcome ♿ Facilities for disabled visitors ✔ No smoking throughout the Museum, diners may smoke on the Terrace (with heating) ⊞ Mastercard/ Eurocard, American Express, Visa, Diners Club, Switch ⋈ Owner: James Thomson

Museum of Scotland Chambers Street Edinburgh EH1 1JF Tel: 0131 225 3003 Fax: 0131 225 0978 E-mail: reservations@tower-restaurant.com Web: www.tower-restaurant.com Located above the new Museum of Scotland at the junction of George IV Bridge and Chambers Street. [D5]

EDINBURGH

The Witchery by the Castle: Winner 2001 Restaurant Award

- *"Come and be spellbound in this very fine eatery."*
- *Stylish modern Scottish cuisine.*

THIS CONTINUES to be one of Edinburgh's gems, with bags of charm and deliciously tempting menus. In the evenings it is an excellent choice for that special occasion, and at lunchtime also offers light menus. James Thomson's wine list is spectacular, incorporating excellent wines from all over the world. The Witchery has six luxurious suites.

Fife crab salad with lime mayonnaise. Honey-roast duck with Savoy cabbage and Ayrshire bacon on sweet potato rösti. Warm dark chocolate tart with praline ice cream.

◗ *Open all year except Christmas Day and Boxing Day* 🏨 *Rooms: 6 en suite* ✖ *Lunch ££ Theatre Supper £ Dinner £££* 💳 *Mastercard/Eurocard, American Express, Visa, Diners Club, Switch* 🗝 *Proprietor: James Thomson; General Manager: Jacquie Sutherland*

Castlehill The Royal Mile Edinburgh EH1 2NF
Tel: 0131 225 5613 Fax: 0131 220 4392
E-mail: reservations@thewitchery.com
Web: www.thewitchery.com
At the top of the Royal Mile, at the gates of Edinburgh Castle. [D5]

EDINBURGH OUTSKIRTS

Caerketton Restaurant

- *"An innovative modern restaurant serving the best of Scottish produce."*
- *Modern Scottish cooking.*

THE DECOR at the Caerketton Restaurant is simple and effective with terracotta walls and green chairs giving a calm and relaxing atmosphere. Proprietors Bob and Susan Woodman, with Chef Scott Donaldson, ensure that fresh produce is served in an innovative style. A true example of Scottish food at its best.

Duo of smoked duck and venison, perched on seasoned avocado mash, drizzled with framboise vinaigrette. Baked whole sea bass en pâté of lemon and herb with coriander and saffron fumet. Fresh warmed strawberries and raspberries with peach sabayon topped with crisp vanilla wafers.

◗ *Open all year except Christmas Day, Boxing Day and 1, 2 Jan Closed Mon* ✖ *Lunch except Mon £ Dinner except Mon ££* 🅥 *Vegetarians welcome* ☀ *Children welcome* ♿ *Facilities for disabled visitors* ✷ *Non smoking dining room* 💳 *Mastercard/Eurocard, American Express, Visa, Switch, Delta* 🗝 *Director/Proprietor: Bob Woodman*

Mauricewood Mains Mauricewood Road Penicuik Midlothian EH26 0NJ
Tel: 01968 670800 Fax: 01968 672670
E-mail: caerketton@mains72.freeserve.co.uk
Web: www.caerketton.com
From the Edinburgh city bypass take the A702 (Lothianburn junction) for 3.7m, turn left at sign (Mauricewood, Belwood, Glencorse) the restaurant is on the right-hand side (after 500 yards). Or take A701 (Straiton junction) for 3.6m, turn right into Belwood Road at Glencorse crossroads, continue to restaurant. [D6]

EDINBURGH OUTSKIRTS

Dalhousie Castle and Spa

- *"Historic castle offering a blend of old and new."*
- *Scottish and French contemporary cooking.*

DATING BACK to the 13th century Dalhousie offers modern comforts with the recent addition of a spa, while at the same time retaining superb features and atmosphere of an historic castle. The Dungeon offers traditional French/Scottish cuisine while the Orangery Conservatory offers modern Scottish and European cooking in an informal atmosphere.

Tartar of West Coast scallops with smoked salmon and land cress salad. Pan-fried Scottish beef with a boudin of foie gras. Iced parfait of Blairgowrie berries with nougatine tuile, heather honey anglaise.

STB ★★★★ Hotel

◐ *Open all year except 2 weeks Jan* 🏚 *Rooms: 32 en suite (inc 5 in Lodge)* 🛏 *DB&B £119.50–£304.50 per room B&B £90–£275 per room* 🆂🅿 *Special rates available* ✗ *Food available all day ££ Lunch from ££ Dinner ££ Orangery Restaurant: Dinner from ££££ Dungeon* Ⓥ *Vegetarians welcome* 🕯 *Children welcome* 🚭 *No smoking in Dungeon Restaurant or bedrooms* 💳 *Mastercard/Eurocard, American Express, Visa, Diners Club, Switch, Delta* 🕴 *Managing Director: Neville Petts*

Bonnyrigg nr Edinburgh Midlothian EH19 3JB Tel: 01875 820153 Fax: 01875 821936 E-mail: enquiries@dalhousiecastle.co.uk Web: www.dalhousiecastle.co.uk A7, 7 miles south of Edinburgh. From traffic lights on A7 at B704 junction. [D6]

EDINBURGH OUTSKIRTS

Houstoun House Hotel

- *"A very pampering experience. A quality hotel a few miles from Edinburgh's City Centre."*
- *Country house cuisine.*

THE RESTAURANT at Houstoun House is situated in the former drawing room, library and great hall on the first floor – all delightful rooms and beautifully furnished with antiques and pictures. The chef presents a sophisticated and well-balanced table d'hôte menu at lunch and an à la carte menu at dinner – his cooking is first-class.

A warm salad of seared scallops with a wild strawberry and black pepper dressing. Pan-fried mallard breast with stir-fried greens with a whisky, soya and lemon sauce. Blackberry delice with bramble and a tamarillo-flavoured ice cream.

STB ★★★★ Hotel

◐ *Open all year* 🏚 *Rooms: 72 en suite* 🛏 *DB&B £77.50–£97.50 B&B £52.50–£72.50* 🆂🅿 *Special rates available* ✗ *Lunch except Sat ££ Dinner ££££* Ⓥ *Vegetarians welcome* 🕯 *Children welcome* ♿ *Facilities for disabled visitors* 🚭 *No smoking dining room available* 💳 *Mastercard/ Eurocard, Visa, Diners Club, Switch* 🕴 *General Manager: Ann Yuille*

Uphall West Lothian Edinburgh EH52 6JS Tel: 01506 853831 Fax: 01506 854220 E-mail: events.houstoun@macdonald-hotels.co.uk Web: www.macdonald-hotels.co.uk Just off M8 motorway at Junction 3. [D6]

EDINBURGH OUTSKIRTS

Howgate Restaurant

- *"Relaxed atmosphere enhanced with fine wine and food set within rural woodland and only 20 minutes from Edinburgh."*
- *Modern Scottish cooking.*

THE À LA CARTE style restaurant operates alongside a cosy intimate bistro with a welcoming open log fire in winter. There is a wide choice of less formal dishes offered on the Bistro menu. The cooking here is excellent, prepared and presented in innovative modern style, with countryside portions. A great place for all the family.

Home-made salmon and dill fish cake on a bed of wilted spinach drenched in a garlic and herb sauce. Scottish sirloin steak marinated in a 'secret sauce' , char-grilled, served with seasonal vegetables and hand-cut chips. Selection of Howgate cheeses (Blue, Brie, St Andrews) with Scottish oatcakes and fresh apple.

◑ Open all year except Christmas Day, Boxing Day, New Year's Day and 2 Jan ✕ Lunch ££ Dinner £££ – reservation recommended Ⓥ Vegetarians welcome ⚹ Children welcome ♿ Facilities for disabled visitors ⊞ Mastercard/ Eurocard, American Express, Visa, Diners Club, Switch, Delta, JCB ⚐ General Manager: Peter Ridgway; Head Chef: Angela Mackenzie

Howgate Nr Penicuik Midlothian EH26 8PY Tel: 01968 670000 Fax: 01968 670000 E-mail: nigel@howgate.f9.co Web: www.howgate.f9.co.uk Situated on B6094 about 1 mile north of Leadburn. [D6]

ELGIN

Mansefield House Hotel

- *"A friendly, comfortable hotel, popular for a business stay or weekend break."*
- *Traditional Scottish cooking, with some French influences.*

CLOSE TO THE CENTRE of Elgin, this completely refurbished and restored former manse provides a comfortable retreat for business and leisure visitors alike. Head Chef, Craig Halliday, presents a well-priced à la carte menu made up of classic Scottish dishes, using market available fish, meat and vegetables.

Smoked trout, tomato and spring onion salad with a horseradish dressing. North Sea halibut baked en papillote with white wine and pink peppercorns. White chocolate parfait on a pool of prune and armagnac coulis.

STB ★★★★ Hotel

◑ Open all year ⌂ Rooms: 21 en suite ⇚ DB&B £60–£90 B&B £40–£70 ⊡ Special rates available ✕ Lunch £ Dinner £££ Ⓥ Vegetarians welcome ⚹ Children welcome ♿ Facilities for disabled visitors ✄ No smoking in restaurant ⊞ Mastercard/Eurocard, American Express, Visa, Switch ⚐ Owners: Mr & Mrs T R Murray

Mayne Road Elgin IV30 1NY Tel: 01343 540883 Fax: 01343 552491 E-mail: reception@mansefieldhousehotel.com Web: www.mansefieldhousehotel.com Just off A96 in Elgin. From Inverness, drive towards town centre and turn right at first roundabout. At mini-roundabout, hotel on right. [D3]

ELLON

**Haddo House,
The National Trust for Scotland**

- *"Wonderful home baking and light lunches enhance the visit to Haddo."*
- *Light lunches, snacks and home baking.*

HADDO HOUSE has the very welcoming Stables tearoom which is high-ceilinged, simply decorated and light and airy. A fine example of the high standards set at The National Trust for Scotland properties. Home baking and traditional soups feature highly on the menu making Haddo House an ideal place to spend the day.

Traditional and alternative home-made soups. A selection of freshly made sandwiches and baguettes filled with Scotland's finest ingredients. Hot Highland fudge cake with toffee sauce and Mackie's ice cream.

STB ★★★ Historic House

◑ *Open weekends only Apr and Oct, Daily 1 May to 30 Sep* ⌷ *Special rates available* ♻ *Licensed – pre-arranged events only* ✘ *Food available all day £ Lunch £* Ⓥ *Vegetarians welcome* ✵ *Children welcome* ♿ *Facilities for disabled visitors* ✂ *No smoking throughout* 🦮 *Guide dogs only* ▣ *Mastercard, Visa* ⋈ *Property Manager: Craig Ferguson*

*Tarves Ellon Aberdeenshire AB41 7EQ
Tel: 01651 851440 Fax: 01651 851888
E-mail: haddo@nts.org.uk
Web: www.nts.org.uk
On the Old Meldrum–Tarves road, take road on left 1 mile outside Tarves. Along 1½ miles drive to Haddo House. [D4]*

EVANTON

Visitor Centre – Storehouse of Foulis: Finalist The Macallan Taste of Scotland Awards 2001

- *"Wholesome, freshly cooked food in interesting picturesque surroundings."*
- *Home cooking.*

STOREHOUSE OF FOULIS is a historic building set in a magnificent site by the sea. The restaurant's atmosphere is light and airy, with panoramic views, where a full range of excellent value, high quality home-made meals and snacks are served. Storehouse specialises in the best of local produce. Also worth visiting – 'The Clan Munro' exhibition.

Lentil and smokey bacon soup. Storehouse fish chowder. Char-grilled fresh salmon with coriander and lime. Open sandwich with hot roast of the day. Highland cheese platter. Strawberry cheesecake. Black Isle beer loaf. Selection of home baking. Hand-made traditional tablet.

STB ★★★★ Visitor Attraction

◑ *Open all year except Christmas and New Year holidays* ♻ *Licensed* ✘ *Food available all day Lunch £ Dinner available for groups of 20–70 (advance booking) £–££* Ⓥ *Vegetarians welcome* ✵ *Children welcome* ♿ *Facilities for disabled visitors* ✂ *No smoking throughout* ▣ *Mastercard/ Eurocard, American Express, Visa, Diners Club, Switch, Delta* ⋈ *Restaurant Manager: Dinah Bolton*

*Foulis Ferry Evanton Ross & Cromarty IV16 9UX
Tel: 01349 830000 Fax: 01349 830033
E-mail: restaurant@storehouseoffoulis.co.uk
Web: www.storehouseoffoulis.co.uk
14 miles north of Inverness on the A9. On the waterfront, 1 mile north of the Cromarty Bridge, just south of Evanton. [C3]*

EYEMOUTH

Churches Hotel

- *"Excellent personal attention in calm luxurious surroundings."*
- *Modern Scottish cooking.*

CHURCHES IS A BEAUTIFUL modern hotel situated in the centre of town overlooking the working harbour. It has been renovated to the highest standard in a contemporary style making for a most memorable experience. This quality is matched by the excellent skilful cooking and use of only the best locally sourced ingredients.

Roasted summer vegetables stacked with melted goats cheese and salad leaves. Mixed seafood platter, fresh from Eyemouth fish market. Medjool dates rolled in coconut rum and demerara sugar, fresh figs, golapes and Mascarpone cheese with lime zest and juice.

STB ★★★★ Hotel

◗ *Open all year except 28 Dec to 12 Jan* 🏨 *Rooms: 6 en suite* 🛏 *DB&B £65–£80 B&B £40–£60* 💷 *Special rates available* ✗ *Food available all day £ Lunch £ Dinner £££* Ⓥ *Vegetarians welcome* ⚲ *Children welcome* ♿ *Facilities for disabled visitors* ✄ *No smoking in dining rooms or bedrooms – smoking permitted in Cocktail Bar only* 🎫 *Mastercard/Eurocard, Visa, Switch, Delta* 🔪 *Owner: Lesley Orson*

Albert Road Eyemouth Berwickshire TD14 5DB Tel: 01890 750401 Fax: 01890 750747 E-mail: lesley@churcheshotel.co.uk Web: www.churcheshotel.co.uk In town centre overlooking Eyemouth harbour. 2 miles from A1, along A1107, 8 miles from Berwick-upon-Tweed, 50 miles from south of Edinburgh. [D5]

FAIRLIE

Fins Seafood Restaurant

- *"Delicious, extremely fresh seafood cooked simply with care and imagination. I will go back!"*
- *Imaginative, modern fish cookery.*

FINS, AND FENCEBAY FISHERIES, is now quite a complex. Many make frequent pilgrimages to enjoy the deft, light cooking of Head Chef Gillian Dick – oysters, squat lobsters, bass, sole, langoustines and fresh trout. A conservatory, in which light meals are available between lunch and dinner during the summer months, has been recently added.

Seared squid with a chilli pepper marinade. Monkfish and salmon in ginger, lime, coconut and coriander. Rhubarb cheesecake with a strawberry and rhubarb compote.

◗ *Open all year except Christmas Day, Boxing Day and New Year's Day Closed Mon* 🏨 *Rooms: 2* ✗ *Lunch except Mon ££ Dinner except Mon £££* Ⓥ *Vegetarians welcome* ⚲ *Children welcome – lunch only* ♿ *Facilities for disabled visitors* ✄ *No smoking in restaurant* 🎫 *Mastercard/Eurocard, American Express, Visa, Switch, Delta* 🔪 *Owner: Jill Thain*

Fencefoot Fairlie Ayrshire KA29 OEG Tel: 01475 568989 Fax: 01475 568921 E-mail: fencebay@aol.com Web: www.fencebay.co.uk On A78, 1 mile south of Fairlie near Largs. [C6]

FALKIRK

La Bonne Auberge Brasserie

- *"Brasserie serving fresh local ingredients in relaxing surroundings."*
- *Modern Scottish with French influences.*

PART OF THE PARK LODGE Hotel, La Bonne Auberge Brasserie is a popular local restaurant serving a sound Scottish menu, with French influences, in an attractive setting. Menus incorporate items from, a more informal contemporary light meal and grill to more traditional main courses. Staff are well trained, friendly and helpful.

Grilled asparagus with Parmesan cheese and balsamic vinegar dressing. Roast breast of duck with a horseradish potato rösti on plum gravy. Port wine trifle, with wild berries and rum ice cream.

STB ★★★ Hotel

◑ *Open all year* 🏨 *Rooms: 55* 🛏 *DB&B £44–£80 B&B £34.50–£65* 🆂 *Special rates available* ✗ *Food available all day £ Lunch £ Dinner £–£££* Ⓥ *Vegetarians welcome* ⚹ *Children welcome* ♿ *Facilities for disabled visitors* 💳 *Mastercard/Eurocard, American Express, Visa, Switch, Delta* 🗡 *General Manager: Anne Bertolini*

The Park Lodge Hotel Camelon Road Falkirk FK1 5RY
Tel: 01324 628331 Fax: 01324 611593
E-mail: park@queensferry.hotels.co.uk
Web: www.theparkhotel.co.uk
Situated on Camelon Road directly opposite Dollar Park. [C5]

FALKIRK

Macdonald Inchyra Hotel

- *"Friendly, relaxed atmosphere in luxurious surroundings."*
- *Choice of bistro or fine dining.*

THERE ARE TWO RESTAURANTS at Inchyra, this modern and extended country house. The Priory Restaurant has a daily changing menu based on the availability of local produce, or visit Peligrino's Bistro for a light meal. Centrally located it is popular with locals and visitors alike.

Warm tartlet of creamed leek and Finnan haddock. Roast rib of Donald Russell beef with Yorkshire puddings and classic chasseur sauce. Chocolate and Cointreau torte served with a chantilly cream and a sauce anglaise.

STB ★★★★ Hotel

◑ *Open all year* 🏨 *Rooms: 107 en suite* 🛏 *DB&B £55–£65 B&B £40–£50 – subject to availability* ✗ *Food available all day Lunch from £ Dinner from £££* Ⓥ *Vegetarians welcome* ⚹ *Children welcome* ♿ *Facilities for disabled visitors* 🚭 *No smoking in restaurant* 💳 *Mastercard/ Eurocard, American Express, Visa, Diners Club, Switch, Solo* 🗡 *General Manager: Steven McLeod*

Grange Road Polmont Falkirk FK2 0YB
Tel: 01324 711911 Fax: 01324 716134
E-mail: info@inchyra-macdonald-hotel.co.uk
Web: www.macdonald-hotels.co.uk
From Edinburgh and the east – leave motorway at junction 5, take junction with Bo'ness sign (A905) on left. Travel ½ mile to roundabout, turn right into Wholeflats Road. After 400 yards take first right for Polmont. Hotel is 400 yards on right. [C5]

FALKLAND

Kind Kyttock's

- *"A trip to Falkland must include a visit to Kind Kyttock's."*
- *Excellent home baking.*

KIND KYTTOCK's is charming. Bert Dalrymple's (owner for over 30 years) baking is divine – he also preserves his own fruits, jams, pickles and chutneys and makes his own soups and more! Kind Kyttock's received the Tea Council's Award of Excellence 2000 and 2001. Winner of The Macallan Taste of Scotland Award 1997.

Kind Kyttock's Scotch broth served with Kind Kyttock's 'famous' home-made brown bread. Delicious salads freshly prepared with the finest ingredients. Scots pancake filled with fresh strawberries and cream.

◑ *Open all year except Christmas Eve to 5 Jan Closed Mon* ✗ *Food available all day except Mon £* Ⓥ *Vegetarians welcome* ⚹ *Children welcome* ✍ *No smoking throughout* ⊞ *Mastercard/Eurocard, American Express, Visa, Switch* Ⓜ *Owner: Bert Dalrymple*

Cross Wynd Falkland Fife KY15 7BE
Tel: 01337 857477 Fax: 01337 857379
E-mail: bert.dalrymple@virgin.net
A912 to Falkland. Centre of Falkland near the Palace, turn up at the Square into Cross Wynd. [D5]

FEARN BY TAIN

Glenmorangie House at Cadboll

- *"Very comfortable 'homely' ambience with the finest local and house garden foods and personal service."*
- *Scottish cuisine.*

GLENMORANGIE HOUSE offers the ultimate in hospitality in a beautiful part of Scotland. Professionally run by Kate Kennedy, the house offers comfort, modern amenities and warmth. Menus are presented in classical style with modern influences, using the finest of locally-sourced and home-grown produce. Wine included in price for dinner.

Mille feuille of Cadboll salmon and Moray Firth crab and lobster. Fillet of Ross-shire beef, creamy leeks and peppercorns spiced cabbage. Chocolate truffle cake with fresh strawberries and sorbet.

STB ★★★★★ Small Hotel

◑ *Open all year – exclusive use available* 🛏 *Rooms: 9 en suite* ⇔ *DB&B £110–£185 B&B £75–£145 Group rates available* ✗ *Lunch from ££ Dinner from ££££ Non residents – with prior booking* Ⓥ *Vegetarians welcome* ⚹ *Children welcome* ✍ *No smoking in dining room and bedrooms* 🐾 *Pets welcome in cottage rooms* ⊞ *Mastercard, American Express, Visa, Switch* Ⓜ *General Manager: Kate Kennedy*

Fearn by Tain Ross-shire IV20 1XP
Tel: 01862 871 671 Fax: 01862 871 625
E-mail: relax@glenmorangieplc.co.uk
Web: www.glenmorangie.com
33 miles north of Inverness on A9. Turn right at roundabout for B9175 Nigg. Drive 2 miles to left turn for Balintore and Hilton. 5 miles through village of Hilton to end of lane. [C3]

FOCHABERS

Baxters Highland Village

- *"Baxters is all things to all people. Choose from delicious juicy scallops or a takeaway sandwich."*
- *Scottish Cooking.*

BAXTER'S SELF-SERVICE Spey Restaurant is spacious and attractive and furnished with pine. It features their own products but also home baking and hot lunch dishes – pancakes are a particular speciality. Within the complex there are speciality shops which are particularly popular with visiting tourists, as well as regular food demonstrations and Baxter Product Tastings.

Rannoch smoked venison with mixed leaves and Baxter's blackcurrant vinaigrette. Grilled ribeye steaks served with mushrooms, tomato, onion rings, salad and herb butter. Strawberry cheesecake.

STB ★★★★ Visitor Attraction

❶ *Open all year except 24 25 Dec and 31 Dec to 4 Jan* ☕ *Licensed* ✗ *Food available all day £ Lunch £ Dinner – large group bookings only* ⓥ *Vegetarians welcome* ☂ *Children welcome* ♿ *Facilities for disabled* ✄ *No smoking throughout* ➥ *Guide dogs only* ⊞ *Mastercard/ Eurocard, Visa, Switch, Delta, Solo* ⓜ *General Manager: Stephen Duncan; Catering Manager: Katrina McCulloch*

Fochabers Moray IV32 7LD
Tel: 01343 820666 Fax: 01343 821790
E-mail: highland.village@baxters.co.uk
Web: www.baxters.co.uk
9 miles from Elgin on the A96 between Inverness and Aberdeen. [D3]

FORRES

Brodie Castle, The National Trust for Scotland

- *"Enjoy home baking – aristocratic style in the home of Brodie of Brodie."*
- *Snacks and home bakes.*

GOOD HOME-MADE soups, rolls and home bakes are the order of the day in Brodie Castle. Enjoy the antique china and paintings which adorn the walls of the Castle tea room. Staff are friendly and helpful.

Curried parsnip soup served with crusty roll. Freshly baked baguette topped with local cheese, bacon and tomato with seasonal leaves. Home-made carrot cake.

STB ★★★ Castle
Green Tourism One Leaf Bronze Award

❶ *Open daily 1 Apr to 30 Sep and weekends only in Oct* ⓢⓟ *Special rates available* ⓤⓛ *Unlicensed* ✗ *Food available during Castle's opening hours £ Lunch £* ⓥ *Vegetarians welcome* ☂ *Children welcome* ♿ *Facilities for disabled* ✄ *No smoking throughout* ⊞ *No credit cards* ⓜ *Catering Manager: Wendy Guild*

Brodie Forres Moray IV36 2TE
Tel: 01309 641371 Fax: 01309 641600
Web: www.nts.org.uk
On A96 between Forres and Nairn. 3 miles west of Forres. [D3]

FORRES

Knockomie Hotel

- *"A comfortable, friendly hotel offering good food and hospitality."*
- *The best of Scottish cooking with French influences.*

KNOCKOMIE HOTEL offers first-rate accommodation and dining. Part of the landscaped gardens are used to supply herbs and salad; vegetables are grown locally. On the daily changing table d'hôte menu, food is local and fresh. The Bistro is more casual than the traditional dining room. The wine list is of especial interest.

Smoked breast of Barbary duck on a bed of baked rhubarb. Roast scallops with lemon and garlic potatoes and braised fennel. Crème brûlée flavoured with saffron, accompanied with honeyed pear.

STB ★★★★ Hotel
Green Tourism Two Leaf Silver Award

◐ *Open all year except Christmas Day*
🏠 *Rooms: 15 en suite* 🛏 *B&B double/twin £122–£160 single £92 per night* 💷 *Special rates available* ✗ *Lunch £ Dinner 5 course menu £££*
Ⓥ *Vegetarians welcome* ✶ *Children welcome*
♿ *Facilities for disabled* ✗ *No smoking in dining room* 💳 *Mastercard/Eurocard, American Express, Visa, Diners Club, Switch, Delta, JCB*
👤 *Resident Director: Gavin Ellis*

Grantown Road Forres Moray IV36 2SG
Tel: 01309 673146 Fax: 01309 673290
E-mail: stay@knockomie.co.uk
Web: www.knockomie.co.uk
1 mile south of Forres on A940. 26 miles east of Inverness. [D3]

FORRES

Ramnee Hotel

- *"A busy traditional hotel, warm and friendly, with good food and lively atmosphere."*
- *Fresh local produce well-presented in modern style.*

THE RAMNEE HOTEL is a lively and bustling town hotel set in two acres of beautiful gardens. Hamblins Dining Room is more formal and food is tempered accordingly. The accompanying wine list is extensive and well-chosen. Lighter more informal meals are available in the very popular 'Tipplings' cocktail lounge. Staff are friendly and helpful.

Smoked chicken and fresh pear presented in crisp filo pastry with a mild chilli dressing. Roast loin of red deer encased in fine Moray ham with a thyme and prune mousseline. Forest fruit and apple crumble served with a cardamom anglaise.

STB ★★★★ Hotel

◐ *Open all year except Christmas Day and 1 to 3 Jan* 🏠 *Rooms: 20 en suite* 🛏 *DB&B £55–£87.50 B&B £32.50–£65* 💷 *Special rates available* ✗ *Lunch £ Dinner ££–£££*
Ⓥ *Vegetarians welcome* ✶ *Children welcome*
✗ *No smoking in restaurant* 💳 *Mastercard/ Eurocard, American Express, Visa, Diners Club, Switch, Delta* 👤 *Director: Garry W Dinnes*

Victoria Road Forres Moray IV36 3BN
Tel: 01309 672410 Fax: 01309 673392
E-mail: ramneehotel@btconnect.com
A96 Inverness-Aberdeen, off bypass at roundabout at eastern side of Forres – 500 yards on right. [D3]

FORT WILLIAM

An Crann B&B and Restaurant

- *"Great home cooking and Highland hospitality at its best."*
- *Imaginative Scottish cooking.*

A CLEVERLY CONVERTED barn, An Crann offers an ever-changing choice of delicious home-made food using local produce. The renovated rooms are very well-appointed and breakfast is one of the best in the Highlands. Stunning views of Ben Nevis and excellent value for money, especially 'early bird' menu (5–6.30 pm).

Salad of hot smoked flaky salmon served on seasonal leaves with a lime and coriander dressing. Pan-fried venison steak with a rowan jelly and blackberry wine jus. Honey, lemon and ginger cheesecake with fruit coulis, fresh fruit and cream. Home-made chocolate truffles.

STB ★★★ Bed & Breakfast

◗ *Open Mar to Oct Restaurant closed Sun* ⌂ *Rooms: 3 en suite* ⊨ *DB&B £25–£40 B&B £18–£20* ✗ *Dinner except Sun ££ early bird except Sun £* Ⓥ *Vegetarians welcome* ✶ *Children welcome* ♿ *Facilities for disabled visitors* ✖ *No smoking throughout* ▣ *Mastercard/Eurocard, Visa, Switch, Solo* ◪ *Proprietor: Sine M Ross*

Seangan Bridge Banavie Fort William PH33 7PB Tel: 01397 773114 E-mail: seangan-chalets@fortwilliam59.freeserve.co.uk A82, 2 miles north of Fort William at traffic lights turn left on to A830 Mallaig road, 1 mile turn right onto B8004 (Gairlochy) Seangan Croft 2 miles after Moorings Hotel. [B4]

FORT WILLIAM

Crannog Seafood Restaurant

- *"Watch the fishing boats, listen to the seagulls and enjoy perfectly cooked Scottish seafood."*
- *Fresh seafood, cooked simply.*

T HERE IS ALWAYS vegetarian, meat and game options but the focus at Crannog is very much on seafood – they have their own smokehouse. Chef Gary Dobbie has a fresh and innovative style that enhances and defines the delicate seafood flavours. A relaxing restaurant with breathtaking views and delightful staff.

Smoked mussels and surf clams presented with lime mayonnaise. Baked Mallaig cod topped with crushed pink peppercorn set on wild rice. Heather cream cheesecake scented with whisky and honey.

◗ *Open all year except Christmas and New Year* ✗ *Lunch £ Dinner ££* Ⓥ *Vegetarians welcome* ✶ *Children welcome* ♿ *Facilities for disabled* ✖ *Smoking area in restaurant* ▣ *Mastercard/Eurocard, Visa, Switch, Solo* ◪ *Managing Director: Finlay Finlayson*

Town Pier Fort William PH33 7PT Tel: 01397 705589 Fax: 01397 705026 E-mail: chef@westhighlandseafood.com Web: www.crannog.net Fort William town pier – off A82 Fort William town centre bypass. [B4]

FORT WILLIAM

The Moorings Hotel

- *"A warm Highland welcome and commitment to fresh local produce."*
- *Bold and imaginative Scottish cooking.*

THE MOORINGS is a coaching inn situated alongside the famous Caledonian Canal, overlooking majestic Ben Nevis. It offers comfortable surrounds and good, hearty food, served by exceptionally warm and friendly staff. Here you can enjoy the best from the Highland larder – fine game and meats, quality vegetables and delicious seafood.

Cured wild salmon gravadlax served with a vanilla butter sauce. Pan-fried saddle of venison served with a celeriac, sweet potato galette and port truffle jus. Caramel parfait with glazed bananas and fruit coulis.

STB ★★★★ Hotel

◗ Open all year 🏠 Rooms: 28 en suite 🛏 DB&B £62–£76 B&B £36–£53 🆂 Special rates available ✗ Food available all day ££ Lunch ££ Dinner £££ Ⓥ Vegetarians welcome ✴ Children welcome ♿ Facilities for disabled ✄ No smoking in dining room 🐕Dogs welcome except in dining areas 🔚 Mastercard/Eurocard, American Express, Visa, Diners Club, Switch, Delta, JCB

*Banavie Fort William PH33 7LY
Tel: 01397 772797 Fax: 01397 772441
E-mail:
reservations@moorings-fortwilliam.co.uk
Web: www.moorings-fortwilliam.co.uk
On the outskirts of Fort William. From Fort William, take A830 Mallaig road for approx 1 mile. Cross the Caledonian Canal and take first right into the village of Banavie. [B4]*

FORT WILLIAM

No 4 Cameron Square

- *"Their delicious home-made chips and ice creams should be one of Fort William's tourist attractions!"*
- *Homely lunches and elegant dinners.*

A COSY DINING ROOM and adjacent bright conservatory ensures a delightful meal experience any time of the year. Accent is on 'home-made' with the majority of ingredients sourced locally. On a sunny day guests can dine 'al fresco' in the attractive 'secret' garden. Coffee and cake is served between lunch and evening service.

Steamed West Coast mussels with garlic and thyme butter. Roast breast of duck with caramelised shallots on a crispy potato galette. Brandied walnut and sultana flan with Tia Maria ice cream.

◗ Open all year except Sun during winter ✗ Food available all day ££ Lunch £ Dinner ££ Ⓥ Vegetarians welcome ✴ Children welcome ♿ Facilities for disabled ✄ No smoking dining area 🔚 Mastercard/Eurocard, American Express, Visa, Diners Club, Switch, Delta 👤 Managing Director: Stewart Leitch

*Cameron Square Fort William Inverness-shire PH33 6AJ
Tel: 01397 704222 Fax: 01397 704448
Web: www.no4-fortwilliam.co.uk
Centrally located in Fort William, Cameron Square is just off the pedestrianised High Street. 'No 4' is next to the Tourist Information Office. [B4]*

GAIRLOCH

Creag Mor Hotel

- *"A little haven of tranquility."*
- *Modern Scottish cooking.*

RAY AND BARBARA Leaver-Hill preside professionally over this attractive hotel with its relaxed atmosphere. The elegant Panorama restaurant offers carefully crafted food by candlelight. Chef Derek MacKenzie's cooking is skilfully executed using the best of available locally sourced produce. A very special place.

Haggis filled filo thistles in cream and malt whisky. Fillet of Aberdeen Angus with salmon mousse set in a pool of lobster bisque. Profiteroles with Drambuie cream and strawberries.

STB ★★★ Hotel

◗ *Open all year* ⊞ *Rooms: 17 en suite* ⇔ *B&B from £30–£55* ⊕ *Special rates available* ✗ *Lunch £ Dinner £££* ✦ *Children welcome* ✍ *No smoking in restaurant* ✦ *Dogs welcome* ⊞ *Mastercard/Eurocard, American Express, Visa, Switch, Delta* ⋈ *Proprietors: Ray & Barbara Leaver-Hill*

Charleston Gairloch Wester Ross IV21 2AW
Tel: 01445 712068 Freephone 0800 5425368
Fax: 01445 712044
E-mail: relax@creagmorhotel.com
Web: www.creagmorhotel.com
Situated in Charleston, ½ mile south of Gairloch. First turning on right when entering Charleston on A832 from Inverness. [B3]

GAIRLOCH

Myrtle Bank Hotel

- *"Watch the local fishing fleet return at sunset whilst enjoying the delightful seafood."*
- *Traditional Scottish cooking.*

MYRTLE BANK is a welcoming and popular hotel with both locals and visitors to the area. Local produce and home-made cooking are the basis of the menu which is balanced and well-priced. Guests have the choice between bar and dining room eating. Local seafood is one of the hotel's specialities.

Warm salad of Lochewe scallops with a saffron cream resting on mixed salad leaves. Medallions of West Coast venison with caramelised shallots and roasted garlic with a red wine jus. Raspberry crème brûlée.

STB ★★★ Small Hotel

◗ *Open all year except New Year's Day* ⊞ *Rooms: 12 en suite* ⇔ *DB&B £56–£62 B&B £36–£44 Special rates available* ✗ *Lunch from £ Dinner from £* ⓥ *Vegetarians welcome* ✦ *Children welcome* ♿ *Facilities for disabled visitors* ✍ *No smoking in dining room* ⊞ *Mastercard, American Express, Visa, Switch* ⋈ *Proprietors: Iain & Dorothy MacLean*

Low Road Gairloch Wester Ross IV21 2BS
Tel: 01445 712004 Fax: 01445 712214
E-mail: myrtlebank@email.msn.com
Web: www.hotelgairloch.com
Close to the centre of Gairloch, just off B2081. [B3]

GLASGOW

Artà

- *"Very stylish, modern bar and restaurant with Spanish influence in the heart of the Merchant City."*
- *Innovative, modern Scottish/Spanish dishes a feature.*

ARTÀ WAS ORIGINALLY the old cheese market and was bought as a shell and converted into this stunning modern venue. There are several choices for the customer here – from a selection of bars to a Tapas Mediterranean restaurant all of which offer a unique and very high quality experience in spectacular surroundings. Booking essential.

Goats cheese and roast garlic salad. Whole grilled sea bass with olive oil and lemon. Sweet pancakes with vanilla ice cream.

◗ *Open all year except Christmas Day, Boxing Day and New Year's Day Closed Mon Tue and open from 5pm Wed to Sun* ✘ *Dinner ££* Ⓥ *Vegetarians welcome* 🆎 *Mastercard/ Eurocard, American Express, Visa, Switch* 🅺 *General Manager: Diane Graham; Head Chef: Michael Smith*

The Old Cheesemarket 13-19 Walls Street Merchant City Glasgow G1 1PA Tel: 0141 552 2101 Fax: 0141 572 0432 E-mail: info@arta.co.uk Web: www.arta.co.uk Artà is on the corner of Walls Street and Bell Street in the cheese market. Walls Street is parallel to High Street to the West and Albion Street to the east, in Glasgow's Merchant City. [C6]

GLASGOW

Babbity Bowster

- *"A taste of the real Glasgow, where fresh Scottish produce and friendly faces create the atmosphere."*
- *Scottish cooking.*

BABBITY BOWSTER is known as one of the 'in places' in Glasgow's city centre. The hotel today has a lively bar on the ground floor, with garden outside; the Schottische Restaurant for more formal dining. Quality food, drink and intellectual conversation is the key to the success of this place, together with Fraser Laurie's personal supervision.

Scottish oysters poached with fish stock and vermouth and topped with breadcrumbs. Fillet of beef on a croûton with a rich port and foie gras sauce. Black and white chocolate terrine with more than a hint of Glayva.

◗ *Open all year except Christmas Day and New Year's Day Note: Restaurant closed Sun evening/Sat lunch* 🏨 *Rooms: 7 en suite* 🛏 *DB&B £60–£85 B&B £50–£70* ✘ *Food available all day £ Lunch £ Dinner ££–£££* Ⓥ *Vegetarians welcome* ✶ *Children welcome* 🆎 *Mastercard/Eurocard, American Express, Visa* 🅺 *Owner: Fraser Laurie*

16-18 Blackfriars Street Glasgow G1 1PE Tel: 0141 552 5055 Fax: 0141 552 7774 E-mail: babbitybowster@gofornet.co.uk In the heart of Glasgow's Merchant City – at the East End of city centre. [C6]

GLASGOW

Bouzy Rouge

- *"An enduring and highly original restaurant idea that continues to offer great modern Scottish food."*
- *Best contemporary Scottish cuisine.*

THE MENU at Bouzy Rouge complements the unique designer (specially made) furniture. It offers many options for both special occasions and day-to-day business and whilst using the best Scottish produce introduces international dishes and themes. There is a very pleasant atmosphere from confident, well-trained staff. Also look out for the speciality nights.

Trio of Scottish puddings, buttered shallots and Orkney cheese sabayon. Perthshire pheasant, apricot and pistachio stuffing, forrester jus. Banana crème brûlée, burnt cream.

◑ *Open all year except New Year's Day* ✘ *Food available all day Lunch £–££ Dinner £–££* Ⓥ *Vegetarians welcome* ⚹ *Children welcome* ♿ *Facilities for non-wheelchair visitors only* 💳 *Mastercard/Eurocard, American Express, Visa, Diners Club, Switch, Delta, Solo, Electron* 🗮 *Proprietors: Alan & Audrey Brown; Managers: Annette & Ewan*

111 West Regent Street Glasgow G2 2RU Tel: 0141 221 8804 Fax: 0141 221 6941 E-mail: reservations@bouzy-rouge.com Web: www.bouzy-rouge.com City centre location on corner of West Regent and Wellington Street. Approach via M8 from Charing Cross and follow one-way system from Sauchiehall Street. [C6]

GLASGOW

The Buttery

- *"A quite outstanding restaurant where the very highest culinary standards are sought and consistently maintained."*
- *Gourmet, Scottish, contemporary.*

THE BUTTERY dates back to 1869 when it was Scotland's first premier restaurant. Stained glass doors lead to the Victorian wood-panelled dining room. Service is impressive. Under chef Ian Mackie, Scottish dishes are exquisitely presented with unusual combinations and lots of interesting textures and flavours. The luncheon menu is excellent value.

Open ravioli of flaked salmon and seared langoustine with sweet vermouth and cream. Sliced roulade of pork fillet stuffed with herb and spinach parfait, haggis timbale, grape chutney, and brandy and green peppercorns. 'The Buttery Grand Dessert' – every dessert on offer miniaturised.

◑ *Open all year except Christmas Day and New Year's Day Closed Sun* ✘ *Lunch except Sun Sat ££ Dinner except Sun £££* Ⓥ *Vegetarians welcome* ⚹ *Smoking of pipes and cigars is preferred in the bar* 💳 *Visa, Diners Club, Switch, Delta*

652 Argyle Street Glasgow G3 8UF Tel: 0141 221 8188 Fax: 0141 204 4639 Argyle Street, just below M8 overpass – Westside. Take Elderslie Street, turn left at mini-roundabout at southern end of street. Restaurant at bottom of street on left. [C6]

GLASGOW

Carlton George Hotel, Windows Restaurant

- *"A peaceful haven in the city centre with rooftop views from Windows Restaurant."*
- *Modern Scottish.*

ONE OF GLASGOW'S newest hotels, the Carlton George combines the art of high quality service and technology to meet today's discerning customers' needs. Windows Restaurant offers a particularly unique experience with views of the city which are matched by a very high standard of cooking and innovative menus.

Seared West Coast scallops, cauliflower purée and basil oil. Char-grilled fillet of Scotch beef set on parsnip rösti, chanterelle mushrooms and red wine essence. Fresh baked lemon tart, fresh raspberries and lime.

STB ★★★★ Hotel

☾ *Open all year except Christmas Day*
🏨 *Rooms: 64 en suite* 🛏 *DB&B £74.50–£85 B&B £49.50–£60* 💷 *Special rates available* ✗ *Food available all day ££ Lunch ££ Dinner £££* Ⓥ *Vegetarians welcome* ⚲ *Children welcome* ♿ *Facilities for disabled visitors* 🐕 *Dogs welcome* 💳 *Mastercard/Eurocard, American Express, Visa, Diners Club, Switch* 🔪 *Restaurant Manager: Brendan Pautz; Chef: Kevin Breslin*

44 West George Street Glasgow G2 1DH
Tel: 0141 354 5070 Fax: 0141 353 6263
E-mail: gmgeorge@carltonhotels.co.uk
Web: www.carltonhotels.co.uk
Follow West George Street towards George Square, 1 block before George Square on left, after Buchanan Street. [C6]

GLASGOW

City Merchant Restaurant

- *"Using the finest Scottish ingredients, Chef Joe Anderson produces one of Glasgow's best meal experiences."*
- *Traditional and contemporary Scottish cooking.*

A WARM AND WELCOMING haven in Scotland's largest city. From Loch Etive mussels to the occasional moonfish caught off Shetland there is a focus on fish and seafood. Meat eaters and vegetarians are also well-catered for with daily changing specials and a seasonally changing à la carte. An inspiring range of wine and whiskies.

Mild sweet pickled West Coast seafood with a Parmesan and herb salad. Saddle of rabbit, crispy Ayrshire bacon, roast shallots, rowanberry glaze, buttered Savoy cabbage and chive creamed potatoes. Home-made clootie dumpling with light Glayva custard.

☾ *Open all year except Christmas Day, Boxing Day, and 1, 2 Jan* ✗ *Food available all day £–££ Lunch £–££ Dinner ££–£££* Ⓥ *Vegetarians welcome* ⚲ *Children over 6 years welcome* ♿ *Facilities for disabled visitors* ✀ *No smoking area in restaurant* 💳 *Mastercard/Eurocard, American Express, Visa, Diners Club, Switch* 🔪 *Head Chef: Joe Anderson; Proprietors: Tony & Linda Matteo*

97 Candleriggs Glasgow G1 1NP
Tel: 0141 553 1577 Fax: 0141 553 1588
E-mail: citymerchant@btinternet.com
Web: www.citymerchant.co.uk
Facing City Halls in Candleriggs, in Glasgow's Merchant City. Candleriggs on right going east along Ingram Street. [C6]

GLASGOW

Corinthian

- *"Splendid opulent bar and restaurant in one of Glasgow's finest historic buildings."*
- *Innovative Scottish with French influences.*

CORINTHIAN is certainly one of Glasgow's most stunning buildings located in the beautiful Merchant City. It hosts a number of different venues all of which have their own particular charm – from the Piano Bar to the Restaurant and even a Private Dining Room. The cooking here is highly innovative and skilled.

Timbale of Scottish crab with plum tomato and shellfish gazpacho dressing. Fillet of beef wrapped in Parma ham with confit potato and red wine shallots. Baked custard and poached peach tart with nutmeg ice cream.

◗ *Open all year* ✖ *Food available all day ££ Lunch ££ Dinner £££* Ⓥ *Vegetarians welcome* ✱ *Children welcome* ♿ *Facilities for disabled visitors* 🔲 *Mastercard/Eurocard, American Express, Visa, Switch, Delta* ▧ *Deputy Manager: Kirsteen Meldrum*

191 Ingram Street Glasgow G1 1DA
Tel: 0141 552 1101 Fax: 0141 559 6826
E-mail: info@corinthian.uk.com
Web: www.corinthian.uk.com
Corinthian is situated on Ingram Street on the edge of Glasgow's city centre and Merchant City. From George Square take South Frederick Street and Corinthian faces you at the end of street. [C6]

GLASGOW

Hilton Glasgow (Camerons Restaurant)

- *"Truly memorable evening in luxurious surroundings."*
- *Exquisite international cuisine.*

CAMERONS RESTAURANT has been refurbished and offers a stylish and soothing ambience. The service is in a class of its own and with Executive Chef James Murphy at the helm a true culinary experience is on offer here. You may also dine informally in Minsky's Restaurant.

Marinated artichoke, mushroom and Roquefort salad. Lamb and lentil broth scented with mint, samosa and floppy cream. Herbed fillet of pork, parsnips, confit shallots, creamy roast potatoes, oatmeal jus. Individual crème brûlée flavoured with Drambuie, fresh raspberries, crisp tuiles.

STB ★★★★★ Hotel

◗ *Open all year* 🏨 *Rooms: 319 en suite* 🛏 *B&B from £125* ✖ *Lunch (Camerons) ££–£££: (Minsky's) from £ Dinner (Camerons) except Sun ££–£££: (Minsky's) from £* Ⓥ *Vegetarians welcome* ✱ *Children welcome* ♿ *Facilities for disabled visitors* 🔲 *Mastercard/ Eurocard, American Express, Visa, Switch*

1 William Street Glasgow G3 8HT
Tel: 0141 204 5555 Fax: 0141 204 5004
Web: www.hilton.com
Access from M8 junction 18, or via Waterloo Street from city centre. [C6]

GLASGOW

The Inn On The Green

- *"Good food in a relaxed friendly atmosphere."*
- *Fine Scottish cuisine.*

A BEAUTIFUL TOWNHOUSE hotel with individually styled designer bedrooms with an independently renowned restaurant in a unique art gallery setting. The menus are extensive, with daily specials making best use of local sourced quality produce, with a Scottish slant. In the evenings enjoy good food accompanied by light jazz piano/vocals.

Sliced breast of warm duck on a cucumber and sesame seed salsa with plum and ginger sauce. Char-grilled breast of spring chicken on salad and new potatoes, tarragon and sun-dried tomato dressing. Orange and Sambucca crème brûlée.

STB ★★★ Small Hotel

◗ *Open all year N.B. Please telephone to ensure restaurant is open during Festive Season* ⚑ *Rooms: 18 en suite* ⛱ *Room Rate £75–£90* ⓢⓟ *Special rates available* ✗ *Lunch – please telephone ahead £ Dinner £££* ⓥ *Vegetarians welcome* ⚡ *Children welcome* ♿ *Facilities for disabled visitors* ⚞ *Smoking discouraged in dining areas* ⊞ *Mastercard/Eurocard, American Express, Visa, Switch, Delta* ⓝ *General Manager: Philip Raskin*

25 Greenhead Street Glasgow G40 1ES
Tel: 0141 554 0165 Fax: 0141 556 4678
E-mail: sales@theinnonthegreen.co.uk
Web: www.theinnonthegreen.co.uk
Located on the edge of Glasgow Green, close to the Peoples' Palace and just off the main London Road arterial route from M74 to city centre. [C6]

GLASGOW

La Bonne Auberge (Holiday Inn Hotel)

- *"City centre French-style brasserie offering skilfully cooked Scottish fare."*
- *Modern Scottish.*

L A BONNE AUBERGE is privately franchised within the city centre Holiday Inn, offering French flair in Parisian style and comfortable surroundings. Guests can relax in L'Orangerie Conservatory. Master Chef David Friel demonstrates great skill in his hand-crafted dishes, using Scottish produce.

Smoked Marbury trout with avocado and apple compote, dill cream. Suprême of Gressingham duck with fondant potato, butternut squash, green beans and plum gravy. Passion fruit tart with local raspberry and yoghurt ice cream.

STB ★★★★ Hotel

◗ *Open all year except Christmas Day and New Year's Day* ⚑ *Rooms: 113 en suite* ⛱ *Room only £120–£170* ⓢⓟ *Special rates available* ✗ *Food available all day Lunch £–££ Dinner from £–££* ⓥ *Vegetarians welcome* ⚡ *Children welcome* ♿ *Facilities for disabled visitors* ⊞ *Mastercard/ Eurocard, American Express, Visa, Diners Club, Switch, Delta* ⓝ *General Manager: Tricia Fitzsimmons*

161 West Nile Street Glasgow G1 2RL
Tel: 0141 352 8310 Fax: 0141 332 7447
E-mail: info@higlasgow.com
Web: www.higlasgow.com
Diagonally opposite Glasgow Royal Concert Hall. [C6]

GLASGOW

Lux

- *"A gastronomic experience achieving consistently high levels of excellence in food and service."*
- *Innovative modern Scottish.*

LUX REFLECTS THE SIMPLICITY of modern establishments but retains the atmosphere of J J Burnet's 19th century architecture. Menus are carefully composed by Chef/Proprietor Stephen Johnson who adds his own special touches, and are enhanced by a well-balanced and informative wine list. Facilities are available for weddings and functions.

Warm baby black pudding with an apple and thyme mash on a strawberry dressing. Orkney salmon on Parmesan mash with baby capers and sun-dried tomato olive oil. Lux crème brûlée with home-made shortbread.

◗ *Open all year except 25, 26 Dec Closed Sun Mon* ✕ *Lunch by arrangement only Dinner except Sun Mon £££* Ⓥ *Vegetarians welcome* ⚹ *Children over 12 years welcome* ▦ *Mastercard/Eurocard, American Express, Visa, Switch, Delta* Ⓝ *Chef/Proprietor: Stephen Johnson; General Manager: Julia Hutton*

1051 Great Western Road Glasgow G12 0XP Tel: 0141 576 7576 Fax: 0141 576 0162 Web: www.lux.5pm.co.uk c2 miles from city centre at entrance to Gartnavel Hospital. Lux is on the first floor above Bar Stazione. [C6]

GLASGOW

Nairns

- *"Fresh Scottish cooking at its best."*
- *Contemporary fusion cuisine.*

THIS IS NICK NAIRN'S flagship. Now on one floor, entered downstairs through garden. Menus are carefully inspired and changed daily. All dishes are cooked to order and created by Head Chef Derek Blair. A testament to his energy and dedication.

Terrine of chicken livers, potato and Parma ham with mustard beignet. Scallops, Skirlie potato, spinach and parsley sauce. Roast pear with honeycomb ice cream and chocolate syrup.

◗ *Open all year except 25, 26 Dec and 1, 2 Jan* ✕ *Lunch except Sun Mon ££ Dinner except Sun Mon £££* Ⓥ *Vegetarians welcome* ⚹ *Children welcome (if they can eat from menu)* ✂ *Diners requested to refrain from smoking until coffee. Cigar and pipe smoking are not permitted* ▦ *Mastercard/Eurocard, American Express, Visa, Diners Club, Switch, Delta* Ⓝ *General Manager: Jim Kerr*

13 Woodside Crescent Glasgow G3 7UL Tel: 0141 353 0707 Fax: 0141 331 1684 E-mail: info@nairns.co.uk Web: www.nairns.co.uk At Charing Cross. Woodside Crescent is off Sauchiehall Street. [C6]

GLASGOW

Pollok House, The National Trust for Scotland: Finalist The Macallan Taste of Scotland Awards 2001

- *"A really charming experience in the centre of Glasgow – a truly lovely spot."*
- *Good quality Scottish cuisine.*

POLLOK HOUSE is a very fine example of the quality visitor experience available at The National Trust for Scotland properties. It is a most beautiful house set amidst spectacular gardens in Pollok Park. The Edwardian Kitchen Restaurant offers good home baking, light refreshments and delightful traditional Scottish dishes – all created fresh on the premises.

Parsnip, fresh ginger and orange soup. Smoked salmon and red onion tart. Warm cinnamon apple cake with raspberry cream.

◗ *Open all year except Christmas Day, Boxing Day, 1 and 2 Jan* ♟ *Licensed* ✖ *Food available all day £ Lunch £ Pre-arranged functions ££* Ⓥ *Vegetarians welcome* ✿ *Children welcome* ♿ *Facilities for disabled visitors* ✖ *No smoking throughout* ▩ *Mastercard, Visa, Switch, Delta* ▨ *Catering Manager: Fiona McLean*

Pollok Country Park 2060 Pollokshaws Road Glasgow G43 1AT
Tel: 0141 616 6410
E-mail: fmclean@nts.org.uk
Web: www.nts.org.uk
Off M77, junction 1 or 2, follow signs for Burrell Collection. 3 miles south of Glasgow city centre. Frequent bus and rail (Pollokshaws West station) from city centre. [C6]

GLASGOW

The Puppet Theatre

- *"Good food in the heart of the West End."*
- *Modern Scottish cooking.*

SITUATED IN THE HEART of Glasgow's West End in a converted mews house providing a varied experience. From cosy to intimate private rooms, to a unique picturesque conservatory boasting an individuality of its own. The menu however varied relies purely on the best Scottish produce, presented creatively to ensure the unique experience throughout the restaurant.

Pan-fried scallops, papaya salad and sweet chilli sauce. Roast fillet of lamb, flageolet bean purée, minted potatoes, rosemary sauce. Iced raspberry soufflé, fruit compote, hot chocolate sauce.

◗ *Open all year except Boxing Day, New Year's Day and 2 Jan Closed Mon* ✖ *Lunch except Mon Sat £–££ Dinner except Mon £££* Ⓥ *Vegetarians welcome* ✿ *Children 12 years and over welcome* ♿ *Facilities for disabled visitors* ✖ *Smoking area, if requested* ▩ *Mastercard/Eurocard, American Express, Visa, Switch, Delta* ▨ *General Manager: Paul Donaldson; Head Chef: Steven Nye*

11 Ruthven Lane Glasgow Hillhead G12 9BG
Tel: 0141 339 8444 Fax: 0141 339 7666
E-mail: puppet@bigbeat.co.uk
Web: www.bigbeat.co.uk
Off Byres Road, opposite Hillhead Underground. [C6]

GLASGOW

Restaurant Rococo

- *"Style and sophistication. A true dining experience."*
- *World-class modern cuisine.*

ONE OF GLASGOW'S newer venues for outstanding cuisine and service, Rococo is set in sumptuous surroundings. No expense has been spared in blending the atmosphere and style into one of Glasgow's top restaurants where you can enjoy a superb wine list of over 300 bins, impeccable service and really skilled cooking.

Parfait of foie gras, toasted brioche. Pan-fried scallops, tamarind, lime and ginger sauce, vegetable noodles. Trio of mini desserts: passion fruit cheesecake, Amaretto Panacotta and mini chocolate mousse.

◗ *Open all year except New Year's Day* ✖ *Lunch ££ Dinner £££* Ⓥ *Vegetarians welcome* ▣ *Mastercard/Eurocard, American Express, Visa, Diners Club, Switch, Delta* ▨ *Proprietors: Alan & Audrey Brown*

West George Street Glasgow G2 2NR
Tel: 0141 221 5004 Fax: 0141 221 5006
E-mail: res@rococoglasgow.com
Web: www.rococoglasgow.com
City centre location on corner of West George and Wellington Street. Approach via M8 from Charing Cross and follow one-way system from Sauchiehall Street. [C6]

GLASGOW

Stravaigin

- *"The café bar is a relaxed and cosmopolitan place to eat and drink all day. Each mouthful promises to be a taste explosion!"*
- *Inspired Scottish eclectic menus.*

COLIN CLYDESDALE is an innovative chef – collecting new ideas and ingredients and adding them to naturally produced local ones. The menus are eclectic and offer excellent value for money, cooking is highly-skilled and dishes are presented with flair. Winner of the Macallan Taste of Scotland Award 1999.

Thai-marinated Ayrshire quail on sesame, ginger, lime dressed glass noodles, with coriander relish. Slow braised Dumfriesshire lamb shank with roast shallot stovies, wild thyme, gravy and mint pea purée. Braw spiced ginger bread with apple, pear compote and Drambuie vanilla custard.

◗ *Open all year except Christmas Day, Boxing Day, 31 Dec and 1 Jan Closed Mon* ✖ *Food available all day, 7 days (Cafe bar) ££ Lunch (restaurant) Fri and Sat only £ Dinner (restaurant) except Mon ££* Ⓥ *Vegetarians welcome* ✶ *Children welcome* ▣ *Mastercard/ Eurocard, American Express, Visa, Diners Club, Switch, Delta* ▨ *General Manager: Carol S Wright*

28 Gibson Street Hillhead Glasgow G12 8NX
Tel: 0141 334 2665 Fax: 0141 334 4099
E-mail: bookings@stravaigin.com
Web: www.stravaigin.com
From M8 junction 17. From city centre take A82, Great Western Road. Turn left down Otago Street. Left onto Gibson Street. 100 yards on left-hand side. [C6]

GLASGOW

Stravaigin 2

- *"Stravaigin 2 offers mouth-watering, truly exciting dishes created using the best of Scotland's larder."*
- *Inspired Scottish with a global twist.*

AS YOU MAY EXPECT from the sister restaurant of The Macallan Taste of Scotland Award winner Stravaigin, this new restaurant is run to the highest of standards set by Colin Clydesdale. Menus are excellent and original, resulting in new and exciting combinations which are cooked and presented with care and skill. Private dining available for groups.

Soft poached Smeeton's free-range duck egg on chapati disk topped with Saag Dahl and a drizzle of Punjabi oil. Seared fillet of organic lamb on Oxacaca white bean and chorizo stew. Deep-fried jeelie piece with Stravaigin 2's own carnation milk ice cream.

◗ *Open all year except Christmas day and New Year's Day* ✕ *Food available all day* ££ *Lunch £–££ Dinner* ££ Ⓥ *Vegetarians welcome* ✻ *Children welcome* ♿ *Facilities for disabled visitors* ✍ *Diners requested to refrain from smoking between 12-2pm and 5-10pm* 💳 *Mastercard/Eurocard, American Express, Visa, Diners Club, Switch, Delta* ⚄ *Managers: Frances Kirk & Ciaran Gourley*

8 Ruthven Lane Glasgow G12 9BG
Tel: 0141 334 7165 Fax: 0141 357 4785
E-mail: booking@stravaigin2.com
Web: www.stravaigin.com
From M8 Junction 17 from city centre, take A82 Dumbarton. Head along Great Western Road 2 miles to Byres Road. Turn Left. Ruthven lane opposite Hillhead Underground. [C6]

GLASGOW

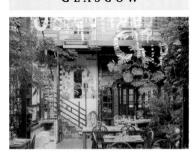

Ubiquitous Chip

- *"Celebrating over 30 years of consistent quality Scottish produce cooked with imagination and style."*
- *Modern Scottish cooking.*

THE 'CHIP' has a spectacular courtyard area, trickling pool, and more traditional dining room. The cuisine marries the traditional and original in innovative recipes, and this variety is complemented by a wine list rated among the top ten in Britain for quality and value. Winner of The Macallan Taste of Scotland Award 2000.

Shellfish custard studded with scallop and langoustine, watercress sauce and pan-fried queenies. Shin of Scotch beef, crushed roast garlic potatoes and lemon vermouth carrots. Banana, rum and butterscotch parfait with chocolate shard.

◗ *Open all year except Christmas Day and 1 Jan* ✕ *Food available all day* Lunch ££ *Dinner £££* Ⓥ *Vegetarians welcome* ✻ *Children welcome* ♿ *Facilities for disabled visitors* 💳 *Mastercard/Eurocard, American Express, Visa, Diners Club, Delta* ⚄ *Proprietor: Ronnie Clydesdale*

12 Ashton Lane Glasgow G12 8SJ
Tel: 0141 334 5007 Fax: 0141 337 1302
E-mail: mail@ubiquitouschip.co.uk
Web: www.ubiquitouschip.co.uk
Behind Hillhead underground station, in a secluded lane off Byres Road in the heart of Glasgow's West End. [C6]

GLASGOW

YES Restaurant, Bar & Café

- *"An exciting city restaurant offering the best modern Scottish food."*
- *Best modern Scottish.*

YES HAS BOTH a very stylish informal brasserie at ground level with a bustling atmosphere and a more formal contemporary and sophisticated restaurant downstairs. Service in both is discreet and professional. The food here is modern and intuitive – original and creative, with a real flair for flavours and outstanding presentation.

Pressed terrine of duck confit with a date chutney. Roast noisette of Perthshire lamb with crushed potatoes, baby vegetables and a rosemary jus. Baked brioche and ginger pudding with rhubarb dressing.

◗ *Open all year except 25, 26 Dec and 1, 2 Jan Closed Sun* ✘ *Lunch except Mon Sat ££ Dinner £££* Ⓥ *Vegetarians welcome* ⚹ *Children welcome* 🎫 *Mastercard/Eurocard, American Express, Visa, Diners Club, Switch, Delta* 🄽 *General Manager: Alan Forrester*

22 West Nile Street Glasgow G1 2PW Tel: 0141 221 8044 Fax: 0141 248 9159 City centre. M8 exit for George Square, turn left at 2nd lights into Port Dundas Road which joins West Nile Street. [C6]

GLASGOW OUTSKIRTS

The Beardmore Hotel

- *"Formal yet relaxed restaurant with really friendly staff."*
- *Imaginative cuisine in an imaginative setting.*

THE BEARDMORE HOTEL has two dining areas: Citrus with its 'funky' retro furnishing and presenting a combination of well-cooked produce, and B Bar Café, with fresh food served quickly from 10am–10pm. Service is efficient, friendly and relaxed. Investor in People Award. Winner of The Macallan Taste of Scotland Award 1996.

Sole fillet gently confited and served with purple potatoes and a curried butter. Pan-fried breast of goose, sautéed cabbage, rösti potato, smoky essence (poached egg optional). Passion fruit raviolis with a crème fraîche and vanilla sorbet.

STB ★★★★ Hotel

◗ *Open all year* 🛏 *Rooms: 168 en suite* 🛌 *DB&B £50–£135 B&B £35–£120* 🆂 *Special rates available* ✘ *Food available all day from £ Lunch from ££ Dinner from ££* Ⓥ *Vegetarians welcome* ✄ *Smoking area in lounge bar* 🎫 *Mastercard/Eurocard, American Express, Visa, Diners Club, Switch* 🄽 *General Manager: Andrew Renouf*

Beardmore Street Clydebank Glasgow G81 4SA Tel: 0141 951 6000 Fax: 0141 951 6018 E-mail: beardmore.hotel@hci.co.uk Web: www.beardmore.hotel.co.uk Between Glasgow and Loch Lomond. Off A82, 8 miles from M8 Junction 19 over Erskine Bridge or approach from Glasgow along Dumbarton Road. [C6]

GLASGOW OUTSKIRTS

East Lochhead Country House & Cottages: Finalist The Macallan Taste of Scotland Awards 2001

- *"Only the highest quality in food and service is good enough at this gem of a place in pretty Renfrewshire."*
- *Very best home-style Scottish cooking.*

EAST LOCHHEAD is a traditional Scottish stone-built farmhouse renovated to the highest modern standards with many delightful touches. Janet and Ross Anderson are accomplished and friendly hosts and Janet is also a skilled cook who uses fruit and vegetables from her own garden and honey from her own bees – fabulous home cooking.

Salmon fish cake on a bed of salad leaves with warm lemon butter sauce. Braised East Lochhead Highland beef in a red wine sauce with herby dumplings. Brown sugar meringues with raspberry sauce.

STB ★★★★ B&B

◗ *Open all year* ▥ *Rooms: 6, 5 en suite* ▤ *DB&B £50–£55 B&B £32.50–£35* ▩ *Special rates available* ▥ *Unlicensed* ✗ *Food available all day ££ Lunch ££ Dinner ££ Dinner/Lunch parties with prior booking* ▼ *Vegetarians welcome* ✿ *Children welcome* ✍ *No smoking throughout* ▧ *Mastercard, American Express, Visa* ▨ *Proprietor: Janet Anderson*

Largs Road Lochwinnoch Renfrewshire PA12 4DX
Tel: 01505 842610 Fax: 01505 842610
E-mail: eastlochhead@aol.com
Web: www.eastlochhead.co.uk
Exit M8 at junction 28a (A737 Irvine). Right on A760. East Lochhead is 2 miles on left-hand side. [C6]

GLASGOW OUTSKIRTS

Gavins Mill Restaurant

- *"Trendy out-of-town rendezvous."*
- *Innovative modern Scottish.*

GAVINS MILL is a 15th Century flour mill that has been sensitively restored, with original elements of the building used as new functional features. The restaurant upstairs is a testimonial to modern design. Cooking is original; staff and management are accomplished; and the chef is highly skilled.

Grilled red mullet on wilted red chard and a rosemary and lemon dressing. Pan-fried breast of corn fed chicken with sautéed asparagus and pancetta. Raspberry crème brûlée.

◗ *Open all year* ✗ *Food available all day ££ Lunch ££ Dinner £££* ▼ *Vegetarians welcome* ♿ *Facilities for disabled visitors* ▧ *Mastercard/ Eurocard, American Express, Visa, Diners Club, Switch, Delta* ▨ *General Manager: Mr Ryan James*

Gavins Mill Road Milngavie Glasgow G62 6NB
Tel: 0141 956 2255 Fax: 0141 943 2488
E-mail: gavinsmill@icscotland.co.uk
Web: www.gavinsmill.co.uk
Near town centre – Gavins Mill is at the bottom of the Tesco car park, off the Glasgow road. [C6]

GLASGOW OUTSKIRTS

Gingerhill

- *"Excellent food in warm, friendly and relaxed setting – well worth the short drive from Glasgow."*
- *Modern Scottish (accent on seafood).*

CHEF/PROPRIETOR Alan Burns has created a delightful dining experience where guests feel like they are relaxing in the home of an old friend. Finest Scottish produce is carefully sourced, freshly prepared to order and served in a simple and unpretentious setting. Excellent value and a real home-from-home.

Pressed smoked fish terrine with crème fraîche caviar. Roasted cod with seared West Coast scallops on butter-braised leeks with a rhubarb dressing. Cabernet chocolate torte with a strawberry and basil salad and anglaise sauce.

◗ *Open all year except Christmas Day, Boxing Day and 1 to 16 Jan Closed Mon Tue* ℠ *Unlicensed – guests welcome to take own wine (corkage £2)* ✕ *Lunch except Mon Tue £–££ Dinner Thu to Sat ££–£££* ✽ *Lunch: smoking permitted in smaller room Dinner: smoking permitted after all guests have eaten* ♞*Guide dogs only* 💳 *Mastercard/Eurocard, Visa, Switch, Delta* ⚅ *Chef/Proprietor: Alan Burns*

1 Hillhead Street Milngavie G62 8AF Tel: 0141 956 6515 Fax: 0141 956 6515 Web: www.gingerhill.co.uk From Milngavie train station car park, walk through underpass into precinct. Hillhead Street is first road (up a hill) on the right. Gingerhill is on the left-hand side. [C6]

GLASGOW (OUTSKIRTS)

Gleddoch House Hotel & Country Estate

- *"Set in an attractive location. Gleddoch offers a relaxed getaway, an ideal golfers retreat."*
- *Modern Scottish cooking.*

GLEDDOCH HOUSE HOTEL's 360-acre estate has an 18-hole golf course, horse riding, clay pigeon shooting and off-road driving. The restaurant is spacious and gracious; the four-course, table d'hôte menu is superbly cooked and presented by chef Brian Graham. The whole food experience is excellent. The hotel has conference and private dining facilities.

Seared king scallops on a filo parcel of roasted root vegetables traced with Oban mussels in white wine pan jus. Roast saddle of Highland venison, sliced pink on a bed of red cabbage and pear compote with blackberry, poivrade sauce. Drambuie parfait on a gratin of winter berries with rich strawberry coulis.

STB ★★★★ Hotel

◗ *Open all year* 🏠 *Rooms: 38 en suite* 🛏 *DB&B £75–£127.50 B&B £99–£180* 💷 *Special rates available* ✕ *Food available all day £–££££ Lunch ££ Dinner ££££* Ⓥ *Vegetarians welcome* ☀ *Children welcome* 💳 *Mastercard/Eurocard, American Express, Visa, Diners Club, Switch* ⚅ *General Manager: Leslie W Conn*

Langbank Renfrewshire PA14 6YE Tel: 01475 540711 Fax: 01475 540201 E-mail: gleddochhouse@ukonline.co.uk M8 towards Greenock. Take B789 Langbank/ Houston exit. Follow signs to left and then right after ½ mile – hotel is on left. [C6]

GLASGOW (OUTSKIRTS)

Uplawmoor Hotel & Restaurant

- *"A friendly unassuming hotel, offering delicious food and real ales!"*
- *Good Scottish cooking.*

THIS IS A WELL-RUN and managed hotel. The lounge bar provides traditional bar meals at lunchtime and evenings whilst the restaurant and adjoining cocktail bar are open in the evening. The à la carte menu, in the restaurant, together with the fortnightly changing table d'hôte, provide a good choice.

Arbroath smokie mousse with lemon dressing. Gaelic steak – prime locally reared fillet on a haggis crouton flamed in whisky with a garlic and onion demi-glaze. Glazed lemon tart.

STB ★★★ Small Hotel

❶ *Open all year except Boxing Day and New Year's Day* 🛏 *Rooms: 14 en suite* 🛏 *DB&B £45–£65 B&B £27.50–£49* 🆘 *Special rates available* ✘ *Food available all day Sun Sat £ Lunch £ Dinner ££* Ⓥ *Vegetarians welcome* 🧒 *Children welcome* 🚭 *No smoking in restaurant Smoking in adjoining Cocktail Bar* 💳 *Mastercard/Eurocard, Visa, Switch, Solo* 🅺 *Proprietor: Stuart Peacock*

Neilston Road Uplawmoor Glasgow G78 4AF Tel: 01505 850565 Fax: 01505 850689 E-mail: enquiries@uplawmoor.co.uk Web: www.uplawmoor.co.uk Just off A736 Glasgow to Irvine road. Approx 4 miles from Barrhead. [C6]

GLENCOE

The Holly Tree Hotel, Seafood & Steak Restaurant

- *"Good food in a relaxing atmosphere, with spacious bedrooms and lochside views."*
- *Skilled handling of seafood.*

LOVINGLY RESTORED in the classical 'Charles Rennie Mackintosh' style. The comfortable restaurant overlooks the floodlit gardens. A varied choice of superb fresh seafood is skilfully prepared; the atmosphere is friendly; the hospitality excellent, all combine to make this a most relaxing place to enjoy the astounding scenery and location.

Whole Loch Linnhe prawns with Marie Rose. Salad of venison with a port and redcurrant juice. Caramel shortcake ice cream.

STB ★★★ Small Hotel

❶ *Open Mar to Nov* 🛏 *Rooms: 10 en suite* 🛏 *DB&B £50–£78 B&B £30–£57.50* 🆘 *Special rates available* ✘ *Dinner from £££* Ⓥ *Vegetarians welcome* 🧒 *Children welcome* ♿ *Facilities for disabled visitors* 🚭 *No smoking in restaurant* 💳 *Mastercard/Eurocard, Visa, Switch, Delta* 🅺 *Manager: Annette McFatridge*

Kentallen by Appin Argyll PA38 4BY Tel: 01631 740292 Fax: 01631 740345 E-mail: stay@hollytree.co.uk Web: www.hollytreehotel.co.uk From Glasgow take the A82 to Glencoe, continue towards Ballachulish Bridge, then take the A828 Oban road to Kentallen. Hotel is 2 miles down this road on right-hand side beside loch. [B5]

GLENDEVON BY DOLLAR

Tormaukin Hotel and Restaurant

- *Long popular with locals, this hidden gem is well worth seeking out."*
- *Accomplished Scottish cooking.*

THIS IDYLLIC 18TH CENTURY Drovers Inn still retains most of its original features. Both menus – an excellent bar menu and imaginative à la carte – feature the finest Scottish produce and represent good value for money. Wine lovers are also well catered for – superb choice 'by the glass'. Newly opened, a patio area to dine alfresco! Walkers welcome.

Fish soup with crab meat, stem ginger and coriander. Pan-cooked loin of venison served on venison haggis, with a port and beetroot gravy. Bread and butter pudding with whisky-soaked raisins, served with fresh cream.

STB ★★★ Small Hotel

◑ *Open all year except Christmas Day* ☗ *Rooms: 12 en suite* ⊨ *DB&B £55–£70 B&B £40–£58* ⏢ *Special rates available* ✗ *Lunch from £ Dinner from ££* Ⓥ *Vegetarians welcome* ✶ *Children Welcome* ♿ *Facilities for disabled visitors* ☙ *Residents' dogs welcome by prior arrangement* ⊞ *Mastercard/Eurocard, American Express, Visa, Switch, Delta* ☖ *Owners: Mr & Mrs Simpson*

Glendevon By Dollar South Perthshire FK14 7JY Tel: 01259 781 252 Fax: 01259 781 526 E-mail: enquiries@tormaukin.co.uk Web: www.tormaukin.com Situated on A823 between Gleneagles and Yetts O' Muckhart. [C5]

GLENFINNAN

Glenfinnan Monument, The National Trust for Scotland

- *"An interesting coffee and home baking stop when touring the West Highlands."*
- *Wholesome Scottish food.*

THIS IS A NEAT little coffee bar with open-plan servery. It has a friendly atmosphere as staff – while on view to customers – serve and prepare the next day's baking. With the customer in mind tables are placed around the window with all seating facing the view of the monument.

Traditional pea and ham soup served with crusty bread. Seasonal vegetable savoury tart. Glenfinnan's famous bran loaf.

STB ★★★ Visitor Attraction

◑ *Open 1 Apr to 31 Oct* ⏢ *Special rates available* ⓤ *Unlicensed* ✗ *Food available all day £ Lunch £* Ⓥ *Vegetarians welcome* ✶ *Children welcome* ♿ *Facilities for disabled visitors* ✅ *No smoking in snack bar* ⊞ *Mastercard, Visa, Switch* ☖ *Property Manager: Dierdre Smyth*

Information Centre Inverness-shire PH37 4LT Tel: 01397 722250 Fax: 01397 722250 Web: www.nts.org.uk A830, 18½ miles west of Fort William. [B4]

GLENLIVET

Minmore House

- *"Victor and Lynne welcome you to Minmore where the food is first-class!"*
- *Classic cuisine of international flair using Scotland's best.*

MINMORE HOUSE is run by Chef Victor Janssen and his wife Lynne. They are enthusiastic hosts who set high standards of hospitality and cooking. Both are passionate about food and this is reflected in the meals at Minmore. Menus are delightful using the best of Scottish ingredients in an innovative way.

Fresh Scottish Scallops à la Victor! Grilled rack of Highland lamb in garlic and rosemary, served in roast fennel and minted hollandaise. Apple and tarragon soufflé in calvados cream.

STB ★★★★ Small Hotel

◑ *Open Easter to mid Nov Closed 2 weeks Nov and all Feb* ⊞ *Rooms: 10 en suite* ⇔ *DB&B £82.50 B&B £55* ⊞ *Special rates available* ✗ *Packed Lunch on request Lunch ££ Dinner £££* Ⓥ *Vegetarians welcome* ☀ *Children welcome* ⊁ *No smoking in restaurant* ⊞ *Mastercard/Eurocard, American Express, Visa, Switch, Delta* ⋈ *Victor & Lynne Janssen*

Glenlivet Banffshire AB37 9DB
Tel: 01807 590378 Fax: 01807 590472
E-mail: minmorehouse@ukonline.co.uk
Web: www.minmorehousehotel.com
Take the A95 from Grantown-on-Spey. Right after 15 miles take B9008 – follow signs to The Glenlivet Distillery. [D4]

GLENROTHES

Balbirnie House Hotel

- *"Charming staff welcome you to a haven of good food and tranquility."*
- *Scottish incorporating European influences.*

WHETHER STAYING or simply visiting for lunch, dinner or afternoon tea, Balbirnie's exceptional staff make all guests feel really special. Enjoy one of over 250 wines to complement the excellent food and finish with your choice of 110 fine malt whiskies. Winner of the Macallan Taste of Scotland Award 1996.

Hot home oak-roasted salmon with marinated local mushrooms and an Arran mustard dressing. Pan-fried loin of venison, with red cabbage, glazed red apple, garlic mash and bramble gravy. Heather honey and Drambuie parfait.

STB ★★★★ Hotel

◑ *Open all year* ⊞ *Rooms: 30 en suite* ⇔ *DB&B £92.50–£154 B&B £92.50–£122.50* ⊞ *Special rates available* ✗ *Lunch £ Dinner £££* Ⓥ *Vegetarians welcome* ☀ *Children welcome* ♿ *Facilities for disabled visitors* ⊞ *Mastercard/ Eurocard, American Express, Visa, Diners Club, Switch, Delta* ⋈ *Proprietors: The Russell Family*

Balbirnie Park Markinch Fife KY7 6NE
Tel: 01592 610066 Fax: 01592 610529
E-mail: balbirnie@breathemail.net
Web: www.balbirnie.co.uk
½ hour equidistant from Edinburgh and St Andrews. Just off A92 on B9130. Follow directions to Markinch Village then Balbirnie Park. [D5]

GLENSHEE

Dalmunzie House Hotel

- *"A visit to Dalmunzie offers relaxation steeped in tradition."*
- *Traditional Scottish cooking.*

DALMUNZIE HOUSE HOTEL's 6,500-acre estate has a 9-hole golf course, fishing, stalking, grouse shooting and the Glenshee ski slopes are close by. The menu is table d'hôte (four/five choices) with a couple of à la carte supplements. The cooking is homestyle but imaginative.

Sautéed Glamis asparagus bruschetta with a chive hollandaise sauce and Scottish smoked salmon. Roast loin of local venison on a mustard and onion mash with root vegetables and pan juices. Blairgowrie strawberry shortbread with vanilla pod ice cream.

STB ★★★ Hotel

◐ Open 28 Dec to 28 Nov ⋔ Rooms: 17, 16 en suite ⊨ DB&B £63–£75 (3 to 6 days) B&B £31–£57 ▥ Special rates available ✗ Lunch £ Dinner ££–£££ Ⓥ Vegetarians welcome ✸ Children welcome & Limited facilities for disabled visitors ⊞ Mastercard/Eurocard, Visa, Switch ▨ Owners: Simon & Alexandra Winton

Spittal of Glenshee Blairgowrie Perthshire PH10 7QG Tel: 01250 885224 Fax: 01250 885225 E-mail: dalmunzie@aol.com Web: www.welcome.to/dalmunzie Approx 20 miles from Blairgowrie on A93 at Spittal of Glenshee – then follow signs. [C4]

GLENSHIEL

Duich House

- *"Sink into the comfort of this interesting home and enjoy good cuisine and hospitality."*
- *Skilful Scottish country house cooking.*

THIS IS A BEAUTIFUL house furnished with antiques collected whilst the owners stayed in Asia. Every thought and care has been put into the room touches making a stay here quite a unique experience. The food is excellent, skilful with some interesting innovations – a real find!

Marbled quails eggs flavoured with smokey tea and served with Szechuan red peppercorns. Sea bass baked with Pernod and stuffed with garlic and fresh dill. Home-made orange sorbet with a leaf of pastry on a bed of sugared fresh berries.

◐ Open Easter to Oct ⋔ Rooms: 2 with private facilities ⊨ B&B £34–£40 ▥ Special rates available ▥ Unlicensed – guests welcome to take own wine ✗ Packed Lunch by prior arrangement £ Dinner except Fri – residents only £££ Ⓥ Vegetarians welcome with prior notice ✦ No smoking throughout ⊞ No credit cards ▨ Operators: Uilleam Mac A'Reudaidh & Anne Kempthorne

Letterfearn Glenshiel Ross-shire IV40 8HS Tel: 01599 555 259 Fax: 01599 555 259/555 333 E-mail: duich@cwcom.net Web: www.milford.co.uk/go/duich.html From the south take the main A87 road to Isle of Skye. On reaching Shiel Bridge turn left following the sign for Ratagan, Letterfearn and Glenelg. After 1 mile take a right turn to Ratagan, Letterfearn and Totaig and travel 3 miles along lochside. Duich House on sharp turn on the left. [B4]

GRANGEMOUTH

The Grange Manor Hotel

- *"Enjoy Scottish cooking of a high standard."*
- *Modern Scottish cooking.*

BILL WALLACE enjoys personally greeting his guests, ensuring that they feel at home in this comfortable hotel. Le Chardon Restaurant offers complex Scottish cooking of high modern standards. Both à la carte and table d'hôte eating are provided, where game and fish feature with light, imaginative sauces alongside traditional meats and poultry.

Home-cured salmon terrine accompanied with a sun-dried tomato and apricot chutney. Steamed breast of pheasant centred with a white truffle and smoked shallot mousseline wrapped in Savoy cabbage. Chilled cappuccino bavaroise with Drambuie parfait set on a banana coulis.

STB ★★★★ Hotel

Open all year Rooms: 37 en suite DB&B £60–£95 B&B £40–£50 Special rates available Food available all day £££ Lunch ££ Dinner £££ Vegetarians welcome Children welcome Facilities for disabled visitors Mastercard/Eurocard, American Express, Visa, Diners Club, Switch, Delta Proprietors: Bill & Jane Wallace

Glensburgh Grangemouth FK3 8XJ
Tel: 01324 474836 Fax: 01324 665861
E-mail: info@grangemanor.co.uk
Web: www.grangemanor.co.uk
Just off M9. To Stirling – exit at junction 5, follow A905 for 2 miles (to Kincardine Bridge). To Edinburgh – exit at junction 6, turn right, 200 metres on right. [C5]

GRANTOWN-ON-SPEY

Ardconnel House

- *"Superb welcome and food with the use of local produce."*
- *French cooking using Scottish produce.*

AWARD-WINNING Ardconnel House is elegantly furnished and decorated with antiques and paintings in keeping with the Victorian style. Run by owners Barbara and Michel Bouchard, Michel is French and brings flair and skill to very good local produce, whilst Barbara skilfully tends to guests' needs. A carefully selected wine list complements the excellent food.

Cider and Stilton soup served with Parmesan croutons. Scottish pheasant with sherry and port sauce. Panettone and banana sticky toffee pudding.

STB ★★★★★ Guest House

Open Easter to 31 Oct Rooms: 6 en suite DB&B £50–£62 B&B £28–£40 Special rates available Residents only Dinner – by arrangement ££ Children over 8 years welcome No smoking throughout Mastercard/Eurocard, Visa Proprietors: Michel & Barbara Bouchard

Woodlands Terrace Grantown-on-Spey PH26 3JU
Tel: 01479 872104 Fax: 01479 872104
E-mail: enquiry@ardconnel.com
Web: www.ardconnel.com
On A95, south west entry to town. [C4]

GRANTOWN-ON-SPEY

Culdearn House Hotel

- *"Scottish food and hospitality at its best."*
- *Innovative, imaginative cooking.*

THIS CHARMING establishment has achieved many accolades and Alasdair and Isobel Little are enthusiastic hosts, and look after their guests very well. New chef Feona MacLean shows dedication and enthusiasm in the preparation of local produce in classic Scots ways. Over 70 malt whiskies are offered and an interesting wine list.

Avocado pear served warm with smoked salmon in a white wine sauce. Breast of Guinea fowl with parsnip potato cakes and a peppercorn and cognac jus. Crème fraîche and vanilla mousse with a syrup of fruits.

STB ★★★★ Hotel
Green Tourism Three Leaf Gold Award

◑ *Open 1 Mar to 30 Oct* 🏨 *Rooms: 9 en suite* 🛏 *DB&B £75* 🆂🅿 *Special rates available* 🍷 *Restricted licence* ✕ *Non-residents – reservations essential Picnic lunches to order Dinner 4 course menu £££* ✄ *No smoking in dining room* 💳 *Mastercard/Eurocard, American Express, Visa, Diners Club, Switch, Delta, JCB* 👤 *Proprietors: Isobel & Alasdair Little*

Woodlands Terrace Grantown-on-Spey Morayshire PH26 3JU
Tel: 01479 872106 Fax: 01479 873641
E-mail: culdearn@globalnet.co.uk
Web: www.culdearn.com
Entering Grantown on A95 from south west, turn left at 30 mph sign. Culdearn faces you. [C4]

GRANTOWN-ON-SPEY

Muckrach Lodge Hotel & Restaurant

- *"Muckrach's restaurants offer excellent food in a peaceful, stylish and relaxing location."*
- *Modern Scottish cooking with continental influence.*

INTERESTING AND SKILFUL cooking is 'the' priority here. Both the fine dining Finlarig Restaurant and the informal Conservatory bistro use the wonderful local produce for which this region is so famous. A distinguished cellar complements the food experience. James and Dawn Macfarlane are friendly hosts.

Dived Mallaig scallops with roast peppers and asparagus in filo pastry. Medallions of Moray beef with tarragon crust on a shallot and port wine reduction. Iced terrine of white and dark Belgian chocolate on a coffee bean sauce.

STB ★★★★ Hotel
Green Tourism Three Leaf Gold Award

◑ *Open all year* 🏨 *Rooms: 13, 12 en suite* 🛏 *DB&B £89–£99 B&B £60–£70* 🆂🅿 *Special rates available* ✕ *Lunch £ Dinner £££* Ⓥ *Vegetarians welcome* ✦ *Children welcome* ♿ *Facilities for disabled visitors* ✄ *No smoking in restaurants* 💳 *Mastercard/Eurocard, American Express, Visa, Diners Club, Switch, JCB* 👤 *Proprietors: James & Dawn Macfarlane*

Dulnain Bridge Grantown-on-Spey Morayshire PH26 3LY
Tel: 01479 851 257 Fax: 01479 851 325
E-mail: info@muckrach.co.uk
Web: www.muckrach.co.uk
3 miles from Grantown-on-Spey on A938 Dulnain Bridge – Carrbridge Road, 400 yards from Dulnain Bridge. [C4]

GRANTOWN-ON-SPEY

The Pines

- *"A charming intimate small hotel offering excellent food and hospitality."*
- *Modern Scottish cooking.*

THE EXPERIENCE at The Pines is one of real Scottish hospitality. Many antiques, fine furnishings and family portraits are to be found here together with interesting 'objets d'art'. Michael and Gwen Stewart make their guests welcome in their fine home with its large landscaped garden in a delightful woodland setting.

Salad of smoked chicken and tomato with parsley pesto dressing. Fillet of Scottish salmon with pistachio on an olive oil and spring onion mash with sweetcorn and red pepper salsa. Crème brûlée with raspberry sorbet in a chocolate tuile.

STB ★★★★ Small Hotel

◗ Open 1 Mar to 31 Oct – or by special arrangement 🏨 Rooms: 8 (7 en suite, 1 with adjacent private facilities) 🍴 DB&B £60–£70 B&B £35–£45 🆂🅿 Special rates available ✕ Dinner £££ – non residents reservation essential Ⓥ Vegetarians welcome ✻ Children over 12 years welcome ✚ No smoking throughout 💳 Mastercard/Eurocard, Visa, Delta 🅺 Owners: Gwen & Michael Stewart

Woodside Avenue Grantown-on-Spey PH26 3JR Tel: 01479 872092 Fax: 01479 872092 E-mail: info@thepinesgrantown.co.uk Web: www.thepinesgrantown.co.uk On entering the town take A939 road to Tomintoul. 1st right. [C4]

GULLANE

Greywalls

- *"A beautiful historic building, set in delightful gardens and offering the best in food and service."*
- *Refined country house cuisine.*

THIS HISTORIC HOTEL'S lovely walled garden complements the serenity of the house itself. Chef Simon Burns' excellent menus are table d'hôte and his cooking is quite inspirational. The wine list is exceptional. Greywalls retains its position as one of Scotland's very special places. Winner of The Macallan Taste of Scotland Award 1999.

Roast dived scallops with a confit of tomato. Fillet of Scottish spring lamb with an aubergine caviar. 'Coffee and doughnuts'.

STB ★★★★ Hotel

◗ Open mid Apr to mid Oct 🏨 Rooms: 23 en suite 🍴 B&B £110–£120 ✕ Lunch ££ Dinner ££££ Ⓥ Vegetarians welcome – prior notice required ✻ Children welcome ♿ Facilities for disabled visitors ✚ No smoking in dining room 💳 Mastercard/Eurocard, American Express, Visa, Diners Club, Switch 🅺 Manager: Sue Prime

Muirfield Gullane East Lothian EH31 2EG Tel: 01620 842144 Fax: 01620 842241 E-mail: hotel@greywalls.co.uk Web: www.greywalls.co.uk At the eastern end of Gullane village (on the A198), signposted left as a historic building. [D5]

HAWICK

Mansfield House Hotel

- *"Warm and friendly host with good food throughout."*
- *Traditional Scottish and contemporary cooking.*

A VICTORIAN MANSION owned and run by the MacKinnon family. Under their supervision Chef David Tate presents well-priced à la carte and 'business lunch' menus in the formal dining room, and bar meals are also available. As well as the usual grills, the à la carte menu features some unusual combinations.

Terrine of oxtail, slowly cooked, boned and set in its own juices. Loin of venison served on crushed garlic, shallot potatoes, butter beans and seasonal greens. Border tayberry mousse with compote of tayberries and Athol brose ice cream

STB ★★★ Small Hotel

◗ Open all year except 26, 27 Dec, 1 and 2 Jan
🏨 Rooms: 12 en suite ⇔ DB&B £45–£75 B&B £30–£55 🆂🅿 Special rates available ✘ Lunch £–££ Dinner ££–£££ 🆅 Vegetarians welcome ⚹ Children welcome ♿ Facilities for disabled visitors ✌ No smoking area in restaurant 💳 Mastercard/Eurocard, American Express, Visa, Diners Club ⚐ Owners: Ian & Sheila MacKinnon

*Weensland Road Hawick TD9 8LB
Tel: 01450 360400 Fax: 01450 372007
E-mail: ian@mansfield-house.com
Web: www.mansfield-house.com
On the A698 Hawick to Kelso road. On the outskirts of the town. [D6]*

HELENSBURGH

Hill House, The National Trust for Scotland

- *"Excellent home baking that is as memorable as Mackintosh's architecture and design."*
- *Fine home baking.*

T HE HILL HOUSE is an excellent example of world renowned architect, Charles Rennie Mackintosh's work. Interestingly, one client of Mackintosh was Glasgow's 'Tearoom Queen', Kate Cranston and it is certain that both Mackintosh and Ms Cranston would approve of the simple elegant style, delicious home baking and delightful service provided in the Hill House tearoom.

A selection of wickedly tempting cakes, biscuits and home-baking along with a variety of quality coffees and teas.

STB ★★★★ Historic House

◗ Open 1 Apr to 31 Oct 🆄🅻 Unlicensed ✘ Food available all day £ ⚹ Children welcome ♿ Facilities for disabled visitors ✌ No smoking throughout 💳 No credit cards ⚐ Property Manager: Anne Ellis

*Upper Colquhoun Street Helensburgh G84 9AJ
Tel: 01436 673900 Fax: 01436 674685
E-mail: aellis@nts.org.uk
Web: www.nts.org.uk
Off B832, between A82 and A814, 23 miles north-west of Glasgow. [C5]*

HELENSBURGH

Kirkton House

- *"A welcoming and tranquil haven with panoramic views across the River Clyde."*
- *Accomplished home cooking.*

STEP BACK IN TIME to a wonderfully restored 18th century converted farmhouse close to Loch Lomond. Relax in front of an open fire or enjoy the breathtaking views whilst Gillian and Stewart Macdonald pamper you with their good humour, delicious home-cooked food, fine wines and whisky. A wonderful place.

Cockles and mussels in brandy cream sauce. Roast 'smoked' Aberfeldy lamb. Raspberry meringue roulade.

STB ★★★★ Guest House

◗ *Open all year except Dec and Jan* 🏠 *Rooms: 6 en suite* 🛏 *DB&B £45.75–£51.25 B&B £29.50–£45* 💷 *Special rates available (when dining in)* 🍷 *Restricted licence* ✕ *Dinner 4 course menu ££ – advance booking required* Ⓥ *Vegetarians welcome* ♣ *Children welcome* ♿ *Facilities for disabled visitors – downstairs rooms only* ✝ *No smoking in dining room* 💳 *Mastercard/Eurocard, American Express, Visa, Diners Club, Delta, JCB, Maestro, Solo* ♨ *Proprietors: Stewart & Gillian Macdonald*

Darleith Road Cardross Argyll & Bute G82 5EZ Tel: 01389 841 951 Fax: 01389 841 868 E-mail: tos@kirktonhouse.co.uk Web: www.kirktonhouse.co.uk Cardross is mid way between Helensburgh and Dumbarton on the north bank of the Clyde. At west end of Cardross village turn north off A814 up Darleith Road. Kirkton House drive is ½ mile on right. [C5]

HOWWOOD

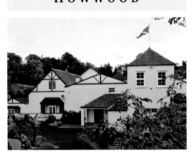

Bowfield Hotel & Country Club

- *"Relaxing, informal atmosphere with leisure facilities."*
- *Traditional food with Scottish influences.*

BOWFIELD HOTEL & Country Club is a refreshingly different country retreat close to town and city attractions. It enjoys many international visitors and is a popular retreat for weekend leisure breaks, combining a well-converted building with modern facilities – pool, spa and gym – and a relaxing dining experience. Imaginative menus using good quality produce cooked with skill and flair.

Tartare of Loch Fyne salmon layered with avocado and onion, topped with dill crème fraîche. Loin of Highland venison wrapped in tarragon mousse and Argyll ham with wild blackcurrant reduction. Iced melon and honey parfait with Drambuie anglaise.

STB ★★★★ Hotel

◗ *Open all year* 🏠 *Rooms: 23 en suite* 🛏 *B&B £48–£68* 💷 *Special rates available* ✕ *Food available all day £ Lunch £ Dinner ££* Ⓥ *Vegetarians welcome* ♣ *Children welcome* ✝ *No smoking in restaurant* 💳 *Mastercard/ Eurocard, American Express, Visa, Diners Club, Switch, Delta* ♨ *General Manager: Aileen Adams*

Howwood Renfrewshire PA9 1DB Tel: 01505 705225 Fax: 01505 705230 E-mail: enquiries@bowfieldcountryclub.co.uk Web: www.bowfieldcountryclub.co.uk From the M8 at Glasgow Airport take A737 (Irvine) for approx 6 miles. Exit left (Howwood) onto B787 then either take second right onto a single track shortcut or drive into Howwood and take right onto B776 for 1 mile to Bowfield at top of hill (large white gateposts). [C6]

HUNTLY

Castle Hotel

- *"An impressive building situated in parkland offering Scottish hospitality and food."*
- *Traditional Scottish cuisine.*

CASTLE HOTEL is owned and run by Linda Meiklejohn and offers a traditional Scottish experience in impressive surroundings. It is set amidst the tranquil surroundings of the River Deveron and the ruins of Huntly Castle. The cooking here is traditional and is served with warm Scottish hospitality.

Smoked salmon cheesecake served with a peach salsa. Chicken with wild mushroom and bacon stuffing and a sweet Marsala sauce. Fresh strawberry and kiwi liqueur salad.

STB ★★★ Hotel

◗ *Open all year except 25 to 27 Dec* ✿ *Rooms: 20 en suite* ⛌ *DB&B £58–£68 B&B £48–£58* ⓈⓅ *Special rates available* ✗ *Food available all day £ Lunch ££ Dinner £££* Ⓥ *Vegetarians welcome* ☀ *Children welcome* ♿ *Facilities for disabled visitors* ✄ *No smoking in restaurant* ✖*Dogs welcome* ▦ *Mastercard/Eurocard, American Express, Visa, Diners Club, Switch, Delta* ◪ *Marketing Manager: Nikki Meiklejohn*

Huntly Aberdeenshire AB54 4SH
Tel: 01466 792696 Fax: 01466 792641
E-mail: castlehot@enterprise.net
Web: www.castlehotel.uk.com
Huntly is situated on the main A96 between Aberdeen and Inverness. Take direct route through Huntly town square and follow signs to Huntly Castle and on to Castle Hotel. [D4]

INVERKEILOR

Gordon's Restaurant with Rooms

- *"The gourmet experience just goes on and on …"*
- *Modern Scottish cooking.*

IN THIS TINY FAMILY RESTAURANT with rooms in the tiny village of Inverkeilor the welcome is big and the gourmet experience huge. Local fish, meats, wild mushrooms and fruits are used to produce imaginative, modern Scottish cooking. Menus change regularly. Winner of The Macallan Taste Of Scotland Award 1999.

Arbroath smokie cheesecake, flavoured with malt whisky and Arran mustard, crème fraîche, heather honey dressing. Fillet of Angus beef with chanterelle and smoked bacon ravioli, red wine jus. Pyramid of chocolate Marquise with mango, orange and cardamom syrup.

STB ★★★★ Restaurant with Rooms

◗ *Open all year except last 2 weeks Jan Closed Mon – residents only* ✿ *Rooms: 2 en suite, 1 private bathroom* ⛌ *DB&B £66.50–£75.50 B&B £40–£47* ✗ *Lunch except Mon Tue Sat – booking essential ££ Dinner except Mon – residents only £££* Ⓥ *Vegetarians welcome* ☀ *Children over 12 years welcome* ✄ *No smoking area in restaurant* ▦ *Mastercard/ Eurocard, Visa* ◪ *Owners: Gordon & Maria Watson*

32 Main Street Inverkeilor by Arbroath Angus DD11 5RN
Tel: 01241 830364 Fax: 01241 830364
E-mail: gordonsrest@aol.com
Web: www.gordonsrestaurant.co.uk
A92 Arbroath to Montrose, turn off at sign for Inverkeilor. [D5]

INVERNESS

Bunchrew House Hotel

- *"Glorious setting, fine architecture and delicious dining make this a wonderful spot to eat and stay."*
- *Excellent Scottish cooking with an imaginative modern flair.*

BUNCHREW HOUSE HOTEL has a magnificent dining room which overlooks the sea. The style of cooking is a fusion of traditional and modern styles and deservedly gaining acclaim. The high standard of furnishing and fittings throughout combined with welcoming staff – makes Bunchrew a very special and enchanting destination.

Pink breast of woodland pigeon wrapped in filo pastry and masked in a port and black truffle sauce. Papillote of salmon and turbot surrounded by a shellfish and caviar sauce spiked with vegetable pearls. Delice of passion fruit accompanied by a caramel cage and poached baby peach.

STB ★★★★ Small Hotel

◐ *Open all year* 🏨 *Rooms: 14 en suite* 🛏 *DB&B £70–£115 B&B £65–£97.50* 🆂 *Special rates available* ✕ *Food available all day £ Lunch ££ Dinner £££* Ⓥ *Vegetarians welcome* ✿ *Children welcome* ✌ *No smoking in restaurant* 🐕 *No dogs in public rooms* 💳 *Mastercard/Eurocard, American Express, Visa, Switch, Delta, JCB* 🅼 *Owners: Janet and Graham Cross*

Bunchrew Inverness IV3 8TA
Tel: 01463 234917 Fax: 01463 710620
E-mail: welcome@bunchrew-inverness.co.uk
Web: www.bunchrew-inverness.co.uk
On A862 Inverness to Beauly. 10 minutes from the centre of Inverness. [C4]

INVERNESS

Cafe 1

- *"Casual yet stylish city centre restaurant."*
- *Modern Scottish fusion.*

CAFE 1 is now in its fourth year, continuity of staff through this period has ensured a high level of development both in the kitchen and in the restaurant. The menus offer freshly prepared local produce with continental and eastern influences. The bistro's ambience is enhanced by its friendly yet professional staff. A popular venue used by locals as well as travellers.

Brochette of king scallops wrapped in bacon, served with balsamic dressed rocket and Parmesan salad. Prime Angus Scotch fillet served on a bed of skirlie topped with red onion marmalade with a red wine jus. Crêpe filled with home-made Malteser ice cream with a butterscotch sauce.

◐ *Open all year except Christmas Day, Boxing Day and New Year's Day Closed Sun* ✕ *Lunch except Sun £ Dinner except Sun ££–£££* Ⓥ *Vegetarians welcome* ✿ *Children welcome* 💳 *Mastercard/Eurocard, Visa, Switch, Delta* 🅼 *Owners: Norman & Karen MacDonald*

75 Castle Street Inverness IV2 3EA
Tel: 01463 226 200 Fax: 01463 716 363
E-mail: info@cafe1.net
Web: www.cafe1.net
Centrally located on Castle Street near castle. [C4]

INVERNESS

Culloden House Hotel

- *"Impeccable service given in a friendly manner."*
- *Top quality Scottish produce in classic French style.*

CULLODEN HOUSE HOTEL is an elegant and imposing country house hotel set in 40 acres of parkland. There is a majestic splendour and romance about the place. The standard of cooking is high, prepared by Chef Michael Simpson who is committed to high quality and menus are classic with traditional French undertones.

Parcel of filo pastry filled with pine nuts and Arran goats cheese. Suprême of Scottish salmon topped with a lemon sole mousse and served with a langoustine sauce. Crème brûlée with Blairgowrie berries.

STB ★★★★ Hotel

❶ Open all year 🏨 Rooms: 28 en suite 🛏 DB&B £190–£340 B&B £145–£270 🆂🅿 Special rates available off season ✗ Food available all day ££££ Lunch ££ Dinner ££££ Ⓥ Vegetarians welcome ☀ Children welcome ✸ No smoking in dining room and lounge 💳 Mastercard/ Eurocard, American Express, Visa, Diners Club, Switch, Delta, JCB 🄼 General Manager/Director: Stephen Davies

Culloden Inverness IV2 7BZ
Tel: 01463 790461 Fax: 01463 792181
E-mail: info@cullodenhouse.co.uk
Web: www.cullodenhouse.co.uk
3 miles from the centre of Inverness, off the A96 Inverness to Aberdeen road. [C4]

INVERNESS

Culloden Moor Visitor Centre Restaurant
The National Trust for Scotland

- *"Bright, friendly self-service restaurant offering home-style dishes freshly made from top quality local produce."*
- *Traditional Scottish.*

THE HISTORIC BATTLEFIELD at Culloden Moor is well worth a visit for its excellent information centre, moorland walks, breathtaking scenery and good cooking in the centres restaurant. Popular with locals as well as visitors.

Cream of potato and leek soup with warm cheese and herb scone. Highland beef and beer stew with dumplings and turnip mash. Rhubarb and white chocolate tart with Mackie's ice cream.

STB ★★★ Visitor Attraction

❶ Open 15 Jan to 31 Dec except 24 to 26 Dec ❢ Licensed ✗ Food available all day £ Lunch £ Ⓥ Vegetarians welcome ☀ Children welcome ♿ Facilities for disabled visitors ✸ No smoking throughout 💳 Mastercard, Visa, Switch, Delta 🄼 Restaurant Manager: Mrs Daska MacKintosh

Culloden Moor Inverness IV2 5EU
Tel: 01463 790607 Fax: 01463 794294
E-mail: dmacintosh@nts.org.uk
Web: www.nts.org.uk
B9006, 5 miles east of Inverness on National Cycle Routes 1 and 7. [C4]

INVERNESS

INVERNESS

Dunain Park Hotel

Glendruidh House Hotel

- *"An excellent welcome and superb service awaits guests to this elegant and comfortable hotel."*
- *First rate Scottish cooking, with assured French influences.*

- *"A homely, small hotel with very personal and helpful service from Michael, and freshly prepared meals from Christine."*
- *Traditional Scottish cooking.*

GUESTS ARE extremely well-cared for at Dunain Park, an elegant Georgian home in peaceful surroundings. Ann and Edward Nicoll ensure a high standard of comfort and cuisine, including fruit and vegetables from their walled garden. An outstanding list of Scottish whiskies will satisfy those in search of the ultimate dram.

THIS IS AN UNUSUAL and attractive small country house set in three acres of woodland and lawns. The elegant dining room with Italian marble fireplace has a relaxed, comfortable ambience. Christine sources local ingredients, mainly organic, prepared without pretentiousness but with great care and love of good food.

Terrine of chicken and Guinea fowl layered with venison, pigeon and hare served with home-made chutney. Medallions of venison rolled in oatmeal and served with a mushroom potato cake and a claret and crème de cassis sauce. Chocolate truffle and Drambuie cake.

Smoked venison with salad and wild rowanberry jelly. Fillet of organic Scottish beef. Rhubarb and apple charlotte with vanilla ice cream.

STB ★★★★ Hotel
Green Tourism Two Leaf Silver Award

STB ★★★★ Small Hotel

❍ *Open all year* ♣ *Rooms: 13 en suite* ⚏ *DB&B £104–£124 B&B £79–£99* ⚏ *Special rates available in the low season* ✗ *Dinner £££* Ⓥ *Vegetarians welcome* ✳ *Well-behaved children welcome* ♿ *Facilities for disabled visitors – residents only* ⦸ *No smoking in dining room* ⊞ *Mastercard/Eurocard, American Express, Visa, Diners Club, Switch, Delta* 🄼 *Owners: Ann & Edward Nicoll*

❍ *Open all year except Christmas Day* ♣ *Rooms: 5 en suite (and 3 en suite rooms in Garden Villa)* ⚏ *DB&B £53.50–£97 B&B £24.50– £67.50* ⚏ *Special rates available* ✗ *Lunch – residents only ££ Dinner – residents only ££–£££* Ⓥ *Vegetarians welcome* ✳ *Children welcome* ♿ *Limited facilities for disabled* ⦸ *No smoking throughout (incl grounds)* ⊞ *Mastercard/ Eurocard, American Express, Visa, Diners Club, Switch, JCB* 🄼 *Proprietors: Michael & Christine Smith*

Inverness IV3 8JN
Tel: 01463 230512 Fax: 01463 224532
E-mail: dunainparkhotel@btinternet.com
Web: www.dunainparkhotel.co.uk
On A82, on left-hand side, 1 mile from the Inverness town boundary. [C4]

by Castle Heather Old Edinburgh Road South Inverness IV2 6AR
Tel: 01463 226499 Fax: 01463 710745
E-mail: tos@cozzee-nessie-bed.co.uk
Web: www.cozzee-nessie-bed.co.uk/intro.html
Two miles from Inverness centre. ½ mile south off Sir Walter Scott Drive. At the second roundabout turn left and take the first right at the 'hotel 300 yards' sign. [C4]

INVERNESS

Ristorante La Riviera

- *"Elegant and intimate restaurant, stunningly decorated – a very special place indeed!"*
- *Innovative, stylish cooking with Italian influences.*

RISTORANTE LA RIVIERA boasts a skilled and experienced team of chefs who prepare the finest local seafood, meat and game with Mediterranean flair, superb attention to detail and the highest standards of service to match. There is an extensive choice from the à la carte and 'prezzo fisso' – these menus will surprise and delight.

Rosette of caramelised scallops with creamy baby spinach, crispy Parma ham and tempura squid. Pot-roasted fillet of beef wrapped in Parma ham with balsamic red onion, pesto and a porcini mushroom sauce. Sweet plum bruschetta with Glayva sauce.

STB ★★★★ Small Hotel

◐ *Open all year ☗ Rooms: 15 en suite ✉ B&B £85–£135 per room ᔕ Special rates available ✕ Food available all day £ Lunch ££ Dinner £££ Ⓥ Vegetarians welcome ✵ Children welcome ♿ Facilities for disabled visitors ⚲ Dogs welcome by prior arrangement ☒ Mastercard/ Eurocard, American Express, Visa, Diners Club, Switch, Delta ⚙ Proprietor: Adrian Pieraccini*

Glenmoriston Town House Hotel
Ness Bank Inverness IV2 4SF
Tel: 01463 223777 Fax: 01463 712378
E-mail: glenmoriston@cali.co.uk
Web: www.glenmoriston.com
Situated on south side of the River Ness, close to city centre and directly opposite Eden Court Theatre. [C4]

INVERNESS

Seafields Restaurant and Grill at The Taste of Moray

- *"Quality Highland grills and seafood specialities cooked to order in a casual setting."*
- *Modern Scottish cooking.*

TASTE OF MORAY has a Seafood and Steak Restaurant, Food Hall and Cookshop. It is run by Robin and Celia Birkbeck and finished to an exceptionally high standard. The restaurant is open all day and offers everything from light refreshments to a full dinner menu, all cooked using fresh local produce.

Char-grilled Aberdeen Angus sirloin steak garni. Diver harvested scallops, wrapped in Morayshire bacon, served with hollandaise sauce. Profiteroles with chocolate sauce.

◐ *Open all year except 25, 26, 31 Dec and 1 Jan N.B. Jan to 1 Apr evening meals by booking only ✕ Food available all day £ Lunch £ Dinner ££ Ⓥ Vegetarians welcome ✵ Children welcome ♿ Limited facilities for disabled visitors ☒ Mastercard/Eurocard, Visa, Switch, Delta ⚙ Proprietors: Robin & Celia Birkbeck*

Gollanfield Inverness IV2 7QT
Tel: 01667 462340 Fax: 01667 461087
E-mail: info@tasteofmoray.co.uk
Web: www.tasteofmoray.co.uk
Between Inverness and Nairn on the main A96.
Inverness 8 miles, Nairn 5 miles. [C4]

INVERNESS

INVERURIE

Woodwards Restaurant

- *"A small restaurant with Celtic charm offering superbly prepared and presented meals."*
- *Modern Scottish cooking.*

WOODWARDS is a tastefully refurbished 'Auld Hoose'. Local produce is very much in evidence and attention to detail prominent. A small corner bar and seating area provide space for waiting – an upstairs bar/lounge provides further seating. Celtic music and good Scottish cooking set the scene for a thoroughly enjoyable dining experience.

Highland haggis in whisky and Arran mustard sauce. Lightly grilled halibut served with fresh egg pasta and a red wine and basil butter jus. Caramelised fruit flan with soft poached berries.

◐ *Open all year* ✕ *Dinner £££* Ⓥ *Vegetarians welcome* ✚ *Children welcome* ✍ *No smoking in restaurant* 🖃 *Mastercard/Eurocard, American Express, Visa, Diners Club, Switch, Delta* ✗ *Proprietor: Kay Frew*

99 Castle Street Inverness IV2 3EA
Tel: 01463 709809 Fax: 01463 709809
E-mail: woodwards@lineone.net
Looking onto historic Castle of Inverness, centre of town, turn right at Town House. Restaurant at the top of Castle Street, on the left. [C4]

Macdonald Thainstone House Hotel

- *"The good food matches the friendliness of the staff – enjoy the elegant atmosphere that is popular with locals and visitors to the North East."*
- *Modern Scottish cuisine.*

AN AWARD-WINNING team offer an extensive table d'hôte menu in 'Simpsons' Restaurant. Portion sizes and the quality of the raw materials are influenced only by the rich farming country within which Thainstone stands. For more informal dining there is Cammie's Bar.

Risotto of fine vegetables with goats cheese and fresh basil. Mille feuille of salmon and aubergine, served with a thyme jus. Poached pear with cinnamon ice cream and a warm claret syrup.

STB ★★★★ Hotel

◐ *Open all year* 🛏 *Rooms: 48 en suite* 🛏 *DB&B £66–£90 B&B £45–£80* ⓈⓅ *Special rates available* ✕ *Food available all day ££–£££ Lunch £££ Dinner ££££* Ⓥ *Vegetarians welcome* ✚ *Children welcome* ♿ *Facilities for disabled visitors* ✍ *No smoking in restaurant* 🖃 *Mastercard/Eurocard, American Express, Visa, Diners Club, Switch, Delta* ✗ *General Manager: Sylvia Simpson*

Inverurie Aberdeenshire AB51 5NT
Tel: 01467 621643 Fax: 01467 625084
E-mail: reservations@thainstone.macdonald-hotels.co.uk
Web: www.macdonaldhotels.co.uk
On A96 north of Aberdeen, 8 miles from airport turn left at first roundabout after Kintore. [D4]

IRVINE

Montgreenan Mansion House Hotel

- *"A gracious stone-built country mansion offering personal comfort and good cooking."*
- *Modern Scottish.*

AN HOTEL SINCE 1981, this 19th century house is set in formal landscaped gardens and pretty grounds in a rural location. Major refurbishing is an ongoing plan. Elegant and gracious, plenty of space and many original architectural features. Good variety of accommodation and eating experiences on offer – bar menu and à la carte dinner.

Savoury crêpe filled with wild mushrooms and asparagus in cream sauce glaze with smoked cheese. Breast of chicken on a bed of sautéed leeks, broccoli and exotic mushrooms with café au lait sauce. Warm butterscotch pot laced with Chantilly cream.

STB ★★★ Hotel

❍ *Open all year* ⌂ *Rooms: 21 en suite* ⇔ *DB&B £80–£160 B&B £80–£120* ⑲ *Special rates available* ✗ *Food available all day ££ Lunch ££ Dinner £££* Ⓥ *Vegetarians welcome* ✻ *Children welcome* ⚭ *No smoking in restaurant* ⑤ *Mastercard/Eurocard, American Express, Visa, Diners Club* Ⓜ *Manager: Kenneth Buchanan*

Montgreenan Estate nr Kilwinning Ayrshire KA13 7QZ
Tel: 01294 557733 Fax: 01294 850397
E-mail: info@montgreenanhotel.com
Web: www.montgreenanhotel.com
Just off the A736, 4 miles north of Irvine. 30 minutes from Glasgow, 20 minutes from Ayr. [C6]

ISLE OF ARRAN

Apple Lodge

- *"The type of place you arrive a guest and return a friend, again and again and again."*
- *High quality home cooking.*

APPLE LODGE is tranquilly located, set in its own appealing gardens from where you can watch wild deer graze. It has been furnished beautifully to a very high standard. Jeannie Boyd creates great food which is served in a friendly and unobtrusive style. Much thought goes into the balancing of meals here.

Salmon and asparagus tart, rocket salad. Fillet of lamb, baby spinach, port, orange and mint sauce, seasonal vegetables, platter garnished with herbs. Honey whisky creams and almond biscuits.

STB ★★★★ Guest House

❍ *Open all year except Christmas week* ⌂ *Rooms: 4 en suite* ⇔ *DB&B £50–£55 B&B £31–£36* ⑲ *Special rates available* ⓤ *Unlicensed – guests welcome to take own wine* ✗ *Packed lunches £ Dinner ££ Residents only* Ⓥ *Vegetarians welcome* ✻ *Children over 12 years welcome* ⚭ *No smoking in dining room and bedrooms* ⑤ *No credit cards* Ⓜ *Proprietor/Chef: Jeannie Boyd*

Lochranza Isle of Arran KA27 8HJ
Tel: 01770 830229 Fax: 01770 830229
E-mail: applelodge@easicom.com
From Brodick, head north and follow the road to Lochranza (around 14 miles). As you enter the village pass the distillery and Apple Lodge is situated 300 yards on the left opposite golf course. [B6]

ISLE OF ARRAN

Argentine House Hotel

- *"Assya is an enthusiastic cook and committed to using quality local produce, along with some international specialities."*
- *Scottish produce with a continental touch.*

ASSYA AND BRUNO Baumgärtner have refurbished this lovely villa to suit the local heritage, making a comfortable and relaxing home which is well cared for. Menus change daily, depending on produce available and guests' taste. Vegetarians are well-cared for and every taste is met. Food combinations are interesting, innovative and well-executed.

Tartar of Orkney herring on Arran oatcakes. Consommé with spinach, garlic and Parmesan. Fillet Wellington (pork) with 5 vegetables. Mousse of dark, brown and white Lindt chocolate.

STB ★★★ Small Hotel

◗ *Open all year* ⌂ *Rooms: 5 en suite* ⇌ *DB&B from £46 B&B from £26* ⅏ *Special rates available* ✗ *Dinner ££–£££ Non-residents – by arrangement* Ⓥ *Vegetarians welcome* ⌖ *No smoking in dining room* ⊞ *Mastercard/ Eurocard, Visa, JCB* ⚑ *Owners: Assya & Bruno Baumgärtner*

Shore Road Whiting Bay Isle of Arran KA27 8PZ
Tel: 01770 700 662 Fax: 01770 700 693
E-mail: info@argentinearran.co.uk
Web: www.argentinearran.co.uk
8 miles south of ferry terminal. First hotel on seafront at village entrance. [B6]

ISLE OF ARRAN

Auchrannie Country House Hotel

- *"Auchrannie offers something for everyone!"*
- *Modern Scottish cooking.*

AUCHRANNIE IS A DELIGHTFUL, comfortable hotel. Brambles Cafe Bar is an informal choice for snacks and meals, and the Garden Restaurant offers formal dining with a well-balanced table d'hôte menu offering a good range of local Scottish meat and fish dishes complemented by fresh vegetables and a daily vegetarian speciality.

Roast scallops with baby fennel and ginger cream. Loin of lamb with mushroom duxelle and air-dried ham, baby spinach and haricot vert served on a claret and redcurrant reduction. Raspberry and Glayva crème brûlée served with lacy tuiles.

STB ★★★★ Hotel
STB ★★★★★ Lodges

◗ *Open all year* ⌂ *Rooms: 28 en suite* ⇌ *DB&B £52.50–£81 B&B £35–£61* ⅏ *Special rates available* ✗ *Food available all day £ Lunch £ Dinner £££* Ⓥ *Vegetarians welcome* ⌖ *Children welcome* ⌖ *Facilities for disabled visitors* ⌖ *No smoking in Garden Restaurant Smoking area in Brambles Café Bar* ⊞ *Mastercard/Eurocard, American Express, Visa, Switch* ⚑ *Managing Director: Iain Johnston*

Brodick Isle of Arran KA27 8BZ
Tel: 01770 302234 Fax: 01770 302812
E-mail: info@auchrannie.co.uk
Web: www.auchrannie.co.uk
One mile north of Brodick Ferry Terminal and 400 yards from Brodick Golf Club. [B6]

ISLE OF ARRAN

Brodick Castle Restaurant, The National Trust for Scotland

- *"Relax and enjoy some homebaking and one of the best views of Arran."*
- *Home cooking and baking.*

I N THE CASTLE itself is the restaurant which offers tasty home-cooked meals and light snacks, all made from locally sourced ingredients. The wonderful home baking is hard to resist. On a sunny day visitors may also sit outside to eat on the terrace and enjoy the magnificent views and grounds.

Traditional soups served with cheese and Arran mustard scones or crusty bread. Casserole of local beef and Arran ale. Traditional hot or cold puddings served with Arran dairy ice cream.

STB ★★★★ Castle

◐ *Open 1 Apr to 31 Oct and winter weekends until 31 Dec* ♟ *Licensed* ✖ *Food available all day £ Lunch £* Ⓥ *Vegetarians welcome* ✻ *Children welcome* ♿ *Facilities for disabled visitors* ✘ *No smoking throughout* 💳 *Mastercard/Eurocard, Visa* ▧ *Property Manager: Mr Ken Thorburn*

Brodick Isle of Arran KA27 8HY
Tel: 01770 302202 Fax: 01770 302312
E-mail: kthorburn@nts.org.uk
Web: www.nts.org.uk
2 miles north out of Brodick on the Lochranza Road. Follow signs for the castle. [B6]

ISLE OF ARRAN

Distillery Restaurant

- *"Smart, well run visitor attraction, offering good quality and value for money food."*
- *Fresh and innovative to suit all tastes.*

T HE DISTILLERY RESTAURANT offers a fine quality of dining but with an informality – to appeal to all tastes and ages. Evening dinner is a candlelit affair with a more formal approach. In the kitchen, Head Chef Garry Noble is skilfully creating some unique yet very appealing dishes alongside the more traditional.

Smoked salmon pearl barley roulade with pickled wild mushrooms and Thai dressing. Pan-roasted haunch of venison with black pudding mash and pickled walnut jus. Iced Arran malt whisky parfait with berry coulis.

STB ★★★★★ Visitor Attraction

◐ *Open 7 days Apr to Oct (with reduced winter hours) Closed Mon evening* ✖ *Food available all day except Mon evening £ Lunch £ Dinner except Mon ££* Ⓥ *Vegetarians welcome* ✻ *Children welcome* ♿ *Facilities for disabled visitors* ✘ *Smoking area in restaurant* 💳 *Mastercard/Eurocard, Visa, Switch, Delta, JCB* ▧ *Head Chef: Gary Noble*

Isle of Arran Distillers Lochranza Isle of Arran KA27 8HJ
Tel: 01770 830264/830328 Fax: 01770 830364
E-mail: visitorcentre@arranwhisky.com
Web: www.arranwhisky.com
From Brodick follow signs to Lochranza. The Distillery Restaurant is located on the upper floor of the visitor centre. [B6]

ISLE OF ARRAN

ISLE OF ARRAN

Kilmichael Country House Hotel

- *"Make Kilmichael your first step off the ferry for unrivalled luxury and some of the best food on Arran."*
- *Superb modern cooking.*

KILMICHAEL IS AN ELEGANT and compact lodge, exquisitely furnished. Partners Geoffrey and Antony are charming hosts. The menus are very interesting and demonstrate French and Italian influences. Every dish has something unique and authentic about it, with piquant flavours and delicately spiced sauces. Service is excellent. Winner of The Macallan Taste of Scotland Award 1998.

Wild mushrooms and quails eggs in Parmesan pastry with rocket and a light dill dressing. Whole sea bream baked in sea salt brine infused with rosemary, garlic and chillies. Damson gin fool with home-made damson ice cream.

STB ★★★★★ Small Hotel

◑ *Open Apr to Oct* 🏠 *Rooms: 8 en suite* 🛏 *DB&B £89.50–£104.50 B&B £60–£75* 💲 *Special rates available* ✕ *Dinner £££ Dinner for non-residents – booking essential* Ⓥ *Vegetarians welcome* ♿ *Facilities for disabled visitors* ✖ *No smoking in dining room and bedrooms* 💳 *Mastercard/Eurocard, Visa, Switch, Delta* 🗡 *Partners: Geoffrey Botterill & Antony Butterworth*

Glen Cloy by Brodick Isle of Arran KA27 8BY
Tel: 01770 302219 Fax: 01770 302068
E-mail: enquiries@kilmichael.com
Web: www.kilmichael.com
From Brodick Pier take road north ½ mile, then turn left at golf course following signs about ¾ mile. [B6]

Kinloch Hotel

- *"Family hotel offering relaxation, with superb views."*
- *Modern Scottish.*

FAMILY OWNED for over 30 years Kinloch offers a warm friendly welcome in a relaxed comfortable atmosphere. It has glorious sea views and leisure facilities, including an indoor swimming pool. A unique feature at Kinloch is the bakery which produces bread and rolls for the restaurant. Fine examples of local produce are presented at Kinloch.

Wild mushroom risotto topped with smoked haddock, served with a mussel beurre blanc. Roast rack of Arran lamb presented with dauphinoise potatoes and a rich Madeira jus. Raspberry crème brûlée complemented with a Granny Smith apple sorbet.

STB ★★★ Hotel

◑ *Open all year* 🏠 *Rooms: 43 en suite* 🛏 *DB&B £59.20–£64 B&B £39.20–£49* 💲 *Special rates available* ✕ *Food available all day £ Lunch £ Dinner £££* Ⓥ *Vegetarians welcome* ♣ *Children welcome* ♿ *Facilities for disabled visitors* ✖ *No smoking in dining room* 🐕 *Dogs welcome – not in public areas* 💳 *Mastercard/Eurocard, American Express, Visa, Diners Club, Switch, Delta* 🗡 *Director: Robbie Crawford*

Blackwaterfoot Isle of Arran KA27 8ET
Tel: 01770 860444 Fax: 01770 860447
E-mail: kinloch@bestwestern.co.uk
Web: www.kinloch-arran.com
At Brodick, take A841 to Corrie then B880 to Blackwaterfoot for 10 miles. Rejoin A841 for ½ mile. Hotel in centre of village. [B6]

ISLE OF ARRAN

Pirates Cove Restaurant & Guest House

- *"A little treasure trove of good food and hospitality."*
- *Traditional and modern Scottish.*

ABANDON SHIP at Pirates Cove and enjoy Scotland's finest fresh produce cooked simply and served with a smile. Susan and Godfrey Hall are delightful hosts and Chef Brian Gracie offers a diverse menu choice from traditional classics (such as home-made savoury pies) to innovative new flavours and combinations which offer good value for money.

Quenelles of haggis, neeps and tatties with a sauce of the Lochranza malt. Fillet of Aberdeen Angus beef, Dunsyre fondue and wild Arran mushrooms. Cranachan with fresh Arran raspberries, home-made shortbread and Talisker whisky.

STB ★★ B&B

◐ *Open all year Closed Mon* 🏠 *Rooms: 2* 🛏 *DB&B £35–£50 B&B £19–£25* 🈺 *Special rates available* ✖ *Morning coffee except Mon £ Lunch except Mon ££ Dinner except Mon £££* Ⓥ *Vegetarians welcome* ✱ *Children welcome* ♿ *Facilities for disabled visitors* ✌ *No smoking in restaurant* 🐕 *Dogs welcome* 🏧 *Mastercard/ Eurocard, Visa, Switch, Delta, JCB, Solo, Maestro* 🔪 *Proprietors: Godfrey & Susan Hall*

Corrie Shore Corrie Isle of Arran KA27 8JA Tel: 01770 302438 Fax: 01770 302438 On leaving the ferry terminal, turn right onto the A841 signposted Blackwaterfoot and Lochranza, follow the A841 until signs for Corrie and Sannox. Pirates Cove is 5 miles along A841 from ferry terminal. [B6]

ISLE OF BENBECULA

Stepping Stone Restaurant

- *"A popular and friendly meeting place for locals and visitors."*
- *A blend of traditional and contemporary Scottish cooking.*

THE STEPPING STONE is an inspirational restaurant. Food is available all day from 10am–9pm including a mixture of sandwiches, rolls and home baking to more substantial meals. In the evening there is also a table d'hôte menu offering three, four or five course options including Scottish cheeses. Take-away food is also available.

Pan-fried local cockles in oatmeal. Roast Uist venison with rowanberry jelly. Home-grown strawberries with whisky cream.

◐ *Open all year – 7 days a week* ✖ *Food available all day £££ Lunch ££ Dinner £££* Ⓥ *Vegetarians welcome* ✱ *Children welcome* ♿ *Facilities for disabled visitors* ✌ *No smoking throughout* 🏧 *Mastercard/Eurocard, Visa, Switch, Delta* 🔪 *Manager: Ewen MacLean*

Balivanich Benbecula Western Isles HS7 5DA Tel: 01870 602659 Fax: 01870 603121 Drive south from Lochmaddy – heading for Benbecula, take sign for Balivanich – after 2½ miles turn into restaurant, just off the main road. [A4]

ISLE OF HARRIS

Leachin House

- *"Fine home cooking with peace and tranquility in abundance."*
- *Modern Scottish cooking.*

THE SKILL AND CARE with which Linda cooks and presents the food is worth a journey to Harris just to eat at Leachin House! Meals have a strong emphasis on local Hebridean produce and are served in a delightful dining room with its original 100 year old wallpaper!

Smoked wild venison with an asparagus salad. Fillet of salmon with a horseradish crust and a chive sauce. Raspberry and hazelnut roulade.

STB ★★★★ Guest House

◑ *Open all year except Christmas and New Year* ⌂ *Rooms: 3 (1 en suite, 1 with private facilities)* ⇔ *DB&B £75 B&B £45* ⬚ *Special rates available* ⬚ *Unlicensed* ✗ *Dinner £££ Residents only* ⚘ *Children over 10 years welcome* ✄ *No smoking in dining room or bedrooms* ⬚ *Mastercard/Eurocard, Visa, Delta* ⬚ *Owners: Linda & Diarmuid Evelyn Wood*

Tarbert Isle of Harris Outer Hebrides HS3 3AH
Tel: 01859 502157 Fax: 01859 502157
E-mail: leachin.house@virgin.net
Web: www.leachin-house.com
1 mile from Tarbert on A859 to Stornoway, signposted at gate. [A3]

ISLE OF HARRIS

Scarista House

- *"Exquisite food, charming service and breathtaking views – Scarista is a truly magical place!"*
- *Creative cooking using the finest ingredients.*

TIM AND PATRICIA MARTIN offer a truly welcoming stay at Scarista House. The cooking is adept and full of flavour and organic produce is used whenever possible. Superb fish and shellfish, fresh vegetables and herbs together with fresh eggs from the hotel's hens and the best of home-made bread.

Ravioli of Sound of Harris langoustines with squat lobster butter sauce. Roast rack of island lamb with heather honey scented gravy, stovies and confit of carrots, parsnips and celery. Floating islands with crème anglaise and raspberry sauce.

STB ★★★★ Guest House

◑ *Open all year closed occasionally in winter* ⌂ *Rooms: 5 en suite* ⇔ *DB&B £94 B&B from £61* ⚘ *Residents and table licence* ✗ *Dinner £££* ⬚ *Vegetarians welcome* ⚘ *Children welcome* ✄ *No smoking in dining room, bedrooms and drawing room; smoking permitted in the library* ⬚ *Mastercard/Eurocard, Visa* ⬚ *Owners: Tim & Patricia Martin*

Isle of Harris HS3 3HX
Tel: 01859 550238 Fax: 01859 550277
E-mail: timandpatricia@scaristahouse.com
Web: www.scaristahouse.com
On A859, 15 miles south-west of Tarbert (Western Isles). [A3]

ISLE OF ISLAY

The Croft Kitchen

- *"A pure delight where fresh local Islay produce is simply prepared and presented."*
- *Modern Scottish.*

THE CROFT KITCHEN offers a daytime menu of home baking, home-made soups, snacks and a good range of daily specials chosen from a blackboard at very reasonable prices. You will also find seafood freshly caught and simply, yet skilfully, prepared. There is a separate menu for dinner in the evening.

Fresh local prawns with garlic mayonnaise, smoked salmon and cream cheese pesto. Islay scallops lightly cooked in butter. Islay venison in a red wine sauce. Raspberry meringue roulade.

● *Open Easter to end Oct Closed mid afternoon Wed and 2nd Thu in Aug (Islay Show Day)* ❢ *Licensed* ✗ *Food available all day £ Lunch £ Dinner ££* Ⅵ *Vegetarians welcome* ✶ *Children welcome* ✔ *No smoking area in restaurant* ⊞ *Mastercard/Eurocard, Visa* ❚ *Joint Proprietors: Joy & Douglas Law*

Port Charlotte Isle of Islay PA49 7UN Tel: 01496 850 230 Fax: 01496 850 230 E-mail: douglas@croftkitchen.demon.co.uk On the main road into Port Charlotte opposite the Museum of Islay Life. [A6]

ISLE OF ISLAY

Glenmachrie Country Guest House

- *"A gastronomic delight aimed to satisfy the largest appetites."*
- *The best of home cooking.*

RELAX in the atmosphere of this family-run working farmhouse. No effort is spared by proprietor, Rachel Whyte, to meet the slightest whim of the guests. Rachel and her family are most attentive hosts. Splendid home cooking is served here with menus including Islay beef and lamb and wonderful home baking.

Timbale of smoked salmon and prawns with an orange and tarragon dressing. Dunlossit pheasant on a bed of caramelised onions drizzled with a redcurrant sauce. Pear, chocolate and frangipane tart with a jug of double cream.

STB ★★★★ Guest House

● *Open all year* 🏠 *Rooms: 5 en suite (2 twin, 3 double)* ⋈ *DB&B from £53 B&B from £30* Ⅶ *Unlicensed – guests welcome to take own wine* ✗ *Dinner ££ Residents only* ✶ *Children over five years welcome* ♿ *Facilities for disabled visitors (ground floor bedroom)* ✔ *No smoking throughout* ⊞ *No credit cards* ❚ *Proprietor: Rachel Whyte*

Port Ellen Isle of Islay PA42 7AW Tel: 01496 302560 Fax: 01496 302560 E-mail: glenmachrie@lineone.net Web: www.glenmachrie.com Midway on A846 between Port Ellen and Bowmore. [B6]

ISLE OF ISLAY

Kilmeny Country Guest House: Finalist The Macallan Taste of Scotland Awards 2001

- *"This beautifully restored home is run by people who really know how to make their guest's welcome."*
- *Unpretentious top quality cuisine.*

MARGARET AND BLAIR ROZGA enjoy a loyal following of guests from all over the world. Margaret is a highly accomplished cook and uses only the finest produce creating mouth-watering dishes. Her menus are well-planned and imaginative demanding skill and careful organisation – all of which she accomplishes single-handedly to great effect.

Grilled 'Loch Gruinart' oysters with a leek and Islay cheese topping. Loin of Colonsay lamb, roasted with rosemary, carved and served with a bramble and port sauce. Steamed marmalade pudding with a whisky and vanilla sauce.

STB ★★★★★ Guest House

◗ *Open all year except Christmas and New Year ⌂ Rooms: 3 en suite ⊯ DB&B £62 B&B £38 ⊠ Special rates available ⊞ Unlicensed – guests welcome to take own wine ✗ Residents only Ⓥ Vegetarians welcome ⊁ No smoking throughout ⊞ No credit cards ⋈ Proprietor: Mrs Margaret Rozga*

Ballygrant Isle of Islay PA45 7QW
Tel: 01496 840 668 Fax: 01496 840 668
E-mail: info@kilmeny.co.uk
Web: www.kilmeny.co.uk
½ mile south of Ballygrant village – look for sign at road end, then ¾ mile up private road. [B6]

ISLE OF LEWIS

Park Guest House & Restaurant

- *"With a focus on Hebridean flair, this is the ideal place to sample freshly prepared seafood, game and meats."*
- *Modern Scottish cooking with a continental influence.*

RODDY AND CATHERINE AFRIN are friendly hosts. Roddy was formerly head chef on an oil rig in the North Sea. His robust à la carte menus use fresh fish from Stornoway and the West Coast fishing boats. Local lamb and venison are cooked to order and skilfully prepared and presented.

Millefeuille of Stornoway black pudding and sweet potato, balsamic dressing. Fillet of halibut with herb crust served on risotto bed. Apple ice cream on a choux pastry ring, butterscotch sauce.

STB ★★★ Guest House

◗ *Open all year except 24 Dec to 5 Jan Note: Restaurant closed Sun Mon ⌂ Rooms: 8, 3 en suite ⊯ DB&B £38.50–£54 B&B £24–£29 ✗ Packed lunches available £ Dinner – residents only ££–£££ Dinner (Restaurant) Tue to Sat £££ Ⓥ Vegetarians welcome ⊀ Children welcome ⅏ Facilities for non-residential disabled visitors ⊞ Mastercard/Eurocard, Visa, Delta ⋈ Proprietor: Catherine Afrin Chef/Proprietor: Roddy Afrin*

30 James Street Stornoway Isle of Lewis HS1 2QN
Tel: 01851 70 2485 Fax: 01851 70 3482
500 yards from ferry terminal. At junction of Matheson Road, James Street and A866 to airport and Eye Peninsula. [B3]

ISLE OF MULL

Calgary Hotel

- *"Matthew and Julia are committed to giving their guests hospitality and very good food in an idyllic location."*
- *Modern Scottish cooking.*

THE SENSITIVELY CONVERTED Calgary Hotel has a warm, cosy environment. The Dovecote Restaurant's à la carte menu changes daily according to seasonal produce available. The accent is on skilful modern cooking in an informal atmosphere. There is also a tearoom, The Carthouse Gallery is open throughout the day for light lunches and home baking.

Rabbit in filo pastry with oranges and olives in a rabbit jus. Roasted fillet of cod on a Pecorino mash potato with buttered spinach, crispy anchovies and chive butter sauce. Lemon and meringue ice cream with tuile biscuits and orange custard.

STB ★★★ Small Hotel

◐ *Open Apr to Oct incl and weekends Mar Nov* ⌂ *Rooms: 9 en suite* ⋈ *DB&B £45–£65 B&B £29–£36* ✗ *Lunch £ Dinner ££* Ⓥ *Vegetarians welcome* ⚘ *Children welcome* ✄ *Smoking discouraged whilst others are eating* ⊞ *Mastercard/Eurocard, Visa, Switch* Ⓜ *Proprietors: Matthew & Julia Reade*

by Dervaig Isle of Mull PA75 6QW
Tel: 01688 400256 Fax: 01688 400256
E-mail: calgary.farmhouse@virgin.net
Web: www.calgary.co.uk
About 4½ miles from Dervaig on B8073, just up the hill from Calgary beach. [B5]

ISLE OF MULL

Druimard Country House

- *"A friendly, well-run country house hotel."*
- *Innovative Scottish.*

THE AMBIENCE OF DRUIMARD, is one of relaxed and comfortable style. Haydn and Wendy Hubbard are true professionals. The elegant award-winning restaurant offers outstanding cuisine and makes full use of the very best of Scottish produce. The serious dedicated approach by the kitchen is demonstrated in details such as home-made breads, sorbets and ice creams.

Aberdeen Angus fillet of beef on an olive oil crouton with Strathdon Blue cheese, port dressing, marinated red onions and rocket salad. Locally dived Mull scallops, saffron cream, leeks, smoked bacon, baby roasted tomatoes. Caramelised orange and lemon cheesecake, orange and Cointreau sauce, home-made tangy lemon ice cream.

STB ★★★★ Small Hotel

◐ *Open end Mar to end Oct* ⌂ *Rooms: 7 en suite* ⋈ *DB&B £65–£80* ♟ *Restaurant licence only* ✗ *Lunch – residents only £ Dinner – non-residents welcome £££* Ⓥ *Vegetarians welcome* ⚘ *Children welcome* ✄ *No smoking in restaurant* ⊞ *Mastercard/Eurocard, Visa, Switch, Delta, JCB, Solo* Ⓜ *Partners: Mr & Mrs H R Hubbard*

Dervaig Isle of Mull PA75 6QW
Tel: 01688 400345 Fax: 01688 400345
E-mail: druimard.hotel@virgin.net
Web: www.druimard.co.uk
Situated adjacent to Mull Little Theatre, well signposted from Dervaig village. [B5]

ISLE OF MULL

ISLE OF MULL

Druimnacroish Hotel

- *"A home-from-home atmosphere set in delightful gardens."*
- *Good quality Scottish cuisine.*

A LAID-BACK, friendly atmosphere surrounds this small spacious hotel with unspoilt views across the glen from every room. Margriet is a welcoming host and Neil's cooking is skilled and assured and something to look forward to after a day exploring Mull. Games and 'wellies' are provided for guests who wish to stroll through the gardens.

Isle of Mull scallops sautéed with white wine and lemon grass. Roast rack of Scottish lamb with a rowanberry gravy. Drambuie and orange parfait.

STB ★★★ Small Hotel

◖ *Open all year* 🏠 *Rooms: 6 en suite*
🛏 *DB&B £49–£59 B&B £32–£42* 🅂🄿 *Special rates available* ✗ *Dinner ££* Ⓥ *Vegetarians welcome* ✂ *No smoking in dining room* 🐾 *Dogs by arrangement* 💳 *Mastercard/ Eurocard, Visa, Switch, Delta* 🅗 *Owners: Neil Hutton & Margriet van de Pol*

Dervaig Isle of Mull PA75 6QW
Tel: 01688 400274 Fax: 01688 400274
E-mail: taste@druimnacroish.co.uk
Web: www.druimnacroish.co.uk
2 miles south of Dervaig on the Salen–Dervaig road. [B5]

Highland Cottage

- *"Fantastic hospitality and a truly memorable dining experience."*
- *Skilled use of modern culinary trends.*

H IGHLAND COTTAGE is a delightful small hotel. It is charming in style with a very high standard throughout and great attention to detail. Josephine Currie is a talented cook who uses excellent produce, her presentation is very professional. Josephine's husband Dave makes his guests feel relaxed and completely at home. Service is impressive.

Risotto of locally smoked haddock. Seared hand-dived scallops, parsnip purée and ginger cream. Raspberry meringue roulade.

STB ★★★★ Small Hotel
Green Tourism One Leaf Bronze Award

◖ *Open all year (restricted opening, winter months)* 🏠 *Rooms: 6 en suite*
🛏 *DB&B £60–£76 B&B £42.50–£66.50* 🅂🄿 *Special rates available* ✗ *Food available all day (residents only) Dinner non residents welcome £££* Ⓥ *Vegetarians welcome* ✿ *Children welcome* ♿ *Facilities for disabled visitors* ✂ *No smoking in dining room* 🐾 *Dogs welcome* 💳 *Mastercard/ Eurocard, Visa, Switch, Delta, JCB* 🅗 *Chef/ Owner: Josephine Currie*

Breadalbane Street Tobermory Isle of Mull PA75 6PD
Tel: 01688 302030 Fax: 01688 302727
E-mail: davidandjo@highlandcottage.co.uk
Web: www.highlandcottage.co.uk
On approaching Tobermory at the roundabout, carry on straight across narrow stone bridge and immediately turn right (signposted Tobermory-Breadalbane Street). Follow road round – Highland Cottage is opposite the Fire Station. [B5]

ISLE OF MULL

The Old Byre Heritage Centre

* *"Welcoming stop with mouth watering bakes."*
* *Home cooking and baking.*

THIS LICENSED tearoom offers a range of light meals, home baking and daily specials, using fresh Mull produce. Vegetarians are well catered for, and meals can be organised for groups by prior arrangement. At the Old Byre orders are placed at the counter, but the food is served at the table for the customer.

Home-made crofter's soup. Tobermory trout with salad and warm roll. Clootie dumpling served warm with cream.

STB ★★★ Visitor Attraction

◐ *Open 24 Mar to 25 Oct* ♟ *Licensed* ✖ *Light meals served throughout day £* Ⓥ *Vegetarians welcome* ⚘ *Children welcome* ⊞ *No credit cards* ⧆ *Joint Owners: Ursula & Michael Bradley*

The Old Byre Dervaig
Isle of Mull PA75 6QR
Tel: 01688 400229
1½ miles from Dervaig. Take Calgary road for ¾ mile, turn left along Torloisk road for ¼ mile, then left down private road following signs.
[B5]

ISLE OF MULL

Tiroran House

* *"A delightful country house hotel set in truly stunning gardens with hospitality to match."*
* *Modern Scottish.*

TIRORAN HOUSE is a charming country house owned and run by Colin and Jane Tindal. They are both welcoming hosts who make the stay at Tiroran a most pleasant and relaxing experience. Colin hosts front of house whilst Jane and a small team prepare excellent dishes using local and Scottish produce.

Seared Sound of Mull scallops with avocado salsa. Roast gigot of Scottish lamb with oatmeal and rosemary stuffing and creamy fennel sauce. Dark chocolate terrine with raspberry coulis and home-grown strawberries.

◐ *Open 1 Apr to 28 Oct* ⌂ *Rooms: 6 en suite* ⇔ *DB&B £66–£77 per person B&B £41–£52 per person* ⑤ *Special rates available* ✖ *Dinner non-residents – by prior arrangement £££* Ⓥ *Vegetarians welcome* ✂ *No smoking throughout* ⊞ *Mastercard/Eurocard, Visa* ⧆ *Proprietors: Colin & Jane Tindal*

Tiroran Isle of Mull PA69 6ES
Tel: 01681 705232 Fax: 01681 705240
E-mail: colin@tiroran.freeserve.co.uk
Web: www.tiroran.com
Turn off A849 Craignure–Iona Ferry road at Kinloch signed 'scenic route to Salen'. Along the B8035 for 4 miles: Tiroran House sign at converted church – 1 mile along minor road.
[B5]

ISLE OF MULL

The Western Isles Hotel

- *"Stunning views and fine service are enjoyed in this grand hotel."*
- *Scottish cooking with continental flair.*

THE WESTERN ISLES HOTEL occupies one of the finest positions set above the village of Tobermory. The bar lunch menu is extensive with a very wide choice. The dinner menu offers four courses on a table d'hôte menu of good, traditional Scottish cooking accompanied by a reasonably priced wine list.

Smoked Tobermory haddock in a puff pastry case, with a lemon and cashew nut sauce. Fine slices of local venison, with walnuts sautéed in hawthorn jelly. White chocolate cheesecake on a lake of rich chocolate sauce.

STB ★★★★ Hotel

◗ *Open all year except 17 to 28 Dec* 🏨 *Rooms: 28 en suite* 🛏 *DB&B £55.50–£122.50 B&B £42–£98* 💷 *Special rates available* ✗ *Bar Lunch £ Dinner £££* Ⓥ *Vegetarians welcome* ✷ *Children welcome* ✠ *No smoking in dining room* 🖾 *Mastercard/Eurocard, American Express, Visa, Switch* 🍴 *Proprietors: Sue & Michael Fink*

Tobermory Isle of Mull PA75 6PR
Tel: 01688 302012 Fax: 01688 302297
E-mail: wihotel@aol.com
Web: www.mullhotel.com
Leaving Tobermory seafront on the Dervaig road take a sharp right and turn halfway up the hillside. [B5]

ISLE OF NORTH UIST

Langass Lodge

- *"You would struggle to find finer quality or fresher seafood anywhere else in Scotland."*
- *Modern Scottish.*

LANGASS LODGE offers the old world comfort of a traditional shooting lodge with the added delights of a dedicated and skilled chef. Chef John Buchanan's daily changing menu features mainly fish dishes and the understated 'selection of seafood' is a memorable experience. The fishing in the area is renowned, naturalists can enjoy the wildlife.

Avocado and fresh crab salad with mint and lemon dressing. Rack of Scottish lamb glazed with heather honey. Fresh lemon tart with crème fraîche.

STB ★★★ Small Hotel

◗ *Open all year except Christmas Day* 🏨 *Rooms: 6 en suite* 🛏 *DB&B £65–£90 B&B £36–£60* ✗ *Food available all day ££ Lunch ££ Dinner £££* Ⓥ *Vegetarians welcome* ✷ *Children welcome* ♿ *Facilities for disabled visitors* 🐾 *Dogs welcome* 🖾 *Mastercard/ Eurocard, Visa, Switch* 🍴 *Manager: Niall Leveson-Gower*

Langass Isle of North Uist The Western Isles HS6 5HA
Tel: 01876 580285 Fax: 01876 580385
E-mail: langasslodge@btconnect.com
Web: www.witb.co.uk/langasslodge.htm
Take the B867 south from Lochmaddy for 10 miles. The hotel is clearly signposted from the main road. [A3]

ISLE OF SKYE

Ardvasar Hotel

- *"A popular spot with locals and visitors who are enjoying the view and a cheerful environment."*
- *Accomplished Scottish cuisine.*

MICHAEL AND CHRISTINE CASS are well settled at Ardvasar, and extend a warm welcome to everyone. The cooking is accomplished using the best of local produce. This is a hotel committed to good hospitality and quality eating. You may choose from relaxed eating in the lounge bar or a more formal dining room setting.

Warm salad of Brie, bacon and olives and cranberry sauce. Fillets of lemon sole with lime and roast strawberries. Dark chocolate pie with Chantilly cream.

STB ★★★ Small Hotel

◑ *Open all year* ⌂ *Rooms: 9 en suite* ⇔ *DB&B £62.50–£72.50 B&B £40–£70* ⑤ℙ *Special rates available* ✖ *Food available all day ££–£££ Lunch £–£££ Dinner ££–£££* Ⓥ *Vegetarians welcome* ✲ *Children welcome* ✖ *No smoking in dining room* ⊨ *Dogs welcome* ⊞ *Mastercard/ Eurocard, Visa, Switch, Delta* ⋈ *Owner: Mrs Christine Cass*

Sleat Isle of Skye IV45 8RS
Tel: 01471 844223 Fax: 01471 844495
E-mail: christine@ardvasar-hotel.demon.co.uk
Short distance from Armadale Ferry close to Armadale Castle and Museum of the Isle. [B4]

ISLE OF SKYE

Atholl House Hotel

- *"A hospitable spot where freshly prepared food is a priority."*
- *Competent Scottish cooking with some Caribbean influences.*

ATHOLL HOUSE HOTEL is situated at the head of Loch Dunvegan and looks out on to the Macleod's Tables. New owners Christine Oliver and John Whittaker have already started to make their own particular mark. The atmosphere is warm and hospitable and Christine's accomplished cooking reflects their past experience on a charter yacht in the Caribbean.

Loch Dunvegan prawns in garlic butter with a salad of Glendale organic leaves. Medallions of Highland lamb with a mint and honey sauce served on a pillow of rosemary and garlic mash. Skye whisky and marmalade pudding.

STB ★★ Small Hotel

◑ *Open 5 Mar to 31 Oct and 15 Dec to 5 Jan* ⌂ *Rooms: 9 en suite* ⇔ *DB&B £50–£66 B&B £34–£48* ⑤ℙ *Special rates available* ✖ *Food available all day £ Lunch £ Dinner £££* Ⓥ *Vegetarians welcome* ✲ *Children welcome* ✖ *No smoking in restaurant* ⊨ *Dogs welcome* ⊞ *Mastercard/Eurocard, American Express, Visa, Switch, Delta* ⋈ *Owners: Christine Oliver & John Whittaker*

Dunvegan Isle of Skye IV55 8WA
Tel: 01470 521219 Fax: 01470 521481
E-mail: reservations@athollhotel.demon.co.uk
Web: www.athollhotel.demon.co.uk
Centre of village of Dunvegan, 1 mile from Dunvegan Castle. [A4]

ISLE OF SKYE

Bosville Hotel

- *"Interesting dishes are created by Chef John Kelly and his team using quality game and seafood."*
- *French cuisine using the best of Scottish produce.*

THE BOSVILLE HOTEL commands fine views from its elevated position and the Chandlery Restaurant produces meals, reflecting the local produce, with some exceptional presentation. Table d'hôte lunch and dinner menus are presented, using local produce wherever possible and featuring a number of Scottish specialities.

Cannelloni of Skye langoustines with squid ink pasta, plum tomatoes and saffron vinaigrette. Poached hare loin on parsnip purée with glazed chestnuts, port wine sauce and gooseberries in brandy. Rhubarb bavarois served with spiced rhubarb compote and oatmeal biscuits.

STB ★★★★ Small Hotel

◗ *Open all year* 🛏 *Rooms: 15 en suite* ⇔ *DB&B £44–£85 B&B £35–£60* 🆂🅿 *Special rates available* ✘ *Food available all day £ Lunch £ Dinner ££* Ⓥ *Vegetarians welcome* ⚘ *Children welcome* ♿ *Facilities for disabled visitors* ✄ *No smoking throughout* 💳 *Mastercard/Eurocard, American Express, Visa, Switch, Delta* 🅽 *Hotel Manager: Donald W Macleod*

9–10 Bosville Terrace Portree Isle of Skye IV51 9DG
Tel: 01478 612846 Fax: 01478 613434
E-mail: bosville@macleodhotels.co.uk
Web: www.macleodhotels.co.uk/bosville/
Town centre, on terrace above Portree harbour. [B4]

ISLE OF SKYE

Cuillin Hills Hotel

- *"Flavoursome dishes can be enjoyed in this well-cared for hotel, which offers good service and commanding views."*
- *French/Scottish traditional.*

THE CUILLIN HILLS has been extensively upgraded and stands in 15 acres of mature private grounds overlooking Portree Bay. Bedrooms are comfortable and decorated to a high standard and public rooms are decorated with quality furnishings. Chef Jeff Johnston's daily changing menu features fresh local produce presented in an imaginative way.

Warm crab Niçoise salad served in fresh artichoke heart with a sauce vierge. Canon of Highland venison with pears poached in mulled wine with gin, redcurrant and juniper berry. Strawberry shortcake with an Atholl brose cream and fresh raspberry coulis.

STB ★★★★ Hotel

◗ *Open all year* 🛏 *Rooms: 30 en suite* ⇔ *DB&B £45–£110 B&B £40–£90* 🆂🅿 *Special rates available* ✘ *Lunch £ Dinner £££* Ⓥ *Vegetarians welcome* ⚘ *Children welcome* ♿ *Facilities for disabled visitors* ✄ *No smoking in restaurant* 💳 *Mastercard/Eurocard, American Express, Visa, Switch, Delta* 🅽 *General Manager: Mr Murray McPhee*

Portree Isle of Skye IV51 9QU
Tel: 01478 612003 Fax: 01478 613092
E-mail: office@cuillinhills.demon.co.uk
Web: www.cuillinhills.demon.co.uk
Turn right ¼ mile north of Portree on A855 and follow hotel signs. [B4]

ISLE OF SKYE

Dunorin House Hotel

- *"You have comfort and choice of well-prepared food at Dunorin with the added attraction of a little corner bar which offers malt whiskies, with good conversation."*
- *Traditional, Scottish island cooking.*

THIS HOTEL ENJOYS panoramic views across Loch Roag to the Cuillin Hills. With many local recipes, the hotel's daily changing table d'hôte menu seeks to make the most of fresh local produce, such as scallops, venison, salmon, beef and lamb. The wine list is reasonably priced and varied.

Loch Dunvegan langoustine cocktail. Roast leg of Skye lamb served with minted pear, gravy and fresh vegetables. Granny's clootie dumpling with home-made custard.

STB ★★★★ Small Hotel

◐ *Open 1 Apr to 15 Nov except 2 weeks Oct* ⌂ *Rooms: 10 en suite* ⇔ *DB&B £50–£68 B&B £36–£45* ⓢⱼ *Special rates available* ♟ *Restricted hotel licence* ✗ *Dinner £££ non-residents – bookings only* Ⓥ *Vegetarians welcome* ⚎ *Children welcome* ⚒ *Facilities for disabled visitors* ⚓ *No smoking in dining room and bedrooms* ⊞ *Mastercard/Eurocard, Visa* ⚑ *Partners: Alasdair & Joan MacLean*

Herebost Dunvegan Isle of Skye IV55 8GZ
Tel: 01470 521488 Fax: 01470 521488
E-mail: stay@dunorin.freeserve.co.uk
Web: www.dunorin.com
From Skye Bridge A87 to Sligachan, then A863 to Dunvegan. 2 miles south of Dunvegan turn left at Roag/Orbost junction, 200m on right. [B4]

ISLE OF SKYE

Hotel Eilean Iarmain

- *"Comfortable beds and well-prepared produce guarantee a good night's sleep."*
- *Modern Scottish cooking.*

OWNED BY SIR IAIN and Lady Noble, this 19th century Victorian inn is located in a truly romantic setting by the seaside of Isle Ornsay. The award-winning restaurant offers an abundance of fresh local produce, specialising in seafood fresh from the harbour and game from the hotel's estate. Bar meals available.

Peat-smoked salmon and tail of langoustine roulade. Saddle of Skye lamb, oatmeal and onion mash, roast shallots, port and thyme jus. Cinnamon-poached seasonal fruits.

STB ★★★ Hotel

◐ *Open all year* ⌂ *Rooms: 16 (all en suite) incl 4 suites* ⇔ *DB&B £91–£121 B&B £60–£90* ⓢⱼ *Special rates available* ✗ *Lunch – booking essential ££ Dinner – advance reservation advisable ££££* Ⓥ *Vegetarians welcome* ⚎ *Children welcome* ⚓ *No smoking in restaurant* ⊞ *Mastercard/Eurocard, American Express, Visa, Switch, Delta, Solo* ⚑ *Proprietors: Sir Iain & Lady Noble*

Isle Ornsay Sleat Isle of Skye Inverness-shire IV43 8QR
Tel: 01471 833 332 Fax: 01471 833 275
E-mail: hotel@eilean-iarmain.co.uk
Web: www.eileaniarmain.co.uk
From Mallaig/Armadale ferry turn right on to A851 for 8 miles, then right at sign Isle Ornsay, hotel is down at waters edge. From Skye Bridge take road to Broadford and turn off left at junction signed A851 to Armadale. Drive 8 miles, turn left at Isle of Ornsay signpost, drive for a ¼ of a mile, hotel situated at harbour front. [B4]

ISLE OF SKYE

Kinloch Lodge

- *"Kinloch Lodge has yet another accolade – the perfect recipe for warmth, hospitality and ambience."*
- *Outstanding traditional cooking with innovative influences.*

HOME OF LORD MACDONALD of Macdonald, Kinloch Lodge is full of portraits of ancestors, old furniture and family treasures. Claire Macdonald, one of Scotland's best known cooks, presents a five-course table d'hôte menu each night using only fresh seasonal produce. Winner of The Macallan Taste of Scotland Award 1998.

Skye scallop terrine with locally-grown watercress and shallot sauce. Roast rack of Highland bred lamb with pinhead oatmeal and cracked black pepper crust, and minty hollandaise. Baked dark and white chocolate cheesecake with bitter orange sauce.

STB ★★★★ Small Hotel

❍ *Open all year except Christmas* 🏠 *Rooms: 14 en suite* 🛏 *DB&B £70–£130 B&B £45–£95* 🆂 *Special rates available* ✗ *Dinner 5 course menu ££££* Ⓥ *Vegetarians welcome – prior notice required* 🕏 *Children welcome by arrangement* ✂ *No smoking in dining room* 💳 *Mastercard/Eurocard, American Express, Visa* 🐾 *Proprietors: Lord & Lady Macdonald*

Sleat Isle of Skye IV43 8QY
Tel: 01471 833214 Fax: 01471 833277
E-mail: kinloch@dial.pipex.com
Web: www.kinloch-lodge.co.uk
8 miles south of Broadford on A851. 10 miles north of Armadale on A851. 1 mile off A851.
[B4]

ISLE OF SKYE

Rosedale Hotel

- *"A warm welcome and good local walking information can be had here – you will need it after eating the enjoyable food."*
- *Modern Scottish.*

THE FIRST FLOOR RESTAURANT has splendid views out over the bay where Chef Kirk Moir presents a daily changing table d'hôte dinner menu offering imaginative dishes, based on fresh local produce. You may even see the fishermen unloading the day's catch which may appear on tomorrow's menu. Service is very good here.

A melody of Skye mussels and prawns in a saffron and white wine velouté. Locally-caught smoked monkfish tails filled with a seafood mousse, wrapped in bacon and set on a duo of pepper sauces. Warm home-made Dundee cake served with marmalade ice cream.

STB ★★★★ Hotel

❍ *Open Apr to Nov* 🏠 *Rooms: 23 en suite* 🛏 *DB&B £57–£72 B&B £36–£51* 🆂 *Special rates available* ✗ *Dinner £££* Ⓥ *Vegetarians welcome* 🕏 *Children welcome* ✂ *No smoking in restaurant and all bedrooms* 🐕 *Dogs welcome by prior arrangement* 💳 *Mastercard/Eurocard, Visa, Switch, Delta* 🐾 *Owners: Paul & Allison Rouse*

Beaumont Crescent Portree
Isle of Skye IV51 9DB
Tel: 01478 613131 Fax: 01478 612531
E-mail: Duncan@achnacraig.freeserve.co.uk
Web: www.Rosedalehotelskye.co.uk
Down in the harbour, 100 yards from village square. [B4]

ISLE OF SKYE

Roskhill House

- *"A home-from-home where the cooking is assured and breakfast is a little special."*
- *Traditional Scottish cooking.*

ROSKHILL HOUSE is a traditional croft house which was built in 1890. The atmosphere is very informal but caring. Proprietor Gillian Griffith offers very warm and sincere Scottish hospitality. Menus are well-thought out and use excellent locally-sourced produce which is then cooked in a sympathetic style.

Roast leg of lamb with garlic and rosemary and seasonal fresh vegetables. Banana bread and butter pudding.

STB ★★★★ Guest House

◐ *Open Mar to Oct* 🏠 *Rooms: 4 (3 en suite, 1 private facilities)* 🛏 *DB&B £41.50–£49.50 B&B £27–£35* 💷 *Special rates available* 🍷 *Restricted hotel licence* ✖ *Residents only Dinner ££* Ⓥ *Vegetarian and special diets catered for* 🕯 *Children over 10 years welcome* 🚭 *No smoking throughout* 💳 *Mastercard/ Eurocard, American Express, Visa, Switch, Delta, JCB, Solo* 🔑 *Proprietor: Gillian Griffith*

by Dunvegan Isle of Skye IV55 8ZD
Tel: 01470 521317 Fax: 01470 521761
E-mail: stay@roskhill.demon.co.uk
Web: www.roskhill.demon.co.uk
2 miles south of Dunvegan on A863, turn off road at River Rosgill. [B4]

ISLE OF SKYE

Rowan Cottage

- *"Well worth the drive down – stunning scenery, comfort and friendliness await you."*
- *Good home cooking.*

ROWAN COTTAGE is home to Ruth Shead and is a delightful, traditional croft house. It is an excellent spot from which to enjoy this beautiful part of Skye and has panoramic views over Loch Slapin. Ruth is an accomplished and enthusiastic cook who serves good home cooking using best local produce.

Home-made parsnip and apple soup. Local-dived Skye scallops in a white wine and mushroom sauce, seasonal vegetables. Sticky toffee pudding with sauce and cream.

STB ★★★★ B&B

◐ *Open 23 Mar to early Nov* 🏠 *Rooms: 3, 1 en suite* 🛏 *DB&B £36.50–£46.50 B&B £20–£25* 🍷 *Licensed* ✖ *Residents only Dinner ££–£££* Ⓥ *Vegetarians welcome* 🚭 *No smoking throughout* 🐕 *Dogs welcome – by arrangement* 💳 *No credit cards* 🔑 *Owner: Ruth Shead*

9 Glasnakille By Elgol Isle of Skye IV49 9BQ
Tel: 01471 866287 Fax: 01471 866287
E-mail: rowan@rowancott.demon.co.uk
Web: www.rowancott.demon.co.uk
From Broadford take the A8083 to Elgol, 15 miles down a single track road. From Elgol take turning to Glasnakille for 2 miles, turn left at the T-junction by phone box. Continue for 100m to the first house on the left. [B4]

ISLE OF SKYE

Skeabost House Hotel

- *"Stylish presentation of skilfully prepared quality local produce is evident in this interesting house."*
- *Contemporary Scottish cooking.*

SKEABOST HOUSE is a comfortable and relaxing hotel located in 30 acres of woodland and landscaped gardens. Under new owners the Heaney family, Skeabost has already carried out some well-chosen and thoughtful refurbishment. Chef Timothy Morris presents stylish menus using good local produce which is skilfully cooked and tastefully presented.

Open ravioli of wild sorrel and local scallops in a parsley pesto. Roasted rack of spring lamb with a Perigourdine truffle farce. Chocolate cappuccino with fresh cherries in Kirsch.

STB ★★★ Hotel

◑ *Open 1 March to 7 Jan* 🏨 *Rooms: 26, 25 en-suite* 🛏 *DB&B £69–86.50 B&B £45–£62.50* 🏷 *Special rates available* ✗ *Lunch £ Dinner £££* Ⅴ *Vegetarians welcome* ✻ *Children welcome* ♿ *Facilities for disabled visitors* ✄ *No smoking in dining room* 🐕 *Dogs welcome by arrangement* 💳 *Mastercard/Eurocard, Visa, Switch, Delta* 🅗 *Owners: Michael & Ann Heaney*

Skeabost Bridge Isle of Skye IV51 9NP
Tel: 01470 532 202 Fax: 01470 532 454
E-mail: skeabost@sol.co.uk.
Web: www.sol.co.uk/s/skeabost
4 miles north of Portree on Dunvegan road.
[B4]

ISLE OF SKYE

The Three Chimneys Restaurant And The House Over-By

- *"A wonderful culinary experience and a celebration of the finest Scottish produce."*
- *Natural skilled Scottish cooking.*

THREE CHIMNEYS is a joy! Fresh Skye seafood is a speciality but lamb, beef, game and a vegetarian option are also offered. The wine list is extensive and carefully compiled. Winner of The Macallan Taste of Scotland Award 1998 and 1999, and Overall Excellence Award 1999.

Bracadale crab risotto. Roast breast of wild mallard, crushed potato with celeriac, spiced red cabbage, plum and port wine sauce. Old- fashioned fruity bread pudding with Caledonian ice cream and sharp orange syrup.

STB ★★★★★ Restaurant with Rooms

◑ *Open virtually all year Closed Sun lunch and lunch in winter months* 🏨 *Rooms: 6 en suite* ✗ *Lunch except Sun ££–££££ Dinner 3 course menu £££–££££* Ⅴ *Vegetarians welcome* ✻ *Children welcome* ♿ *Disabled access* ✄ *No smoking in restaurant* 💳 *Mastercard/Eurocard, American Express, Visa, Switch* 🅗 *Owners: Eddie & Shirley Spear*

Colbost by Dunvegan Isle of Skye IV55 8ZT
Tel: 01470 511258 Fax: 01470 511358
E-mail: eatandstay@threechimneys.co.uk
Web: www.threechimneys.co.uk
4 miles west of Dunvegan on B884 road to Glendale. Look out for Glendale Visitor Route signs. [A4]

ISLE OF SKYE

Viewfield House

- *"An enjoyable meal in an elegant dining room with good company."*
- *Traditional Scottish with modern influences.*

VIEWFIELD has been a family home for over five generations and many original features remain. Your host is Hugh Macdonald who welcomes you into his home with real Highland hospitality. The cooking here is exceptional and highly skilled using only the best produce prepared and presented with an innovative twist and successfully executed.

Pan-fried scallops with tarragon butter. Saddle of venison with hawthorn sauce. Elderflower cake with fresh Skye strawberries.

STB ★★★ Small Hotel

◑ *Open mid Apr to mid Oct* ⌂ *Rooms: 12, 10 en suite* ⊟ *DB&B £55–£65 B&B £35–£47.50* ⑤ *Special rates available* ✗ *Dinner ££* Ⅴ *Vegetarians welcome* ⚹ *Children welcome* ♿ *Facilities for disabled visitors* ✔ *No smoking in dining room* 🐕 *Dogs welcome* 🖃 *Mastercard/ Eurocard, Visa, Switch, Maestro, JCB* ⓜ *Chef/ Proprietors: Mr Hugh Macdonald & Mrs Linda Macdonald*

Portree Isle of Skye IV51 9EU
Tel: 01478 612217 Fax: 01478 613517
E-mail: info@viewfieldhouse.com
Web: www.viewfieldhouse.com
Viewfield House is located off the main road from Kyleakin to Portree, as you approach Portree. [B4]

ISLE OF SOUTH UIST

Orasay Inn

- *"Delicious home cooking with a focus on simply prepared local seafood."*
- *Scottish home cooking.*

ORASAY INN is a modern house which has been extended to form a small country hotel. The dining room commands stunning views across the Minch and also to the mountains of South Uist. There is also a very comfortable lounge in which to relax and enjoy the comforts in front of the peat fire.

Lochcarnan Bay Platter: a mix of Hebridean shellfish, lightly battered and served with home-made tartare sauce. Partan Chicken: Uist crabmeat stuffed inside a breast of chicken and served on a bed of diced, oatmeal potatoes. Home-made hot chocolate fudge cake with fresh cream or ice cream.

STB ★★ Inn

◑ *Open all year except Christmas Day* ⌂ *Rooms: 9 en suite* ⊟ *DB&B £34–£75 B&B £29–£65* ⑤ *Special rates available* ✗ *Food available all day £–££ Lunch £ Dinner ££* Ⅴ *Vegetarians welcome* ⚹ *Children welcome* ♿ *Facilities for disabled visitors* ✔ *No smoking in dining room* 🖃 *Mastercard/Eurocard, American Express, Visa, Switch, Delta, JCB* ⓜ *Proprietors: Alan & Isobel Graham*

Lochcarnan Isle of South Uist Western Isles HS8 5PD
Tel: 01870 610298 Fax: 01870 610390
E-mail: orasayinn@btinternet.com
20 miles from Lochboisdale A865, 24 miles from Lochmaddy. [A4]

ISLES OF ORKNEY

Cleaton House Hotel

- *"This house is set in splendid isolation, with food and hospitality to make the trip even more worthwhile."*
- *Modern Scottish cuisine using high quality Orcadian produce.*

A REGULAR roll-on, roll-off ferry service connects Westray to Kirkwall, and Cleaton's owner Malcolm Stout is happy to meet you at the pier. Chef Lorna Reid marries her experience with outstanding local ingredients, producing quality cuisine complemented by Malcolm's wine list. In season, herbs and vegetables come from the hotel's vegetable garden.

Open lasagne of crab, mussel and squid in lime-scented butter sauce. Orkney fillet steak topped with onion marmalade, garnished with straw sweet potato chips and sautéed mushrooms. Sticky toffee pudding, toffee sauce and home-made chocolate ripple ice cream.

STB ★★★★ Small Hotel
Green Tourism Three Leaf Gold Award

❍ *Open all year except Nov and Christmas Day* 🏠 *Rooms: 6 en suite* 🛏 *DB&B £57–£67.50 B&B £34.50–£45* 💷 *Special rates available* ✖ *Lunch £ Dinner ££* Ⓥ *Vegetarians welcome – notice preferred* 🧒 *Children welcome* ♿ *Facilities for disabled visitors* 🚭 *No smoking in dining room or bedrooms* 💳 *Mastercard/ Eurocard, Visa, Switch, Delta* 🁢 *Proprietor: Malcolm Stout*

Westray Orkney KW17 2DB
Tel: 01857 677508 Fax: 01857 677442
E-mail: cleaton@orkney.com
Web: www.cleatonhouse.com
5 miles from Rapness (Westray) Ferry terminal. [D1]

ISLES OF ORKNEY

Creel Restaurant & Rooms

- *"Excellent food prepared by a master of his art, served in pleasant surroundings overlooking the harbour."*
- *Innovative modern cooking with a hint of Orcadian influence.*

T HIS SMALL, family-run restaurant has an international reputation. Menus change daily to suit the supply of fresh produce. Alan Craigie cooks with great skill and the Creel has rightly become a place of pilgrimage for gourmets, but its cheerful understated ambience remains unchanged. Winner of The Macallan Taste of Scotland Award 1997.

Green crab bisque. Fillet of beef with onion marmalade. Strawberry shortcake.

STB ★★★ Restaurant with Rooms
Green Tourism Three Leaf Gold Award

❍ *Open weekends Oct to Mar except Jan: daily Apr to Sep – advisable to book, especially in low season Closed Christmas Day and Boxing Day, Jan, Feb and 3 weeks Oct* 🏠 *Rooms: 3 en suite* 🛏 *B&B £33–£35* ✖ *Dinner £££* Ⓥ *Vegetarians welcome* 🧒 *Children 5 years and over welcome* 🚭 *No smoking in restaurant* 💳 *Mastercard/Eurocard, Visa, Switch, Delta* 🁢 *Owners: Joyce & Alan Craigie*

Front Road St Margaret's Hope Orkney KW17 2SL
Tel: 01856 831 311
E-mail: alan@thecreel.freeserve.co.uk
Web: www.thecreel.co.uk
Take A961 south across the Churchill Barriers into St Margaret's Hope. 14 miles from Kirkwall. [D2]

ISLES OF ORKNEY

Foveran Hotel & Restaurant

- *"A comfortable hotel offering friendliness, informality and great food."*
- *Modern Scottish with Orcadian influence.*

UNDER NEW OWNERS, the Doull family, the Foveran Hotel and Restaurant has continued to develop its reputation for excellent Orcadian hospitality and good food. The atmosphere is relaxed and the cooking is skilled, making best use of local Orcadian produce and presenting it with a contemporary flair.

Pan-seared scallops, accompanied with crisp parsnip shavings and traditional bannocks. Prime Orkney fillet steak with onions, haggis, light pastry lattice, finished with a creamy whisky sauce. Orkney ice cream terrine with summer berry yoghurt and a raspberry coulis.

STB ★★★ Small Hotel

◐ *Open all year except Christmas Day and New Year's Day Closed Sun Mon when no residents* 🏨 *Rooms: 8, 7 en suite* 🛏 *DB&B £55–£65 B&B £35–£45* ✕ *Lunch – residents by arrangement £ Dinner £££* Ⓥ *Vegetarians welcome* ⚭ *Children welcome* ⚬ *Limited facilities for disabled guests* ✌ *Smoking in lounge only* 🖸 *Mastercard/Eurocard, Visa, Switch, Solo* 🅼 *Proprietors: The Doull Family*

St Ola Kirkwall Orkney KW15 1SF
Tel: 01856 87 2389 Fax: 01856 87 6430
E-mail: foveranhotel@aol.com
Web: www.foveranhotel.co.uk
From Kirkwall take the A964 to Orphir, carry on this route for approx 3 miles passing the Scapa Distillery on your way. Hotel signpost on right-hand side. [D2]

ISLES OF ORKNEY

Orkney Hotel

- *"Charming and attentive staff, good food and a friendly atmosphere is offered at this hotel."*
- *Modern Scottish.*

THE ORKNEY HOTEL has central Kirkwall's only Taste of Scotland restaurant. It serves superb local produce imaginatively and attentively in comfortable surroundings. The hotel is close to St Magnus Cathedral at the ancient heart of Orkney's capital.

Twice baked Grimbister cheese soufflé with a saffron olive oil. Organic Orkney salmon with a king scallop, rested on crab stovies and a lemon butter sauce. Dark Island clootie dumpling with fresh custard.

STB ★★★ Hotel
Green Tourism One Leaf Bronze Award

◐ *Open all year except 1 to 3 Jan* 🏨 *Rooms: 30 en suite* 🆂 *Special rates available* ✕ *Open to non-residents Lunch except Oct to Apr ££ Dinner £££* Ⓥ *Vegetarians welcome* ⚭ *Children welcome* ✌ *No smoking in restaurant* 🖸 *Mastercard/Eurocard, Visa, Switch, Delta, JCB* 🅼 *Owners: The Spence Family*

40 Victoria Street Kirkwall Orkney KW15 1DN
Tel: 01856 873477 Fax: 01856 872767
E-mail: info@orkneyhotel.co.uk
Web: www.orkneyhotel.co.uk
Located in Victoria Street, the very heart of Orkney's capital, Kirkwall. 150 metres from St Magnus Cathedral. [D2]

ISLES OF ORKNEY

ISLES OF SHETLAND

Woodwick House

- *"A special peaceful place with home-cooked food."*
- *Orcadian produce imaginatively prepared.*

WOODWICK HOUSE is a welcoming country house set in 12 acres of bluebell woodland with a burn that cascades down to a secluded bay. Candlelit meals are prepared with care using prime quality local produce and seafood. Situated on Orkney's West Mainland, Woodwick is an excellent place from which to explore these ancient islands.

Local mussels steamed with fresh thyme and parsley. Freshly opened scallops seared with ginger and spring onion served with a cream wine sauce and fresh locally grown vegetables. Hazelnut meringue with Orkney cream and Rousay strawberries.

STB ★★★ Small Hotel

◗ *Open all year* ♨ *Rooms: 7, 4 en suite* ♨ *DB&B £40–£70 B&B £28–£48* ✖ *Lunch ££ Dinner ££–£££* Ⓥ *Vegetarians welcome* ♣ *Children welcome* ♿ *Facilities for disabled visitors* ✄ *No smoking in dining room* 💳 *Mastercard/Eurocard, Visa, Delta* 🅺 *Co-Proprietor: Ann Herdman*

Evie Orkney KW17 2PQ Tel: 01856 751 330 Fax: 01856 751 383 E-mail: woodwickhouse@appleonline.net Web: www.orknet.co.uk/woodwick From A965 Stromness–Kirkwall road, turn off at Finstown towards Evie. After 7 miles, turn right at sign to Woodwick House. Follow sign first left, taking the track past the farm and continue on to the house amongst the trees. [D2]

Almara

- *"Feel cared for and well-fed here at Almara."*
- *Traditional home cooking.*

MARCIA's HOSPITALITY is a true reflection of her commitment to make every single guest's experience of Shetland a memorable one. The guest house is unlicensed, however guests are most welcome to take their own wine. Cooking here is accomplished yet kept simple, making the best of what is available locally. This is a little treasure.

Deep-fried squid with chilli coleslaw. Valhalla Casserole – Shetland lamb, marinated and braised in Unst ale. Almara crumble – stuffed apricots topped with a crunchie crumble.

STB ★★★★ B&B
Green Tourism Three Leaf Gold Award

◗ *Open all year* ♨ *Rooms: 3, 2 en suite* ♨ *DB&B £34 B&B £22* ⓢⓟ *Special rates available* Ⓤ *Unlicensed – guests welcome to take own wine* ✖ *Dinner ££ Residents only* Ⓥ *Vegetarians welcome* ♣ *Children welcome* ✄ *No smoking in bedrooms, sitting room and dining room* 💳 *No credit cards* 🅺 *Proprietor: Marcia Williamson*

Upper Urafirth Hillswick Shetland ZE2 9RH Tel: 01806 503 261 Fax: 01806 503 261 E-mail: almara@zetnet.co.uk Web: www.users.zetnet.co.uk/almara/ Follow the A970 north to Hillswick. 1½ miles before Hillswick follow signs to Upper Urafirth and Almara. [E2]

ISLES OF SHETLAND

Busta House Hotel

- *"A peaceful retreat with wonderful views and fine hospitality."*
- *Scottish with Modern influences.*

THIS HISTORIC SHETLAND house is under the new ownership of Joe Rocks and continues to offer an excellent experience in one of Scotland's most northerly establishments. Chef Pat Shaw prepares and presents food to the highest of standards and as expected makes excellent use of local Shetland produce.

Home made leek and potato soup. Grilled Shetland salmon with citrus butter. Lemon meringue pie.

STB ★★★ Hotel
Green Tourism Two Leaf Silver Award

◑ *Open all year* ⌂ *Rooms: 20 with private facilities* ⇔ *On application* ⑲ *Special rates available* ✗ *Bar lunch £–££ Dinner ££–£££* Ⓥ *Vegetarians welcome* ☂ *Children welcome* ✦ *No smoking in dining room* ⊞ *Mastercard/ Eurocard, American Express, Visa,* ⋈ *Joe & Veronica Rocks*

Busta Brae Shetland ZE2 9QN
Tel: 01806 522 506 Fax: 01806 522 588
E-mail: reservations@bustahouse.com
Web: www.bustahouse.com
On the Muckle road. 1 mile off A970 Hillswick road. [E2]

ISLES OF SHETLAND

Monty's Bistro

- *"The style is informal, the cooking is excellent – what a combination!"*
- *Modern Scottish cooking.*

MONTY'S IS INTIMATE with a wonderful atmosphere. The original stone walls and floor set the mood for a relaxed, informal eating experience. The menu and blackboard specialities are well-balanced and full of Shetland's finest ingredients. Guests at Monty's benefit from Raymond's in-depth knowledge of cooking and his accomplished, innovative style.

Cup of crab cappuccino with Glenmorangie whisky. Seared monkfish tails in Creole spices on mango salsa, salad, warm baby potatoes. Baked rhubarb and ginger cheesecake with lightly whipped double cream.

◑ *Open all year except Christmas Day, Boxing Day, 1 Jan, last Wed in Feb, last week Oct and 1st week Apr Closed Sun Mon* ✗ *Lunch except Sun Mon £ Dinner except Sun Mon ££* Ⓥ *Vegetarians welcome* ☂ *Children welcome* ✦ *No smoking throughout* ⊞ *Mastercard/ Eurocard, Visa, Switch, Delta, JCB* ⋈ *Proprietor: Raymond Smith*

5 Mounthooly Street Lerwick Isles of Shetland ZE1 OBJ
Tel: 01595 696555 Fax: 01595 696955
Centre of Lerwick, behind Tourist Information Centre. Up Mounthooly Street, approx 20 metres on the left. [E2]

JEDBURGH

Jedforest Hotel

- *"Patrick Bardoulet is an excellent and innovative chef. Every dish was a delight!"*
- *Modern Scottish.*

AN ELEGANT, SMALL country house with excellent accommodation and beautifully refurbished, this is actually the first hotel in Scotland on the A68. A gastronomic experience awaits in Bardoulets Restaurant where the team of chefs create outstanding Scottish cuisine. The hotel is ideally suited for golfing and fishing on its own stretch of the River Jed.

Roulade of smoked fish with lime, coriander and yoghurt. Aberdeen Angus fillet with potato pancake, wild mushrooms, shallot's confit and port jus. Caramelised lemon torte with home-made vanilla ice cream.

STB ★★★★ Small Hotel

◑ *Open all year* 🏠 *Rooms: 8 en suite* 🛏 *DB&B £62–£77 B&B £42.50–£57.50* 🍴 *Special rates available* ✗ *Lunch ££ Dinner £££* Ⓥ *Vegetarians welcome* ✄ *Smoking restricted to residents lounge and bar only* 💳 *Mastercard/Eurocard, American Express, Visa, Diners Club, Switch, Delta* 🅧 *Owners: Samuel & Patricia Ferguson*

Nr Jedburgh Roxburghshire TD8 6PJ
Tel: 01835 840222 Fax: 01835 840226
E-mail: mail@jedforesthotel.freeserve.co.uk
Web: www.jedforesthotel.freeserve.co.uk
200 metres from A68, main tourist route from Newcastle to Edinburgh. 7 miles north of border and 3 miles south of Jedburgh. [D6]

KELSO

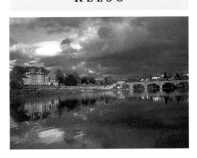

Ednam House Hotel

- *"Relax and enjoy the unique views of the River Tweed."*
- *Traditional and modern Scottish cooking.*

PROPRIETOR/CHEF Ralph Brooks describes his cooking as 'straightforward, but along classical lines', creating original dishes using unusual ingredients such as Berwickshire ostrich and wood pigeon, fashioning his menus from the fresh ingredients he can obtain locally and seasonally. At this hotel the customer comes first.

Loch Awe mussels steamed with Pernod and garlic. Braised shank of Tweed Valley lamb in its rich gravy. Drambuie mousse served with raspberry coulis.

STB ★★★ Hotel
Green Tourism One Leaf Bronze Award

◑ *Open all year except Christmas and New Year* 🏠 *Rooms: 30 en suite* 🛏 *DB&B £60–£76.50 B&B £42–£59* 🍴 *Special rates available* ✗ *Food available all day £–££ Lunch £ Dinner ££* Ⓥ *Vegetarians welcome – prior notice required* 🧒 *Children welcome* 💳 *Mastercard/Eurocard, Visa, Switch* 🅧 *Proprietors: R A & R W Brook*

Bridge Street Kelso TD5 7HT
Tel: 01573 224168 Fax: 01573 226319
E-mail: ednamhouse@excite.co.uk
Web: www.ednamhouse.com
Situated on Bridge Street, halfway between town square and abbey. [D6]

KELSO

The Roxburghe Hotel, Golf Course and Fairways Brasserie

- *"The perfect 19th Hole. Fairways Brasserie is an exciting new venture for the Roxburghe Hotel. Good value food in a relaxed atmosphere with brilliant views of the golf course."*
- *Modern Scottish.*

ALTHOUGH AN IMPOSING mansion, the Roxburghe retains the common touch. Fine dining in the hotel restaurant and less formal in Fairways Brasserie (opened 2001 in the Clubhouse). Both restaurants offer well-constructed and interesting menus innovatively prepared. Cooking here is contemporary with dishes which are presented in a creative and innovative way all using finest Borders produce.

Smoked salmon and leek quiche with saffron hollandaise. Loin of Border lamb with a light herb and tomato sauce. Toffee apple tart with clotted cream.

STB ★★★★ Hotel

◗ Open all year ⌂ Rooms: 22 en suite ⇔ B&B £120–£255 ⑤ℙ Special rates available ✕ Lunch £–£££ Dinner £–£££ Ⓥ Vegetarians welcome ⚡ Children welcome ✄ No smoking in dining room. Smoking permitted in Fairways. ⊞ Mastercard/Eurocard, American Express, Visa, Diners Club, Switch ⚑ General Manager: William Kirby

Kelso Roxburghshire TD5 8JZ
Tel: 01573 450331 Fax: 01573 450611
E-mail: hotel@roxburghe.net
Web: www.roxburghe.net
At village of Heiton, on A698 Kelso-Jedburgh road. Signposted at western end of village. [D6]

KELTY BY DUNFERMLINE

The Butterchurn

- *"Informal eating experience serving fresh home-cooked meals with excellent facilities for children."*
- *Fresh home-style cooking.*

THE PLAIN WHITEWASHED steading conceals the treasures within: The Scottish Food and Craft Centre specialising in Scottish Food Products. Food and Craft demonstrations are a regular feature throughout the year, including printing classes. Excellent fresh home-cooked meals are served all day. There is also an outdoor play area and paddock with unusual animals.

Liver with mustard sauce and spring onion mash. Gressingham duck with home-made kiwi and apple jam. Lemon meringue pie.

STB ★★★★ Visitor Attraction

◗ Open all year except 25, 26 Dec and 1, 2 Jan ⚑ Licensed ✕ Food available all day £ Lunch ££ Dinner ££ Ⓥ Vegetarians welcome ⚡ Children welcome ✄ Facilities for disabled visitors ⊞ Mastercard/Eurocard, Visa, Switch, Delta ⚑ Proprietors: Mr & Mrs K Thomson

Cocklaw Mains Farm Kelty Fife KY4 0JR
Tel: 01383 830169 Fax: 01383 831614
E-mail: enquiries@butterchurn.co.uk
Web: www.butterchurn.co.uk
Just off the M90 motorway at junction 4 on B914. 500 yards west of junction. [D5]

KENMORE

KENTALLEN

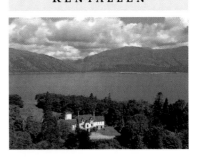

The Kenmore Hotel

- *"Scotland's oldest inn offers good food and hospitality."*
- *Traditional Scottish cooking.*

THIS IS SCOTLAND'S oldest inn, established in 1572, and overlooks the 17th century Kenmore Bridge. The inn has been, and continues to be, renovated to a high standard. All food served in the Taymouth Restaurant is traditional, with some innovations, and all using excellent quality, locally sourced ingredients.

Quenelles of chicken liver pâté with fan of smoked duck breast and pink peppercorn vinaigrette. Oven-baked fillet of Tay salmon with prawn and herb mousse and saffron cream sauce. Mango crème brûlée with quenelle of strawberry ice cream.

STB ★★★ Hotel

◐ *Open all year* 🏠 *Rooms: 40 en suite* 🍴 *DB&B £55–£60 B&B £35–£40* 🅿 *Special rates available* ✗ *Food available all day £ Lunch £ Dinner ££* Ⓥ *Vegetarians welcome* ⚡ *Children welcome* ♿ *Facilities for disabled visitors* ✖ *No smoking in restaurant* 🐕 *Dogs welcome* 🅱 *Mastercard/Eurocard, American Express, Visa, Switch* ⚑ *Director & General Manager: John Hiroz*

The Square Kenmore nr Aberfeldy Perthshire PH15 2NU
Tel: 01887 830 205 Fax: 01887 830 262
E-mail: reception@kenmorehotel.co.uk
Web: www.kenmorehotel.com
From A9 At Ballinluig take A827. Kenmore Hotel is situated in Square at Kenmore. [C5]

Ardsheal House

- *"This family-owned and run country estate house combines a relaxed ambience with fine food."*
- *Innovative country house cooking.*

ARDSHEAL HOUSE is set within 800 acres of ancient woodlands and spectacular scenery. The home of Neil and Philippa Sutherland is opened to guests who enjoy the naturally warm atmosphere combined with attentive service. Philippa is an accomplished cook and the tempting menus change daily. Winner of The Macallan Taste of Scotland Award 1996.

Cauliflower soufflé. Roast sea bass with basil and lemon. Date pudding.

STB ★★★★ Small Hotel

◑ *Open all year except Dec to Feb – when open by prior arrangement only* 🏠 *Rooms: 6 en suite* 🍴 *DB&B from £75 B&B from £47.50* 🍷 *Restricted hotel licence* ✗ *Dinner £££* Ⓥ *Vegetarians welcome* ✖ *No smoking in dining room* 🅱 *Mastercard/Eurocard, American Express, Visa* ⚑ *Neil & Philippa Sutherland*

Kentallen of Appin Argyll PA38 4BX
Tel: 01631 740227 Fax: 01631 740342
E-mail: info@ardsheal.co.uk
Web: www.ardsheal.co.uk
On A828 Oban road, 4 miles south of Ballachulish Bridge, 28 miles north of Oban. About 1 mile up private road, signposted at main road. [B5]

KILCHRENAN

Ardanaiseig Hotel

- *"This grand house has its own special aura, the food preparation is highly skilled with great attention to quality of produce."*
- *Very experienced and beautifully presented modern Scottish cooking.*

STYLE AND OPULENCE are key words to describe this secluded and grand hotel. In the dining room true Scottish hospitality is delivered by Chef Gary Goldie who selects only the best local produce, presented with flair and sophistication. Everything about Ardanaiseig is exquisite from the gardens and nature reserve to the tiniest details.

Smoked haddock ravioli, meaux mustard sauce and crispy leek. Roast squab, braised cabbage, pomme fondant, confit garlic, thyme jus gras. Hot chocolate fondant with caramelised milk ice cream.

◗ *Open all year except 2 Jan to 14 Feb* 🏠 *Rooms: 16 en suite* 🛏 *DB&B from £65 (3 night special) B&B £42–£128* ✖ *Food available all day from £ Lunch from ££ Dinner ££££* 💳 *Mastercard/Eurocard, American Express, Visa, Diners Club* 👤 *General Manager: Robert Francis*

Kilchrenan By Taynuilt Argyll PA35 1HE
Tel: 01866 833 333 Fax: 01866 833 222
E-mail: ardanaiseig@clara.net
Web: www.ardanaiseig-hotel.com
1 mile east of Taynuilt, turn sharp left. Follow B845 to Kilchrenan. At Kilchrenan Inn turn left – 3 miles on single track road to Ardanaiseig. [B5]

KILCHRENAN

Roineabhal Country House Bed and Breakfast

- *"Arrive hungry and do justice to the wonderful home cooking!"*
- *Innovative Scottish cooking.*

OWNERS Roger and Maria have created a warm and hospitable feel here. The house, built in the style of a ski chalet, reflects many years spent in Canadian and French ski resorts. The interior is warm, welcoming and very stylish. From home baking to dinner the food is excellent.

Roast smoked salmon and tomato risotto. Braised haunch of venison with rowan and ginger, beetroot and runner beans from the garden and good old vegetable mash. Rhubarb and raspberry brûlée.

STB ★★★★ B&B

◗ *Open Jan to Oct* 🏠 *Rooms: 3 en suite* 🛏 *DB&B £58–£73 B&B £30–£45* 💷 *Special rates available* 🍷 *Unlicensed - guests welcome to take own wine* ✖ *Residents only Packed Lunch available Dinner £££* Ⓥ *Vegetarians welcome (organic produce available at a little extra cost)* ☀ *Children welcome* ♿ *Facilities for disabled visitors* 🚭 *No smoking – except on covered verandas* 🐕*Dogs welcome* 💳 *Mastercard/Eurocard, Visa, Switch* 👤 *Owner: Maria Soep*

Kilchrenan, by Taynuilt Argyll PA35 1HD
Tel: 01866 833 207 Fax: 01866 833 474
E-mail: maria@roineabhal.com
Web: www.roineabhal.com
Take the A82 from Glasgow to Crianlarich. Then take A85 to Oban, turning off at Taynuilt onto B845. Follow single track road 6 miles. Roineabhal entrance 50m beyond Kilchrenan village sign. [B5]

KILCHRENAN

Taychreggan Hotel Ltd

- *"One of Scotland's stylish hidden gems with mesmerising views and delicious foods."*
- *Elegant modern British cuisine.*

TAYCHREGGAN is a wonderful place in a stunning location. It retains a sense of peace and history where visitors feel like house guests. Experienced chefs present imaginative fine cuisine in the hotel's dining room, whilst more simple bar lunches are no less carefully prepared. All complemented with an award-winning wine list.

Seared Mull Bay scallop brochette. Best end of Argyll lamb with a black olive and tomato dauphinoise. Mixed berry pudding with banana ice cream.

STB ★★★★ Hotel

● *Open all year* ⌂ *Rooms: 19 en suite* ⇔ *B&B £57.50–£107.50* ⑳ *Special rates available* ✗ *Lunch ££ Dinner 5 course menu £££* Ⓥ *Vegetarians welcome* ✔ *No smoking in dining room* ⊞ *Mastercard/Eurocard, American Express, Visa, Switch* ⊠ *Proprietor: Annie Paul*

Kilchrenan Taynuilt Argyll PA35 1HQ
Tel: 01866 833 211/366 Fax: 01866 833 244
E-mail: taychreggan@btinternet.com
Web: www.taychregganhotel.co.uk
Leave A85 at Taynuilt on to B845 through village of Kilchrenan to the lochside. [B5]

KILLIN

The Ardeonaig Hotel and Restaurant

- *"Well worth the drive. Breathtaking scenery and superb food."*
- *Classic French cuisine using the best Scottish produce."*

WITH ITS MAGNIFICENT views and attractive grounds leading to the water's edge, Ardeonaig is a delightful new addition to this Guide. There are several cosy sitting rooms where guests may unwind. Chef Grant Walker is dedicated to the use of top quality Scottish produce – his cooking is first-class.

Foie gras on a bed of mizuna with Puy lentils, balsamic vinegar dressing. Roasted loin of lamb, onion and garlic purée, polenta, fresh garden peas, thyme jus. Hot chocolate tart, coffee bean anglaise and coconut ice cream.

STB ★★★ Small Hotel

● *Open all year Closed 21 to 29 Dec and 7 to 20 Jan incl* ⌂ *Rooms: 10 en suite* ⇔ *DB&B from £75 B&B from £50* ⑳ *Special rates available* ✗ *Lunch ££ Dinner ££££* Ⓥ *Vegetarians welcome* ☆ *Children welcome – over 8 years in dining room after 7pm* ♿ *Facilities for disabled* ✔ *No smoking in dining room* ♞ *Dogs welcome – not in restaurant or public rooms* ⊞ *Mastercard/ Eurocard, Visa, Switch, Delta* ⊠ *General Manager: Mandy Exley*

South Loch Tay Side by Killin Perthshire FK21 8SU
Tel: 01567 820 400 Fax: 01567 820 282
E-mail: ardeonaighotel@btinternet.com
Web: www.ardeonaighotel.co.uk
Located midway between Kenmore and Killin on the south shore road of Loch Tay. From Killin, take the south shore road for 7 miles. From Kenmore, take the south shore road for 9 miles. [C5]

KILLIN

Killin Hotel

- *"Delightfully relaxing spot and an ideal centre for outdoor pursuits."*
- *Traditional Scottish cooking.*

THE KILLIN HOTEL sits on the banks of the river Lochay. It has recently been refurbished by the Garnier family and all rooms are en suite. The Riverview Bistro is suitably named and its informal style leads to a relaxed dining experience where the daily changing menu offers a good choice to suit all tastes.

Baked field mushrooms, baked in Gruyère cheese and topped with salsa. Venison Glen Lochay: venison fillets served with sweet red cabbage and redcurrant on a wild berry jus. Drambuie parfait: Chef's mousse on a biscuit base.

STB ★★ Hotel

◑ *Open all year* 🏮 *Rooms: 32 en suite* 🛏 *DB&B from £42 B&B £26–£29* 💷 *Special rates available* ✗ *Lunch £ Dinner £–££* Ⅵ *Vegetarians welcome* ☘ *Children welcome* ♿ *Facilities for disabled visitors* 🐕 *Dogs welcome* 💳 *Visa, Diners Club, Switch, Delta* ⚑ *General Manager: Neil Addison*

Main Street Killin Perthshire FK21 8TP
Tel: 01567 820296 Fax: 01567 820647
E-mail: killinhotel@btinternet.com
Web: www.killinhotel.com
Follow A85 Crianlarich/Lochearnhead then take A827 to Killin. Hotel is on the right at end of the village. [C5]

KINCARDINE-ON-FORTH

The Unicorn Inn

- *"Fine dining in relaxing atmosphere."*
- *Modern Scottish cooking.*

TONY BUDDE, Chef/Patron, prepares and presents dishes in an innovative style. There is a casual menu at lunchtime and a separate dinner menu in the evening. The Unicorn has been a restaurant for over 100 years but has now been modernised offering a comfortable and relaxed venue in which to enjoy good food.

Vegetarian haggis with tatties and neeps served in a whisky and barley broth. Rack of tender Scottish lamb, lightly marinated and resting on creamed sweet potato and baby vegetables. Raspberries topped with cranachan ice cream.

◑ *Open all year except Christmas Day, Boxing Day and 1, 2 Jan; 3rd week in Jan and 3rd week in July Closed Sun Mon* ✗ *Lunch except Sun Mon ££ Dinner except Sun Mon £££* Ⅵ *Vegetarians welcome* ☘ *Children welcome - 12 years and over at dinner* 🚭 *No smoking in restaurant area* 🐕 *Guide Dogs only* 💳 *Mastercard/Eurocard, Visa, Diners Club, Switch, Delta* ⚑ *Chef/Patron: Tony Budde*

15 Excise Street Kincardine-on-Forth Fife FK10 4LN
Tel: 01259 739 129 Fax: 01259 739 129
Restaurant is situated in the centre of the village. Turn left at the end of the shops on Elphinston Street. [C5]

KINCRAIG

KINGUSSIE

March House

- *"A quiet, secluded and comfortable hideaway, near Aviemore."*
- *Simple home cooking.*

MARCH HOUSE has a spacious pine conservatory providing an idyllic candlelit setting for dinner. It is owned and enthusiastically run by Caroline Hayes, whose cooking and baking matches the fresh atmosphere of the house. Using all fresh local produce, she presents a very well-priced table d'hôte menu. Small lunch party bookings welcome.

Broccoli soufflé with hollandaise and roasted pine nuts. Lightly poached salmon with lemon risotto and a creamy fresh spinach, watercress and smoked salmon sauce. Crêpes with caramelised oranges and home-made ice cream with Grand Marnier.

STB ★★★ Guest House

◗ *Open all year except 26 Nov to 26 Dec* ▥ *Rooms: 6, 5 en suite* ⬱ *DB&B £37–£42 B&B £20–£25* ⓢⓟ *Special rates available* ▥ *Unlicensed – guests welcome to take own wine* ✕ *Lunch – pre-arranged parties ££ Dinner – reservations essential for non-residents ££* Ⓥ *Vegetarians welcome* ✶ *Children welcome* ✌ *Smoking permitted in the woodshed* 🎫 *Mastercard, Visa* Ⓜ *Proprietor: Caroline Hayes*

Feshiebridge Kincraig Inverness-shire PH21 1NG Tel: 01540 651388 Fax: 01540 651388 Mobile: 07890 532150 E-mail: caroline@marchhse01.freeserve.co.uk Web: www.kincraig.com/march.htm From Kincraig follow B970 to Feshiebridge. Cross the bridge and climb until red telephone box on right. Turn right and follow no through road for ½ mile. Turn first left down drive. [C4]

The Cross

- *"Inspirational and exciting food of an exceptional standard. Well worth a visit."*
- *Innovative Scottish cooking.*

RUTH HADLEY is a member of the Master Chefs of Great Britain and treats ingredients with a deft yet experimental energy. She often uses less common produce and grows her own herbs. Tony Hadley makes a nightly selection of wines from one of the best cellars in Scotland.

Diver caught scallops, flash sautéed with a vegetable and noodle salad. Venison 'Francatelli' – fillet of local wild red deer pan-fried with port and redcurrants. Pear and butterscotch tart alongside a tanka bean ice cream.

◗ *Open 1 Mar to 1 Dec Closed Tue* ▥ *Rooms: 9 en suite* ⬱ *DB&B £95–£115* ✕ *Dinner except Tue ££££* Ⓥ *Vegetarians welcome – prior notice preferred* ♿ *Facilities for non-residential disabled visitors* ✌ *No smoking in dining room and bedrooms* 🎫 *Mastercard/Eurocard, Visa, Switch, Delta* Ⓜ *Partners/Proprietors: Tony & Ruth Hadley*

Tweed Mill Brae Ardbroilach Road, Kingussie Inverness-shire PH21 1TC Tel: 01540 661166 Fax: 01540 661080 E-mail: fabulousfood@thecross.co.uk Web: www.thecross.co.uk From traffic lights in centre of village, travel uphill along Ardbroilach Road for c. 300 yards, then turn left down private drive (Tweed Mill Brae). [C4]

KINGUSSIE

The Osprey Hotel

- *"A warm, friendly, comfortable hotel with very good food."*
- *Traditional Scottish cooking with French influences.*

ATTENTION TO DETAIL, good food and a fine cellar are all features of the Osprey which bring so many guests back to the hotel time after time. Aileen Burrow always cooks to order with skill and imagination showing in dishes. The Burrows are friendly accomplished hosts.

Crab cakes with a lime and coriander dressing. Guinea fowl with port and blueberry sauce served with potato and apple rösti. Raspberries with a lemon Mascarpone cream in a chocolate crust.

STB ★★★ Small Hotel

◑ *Open all year* 🏨 *Rooms: 8 en suite* 🛏 *DB&B £42–£56 B&B £24–£36* 🆂🅿 *Special rates available* ✗ *Dinner £££* Ⓥ *Vegetarians welcome* 🧒 *Children over 10 years welcome* ♿ *Facilities for disabled visitors* 🚭 *No smoking in dining room and most bedrooms* 💳 *Mastercard/ Eurocard, American Express, Visa* 🔪 *Proprietors: Robert & Aileen Burrow*

Ruthven Road Kingussie PH21 1EN
Tel: 01540 661510 Fax: 01540 661510
E-mail: aileen@ospreyhotel.co.uk
Web: www.ospreyhotel.co.uk
South end of Kingussie main street. [C4]

KINLOCH RANNOCH

Bunrannoch House

- *"A peaceful location offering a warm welcome, good food and hospitality to match."*
- *Creative Scottish cooking.*

BUNRANNOCH STANDS in the shadow of the 'sleeping giant' mountain near Loch Rannoch. The cosy lounge with log fires complements the delicious aromas from the kitchen. Jennifer Skeaping is the Chef/Proprietor and her good cooking and friendly manner assure you of an enjoyable stay. The menus change daily, fresh food is sourced locally and tastefully prepared.

Three cheese tartlets with smoked venison. Tender lamb fillets in Madeira sauce garnished with sautéed kidneys and mushrooms. Lacy oat biscuits topped with heather honey and whisky ice cream and strawberries.

STB ★★ Guest House

◑ *Open all year except Christmas and New Year* 🏨 *Rooms: 7, 5 en suite* 🛏 *DB&B £36–£40 B&B £22–£25* 🆂🅿 *Special rates available* ✗ *Dinner ££* Ⓥ *Vegetarians welcome – prior notice required* 🚭 *No smoking throughout* 💳 *Mastercard/Eurocard, Visa* 🔪 *Proprietor: Jennifer Skeaping*

Kinloch Rannoch Perthshire PH16 5QB
Tel: 01882 632407 Fax: 01882 632407
E-mail: bun.house@tesco.net
Web: www. bunrannoch.co.uk
Turn right after 500 yards on Schiehallion road, just outside Kinloch Rannoch off B846. White 3-storey building on left-hand side. [C5]

KINROSS

Carlin Maggie's

- *"Excellent food and friendly hospitality."*
- *Good cooking with international accent.*

THE RESTAURANT OFFERS well presented Scottish local produce, with an international twist. Check blackboard for daily specials. Carlin Maggie was a local witch who to this day reputedly helps serve the coffee! Look out for themed evenings offering three-course dinners throughout the year.

Loch Rannoch smoked venison with a sweet and sour gooseberry compote. Poached suprême of chicken stuffed with apple-flavoured black pudding on a cider crème fraîche sauce. Blairgowrie raspberry cheesecake with a Drambuie cranachan cream.

◗ *Open all year except 1, 2 Jan and 30 Oct to 7 Nov Closed Mon* ✖ *Lunch except Mon £ Dinner except Mon £££* Ⓥ *Vegetarians welcome* ☀ *Children welcome* ♿ *Facilities for disabled visitors* 🖃 *Mastercard/Eurocard Visa, Switch, Delta, Solo, Visa Electron* ⛿ *Proprietors: Roy & Carol Smith*

191 High Street Kinross Tayside KY13 8DB Tel: 01577 863652 Fax: 01577 863652 Exit M90 at Junction 6 into town centre. Turn right at mini roundabout on to B966. Restaurant ¼ mile on left. [D5]

KINROSS

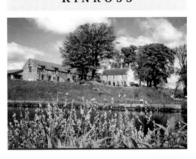

Grouse & Claret Restaurant

- *"Seasonal game and shellfish are a speciality of the house - beautifully prepared and presented."*
- *Modern Scottish cooking with some oriental flavours.*

THE RESTAURANT offers modern Scottish cooking, beautifully presented, including traditional and speciality dishes, such as seasonal game and fresh shellfish, using local produce with a daily vegetarian choice. Tastes of the orient are available in a monthly banquet. The detached accommodation is comfortable and of a good standard, with some bedrooms overlooking the trout lochans.

Cheese soufflé with Scottish cheeses and garden herbs. Fillet of pork with pack choi, stir fry vegetables, black bean and ginger sauce. Gooseberry cobbler with crème anglaise.

STB ★★★ Restaurant with Rooms

◗ *Open all year except Boxing Day, New Year's Day and 2 weeks Jan Note: Closed Sun night and all day Mon* 🏠 *Rooms: 3 en suite* 🛏 *DB&B £55–£65 B&B £32.50–£39* ⛾ *Table licence* ✖ *Lunch except Mon ££ Dinner except Sun Mon ££–£££* Ⓥ *Vegetarians welcome* ☀ *Children welcome* ♿ *Facilities for disabled visitors* ✚ *No smoking in restaurant* 🖃 *Mastercard, Visa* ⛿ *Proprietors: Vicki & David Futong*

Heatheryford Kinross KY13 0NQ Tel: 01577 864212 Fax: 01577 864920 E-mail: grouseandclaret@lineone.net Exit at Junction 6 M90 then 1st left on A977 (opposite service station). [D5]

KIRKBEAN BY DUMFRIES

Cavens

- *"Warm and friendly country house hotel."*
- *Freshly cooked local produce in modern style.*

CAVENS IS the comfortable home of Angus and Jane Fordyce and is set in six acres of mature gardens. It is ideally located for visiting the Solway Coast. Freshly prepared local produce is presented in fine dining style. Guests can relax in one of the sitting rooms in front of a 'real' fire.

Salad of avocado, beans and leaves, topped with a lightly poached egg. Rack of Galloway lamb with a Dijon, thyme and oatcake crust. Home-made pannacotta with Caven's basil syrup.

STB ★★★ Small Hotel

◐ *Open all year* 🏨 *Rooms: 8 en suite* 🛏 *DB&B £50–£80 B&B £35–£50* 🆂🅿 *Special rates available* ✕ *Lunch by arrangement £££ Dinner £££* Ⓥ *Vegetarians welcome* ✵ *Children welcome* 🚭 *No smoking in dining room* 🐕 *Dogs welcome by arrangement* 💳 *Mastercard/ Eurocard, Visa, Switch, Delta, JCB* 🔪 *Owners: Angus & Jane Fordyce*

Kirkbean Dumfriesshire DG2 8AA
Tel: 01387 880 234 Fax: 01387 880 467
E-mail: enquiries@cavens-hotel.co.uk
Web: www.cavens-hotel.co.uk
From Dumfries follow the A710 south for 12 miles to the village of Kirkbean. On entering the village hotel is clearly signed. [C7]

KIRKCALDY

Dunnikier House Hotel

- *"A popular hotel serving à la carte lunches and dinners, also an extensive bar lunch menu."*
- *Elegant Scottish cuisine.*

DUNNIKIER is set in the grounds of Dunnikier Park with spectacular views of the Firth of Forth. Proprietor Barry Bridgens is only too happy to help with the guests' needs. This personal attention, which includes a warm welcome combined with delicious food, makes for a very comfortable destination. Popular with business and sporting guests.

Warm salad of pigeon and black pudding with a balsamic dressing. Loin of venison surrounded by a pheasant and wild mushroom parfait, served with fondant potato, red cabbage, caramelised shallots and a red wine jus. Caramelised banana sandwiched between layers of shortbread.

STB ★★★ Small Hotel

◐ *Open all year* 🏨 *Rooms: 14 en suite* 🛏 *DB&B £60–£80 B&B £45* 🆂🅿 *Special rates available* ✕ *Food available all day £ Lunch ££ Dinner £££* Ⓥ *Vegetarians welcome* ✵ *Children welcome* 🚭 *No smoking in restaurant* 💳 *Mastercard/ Eurocard, American Express, Visa, Diners Club, Switch, Delta* 🔪 *Partners: Barry Bridgens & Kay Garbutt*

Dunnikier Park Kirkcaldy KY1 3LP
Tel: 01592 268393 Fax: 01592 642340
E-mail: recp@dunnikier-house-hotel.co.uk
Web: www.dunnikier-house-hotel.co.uk
Situated to the north of Kirkcaldy town in the grounds of Dunnikier Park. From the A92, 2 miles from Kirkcaldy west exit. 1 mile from Kirkcaldy east exit. [D5]

KIRKCUDBRIGHT

The Selkirk Arms Hotel

- *"Small town hotel offering local produce and courteous, friendly service."*
- *Modern Scottish.*

THIS PLACE IS A GEM. The cuisine is excellent, innovative and inspired and the dishes presented are of superb quality, enhanced by professional and courteous service. This is a small town hotel with good facilities but with a restaurant which is worth going out of your way to enjoy.

Pan-fried breast of pigeon on a bed of roast vegetables and a red wine jus. Seared local king scallops on a herb salad with a dill and elderflower cream. White chocolate cheesecake flavoured with Glayva set on a chocolate shortbread.

STB ★★★★ Small Hotel

◐ *Open all year except Christmas night*
🏨 *Rooms: 16 en suite* 🛏 *DB&B £60–£65 B&B £45–£62* 🆂🅿 *Special rates available* ✗ *Lunch £ Dinner £££* Ⓥ *Vegetarians welcome* ⚡ *Children welcome* ♿ *Facilities for disabled visitors* ✘ *No smoking in restaurant* 💳 *Mastercard/Eurocard, American Express, Visa, Diners Club, Switch, Delta, JCB* 🅽 *Partners: John & Susan Morris*

High Street Kirkcudbright Dumfries & Galloway DG6 4JG
Tel: 01557 330402 Fax: 01557 331639
E-mail: reception@selkirkarmshotel.co.uk
Web: www.selkirkarmshotel.co.uk
At the east end of the High Street in the old part of the town. [C7]

KIRKMICHAEL

Strathardle Inn

- *"A traditional Scottish inn in quiet and scenic surroundings."*
- *Scottish cooking.*

UNDERGOING A COMPLETE refurbishment programme Strathardle Inn is receiving caring attention from Nick and Myra Ibbotson, who are the new owners. It is located in delightful surroundings and the food here is traditional, with some modern twists and served in hearty portions as expected from an inn. The Ibbotsons are friendly and accommodating hosts.

Shetland crab cakes with Bloody Mary relish. Roast rack of Glenfernate lamb on honey soused vegetables with a heather ale jus. Fresh Blairgowrie raspberries with a lemon and elderflower wine syllabub and lime madeleines.

STB ★★ Inn

◐ *Open all year Closed Mon* 🏨 *Rooms: 5 en suite* 🛏 *DB&B £40–£55 B&B £25–£35* 🆂🅿 *Special rates available* ✗ *Lunch except Mon £ Dinner except Mon ££* Ⓥ *Vegetarians welcome Special diets catered for* ⚡ *Children welcome* ♿ *Facilities for disabled visitors* ✘ *No smoking in restaurant* 🐕 *Dogs welcome* 💳 *Mastercard/ Eurocard, Visa, Switch, Delta* 🅽 *Proprietors: Nick & Myra Ibbotson*

Kirkmichael Perthshire PH10 7NS
Tel: 01250 881224 Fax: 01250 881373
E-mail: bookings@strathardleinn.co.uk
Web: www.strathardleinn.co.uk
On A924 between Pitlochry and Blairgowrie, ¼ mile south of Kirkmichael village. [C4]

KIRRIEMUIR

Lochside Lodge & Roundhouse Restaurant

- *"A fine eating experience, presented by a Master Chef of Great Britain."*
- *Skilled, creative cooking.*

SET IN a beautiful location, Lochside Lodge is a converted farm steading which is now a fine restaurant and bar with accommodation. Guests may enjoy food served informally in the Steading Bar or in the more formal setting of the Roundhouse Restaurant. There is also accommodation in the converted hay loft.

Dunsyre Blue cheese brûlée, old-fashioned plum chutney, crème fraîche. Saddle of Angus lamb, mint-flavoured ratatouille, port wine, fresh redcurrant reduction. Glazed lemon and orange tart, organic honeycomb ice cream, peppered berries.

STB ★★★ Restaurant with Rooms

◗ *Open all year except 1 and 2 Jan Closed Mon 1 Oct to Apr ⌂ Rooms: 4 with private facilities ⇔ DB&B £35–£50 B&B £25–£35 ⓢ Special rates available ✗ Lunch ££ Dinner ££ Ⓥ Vegetarians welcome ⁎ Children welcome ⑃ Facilities for disabled visitors ⌥ Smoking in bar only ⌁ Dogs welcome ⓔ Mastercard/Eurocard, Visa, Switch, Delta ⧊ Owners: Gail & Graham Riley*

Bridgend of Lintrathen by Kirriemuir Angus DD8 5JJ
Tel: 01575 560340 Fax: 01575 560202
E-mail: enquiries@lochsidelodge.com
Web: www.lochsidelodge.com
From Alyth, take B954 towards Glenisla. Keep on B954 for 5 miles. Follow signs to Peel Farm, past Lintrathen Loch, follow road into Lintrathen. Lochside Lodge on right-hand side. [D4]

KISHORN

Shore House

- *"First-class accommodation and fine dining in spectacular scenery."*
- *Fine dining in homely atmosphere.*

THIS BEAUTIFUL HOUSE sits on the shore at Kishorn, where a quality of cuisine – seldom encountered in small guest houses – is available. The food is outstanding, carefully sourced and lovingly prepared by Douglas in the kitchen. Attention to detail is evident throughout Shore House. Somewhere to relax, unwind and enjoy good food and then return to!

Twice baked Tobermory Cheddar cheese soufflé and salad leaves tossed in dill and lime dressing. Baked haunch of Highland venison with rowanberry and claret sauce. Achintraid raspberry and strawberry shortcake with Achmore Farm crème fraîche.

STB ★★★★★ Guest House

◗ *Open 9 Apr to 8 Oct ⌂ Rooms: 3 en suite ⇔ DB&B £56–£62 B&B £35–£36.50 ⓢ Special rates available ✗ Dinner £££ Residents only Ⓥ Vegetarians welcome ⌥ No smoking throughout ⓔ Mastercard/Eurocard, Visa ⧊ Chef/Proprietors: Maureen & Douglas Gray*

Kishorn Strathcarron Wester Ross IV54 8XA
Tel: 01520 733333 Fax: 01520 733333
E-mail: taste@shorehouse.co.uk
Web: www.shorehouse.co.uk
Kishorn is almost midway between Shieldaig and Lochcarron on the A896. From Shieldaig, 10 miles south to Kishorn, take right turning signposted Achintraid, Shore House approx ¼ mile along this road on the right. [B4]

KNOYDART

Doune

- *"More than a special place to stay, Doune is a complete experience that should not be missed."*
- *Skilled seafood cooking with a very Scottish edge.*

FROM THE MOMENT you board the boat that takes you to Doune you know it is going to be an experience seldom duplicated. The atmosphere is relaxed and informal and the food is superb. It is the ideal base for walkers, divers and those who just need to escape the hum of city life.

Fresh Doune Bay crab with mixed leaf and herb salad from the garden. Freshly baked granary rolls. Light puff pastry pie of tender Knoydart venison with port and mushrooms. Home-made lemon curd pavlova with Doune raspberries.

STB ★★★ Guest House

❍ *Open 15 Apr to 30 Sept* 🏨 *Rooms: 3 with private facilities* 🛏 *DB&B £48–£55 (incl packed lunch) min 3 night stay* ✕ *Lunch by arrangement ££ Dinner ££* Ⓥ *Vegetarians welcome* ⚲ *Children welcome* 💳 *Mastercard. Visa* ⊠ *Partner: Liz Tibbetts*

Doune Knoydart By Mallaig Inverness-shire PH41 4PL
Tel: 01687 462 667 Fax: 01687 462 667
E-mail: liz@doune-marine.co.uk
Web: www.doune-marine.co.uk
At Mallaig go to the public steps at the small boat pier (not the Skye ferry pier) to meet Doune's boat at the time arranged when the booking was made. [B4]

KNOYDART

The Old Forge

- *"Hearty and flavoursome dishes await you at this quaint little pub – a special wee place!"*
- *Assured Scottish cooking bistro-style.*

THE OLD FORGE is acclaimed by The Guinness Book of Records as 'Britain's Remotest Pub'. It offers some of the freshest seafood and game from local sources. An ideal stop when on Knoydart for hill walkers, sailors and fishermen. A special board offers catches as they are landed. Specialist beers and great malt whiskies.

Fresh Loch Nevis langoustines, mixed leaf home-grown herb salad, home-made dipping sauce. Pan-seared Black Isle ostrich steak, fresh rosemary, rose rowan jelly, new potatoes and buttered garden vegetables. Whisky honey and oatmeal ice cream.

❍ *Open all year except Christmas Day*
🍷 *Licensed* ✕ *Lunch ££ Dinner ££*
Ⓥ *Vegetarians welcome* ⚲ *Children welcome*
♿ *Facilities for disabled visitors* 🐕 *Dogs welcome* 💳 *Mastercard, Visa, Switch, Delta, Solo* ⊠ *Proprietors: Ian & Jackie Robertson*

Inverie Knoydart by Mallaig PH41 4PL
Tel: 01687 462267
E-mail: info@theoldforge.co.uk
Web: www.theoldforge.co.uk
From Fort William, take A830 Road to the Isles heading for Mallaig. Pick up Motor Vessel Western Isles (Bruce Watt 01687 462233) for Inverie or phone Ian Robertson at the pub for boat charters. Train access from south Glasgow/Edinburgh heading for Fort William. Change for Fort William to Mallaig. Short boat journey. Restaurant approx 50m from pier. [B4]

KNOYDART

Pier House

- *"A small friendly restaurant and guest house with a delicious and varied menu on offer."*
- *Imaginative cooking.*

THE PIER HOUSE is a most welcoming restaurant which has been well-maintained and cared for by Gwen Barrell and Murray Carden, the proprietors. They are caring and thoughtful hosts and have a complete commitment to quality, using only the best local produce which they prepare and present with style and appeal.

Loch Nevis scallops with crispy Scottish bacon and fresh home-made organic bread. Pier House seafood platter of langoustines and brown crab with home-grown salad. Home-made whisky crunch ice cream.

STB ★★ Guest House

◗ *Open all year – recommend booking ahead* 🏠 *Rooms: 4, 2 en suite* 🛏 *DB&B £35–£45 B&B £25–£35* ✗ *Breakfast Packed Lunch £ Lunch except Sun - booking essential ££ Dinner ££* Ⓥ *Vegetarians very welcome* ☀ *Children welcome* 🖶 *Please enquire at booking stage* 🅜 *Owners: Gwen Barrell & Murray Carden*

Inverie Knoydart by Mallaig Inverness-shire PH41 4PL
Tel: 01687 462347 Fax: 01687 462347
E-mail: eatandstay@thepierhouse.co.uk
Web: www.thepierhouse.co.uk
Central to village of Inverie. Access by regular ferry from Mallaig, or 17 mile walk from Kinlochourn. Recommend telephoning for information. [B4]

KYLE OF LOCHALSH

The Seafood Restaurant

- *"Skilfully prepared seafood is on offer while you enjoy views to the Skye Bridge and the activities of the station platform."*
- *Freshly cooked, good quality food.*

THE MENU HERE consists mainly of fish and shellfish (Jann's husband landing his catch daily) there are also meat and vegetarian dishes and a daily blackboard special. In the peak season there is a breakfast and lunch menu. You are advised to check opening hours as they vary depending on the time of year.

Queen scallops in oatmeal: Lochcarron queenies rolled in oatmeal, deep-fried and served with lemon. Seafood kebabs: fresh monkfish, scallops and langoustines grilled and served with a dill and orange sauce. Home-made ice cream: Skye whisky and honey ice cream served with shortbread.

◗ *Open Easter to Oct* 🍷 *Table licence* ✗ *Lunch £ Dinner ££* Ⓥ *Vegetarians welcome* ☀ *Children welcome* ♿ *Limited facilities for disabled visitors* 🚭 *No smoking in restaurant* 🖶 *Mastercard/ Eurocard, Visa* 🅜 *Owner: Jann Macrae*

Railway Buildings Kyle of Lochalsh Ross-shire IV40 8XX
Tel: 01599 534813 Fax: 01599 577230
E-mail: thescottishtouristboardwww.host.co.uk
At Kyle of Lochalsh railway station on platform 1. Parking on slipway to station. [B4]

LAIDE

The Old Smiddy Guest House

- *"Relax, unwind and enjoy a stay here with delicious food and welcoming hosts."*
- *Imaginative, creative, Scottish home cooking.*

THE OLD SMIDDY is a small, personally run establishment. Kate and Steve Macdonald work together to ensure their guests have a pleasurable stay where great food is on offer. Home-made breads, scones, oatcakes and delicious desserts make the Old Smiddy a gem of a place to stay. Winner of The Macallan Taste of Scotland Award 1999.

Grilled red pepper and saffron soup with chilli cream. Trio of monkfish, turbot and salmon with langoustine and fennel sauce, served with Parmesan and lovage potatoes and rocket and oak leaf salad leaves. Fresh garden strawberry ice cream and raspberry almond torte.

STB ★★★★ Guest House

◑ *Open Mar until Nov* 🏠 *Rooms: 3 en suite* 🛏 *DB&B £60–£70* 🍷 *Unlicensed – guests welcome to take own wine* ✘ *Dinner £££* 🅥 *Vegetarians welcome* ✄ *No smoking throughout* 💳 *No credit cards* 🅜 *Proprietors: Kate & Steve Macdonald*

Laide Ross-shire IV22 2NB
Tel: 01445 731425 Fax: 01445 731696
E-mail: oldsmiddy@aol.com
Web:
www.s-h-systems.co.uk/hotels/oldsmid.html
On the main road at Laide, on the A832
Gairloch–Braemore road. [B3]

LARGS

The Moorings Hotel

- *"Friendly hotel with lovely views over to Arran and Cumbrae."*
- *Modern Scottish.*

SITUATED ON THE SEAFRONT at Largs overlooking the Clyde and the islands beyond. The Moorings Hotel offers comfortable surrounds and good food with exceptionally warm and friendly staff. Here you can enjoy the best of local produce - fine game and meats, quality vegetables and delicious seafood. The beer garden offers stunning views of the Clyde Estuary.

Smoked Highland venison resting on a simple salad with lardons of bacon and a light raspberry drizzle. Red mullet oven-baked, set on a bed of Mediterranean vegetables with a pesto and balsamic dressing. Pavlova nests: fresh berry pavlova with strawberry coulis.

◑ *Open all year* 🏠 *Rooms: 8 en suite* 🛏 *B&B £35–£50 per person* 💷 *Special rates available* ✘ *Food available all day £ Lunch £ Dinner ££* 🅥 *Vegetarians welcome* ✱ *Children welcome* ♿ *Facilities for disabled visitors* 💳 *Mastercard/ Eurocard, Visa, Switch* 🅜 *Owners: Jean & Douglas Kerr*

2 May Street Largs KA30 8EB
Tel: 01475 672672 Fax: 01475 670050
E-mail: mooringshotel@yahoo.co.uk
Web: www.moorings-hotel.co.uk
Follow M8 (Greenock) then join A78 to Largs. Hotel on right leaving Largs. (C6)

LAUDER

The Lodge at Carfraemill

- *"A gourmet trip back in time, with fantastic quality and all mod cons."*
- *Traditional Scottish home cooking with flair.*

SINCE CARFRAEMILL was taken over by its present owner in 1997, it has undergone extensive renovation and modernisation. Jo Sutherland makes sure this is a most welcoming place for visitors, diners, locals and travellers, with comfortable surroundings and good food. The menus, with a strong emphasis on local produce, change regularly and meals are presented with flair.

Marinated Scottish salmon and deep-fried oysters surrounded by a citrus butter sauce. Roast loin of roe deer on a bed of crispy vegetables served with a game and chocolate sauce. Squidgy meringue cake drizzled with a fresh strawberry and elderflower coulis.

STB ★★★★ Small Hotel

◗ *Open all year* 🏠 *Rooms: 10 en suite* 🛏 *DB&B £50–£70 B&B £35–£55* 🆂 *Special rates available* ✖ *Food available all day £ Lunch £ Dinner ££* Ⓥ *Vegetarians welcome* ⚥ *Children welcome* ⚭ *No smoking area in restaurant and no smoking in bedrooms* 🈁 *Mastercard/ Eurocard, American Express, Visa, Diners Club, Switch, Delta* 🅺 *Owner: Jo Sutherland*

Lauder Berwickshire TD2 6RA
Tel: 01578 750750 Fax: 01578 750751
E-mail: enquiries@carfraemill.co.uk
Web: www.carfraemill.co.uk
Situated at the junction of the A68/A697, just 21 miles south of Edinburgh, 80 miles north of Newcastle and 70 miles from Glasgow. [D6]

LETHAM NR CUPAR

Fernie Castle Hotel

- *"Fernie Castle sits on the bow of Fife and has wonderful surroundings and good Scottish food."*
- *Modern Scottish.*

FERNIE CASTLE is over 450 years old, has great character and has been refurbished to a very high standard throughout. The Auld Alliance room is the ideal setting for a formal dinner with its Georgian chandelier and candles. Menus are traditional and uncomplicated but well executed using high quality produce.

Black pudding and clapshot cake with an Arran grain mustard sauce. Roast sea bass fillet with a pesto herb crust. Poached Prince Charlie pears in a sloe berry coulis with fresh mint ice cream.

STB ★★★★ Hotel

◗ *Open all year* 🏠 *Rooms: 20 en suite* 🛏 *DB&B £62.50–£95 B&B £40–£75* 🆂 *Special rates available* ✖ *Lunch £ Dinner £££* Ⓥ *Vegetarians welcome* ⚥ *Children welcome* ⚭ *No smoking in dining room* 🐕 *Dogs welcome* 🈁 *Mastercard/ Eurocard, American Express, Visa, Switch, Delta* 🅺 *Neil and Mary Blackburn*

Letham Nr Cupar Fife KY15 7RU
Tel: 01337 810381 Fax: 01337 810422
E-mail: mail@ferniecastle.demon.co.uk
Web: www.ferniecastle.demon.co.uk
From Edinburgh follow signs to Glenrothes, then take the Tay Bridge, onto the A92, then 1 mile past Letham. 'Fernie Castle' is on the right. [D5]

LINLITHGOW

Livingston's Restaurant

- *"Small restaurant offering excellent food and service in pleasant relaxed surroundings."*
- *Modern Scottish cooking.*

ORIGINAL STONE WALLS and antique tables and chairs provide a special ambience for interesting and imaginative cooking using fresh, local produce. A large conservatory overlooks well-kept lawns and garden. Winner of The Macallan Taste of Scotland Award 2000.

Fillet of Scottish salmon with Champagne and strawberries. Saddle of wild Highland venison served with a bramble jus and vegetable brochette. Caramelised baby pineapple with pineapple sherbet and caramel sauce.

◐ Open all year except 2 weeks Jan, 1 week Jun and 1 week Oct Closed Sun Mon ✕ Lunch except Sun Mon £ Dinner except Sun Mon £££ 🅥 Vegetarians welcome ✱ Children over 8 years welcome – evenings ♿ Facilities for disabled visitors ⚟ Smoking permitted in conservatory 💳 Mastercard/Eurocard, Visa, Switch 🅜 Managers: Derek Livingston & Fiona Livingston

52 High Street Linlithgow EH49 7AE
Tel: 01506 846565 Fax: 01506 846565
At eastern end of the High Street opposite the Post Office. [C5]

LINLITHGOW

Marynka Restaurant

- *"Delightful small town restaurant."*
- *Modern Scottish.*

MARYNKA is the Polish diminutive for Mary which is particularly appropriate given the historical connections with Mary Queen of Scots. Chef Catriona Staddon (who has Polish connections) prepares innovative dishes using fresh local produce, whilst partner David Nisbet's hospitably tends to customers and front-of-house.

Marynka pickled herring with soured cream, served with a shot of frozen vodka. Baked fillet of pork with pistachio stuffing, caramelised apricots and red wine sauce. Damson crème brûlée with home-made shortbread.

◐ Open all year except Christmas Day, Boxing Day and first 2 weeks Jan Closed Sun Mon ✕ Lunch except Sun Mon £ Dinner except Sun Mon ££ 🅥 Vegetarians welcome ♿ Facilities for disabled visitors ⚟ Diners requested to refrain from smoking at lunchtime and before 9.30pm 💳 Mastercard/Eurocard, American Express, Visa, Switch, Delta 🅜 Owners: Catriona Staddon & David Nisbet

57 High Street Linlithgow EH49 7ED
Tel: 01506 840123
E-mail: eat@marynka.com
On the opposite side of the High Street from the Palace, close to the Cross and next door to the Royal Bank of Scotland. [C5]

LOCH LOMOND

Cameron House Hotel and Country Estate

- *"A traditional Scottish country house hotel feel with international resort facilities on the shores of Loch Lomond."*
- *Modern contemporary cooking.*

A LUXURY HOTEL on the shore of Loch Lomond. Executive Chef Peter Fleming presents a highly sophisticated, imaginative menu in the hotel's main restaurant, the elegant Georgian Room. Smolletts Restaurant offers a wide variety of dishes from an à la carte menu; bar meals are available in Breakers Bar at the Marina.

Roast langoustine tails, beside a crab risotto surrounded by a shellfish cream. Roast saddle of Scottish lamb accompanied by a sweet potato galette on onion chutney and port essence. Hot passion fruit soufflé served with exotic fruit sorbet.

STB ★★★★ Hotel
Green Tourism Two Leaf Silver Award

◗ *Open all year N.B. Georgian room closed all day Mon ♦ Rooms: 96 en suite ⇔ DB&B £200–£265 B&B £180–£245 ✖ Food available all day £–££££ Lunch ££ Dinner ££££ Ⓥ Vegetarians welcome ★ Children welcome ♿ Facilities for disabled visitors ✄ Smoking in public areas only ⊞ Mastercard/ Eurocard, American Express, Visa, Diners Club ◪ Executive Chef: Peter Fleming*

Loch Lomond Dunbartonshire G83 9QZ Tel: 01389 755565 Fax: 01389 759522 E-mail: devere.cameron@airtime.co.uk Web: www.cameronhouse.co.uk On A82 near Balloch, on the banks of Loch Lomond. At Balloch roundabout follow signs for Luss. Approx 1 mile, first right. [C5]

LOCH LOMOND

The Coach House Coffee Shop: Winner 2001 – Light Bite Award

- *"A fine example of Scottish hospitality with mouth watering home baking, giant scones and muffins. A truly fun experience."*
- *Home baking and light meals.*

A WARM WELCOME is extended by the kilted Mr Groves whilst his wife Rowena supervises the making of delicious hearty snacks, home-made soups, light meals and good home baking. Hand-made soft bread rolls are filled with chunky ham, honey-roasted on the premises and eggs from their own free-range Black Rock hens.

Carrot and parsnip soup served with a hunk of bread. Leek and cheese quiche served with salad, coleslaw and fresh or garlic bread. Victoria sandwich. Caffe latte: single espresso with steamed milk and a little frothed milk.

◗ *Open all year ☖ Unlicensed ✖ Food available all day £ Lunch £ Ⓥ Vegetarians welcome ★ Children welcome ♿ Facilities for disabled visitors ✄ No smoking throughout ☂ Dogs welcome ⊞ Mastercard/ Eurocard, American Express, Visa, Switch, Delta, Solo ◪ Proprietors: Gary & Rowena Groves*

Luss Loch Lomond Argyll G83 8NN Tel: 01436 860341 Fax: 01436 860336 E-mail: enquiries@lochlomondtrading.com Web: www.lochlomondtrading.com Turn off A82 (Glasgow to Crianlarich) at signpost for Luss. Park in car park, walk into the village and look for the church. [C5]

LOCH LOMOND

LOCHCARRON

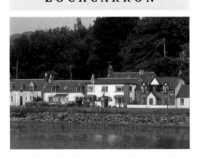

Lodge on Loch Lomond Hotel and Restaurant

- *"Friendly and relaxed atmosphere in stunning location."*
- *Modern Scottish cooking.*

SET IN A PARTICULARLY stunning location, the hotel's addition of balconies, built in 2001, maximise the Loch Lomond effect. The bar and restaurant overlook the loch and present menus which offer something to suit every taste. Cooking is skilled, presentation is attractive, and imaginative use is made of local produce.

Pale smoked haddock and scallion risotto in a Parmesan basket. Baked Perthshire lamb in bread with braised Puy lentils, beetroot jus. Steamed chocolate pudding with 'Crunchie' ice cream.

STB ★★★ Hotel

◗ *Open all year* ⌂ *Rooms: 29 en suite* ⇔ *DB&B £55–£85 B&B £30–£63* ⊞ *Special rates available* ✗ *Food available all day ££ Sun Lunch £ Buffet Lunch except Sun £ Dinner ££* Ⓥ *Vegetarians welcome* ⚤ *Children welcome* ⛿ *Facilities for disabled visitors* ⚮ *No smoking in restaurant* ⊟ *Mastercard/Eurocard, American Express, Visa, Switch, Delta* ⚑ *Manager: Niall Colquhoun*

Luss Argyll G83 8PA
Tel: 01436 860201 Fax: 01436 860203
E-mail: lusslomond@aol.com
Web: www.loch-lomond.co.uk
In the village of Luss on the A82 main route along Loch Lomond side. Well-signposted. [C5]

Rockvilla Hotel & Restaurant

- *"Lovely views from both the lounge bar and the restaurant combined with flavoursome wholesome menus."*
- *Traditional Scottish cooking.*

GOOD FOOD and warm hospitality comes naturally to Ken and Lorna Wheelan. An à la carte dinner menu offers excellent value and good choices. Rockvilla offers guests a good selection of traditional foods at affordable prices. After a hearty breakfast guests are well set up for a day's exploring the dramatic West Highlands.

Hot-smoked Highland venison on sweet charentais melon garnished with quails eggs and juniper chutney. Lochcarron prawn and scallops thermidor with a timbale of saffron basmati rice. Citrus crêpes with home-made orange marmalade ice cream and citrus and Grand Marnier sauce.

STB ★★★ Small Hotel

◗ *Open all year except Christmas Day and 1 Jan (Restaurant closed 30 Sept to Easter)* ⌂ *Rooms: 3 en suite* ⇔ *B&B £24–£30* ⊞ *Special rates available* ✗ *Lunch £ Dinner ££* Ⓥ *Vegetarians welcome* ⚤ *Children welcome* ⚮ *No smoking in restaurant* ⊟ *Mastercard/ Eurocard, American Express, Visa, Switch, Delta, JCB* ⚑ *Proprietors: Lorna & Kenneth Wheelan*

Main Street Lochcarron IV54 8YB
Tel: 01520 722379 Fax: 01520 722844
E-mail: rockvillahotel@btinternet.com
Web: www.rockvilla-hotel.com
Situated in centre of village, c. 20 miles north of Kyle of Lochalsh. [B4]

LOCHGILPHEAD

Fascadale House

- *"Spacious, luxurious ambience and high quality cooking."*
- *Stylish imaginative food.*

SET ON THE SHORES of picturesque Loch Fyne this magnificent Victorian country house with it's grand interior is elegant, homely and relaxing. The cuisine offered meets an excellent standard with locally sourced produce enhancing the stylish, well-prepared and imaginative menus. Alternative cottage accommodation is available within the gardens.

Haddock and prawn chowder with home-baked bread. Rack of Argyll lamb with baby leeks and crushed potatoes. White chocolate and raspberry tart.

STB ★★★★ B&B

◐ *Open all year* 🏠 *Rooms: 4, 2 en suite* 🛏 *DB&B £42–£60 B&B £25–£35* 🆂🅿 *Special rates available* ♟ *Licence pending* ✗ *Dinner ££* Ⓥ *Vegetarians welcome* ✱ *Children welcome* 🚭 *No smoking throughout* 🐕*Dogs welcome by arrangement* 💳 *Mastercard/Eurocard, Visa, Delta* 🔪 *Owner: Kay Davies*

Tarbert Road Ardrishaig Lochgilphead Argyll PA30 8EP
Tel: 01546 603845 Fax: 01546 602152
E-mail: kay@fascadale.com
Web: www.fascadale.com
From Lochgilphead take A83 south to Campbeltown, through Ardrishaig. Go over the Crinan canal swing bridge and Fascadale is 1 mile further, on the right-hand side. [B5]

LOCHINVER

The Albannach

- *"An experience not to be missed when in Lochinver. A very special place with very special hosts."*
- *Contemporary Scottish cooking with French influences.*

THE ALBANNACH is a haven for some of the best hospitality and food to be had. A superb, balanced, set dinner using local produce is served by candlelight. Colin is a charming host whilst Lesley is dedicated to providing fine cuisine. Winner of The Macallan Taste of Scotland Award 1998 and Overall Excellence Award 1998.

Wood pigeon, spiced red cabbage, wild mushroom ravioli, game chocolate sauce. Roast Lochinver monkfish and scallops, vermouth sabayon, saffron and seaweed rice. Caramelised apple tartlet, apple and calvados gelato, apple crisps, apple and vanilla, and caramel sauces.

STB ★★★★ Small Hotel

◐ *Open last 2 weeks Mar to 27 Dec* 🏠 *Rooms: 5 en suite* 🛏 *DB&B £87–£117* 🆂🅿 *Special rates available* ♟ *Table licence* ✗ *Dinner 5 course menu ££££ Non-residents welcome – booking essential* Ⓥ *Vegetarians welcome – by prior arrangement* ✱ *Children over 12 years welcome* 🚭 *No smoking throughout* 💳 *Mastercard/ Eurocard, Visa, Switch, Delta, JCB* 🔪 *Chef/ Proprietors: Lesley Crosfield & Colin Craig*

Lochinver Sutherland IV27 4LP
Tel: 01571 844 407 Fax: 01571 844 285
E-mail: the.albannach@virginnet.co.uk
From Lochinver follow signs for Baddidarroch. After ½ mile, pass turning for Highland Stoneware, turn left for the Albannach. [B3]

LOCHINVER

Inver Lodge Hotel

- *"Panoramic views over the bay await you in this modern hotel, where comfort and style is evident."*
- *Modern Scottish cooking.*

INVER LODGE is a luxuriously furnished hotel where the food is innovative and of a high standard. Attentive staff will make sure your every need is taken care of. Local produce features on both lunch and dinner menus. Great care and effort goes into every aspect of Inver Lodge's hospitality.

Hand-dived Lochinver sea scallops, tian of summer vegetables and a lemon butter sauce. Gâteau of Buccleuch beef fillet layered with haggis and foie gras, Glayva jus lie. Drambuie and raspberry crème brûlée.

STB ★★★★ Hotel

◗ *Open Easter to 1 Nov* 🏨 *Rooms: 20 en suite* 🛏 *DB&B £95–£125 B&B £70–£110* 🆂🅿 *Special rates available* ✗ *Lunch £ Dinner £££* ⓥ *Vegetarians welcome* ✕ *No smoking in dining room* 💳 *Mastercard/Eurocard, American Express, Visa, Diners Club, Switch, Delta, JCB* 🔏 *General Manager: Nicholas Gorton*

Iolaire Road Lochinver Sutherland IV27 4LU
Tel: 01571 844496 Fax: 01571 844395
E-mail: stay@inverlodge.com
Web: www.inverlodge.com
A837 to Lochinver, first turn on left after village hall. ½ mile up private road to hotel. [B3]

LOCKERBIE

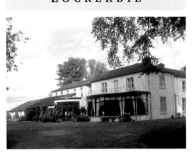

Dryfesdale Hotel

- *"Excellent use of fresh, local produce combined with warm hospitality in splendid surroundings."*
- *Modern Scottish.*

UNDER the ownership of Clive and Heather Sturman, Dryfesdale is set in five acres of delightful grounds. Cooking here is skilled and guests may enjoy their meals in the newly extended restaurant which offers unsurpassed views of the surrounding countryside. Very high standards throughout.

Local oak-smoked salmon cured in Macallan whisky and served with caper berries. Tournedos of Buccleuch beef topped with a blue cheese and spinach cream. Kirkhill Scottish cheeseboard: Scottish cheeses with oatcakes, accompanied by julienne of celery and grapes.

STB ★★★★ Hotel

◗ *Open all year except Boxing Day* 🏨 *Rooms: 15 en suite* 🛏 *DB&B from £122 B&B from £85* 🆂🅿 *Special rates available* ✗ *Lunch ££ Dinner £££* ⓥ *Vegetarians welcome* ✲ *Children welcome* ♿ *Facilities for disabled visitors* ✕ *No smoking in restaurant* 🐕 *Dogs welcome* 💳 *Mastercard/Eurocard, Visa, Switch, Delta* 🔏 *Owner: Mr Clive Sturman*

Dryfebridge Lockerbie Dumfries DG11 2SF
Tel: 01576 202427 Fax: 01576 204187
E-mail: reception@dryfesdalehotel.co.uk
Web: www.dryfesdalehotel.co.uk
¼ mile from junction 17 at Lockerbie on the Carlisle to Glasgow stretch of the M74. The hotel is well signposted from the motorway roundabout. [D6]

LOCKERBIE

Scott's At The Crown

- *"Bright bistro-style restaurant offering home cooking of local produce with an impressive range of wines all at modest prices."*
- *Homely style Scottish cooking.*

SCOTT'S RESTAURANT is centrally located and has been recently refurbished to give a relaxed and informal atmosphere with quiet and effectively simple decor. Chef/Proprietor Ralph Scott specialises in homely style cooking skilfully prepared using fresh produce. Specialities include an excellent selection of Solway seafood and Galloway and Border beef and lamb dishes.

Monkfish and smoked salmon terrine. Scott's medallions of beef: tender fillet steak sliced and pan-fried with onions, mushrooms and red wine, in a rich glaze. Home-made cranachan ice cream: raspberries, honey, Drambuie and oatmeal, folded with home-made ice cream.

Open all year except Christmas Day and 1 Jan ✕ Lunch £ Dinner ££ Ⓥ Vegetarians welcome Children welcome ♿ Facilities for disabled visitors No smoking in restaurant Mastercard, Visa, Switch, Delta, Solo, JCB, Electron Chef/Owner: Mr Ralph MacDonald Scott

95 High Street Lockerbie DG11 2JH
Tel: 01576 202948
High Street in Lockerbie, at back of Crown Hotel. [D6]

LOCKERBIE

Somerton House Hotel

- *"Friendly atmosphere, with fine home-cooked food."*
- *Classic contemporary.*

AT SOMERTON HOUSE HOTEL, diners have the choice of eating in the extensive cosy lounge where a bar menu is available; the conservatory; and in the delightful dining room where a full à la carte is served. The food is hearty and the dishes familiar but served with some style in these pleasant surroundings.

Lowland Ham and Haddie: a local speciality of smoked haddock and ham in a cream sauce topped with croutons, tomato and cheese. Fillet of ostrich with a creamy tarragon sauce. Meringue and mango roulade.

STB ★★★ Small Hotel

Open all year Rooms: 11 en suite B&B £26–£35 ✕ Lunch £ Dinner ££–£££ Ⓥ Vegetarians welcome Children welcome No smoking in dining room Mastercard/Eurocard, American Express, Visa, Diners Club Proprietors: Alex & Jean Arthur

35 Carlisle Road Lockerbie DG11 2DR
Tel: 01576 202583/202384 Fax: 01576 204218
E-mail: somerton@somertonhotel.co.uk
Web: www.somertonhotel.co.uk
Follow High Street eastwards towards M74, 1 mile from town centre. [D6]

MALLAIG

MELROSE

The Fish Market

- *"Skilled preparation of freshly landed seafood from the boats in the nearby harbour."*
- *Imaginative Scottish cooking.*

THE FISH MARKET is relatively young and everything is fresh and clean. Items from large white bowls of prawns to fresh haddock and fries are served, with home baking for teas and coffees. Sandra McLean makes the very best of the plentiful supplies of fresh produce to ensure diners enjoy her cooking at its best.

Hebridean shellfish broth (oatmeal and leek soup with whole prawns, mussels, scallops and oysters). Pan-fried scallops with saffron and dill, with whole lemon sole stuffed with fresh prawns. Sticky toffee pudding with fresh cream or Orkney ice cream.

◗ *Open all year except Christmas Day, 31 Dec and New Year's Day* ✕ *Lunch £–££ Dinner £–££* Ⓥ *Vegetarians welcome* ✵ *Children welcome* ♿ *Facilities for disabled visitors* ⊞ *Mastercard/ Eurocard, Visa, Switch, Delta* ⋈ *Proprietor: Sandra McLean*

Station Road Mallaig PH41 4QS
Tel: 01687 462299 Fax: 01687 462623
In the centre of village overlooking the harbour. A two minute walk from railway station and five minutes from ferry terminal. [B4]

Burts Hotel

- *"Warm Borders hospitality with consistently good, imaginative Scottish cooking."*
- *Modern Scottish cooking.*

BURTS HOTEL is run by Graham, Anne, Nicholas and Trish Henderson, professional and friendly hosts. Their restaurant has an excellent local reputation. Daily changing lunch and dinner menus are innovative and prepared by a skilled chef who knows how to balance preparation and presentation whilst enhancing flavours.

Brandade of lobster and cod served on a king prawn and Champagne jelly. Canon of venison with a black trumpet mushroom mousse accompanied with seared king scallops. Fresh Border raspberry tartlet with a lemon yoghurt cream.

STB ★★★★ Small Hotel

◗ *Open all year except Boxing Day* ⊞ *Rooms: 20 en suite* ⇔ *DB&B £60–£69 B&B £44–£52* SP *Special rates available* ✕ *Lunch except Christmas Day and Boxing Day ££ Dinner except Christmas Day and Boxing Day £££* Ⓥ *Vegetarians welcome* ✵ *Children welcome* ⋊ *No smoking in restaurant* ⊞ *Mastercard/ Eurocard, American Express, Visa, Diners Club, Switch, Delta, JCB* ⋈ *Owners: The Henderson Family*

Market Square Melrose Scottish Borders TD6 9PL
Tel: 01896 822285 Fax: 01896 822870
E-mail: burtshotel@aol.com
Web: www.burtshotel.co.uk
B6394, 2 miles from A68, 38 miles south of Edinburgh. [D6]

MELROSE

Dryburgh Abbey Hotel

- *"An exciting new chef at Dryburgh Abbey Hotel creating outstanding dishes using only the best local produce."*
- *International and modern Scottish.*

DRYBURGH ABBEY HOTEL is an impressive red sandstone baronial mansion. In the spacious, elegant Tweed Restaurant, new Head Chef Hugh Miller offers a table d'hôte menu which changes daily and uses only fresh local produce. During the day, light meals are also available in the courtyard bar and hotel lounges.

Home-cured gravadlax, salad greens, sweet mustard and dill dressing. Roast saddle of venison, compote of cranberries and pink peppercorn hollandaise. Iced tiramisu parfait with cappuccino ice cream.

STB ★★★★ Hotel

◐ *Open all year* 🏨 *Rooms: 37 en suite* 🛏 *DB&B £54–£98 B&B £40–£85* 🅟 *Special rates available* ✗ *Food available all day £ Lunch from £–££ Dinner from £££* Ⓥ *Vegetarians welcome* 🧒 *Children welcome* ♿ *Facilities for disabled visitors* ⊁ *No smoking in restaurant* 💳 *Mastercard/Eurocard, American Express, Visa, Switch, Delta, JCB* 🛅 *General Manager: Matthew Grose*

St Boswells Melrose Scottish Borders TD6 0RQ
Tel: 01835 822261 Fax: 01835 823945
E-mail: enquiries@dryburgh.co.uk
Web: www.dryburgh.co.uk
Off A68 at St Boswells onto B6404. 2 miles turn left onto B6356. Continue for 1½ miles, hotel signposted. [D6]

MOFFAT

Well View Hotel

- *"An excellent example of natural cooking with Scottish produce."*
- *Modern Scottish cooking.*

AT WELL VIEW prior reservation is essential for lunch and dinner. The six course taster dinner menu demonstrates an inventive approach to more familiar dishes, accompanied by light fruity sauces and dressings. John Schuckardt has a good knowledge of wine and has over 100 Bins available. German and a little French spoken.

Fillet of Galloway salmon with a horseradish crust and a dill and Chardonnay sauce. Fillet of Stobo beef on a bed of roasted root vegetables with a red wine jus. Selection of fine cheeses and desserts.

STB ★★★★ Hotel

◐ *Open all year* 🏨 *Rooms: 6 en suite* 🛏 *DB&B £62–£90 B&B £34–£65* 🅟 *Special rates available* ✗ *Lunch except Sat ££ Dinner 6 course menu £££* Ⓥ *Vegetarians welcome* 🧒 *Children over 5 years welcome at dinner* ⊁ *No smoking throughout* 💳 *Mastercard/ Eurocard, American Express, Visa* 🛅 *Owners: Janet & John Schuckardt*

Ballplay Road Moffat DG10 9JU
Tel: 01683 220184 Fax: 01683 220088
E-mail: info@wellview.co.uk
Web: www.wellview.co.uk
Leaving Moffat take A708. At crossroads, left into Ballplay Road – hotel on right. [D6]

MUIR OF ORD

Ord House Hotel

- *"A 17th century country house of character offering guests a homely and relaxing stay."*
- *Good country cooking.*

BUILT IN 1637 and retaining original features, Ord House is a country home away from home with log fires, comfy chairs and beautiful grounds. Enjoy well-prepared fresh local produce including fish, game and meat, as well as fruit, vegetables and herbs from the walled garden in season. Fluent French is spoken.

Salad of smoked halibut and gravadlax with dill sauce. Roasted salmon fillet wrapped in prosciutto with herby lentils, spinach and yoghurt. Pavlova roulade with raspberries and crème pâtissière.

STB ★★ Small Hotel

❍ *Open 1 May to 20 Oct* 🏠 *Rooms: 10 en suite* 🛏 *DB&B £59–£71 B&B £38–£48* ✕ *Lunch £ Dinner 4 course menu £££* Ⓥ *Vegetarians welcome* ☀ *Children welcome* ✄ *No smoking in dining room* 💳 *Mastercard/Eurocard, American Express, Visa* 🅽 *Proprietors: John & Eliza Allen*

Muir of Ord Ross-shire IV6 7UH
Tel: 01463 870492 Fax: 01463 870492
E-mail: eliza@ord-house.com
Web: www.ord-house.com
On A832 Ullapool-Marybank, ½ mile west of Muir of Ord. [C4]

NAIRN

Cawdor Tavern

- *"Diners come from far and wide to eat here – with such delicious food and warm welcome it is not surprising."*
- *The best of traditional Scottish fare.*

CAWDOR TAVERN is a traditional country pub in a building which was originally the old castle workshop. Open log fires and a wood burning stove give a warm welcome to complement some real quality bar meals. The restaurant offers modern Scottish cuisine using fresh, local produce. Popular with locals and visitors.

Crab and prawn risotto with pesto marie rose. Loin of prime Scottish lamb on black pudding mousseline with rhubarb chutney and lovage jus. Warm Belgian chocolate and marshmallow tart with Drambuie crème anglaise.

❍ *Open all year except 25 and 26 Dec* ✕ *Lunch £ Dinner ££* Ⓥ *Vegetarians welcome* ☀ *Children welcome* ✄ *Facilities for disabled visitors* ✄ *No smoking area in restaurant* 💳 *Mastercard/ Eurocard, American Express, Visa, Diners Club, Switch* 🅽 *Proprietor: Norman Sinclair*

Cawdor Nairn IV12 5XP
Tel: 01667 404 777 Fax: 01667 404 777
Web: www.cawdortavern.com
Turn off A96 to Cawdor. Tavern is clearly signposted. [C3]

NAIRN

Golf View Hotel & Leisure Club

- *"Dining in the conservatory on a hot summer's evening overlooking the sea – quite Mediterranean."*
- *Modern Scottish cooking.*

THE GOLF VIEW is within an hour's drive of 25 golf courses. Its leisure club has a magnificent pool and Nautilus equipped gym. Fish and shellfish feature strongly on the restaurant's nightly-changing table d'hôte menu, as well as locally-sourced meat and game. Vegetarian dishes show great imagination. The Conservatory serves food all day.

Isle of Skye squid, roasted with a lemon and herb stuffing, served with a curried lobster and crab relish. Fillet of Sutherland venison, with a shallot rösti and a chanterelle casserole. Trilogy of chocolates.

STB ★★★★ Hotel
Green Tourism Two Leaf Silver Award

◐ *Open all year* 🏨 *Rooms: 44 en suite* 🛏 *DB&B £76–£99 B&B £54–£77* 💷 *Special rates available* ✗ *Food available all day £–££ Lunch £–££ Dinner 4 course menu £££* Ⅴ *Vegetarians welcome* ⚬ *Children welcome* ♿ *Facilities for disabled visitors* ✳ *No smoking in restaurant and conservatory* 💳 *Mastercard/Eurocard, American Express, Visa, Diners Club, Switch* 🎫 *Operations Director: Greta Anderson*

Seabank Road Nairn IV12 4HD
Tel: 01667 452301 Fax: 01667 455267
E-mail: rooms@morton-hotels.com
Web: www.morton-hotels.com
At west end of Nairn. Seaward side of A96. Turn off at large Parish Church. Hotel on right. [C3]

NAIRN

The Newton Hotel & Highland Conference Centre

- *"The conference facilities at the Newton Hotel are superb, sound food and comfortable accommodation makes a stay memorable."*
- *Modern Scottish.*

THE NEWTON HOTEL is set in 21 acres of secluded grounds with magnificent views over the Moray Firth and the Ross-shire Hills beyond. The restaurant offers interesting menus focusing on best use of local produce, which are treated skilfully and imaginatively by the chef.

Pan-seared crab cake rolled in brioche crumbs presented over wilted baby spinach, ribboned with ginger butter sauce. Pot-roasted loin of venison with beetroot and cranberries. Orange suet pudding with chocolate sauce and a vanilla pod ice cream.

STB ★★★★ Hotel
Green Tourism Two Leaf Silver Award

◐ *Open all year* 🏨 *Rooms: 57 en suite* 🛏 *DB&B £76–£99 B&B £54–£77* 💷 *Special rates available* ✗ *Food available all day £££ Lunch £ Dinner £££* Ⅴ *Vegetarians welcome* ⚬ *Children welcome* ♿ *Facilities for disabled visitors* ✳ *No smoking in restaurant* 💳 *Mastercard/Eurocard, American Express, Visa, Diners Club, Switch* 🎫 *General Manager: Kevin Reid*

Inverness Road Nairn IV12 4RX
Tel: 01667 453144 Fax: 01667 454026
E-mail: info@morton-hotels.com
Web: www.morton-hotels.com
West of Nairn town centre on A96. [C3]

NAIRN

Sunny Brae Hotel

- *"A charming, small, friendly hotel with delicious home cooking and wonderful attention to guests' comfort and needs."*
- *Scottish cooking with European flair.*

EVERYTHING AT SUNNY BRAE is top quality. Ian and Sylvia pride themselves in looking after their guests well. Though small, the hotel has a high degree of luxury. Sylvia who is German is the chef – the menus have a distinct European influence with a strong emphasis on quality local produce.

Aultbea smoked monkfish salad with galia melon and strawberries marinated in balsamic and honey. Ragoût of wild Highland venison served with a rosemary infused red wine sauce on puréed parsnip. Raspberry and Drambuie parfait with crème anglaise.

STB ★★★★ Small Hotel
Green Tourism Two Leaf Silver Award

◗ *Open Mar to Oct* 🏠 *Rooms: 9 en suite* 🍴 *DB&B £57.50–£66.50 B&B £35–£44* 💷 *Special rates available* ✕ *Lunch residents only ££ Dinner non residents booking essential ££* Ⓥ *Vegetarians welcome* ✹ *Children welcome* ♿ *Limited facilities for disabled visitors* ✹ *Smoking in lounge only* 💳 *Mastercard/ Eurocard, Visa, Switch, Delta, JCB* ⚑ *Owners: Sylvia & Ian Bochel*

Marine Road Nairn IV12 4EA Tel: 01667 452309 Fax: 01667 454860 E-mail: tos@sunnybraehotel.com Web: www.sunnybraehotel.com Follow A96 Aberdeen-Inverness road through Nairn, at roundabout carry straight onto Marine Road, hotel on left. [C3]

NETHY BRIDGE

Mountview Hotel

- *"A delightful hotel offering Highland hospitality and fine food."*
- *Modern Scottish.*

THE MOUNTVIEW is a great spot from which to admire and explore all that this stunning part of the Highlands has to offer. It is traditional and comfortable with meals served in the restaurant or residents dining room. Cooking is skilled making good use of locally sourced produce.

Red onion and goats cheese tart with mixed leaves and a walnut dressing. Fillet of sea bass with a green grape and sorrel sauce. Ginger and black treacle pudding with ginger sauce.

STB ★★★ Small Hotel

◗ *Open all year except Christmas Day Restaurant closed Mon Tue* 🏠 *Rooms: 12, 11 en suite* 🍴 *B&B from £29.50* 💷 *Special rates available* ✕ *Dinner except Mon Tue ££* Ⓥ *Vegetarians welcome* ✹ *Children welcome* ✹ *No smoking in public rooms* 💳 *Mastercard/ Eurocard, American Express, Visa, Diners Club, Switch, Delta* ⚑ *Owner: Mrs Caryl Shaw*

Nethy Bridge Inverness-shire PH25 3EB Tel: 01479 821248 E-mail: mviewhotel@aol.com Web: www.members.aol.com/mviewhotel 10 miles north-east of Aviemore, leave A9 north of Aviemore and reach Nethybridge via Boat of Garten. The Mountview Hotel is well-signposted on the main road through the village. [C4]

NEWBURGH

Udny Arms Hotel

- *"Good food and wine to make a day's fishing or golf complete."*
- *Creative Scottish cooking.*

IN THE SPLIT-LEVEL bistro Chef Scott Kinghorn changes the extensive à la carte menu every season, which also includes a handful of 'specials' that change daily. Only fresh local produce is used. There is a Café Bar and Cocktail Bar where bar food is served at alternative prices. Member of the Certified Aberdeen Angus Scheme.

Fresh scallops with garlic and vermouth butter sauce. Roast Shetland salmon fillet served with tempura of oyster, crab claw, sesame oil and soya dressing. Chocolate mocha torte and espresso ice cream.

STB ★★★ Hotel

◗ *Open all year except Christmas Night and Boxing Night* 🛏 *Rooms: 26 en suite* 🛏 *DB&B £80–£120 B&B £45–£85 per room per night* 🆂🅿 *Special rates available* ✖ *Lunch £ Dinner ££* 🆅 *Vegetarians welcome* ✹ *Children welcome* ♿ *Limited facilities for disabled visitors* 💳 *Mastercard/Eurocard, Visa, Diners Club, Switch, Delta, JCB* 🄼 *Sole Owners/Proprietors: Denis & Jennifer Craig*

Main Street Newburgh Aberdeenshire AB41 6BL
Tel: 01358 789444 Fax: 01358 789012
E-mail: enquiry@udny.demon.co.uk
Web: www.udny.co.uk
On A975, 2½ miles off A90 Aberdeen-Peterhead – 15 minutes from Aberdeen.[D4]

NEWTON STEWART

The Black Sheep Inn

- *"Warm Galloway hospitality in relaxing atmosphere."*
- *Modern Scottish.*

THE BLACK SHEEP INN is a stone built courtyard dating back to the 1800s. Award-winning Chef Paul Somerville prepares, presents and serves traditional Scottish food in a innovative modern style making excellent use of natural food from Galloway. The atmosphere is relaxing with modern decor enhanced with a selection of prints by local artists.

Seared Kirkcudbright king scallops with asparagus, poached egg and a chivry sauce. Braised lamb shank with roast shallots, garlic and rosemary mash and a port enriched jus. Apple and calvados iced parfait with brandy snaps and a passion fruit coulis.

STB ★★★★ Self Catering

◗ *Open all year except Boxing Day and 2 Jan* 🛏 *6 self-catering lodges (catering for 24)* 🆂🅿 *Special rates available* ✖ *Lunch ££ Dinner £££* 🆅 *Vegetarians welcome* ✹ *Children welcome* ♿ *Facilities for disabled visitors* 🚭 *No smoking in restaurant* 🐕 *Dogs welcome* 💳 *Mastercard/Eurocard, Visa, Switch, Visa Electron, Solo* 🄼 *Director: Alistair MacMillan*

Nether Barr Steadings Ltd Nether Barr Newton Stewart DG8 6AU
Tel: 01671 404326 Fax: 01671 404860
E-mail: info@netherbarr.co.uk
Web: www.netherbarr.co.uk
½ mile from Newton Stewart roundabout on the A714 Wigtown road. [C7]

NEWTON STEWART

Corsemalzie House Hotel

- *"Friendly and efficient, ensuring guests have an enjoyable stay."*
- *Modern Scottish cooking.*

CORSEMALZIE is an excellent example of an 19th century country mansion. Chef David Alexander offers interesting and innovative dishes using fresh local produce and vegetables from the hotel's garden. Menus are complemented by a carefully chosen wine list. Corsemalzie also has its own game, fishing and shooting.

Tian of avocado and potted shrimp flavoured with coriander and lime with sauce gazpacho. Seared medallions of local venison served with sweet pickled red cabbage, fondant potato and grand-veneur sauce. Frozen prune and armagnac parfait with an Earl Grey Syrup.

STB ★★★★ Hotel

◗ *Open 1 Mar to 20 Jan except Christmas Day and Boxing Day* 🏨 *Rooms: 14 en suite* 🛏 *DB&B from £59.50 B&B £40–£49.50* 💷 *Special rates available* ✕ *Lunch £–££ Dinner £££* 🎫 *Vegetarians welcome* ☂ *Children welcome* ♿ *Facilities for disabled visitors – ground floor only* ✂ *No smoking in dining room* 💳 *Mastercard/Eurocard, American Express, Visa, Switch, Delta* 🗝 *Proprietor: Peter McDougall*

Port William Newton Stewart DG8 9RL
Tel: 01988 860 254 Fax: 01988 860 213
E-mail: corsemalzie@ndirect.co.uk
Web: www.lighthousehotel.co.uk
Halfway along B7005 Glenluce-Wigtown, off A714 Newton Stewart-Port William or A747 Glenluce-Port William. [C7]

NEWTON STEWART

Kirroughtree House

- *"Gourmet Scottish cooking presented with perfection."*
- *Gourmet Scottish cooking.*

KIRROUGHTREE has two dining rooms reached from the panelled lounge. Head Chef Rolf Mueller was trained in Switzerland and has a distinctive modern Scottish, with French influence, style of cooking. The menus are short, creative and well-balanced. Everything at Kirroughtree is done to the highest standards – polished and professional without being stuffy.

Grilled Solway scallops with vegetable relish and beurre blanc. Orange and ginger marinated breast of Gressingham duck served with galette potato, tomato fondue, Savoy cabbage and baby turnips, surrounded by a rich port sauce. Pear tarte tatin drizzled with sauce legere.

STB ★★★★ Hotel

◗ *Open mid Feb to 3 Jan* 🏨 *Rooms: 17 en suite* 🛏 *DB&B £70–£100 B&B £60–£85* 💷 *Special rates available* ✕ *Lunch – booking essential ££ Dinner 4 course menu £££* 🎫 *Vegetarians welcome – prior notice required* ☂ *Children over 10 years welcome* ✂ *No smoking in dining rooms* 💳 *Mastercard/Eurocard, Visa, Switch* 🗝 *Manager: James Stirling*

Newton Stewart DG8 6AN
Tel: 01671 402141 Fax: 01671 402425
E-mail: info@kirroughtreehouse.co.uk
Web: www.mcmillanhotels.com
From A75 take A712 New Galloway road, hotel 300 yards on left. [C7]

NEWTONMORE

Eagle View Guest House

- *"A cosy place with imaginative home cooking."*
- *Creative home cooking.*

NICKY DRUCQUER has created a Highland Haven in the Eagle View Guest House – 'Monarch of the Glen' country. She creates the most interesting and imaginative of dishes offering value for money, with a homely atmosphere and a knowledge of the area – and good food! Nicky has a flair and skill of produce.

Pea soup with minted cream. Ragoût of pigeon in rowanberry jelly with onion marmalade on a bed of olive mash. Gooseberry and lemongrass ice cream with ginger snap.

STB ★★★ Guest House

❶ *Open all year except second fortnight in Oct and Christmas night Closed Sun dinner* ⌂ *Rooms: 5, 3 en suite* ⇥ *DB&B £37.50–£39.50 B&B £20–£22* ⑲ *Special rates available* ⑪ *Unlicensed – Guests welcome to take own wine* ✗ *Dinner except Sun ££ Open to non-residents – booking essential* Ⓥ *Vegetarians welcome* ⚐ *Children welcome* ♿ *Limited facilities for disabled visitors* ✗ *No smoking throughout* ⚑*Dogs welcome – please advise at time of booking* ⊞ *Mastercard, Visa* ⚙ *Proprietor: Nicky Drucquer*

Perth Road Newtonmore PH20 1AP
Tel: 01540 673675
E-mail: eagleview@aol.com
Web: www.newtonmore.com/eagleview
At the south end of the village. First guest house on the right-hand side, if coming north. [C4]

OBAN

Ards House

- *"For comfort, cuisine and cosy atmosphere, Ards House has it all. It's unsurpassed."*
- *Traditional Scottish cooking.*

ARDS HOUSE stands on the water's edge with views over Loch Etive to Ardmuchnish Bay. Guests are made very welcome by the owners, John and Jean Bowman, and are treated like friends. John is an innovative cook and uses only fresh local ingredients to produce meals of the highest standard. Set menu changes daily.

Aberdeen smoked cod en croûte with a coconut and lime velouté. Roast rack of Scottish lamb with a minted red wine jus. White chocolate pudding with a dark chocolate and orange sauce.

STB ★★★ Small Hotel

❶ *Open Feb to mid Nov* ⌂ *Rooms: 7 (6 en suite, 1 with private facilities)* ⇥ *DB&B £58–£64 B&B £35–£47* ⑲ *Special rates available* ❢ *Restricted licence* ✗ *Dinner 4 course menu £££ Non-residents – by arrangement* Ⓥ *Vegetarians and special diets catered for – by arrangement* ⚐ *Young adults over 16 years old welcome* ✗ *No smoking throughout* ⊞ *Mastercard/Eurocard, Visa, Switch, Delta, JCB* ⚙ *Proprietors: John & Jean Bowman*

Connel by Oban PA37 1PT
Tel: 01631 710255
E-mail: jb@ardshouse.demon.co.uk
Web: www.ardshouse.com
On main A85 Oban–Tyndrum, 4½ miles north of Oban. [B5]

OBAN

Barcaldine House

- *"Quiet and secluded, a place where you can totally relax."*
- *Contemporary Scottish.*

BARCALDINE HOUSE has been tastefully renovated to the highest standards whilst retaining many original features. Nowhere better to relax than in the elegant drawing room. Barcaldine offers a warm welcome, and good food prepared by Chef Gary Smith. All tastes are catered for in a contemporary style. Six self-catering cottages available in hotel grounds.

Ravioli of haggis with neep and tattie velouté. Roast monkfish tail on a smoked haddock pattie with asparagus and chive cream. Glazed orange and lemon tart on a pool of damson and sloe gin coulis.

STB ★★★★ Small Hotel

◐ *Open all year Restaurant closed Mon evening* 🏨 *Rooms: 7 en suite* 🛏 *DB&B £55–£75 B&B £40–£60* 🆂🅿 *Special rates available* ✗ *Lunch – bookings of 10 people or more only ££ Dinner except Mon £££* Ⓥ *Vegetarians welcome* ☀ *Children welcome* ♿ *Facilities for disabled* ✂ *No smoking in dining room* 🐾 *Dogs welcome* 💳 *Mastercard/Eurocard, Visa, Switch, Delta, Solo, Visa Electron* 🔪 *Chef Manager: Gary Smith; Manager: Wendy Graham*

Barcaldine By Oban PA37 1SG
Tel: 01631 720219 Fax: 01631 720219
E-mail barcaldine@breathe.co.uk
Web: www.countrymansions.com
A828 Barcaldine village, driveway 1m north of Sealife Centre – driveway on right. Hotel is ¼m along driveway. [B5]

OBAN

Blarcreen Farm Guest House

- *"Victorian farmhouse comforts within a peaceful location."*
- *Scottish gourmet cooking.*

NESTLING ON the shores of Loch Etive, Blarcreen Farm Guest House is the ideal place to relax within tranquil countryside. It has been lovingly and beautifully furnished in keeping with the Victorian period and features of this substantial home. Four-poster king size beds and tasty hearty cooking from Johanna and Bruce guarantee an enjoyable stay.

Peppered tomato soup with red wine. Fresh Loch Etive trout with glazed almonds, sweet potatoes and ginger. Chilled rhubarb fool with brandy and warm baked meringue.

STB ★★★★ B&B

◐ *Open from 1 Mar to 31 Dec* 🏨 *Rooms: 3 en suite* 🛏 *DB&B £42–£55 B&B £29.50–£38* 🆂🅿 *Special rates available* 🍷 *Unlicensed* ✗ *Residents only Packed Lunch £ Dinner ££* Ⓥ *Vegetarians welcome* ✂ *No smoking throughout* 💳 *Mastercard/Eurocard, Visa* 🔪 *Proprietor: Johanna Lace-DeVere; Partner: Bruce Lace-DeVere*

Ardchattan Oban PA37 1RG
Tel: 01631 750272 Fax: 01631 750272
E-mail: j.lace@blarcreenfarm.demon.co.uk
Web: www.blarcreenfarm.com
From Edinburgh or Glasgow take A85 Oban road to Connel, under Connel Bridge, turn left signposted Fort William. After bridge right immediately for Ardchattan Priory. Follow single track loch road for 6 miles following signs for Bonawe. Blarcreen right-hand side. [B5]

OBAN

The Gathering Restaurant and O'Donnells Irish Bar

- *"Good value for money at this cosy, interesting restaurant, especially for the early birds!"*
- *Good, simple cooking with imagination.*

FIRST OPENED IN 1882 as a supper room for the famous annual Gathering Ball, the Gathering has a distinguished pedigree and is rightly popular with Oban's many tourists. First-class, straightforward dishes use local meat and seafood, as well as imaginative starters and popular 'lighter bites'. The wine list is well-chosen and fairly priced.

Ocean Bounty Platter: combination of mussels, oysters, langoustines, salmon, herring. Prime Scottish fillet steak, flame-grilled. Highlander ice cream: whisky, honey and oatmeal ice cream.

◗ *Open Easter to New Year except Christmas Day, New Year's Day and some Suns Closed Sun off-season – please telephone Note: closed to public last Thu in Aug* ✕ *Bar lunch £–££: Bar evening meals £ off-season by reservation Dinner (Restaurant) ££–£££* Ⓥ *Vegetarians welcome* ♣ *Children welcome* ♿ *Facilities for disabled visitors* ✲ *No smoking in restaurant* 🆔 *Mastercard/Eurocard, American Express, Visa, Switch, Delta, JCB* Ⓜ *Owner/Chef: Elaine Cameron*

Breadalbane Street Oban PA34 5NZ
Tel: 01631 565421/564849/566159
Fax: 01631 565421
E-mail: gatheringoban@aol
Entering Oban from A85 (Glasgow) one-way system. Turn left at Deanery Brae into Breadalbane Street (signs for swimming pool etc.) then right at bottom of Deanery Brae. [B5]

OBAN

Loch Melfort Hotel and Restaurant

- *"Breathtaking views and superb food."*
- *Imaginative Scottish cuisine.*

LOCH MELFORT is the place to be for peace and tranquility where the landscape is mesmerising. Local fish and shellfish feature in the daily changing menus. Formal dining is available in the restaurant and more relaxed bar meals are served in the Skerry Bistro.

Seared Islay scallops, braised fennel and ginger cream. Pan-fried loin of venison, roasted barley and wild mushroom risotto, chocolate game jus. Poached pear, mulled wine syrup and cinnamon and honey ice cream.

STB ★★★★ Hotel

◗ *Open all year* 🏠 *Rooms: 26 en suite* 🛏 *DB&B £45–£89 B&B £39–£59* 🆂🅿 *Special rates available* ✕ *Food available all day Lunch from £ Dinner £££* Ⓥ *Vegetarians welcome* ♣ *Children welcome* ♿ *Limited facilities for disabled visitors* ✲ *No smoking in restaurant* 🐕*Well behaved dogs welcome – not permitted in public rooms* 🆔 *Mastercard/Eurocard, American Express, Visa, Switch, Delta* Ⓜ *Owner: Nigel & Kyle Schofield*

Arduaine by Oban Argyll PA34 4XG
Tel: 01852 200 233 Fax: 01852 200 214
E-mail: lmhotel@aol.com
Web: www.loch-melfort.co.uk
On A816, 19 miles south of Oban. [B5]

OBAN

OBAN

The Manor House

- *"Excellent service and skilled cooking in delightful surroundings."*
- *Modern Scottish with French influences.*

MANOR HOUSE retains much of the charm and atmosphere of the past and is a delightful hotel in a stunning location. Now under new ownership it is receiving the care and upgrading deserving of such a special place. It offers a five course table d'hôte dinner menu which changes daily with seasonal variations.

Rilette of poached and smoked salmon with crème fraîche and red onions. Half Hebridean lobster with courgette ribbons, with a light Orkney Cheddar and Drambuie sauce. Shortbread tower with Chantilly cream, bananas and toffee sauce.

STB ★★★★ Small Hotel

◑ *Open all year Closed Sun 3pm to Tue 6pm during Nov to Feb* 🏠 *Rooms: 11 en suite* 🛏 *DB&B £58–£80 B&B £30–£55 Single rates on application* 🆂🅿 *Special rates available* ✗ *Lunch ££ Dinner £££* Ⓥ *Vegetarians welcome* 🧒 *Children 12 years and over welcome* ✿ *No smoking in dining room and bedrooms* 🐕*Dogs welcome by arrangement* 💳 *Mastercard, American Express, Visa, Switch, Delta* 🔪 *Manageress: Gabriella Wijker*

Gallanach Road Oban PA34 4LS
Tel: 01631 562087/562661 Fax: 01631 563053
E-mail: manorhouseoban@aol.com
Web: www.manorhouseoban.com
Oban, Gallanach Road. Follow signs for Oban ferry terminal. Manor House is 200 yards past the ferry terminal entrance. [B5]

The Waterfront Restaurant

- *"Quality fresh seafood in a relaxed bistro style restaurant."*
- *Bold and skilled seafood.*

THE MOTTO here is 'from the pier to the pan as fast as you can'! The first floor restaurant has commanding views over Oban Bay and the Sound of Mull. The chef is 'on view' preparing fresh seafood for lunch/dinner. All produce is carefully cooked to order and presented professionally in a relaxed atmosphere. Member Scotland the Brand.

Seil Island oysters, natural with lemon or grilled with Parmesan. Sea bass with wok-fried vegetables and roasted pepper dressing. Caramelised peanut brûlée.

◑ *Open Easter to Christmas* ✗ *Lunch – depending on choice £–££££ Dinner £–££££* Ⓥ *Vegetarians welcome* 🧒 *Children welcome* 🐕 *Guide dogs welcome* 💳 *Mastercard/Eurocard, American Express, Visa, Switch* 🔪 *Head Chef/Manager: Alex Needham*

No 1 The Pier Oban Argyll PA34 4LW
Tel: 01631 563110 Fax: 01631 563110
Approaching Oban from north or south. Look out for the clock tower – park wherever you can and head for railway and ferry pier. Restaurant is well-signposted from start of pier. [B5]

OBAN

Willowburn Hotel

- *"Peace and tranquility enhanced by superb food."*
- *Outstanding Scottish cooking.*

THIS COMFORTABLE small hotel stands in 1½ acres of garden which leads down to Clachan Sound. Guests are made very welcome and treated like friends. Menus change daily and Chef/Proprietor Chris Mitchell uses only the freshest local produce. Herbs, soft fruits and vegetables are from the hotel's garden.

Lobster and scallop sausages with frothy saffron sauce. Pork roasted in milk with garlic and rosemary, served with caramelised apple. Single bean chocolate and raspberry dessert with lemon Mascarpone.

STB ★★★★ Small Hotel

⦿ Open 1 Mar to 2 Jan 🏠 Rooms: 7 en suite 🛏 DB&B £50–£60 ▨ Special rates available for longer stays ✕ Lunch – residents only £ Dinner £££ Ⓥ Vegetarians welcome ✽ Well-behaved children welcome ⅍ No smoking throughout ▣ Mastercard/Eurocard, Visa, Switch, Delta, JCB ◪ Proprietors: Jan Wolfe & Chris Mitchell

Clachan-Seil by Oban Argyll PA34 4TJ
Tel: 01852 300276 Fax: 01852 300597
E-mail: willowburn.hotel@virgin.net
Web: www.willowburn.co.uk
On the Island of Seil, near Oban, just a few 100 yards from 'The Bridge over the Atlantic'. [B5]

OBAN

Yacht Corryvreckan

- *"The unique Taste of Scotland yacht, Douglas and Mary well deserve their wonderful reputation for fine food and great company."*
- *Best fresh home cooking.*

PEOPLE KEEP RETURNING again and again to this enchanting experience. You do not know where you will go – it depends on the morning wind – but wherever it will be Mary and Douglas have been before and know where to source the best herbs, fruit and seafood, not to mention the best sheltered bays and captivating views. Feast your eyes and your appetite while discovering Scotland's islands.

A salad of fresh and smoked salmon, with strawberries. Venison, peppered with crushed juniper, with a wild berry sauce. Zingy lime parfait.

⦿ Open Apr to Oct 🏠 Cabins: 5 twin berth cabins, 3 heads with shower 🛏 DB&B £465–£525 per person for 1 week cruise – all incl ▨ Special rates available for whole boat charter ▥ Unlicensed – wine available with dinner ⅍ No smoking below deck ▣ Parking available ▣ No credit cards ◪ Proprietors: Douglas & Mary Lindsay

Dal an Eas Kilmore Oban Argyll PA34 4XU
Tel: 01631 770246 Fax: 01631 770246
E-mail: yacht.corryvreckan@virgin.net
Web: www.corryvreckan.co.uk [B5]

OLDMELDRUM

Meldrum House Hotel

- *"Step back in time, sample Meldrum's culinary delights amidst historic surroundings."*
- *Creative Scottish cooking.*

RESIDENT PROPRIETORS Douglas and Eileen Pearson are attentive and courteous hosts who make you very welcome to their home. Residents and non-residents can enjoy an imaginative and well-constructed four course table d'hôte menu carefully overseen by enthusiastic Chef Mark Will. To complement the meal there is a comprehensive, reasonably priced wine list.

Rabbit, hare and rosemary parfait with rowanberry sauce. Pan-seared fillet of local beef with goats cheese, asparagus and sloe gin sauce. Summer fruit pudding with Mascarpone.

STB ★★★ Hotel

◐ *Open all year* 🏠 *Rooms: 9 en suite* 🛏 *DB&B £114–£124 B&B £105–£115* 🆂 *Special rates available* ✕ *Lunch ££ Dinner £££* Ⓥ *Vegetarians welcome* ✚ *Children welcome* ♿ *Facilities for disabled visitors* ✄ *No smoking in restaurant* 🔡 *Mastercard/Eurocard, Visa, Switch* 🈲 *Proprietors: Douglas & Eileen Pearson*

Oldmeldrum Aberdeenshire AB51 OAE
Tel: 01651 872294 Fax: 01651 872464
E-mail: dpmeldrum@aol.com
Web: www.meldrumhouse.com
Main gates on A947 (Aberdeen to Banff road).
1 mile north of Old Meldrum. 13 miles north of Aberdeen airport. [D4]

ONICH BY FORT WILLIAM

Allt-nan-Ros Hotel

- *"A well-run family hotel offering a fine culinary experience."*
- *Modern Scottish cooking.*

ALLT-NAN-ROS is an attractive 19th century shooting lodge personally run by James and Fiona Mcleod. The dining room is ideally situated on an elevated position offering an ever changing view from the well-appointed dining room. Menus offer a range of familiar Scottish dishes presented in an imaginative and innovative style.

Soufflé of diver scallop mousse with a buttered sauce of the hotel's smoked oysters and oyster beignets. Crépinettes of Lochaber lamb loin flavoured with wild garlic, potato soufflé, haggis fritters, jus of home-made grain mustard. Oven-baked white peach filled with a balsamic ice cream served in a chilled elderflower soup.

STB ★★★★ Hotel

◐ *Open 1 Jan to 10 Nov* 🏠 *Rooms: 20 en suite* 🛏 *DB&B £60–£80 B&B £38–£55* 🆂 *Special rates available* ✕ *Lunch from £ Dinner 5 course menu from £££* Ⓥ *Vegetarians welcome* ✄ *No smoking in dining room* 🔡 *Mastercard/Eurocard, American Express, Visa, Diners Club, Switch, JCB* 🈲 *Proprietors: James & Fiona Macleod*

Onich Fort William Inverness-shire PH33 6RY
Tel: 01855 821 210 Fax: 01855 821 462
E-mail: allt-nan-ros@zetnet.co.uk
Web: www.allt-nan-ros.co.uk
On A82, 10 miles south of Fort William. [B4]

ONICH BY FORT WILLIAM

Cuilcheanna House

- *"Enjoy the views over Loch Linnhe and savour the skilled cuisine on offer."*
- *Creative Scottish fayre.*

THIS SMALL, PERSONALLY-RUN hotel welcomes visitors to savour the excellent Scottish fayre on offer. Proprietors, Linda and Russell Scott, are friendly hosts. A set four course dinner is enhanced by Russell's unusual wine list. A fine selection of malts are also available in this former farmhouse which dates back to the 17th Century.

Baked crab ramekins with an Isle of Mull Cheddar crust. Breast of Guinea fowl roasted with coriander seeds and oregano, served with a redcurrant and red wine reduction. Little butterscotch creams and Cuilcheanna shortbread.

STB ★★★★ Small Hotel

◗ *Open Easter to end Oct* ⌂ *Rooms: 7 en suite* ⊨ *DB&B £47–£50* ▣ *Special rates available* ✗ *Residents only Dinner 4 course menu ££* Ⓥ *Vegetarians welcome* ✔ *No smoking throughout* ▦ *Mastercard/Eurocard, Visa, Switch, Delta* ◪ *Proprietors: Linda & Russell Scott*

Onich Fort William Inverness-shire PH33 6SD
Tel: 01855 821226
E-mail: relax@cuilcheanna.freeserve.co.uk
Web: www.cuilcheanna.co.uk
Signposted 300m off A82 in village of Onich – 9 miles south of Fort William. [B4]

ONICH BY FORT WILLIAM

Four Seasons Bistro & Bar

- *"Well-cooked local food is on offer at this popular bistro with its open fire in the restaurant."*
- *Modern home style Scottish cooking.*

A FRIENDLY FAMILY RUN business offering local produce makes the Four Seasons a popular base for hillwalkers and families. Well-cooked dishes to suit all tastes. The Four Seasons Bistro and Bar is well worth a visit.

Fresh local langoustine with a sweet chilli and garlic sauce. Noisettes of lamb with a roasted garlic, red wine and rosemary jus. Home-made clootie dumpling with Orkney ice cream or cream.

◗ *Open Christmas and New Year period Winter limited opening until Easter* Ⓥ *Vegetarians welcome* ✚ *Children welcome* ♿ *Facilities for disabled visitors* ✔ *No smoking in eating areas* ▦ *Mastercard/Eurocard, American Express, Visa* ◪ *Manageress: Susan Heron*

Inchree Onich by Fort William PH33 6SE
Tel: 01855 821393 Fax: 01855 821287
E-mail: enquiry@restaurant-scotland.com
Web: www.restaurant-scotland.com
8 miles south of Fort William. Take Inchree turn-off, ¼ mile south of Corran Ferry, then 250 yards. [B4]

ONICH BY FORT WILLIAM

The Lodge On The Loch Hotel

- *"A Highland hotel offering stylish food in beautiful surroundings."*
- *Stylish Scottish cooking.*

THIS IS A HAVEN for all types of guests. A very relaxed, warm atmosphere all managed by professional husband and wife team Jamie and Jackie Burns. The decor reflects the beauty of the surrounding gardens and countryside. Bedrooms are comfortable and the dining room has delightful loch views. Fine food is served in the classically designed restaurant.

Avocado and crab meat sushi, seasoned with hot wasabi paste and pickled pink ginger. Pan-fried breast of Argyll duck, minted girotte cherries and caraway scented cabbage. Raspberry bread pudding, summer berry compote and clotted cream.

STB ★★★★ Hotel

◗ Open Apr to Oct also open Christmas and New Year ☷ Rooms: 20, 18 en suite ⬌ DB&B £69.50–£100 ⓢⓟ Special rates available ✗ Light lunch £ Dinner 4 course menu £££ Ⓥ Vegetarians welcome ⚲ Children over 12 years welcome ♿ Facilities for disabled visitors ✙ No smoking in dining room ⊞ Mastercard/ Eurocard, Visa, Switch, Delta ⚑ Managers: Jamie & Jackie Burns

Onich nr Fort William The Scottish Highlands PH33 6RY
Tel: 01855 821237 Fax: 01855 821463
E-mail: reservations@freedomglen.co.uk
Web: www.freedomglen.co.uk
On A82, 1 mile north of the Ballachulish Bridge. [B4]

ONICH BY FORT WILLIAM

Onich Hotel

- *"Relaxed and friendly atmosphere with a range of dishes to suit all tastes."*
- *Blends of traditional and contemporary Scottish.*

IDEALLY LOCATED on the shores of Loch Linnhe, the hotel is well maintained from the interior to the well-tended gardens. The management's commitment to all aspects of the hotel is evident – from the calibre of staff to the quality of produce and cooking from the kitchen offering a fine all round experience.

Highland terrine with black pudding, pear chutney and pickled cucumber, finished with a balsamic jus. Breast of pheasant filled with apricot and pistachio mousse, wild mushroom risotto cake and calvados cream. Drambuie and vanilla panna cotta with caramelised oranges.

STB ★★★★ Small Hotel

◗ Open all year ☷ Rooms: 25 en suite ⬌ DB&B £57–£76 B&B £34–£53 ⓢⓟ Special rates available ✗ Bar meals available all day ££ Dinner £££ Ⓥ Vegetarians welcome ⚲ Children welcome ♿ Facilities for disabled visitors ✙ No smoking in restaurant ⚑Dogs welcome – not allowed in dining areas ⊞ Mastercard/Eurocard, American Express, Visa, Diners Club, Switch, Delta ⚑ Managing Director: Stewart Leitch

Onich by Fort William PH33 7RY
Tel: 01855 821214 Fax: 01855 821484
E-mail: enquiries@onich-fortwilliam.co.uk
Web: www.onich-fortwilliam.co.uk
On A82 in the village of Onich on the shores of Loch Linnhe – 12 miles south of Fort William. [B4]

PAISLEY

Makerston House

- *"Simple cooking using fresh local ingredients – try the home-made oatcakes!"*
- *Scottish home cooking.*

MARY McCUE was housekeeper at Makerston in the past and now welcomes guests in her amicable style making them feel part of the family. Food is prepared and presented in simple style with attention to flavour and quality of ingredients. There is also much home baking here to be enjoyed 'in the jewel in Paisley's crown'.

Red pepper soup. Roast leg of lamb and poached minted pear with gratin dauphinoise, courgette and carrot batons and rosemary and thyme. Pavlova.

❶ *Open 3 Jan to 24 Dec* 🏨 *Rooms: 11, 8 en suite* 🛏 *DB&B from £55 B&B from £37.50* 🆂🅿 *Special rates available* ✕ *Lunch – pre booking for private functions ££ Dinner – pre booking necessary* Ⓥ *Vegetarians welcome* 🧒 *Children welcome* 🚭 *No smoking in dining room* 💳 *Eurocard, Visa* 🔪 *Owner: Mrs Mary McCue*

19 Park Road Paisley PA2 6JP
Tel: 0141 884 2520 Fax: 0141 884 2520
E-mail: stay@makerston.co.uk
Web: www.makerston.co.uk
Less than 5 miles from Glasgow Airport. Follow signs to Paisley University then to shopping centre, turn right into Falside Road, continue uphill until Park Road and house is on right hand side. [C6]

PEAT INN

The Peat Inn

- *"Behind the neat white facade of this old inn lies the ultimate Scottish culinary experience."*
- *Unpretentious top quality modern cuisine.*

CHEF AND OWNER David Wilson has created a world-class restaurant whose name is synonymous with good food. All ingredients are of the utmost freshness and quality and, with tremendous flair, transformed into truly memorable dishes. His wine list is formidable but provides great choice and value for money.

Roasted scallops on leek, potato and smoked bacon with pea purée. Peat Inn 'cassoulet' of lamb, pork and duck with flageolet beans. Caramelised banana on a banana cake with coconut ice cream.

STB ★★★★★ Restaurant with Rooms

❶ *Open all year except Christmas Day and New Year's Day Closed Sun Mon* 🏨 *Suites: 8 en suite* 🛏 *DB&B £90–£98, £65–£95* ✕ *Lunch except Sun Mon 3 course menu ££ Dinner except Sun Mon 3 course menu £££* Ⓥ *Vegetarians welcome* 🧒 *Children welcome* ♿ *Facilities for disabled visitors* 🚭 *No smoking in dining rooms* 💳 *Mastercard/Eurocard, American Express, Visa, Switch* 🔪 *Partners: David & Patricia Wilson*

Peat Inn by Cupar Fife KY15 5LH
Tel: 01334 840206 Fax: 01334 840530
E-mail: reception@thepeatinn.co.uk
Web: www.standrews.co.uk/hotelspeatinn.htp
At junction of B940/B941, 6 miles south west of St Andrews. [D5]

PEEBLES

Castle Venlaw Hotel

- *"A relaxed and informal hotel, well worth the hike to the top of the hill."*
- *Modern Scottish.*

CASTLE VENLAW is owned and run by John and Shirley Sloggie, both experienced and professional hoteliers. It has been totally refurbished to a very high standard whilst retaining many original features. It offers a warm welcome, comfortable surroundings and good food prepared by Chef Alex Burns in a traditional style with contemporary undertones.

Stack of egg and char-grilled peppers, with pepper purée and coriander essence. Pan-fried cannon of venison presented on mint mash, glazed vegetables and local ale jus. Chocolate croissant pudding with marmalade syrup and vanilla cream.

STB ★★★★ Small Hotel

◑ *Open all year* 🏨 *Rooms: 13 en suite* 🛏 *DB&B £65–£95 B&B £60–£85* 🆂 *Special rates available* ✕ *Lunch ££ Dinner £££ Non-Residents welcome* Ⓥ *Vegetarians welcome* ⚘ *Children welcome* ✌ *No smoking in dining room and bedrooms* 🐾 *Dogs welcome* 💳 *Mastercard/ Eurocard, Visa, Switch, Delta* 👤 *Proprietors: John & Shirley Sloggie*

Edinburgh Road Peebles EH45 8QG
Tel: 01721 720384 Fax: 01721 724066
E-mail: enquiries@venlaw.co.uk
Web: www.venlaw.co.uk
From Peebles take the Edinburgh road A703, hotel is ¾ mile on the right. From Edinburgh follow A703 to Penicuik and Peebles, the hotel drive is on the left just after the 30 mph sign as you enter Peebles. [D6]

PEEBLES

Cringletie House Hotel

- *"The only disappointment at Cringletie is having to leave. Fantastic food, service and comforts."*
- *Modern Scottish cooking.*

CRINGLETIE HOUSE has been carefully restored to retain its 19th century features, retaining family portraits in the main room. The atmosphere here is both relaxing and romantic with attention to detail in both service and carefully designed menus. The food here is superb with great flavours and excellent use of Scottish produce.

Savarin of lemon sole with seared scallops complemented by an aniseed infused shellfish froth. Oven-roasted rack of Yarrow Valley lamb on a scorronera mash with beetroot mousse and a juniper berry jus. Consommé of Cringletie garden rhubarb with summer fruits and iced Macallan parfait.

STB ★★★★ Hotel

◑ *Open all year* 🏨 *Rooms: 14 en suite* 🛏 *DB&B £200 per room B&B £150 per room* 🆂 *Special rates available* ✕ *Lunch ££ Dinner ££££* Ⓥ *Vegetarians welcome* ⚘ *Children welcome* ✌ *No smoking in restaurant* 💳 *Mastercard/Eurocard, American Express, Visa, Switch, Delta* 👤 *General Manager: Kellie Bradford*

Peebles Borders EH45 8PL
Tel: 01721 730 233 Fax: 01721 730 244
E-mail: enquiries@cringletie.com
Web: www.cringletie.com
From Peebles take A703, hotel 2 miles on left. [D6]

PEEBLES

Sunflower Restaurant

- *"The Sunflower has a very enthusiastic chef, offering meals or snacks to tempt any taste buds."*
- *Modern-style cooking.*

THE SUNFLOWER is a lovely, bright and colourful restaurant which suits all ages. The restaurant is ideal for everything from morning coffee, afternoon tea or a light lunch – ranging from soup and sandwiches to dish of the day – to delicious, artistic dinners. Service is excellent and complements the enthusiasm of the chef.

Mille feuille of seafood with ginger reduction. Glazed sesame duck with plum and yellow pepper confit. Passion fruit mousse with caramel crack and mango sauce.

◗ *Open all year except Christmas Day, Boxing Day and 1, 2 Jan Closed Sun between Jan to Apr* ✕ *Food available all day £ Lunch £ Dinner except Sun to Wed £££* Ⓥ *Vegetarians welcome* ✸ *Children welcome* ✘ *No smoking in restaurant; smoking room available* ▣ *Mastercard/Eurocard, American Express, Visa, Diners Club, Switch, Delta* ▮ *Chef/ Manager: Valerie Brunton*

4 Bridgegate Peebles Peeblesshire EH45 8RZ
Tel: 01721 722420
E-mail: kenny@kmphoto.co.uk
Web: www.kmphoto.co.uk/Sunflower.htm
From Peebles High Street, turn down the Northgate, take first left into the Bridgegate. The Sunflower Restaurant is situated on the right. [D6]

PERTH

63 Tay Street Restaurant: Winner 2001 – Best Newcomer Award

- *"The expertly handled dishes are a memorable experience."*
- *Scottish and international cooking.*

THIS IS AN EXCITING new addition to the Perth restaurant scene, with its minimalist contemporary look, wooden floors and quality white linen and modern art wall hangings. Everything here is of the highest standard, especially evident in the sourcing of the best produce. Skill and care in preparation is second to none.

Seared Skye scallops, tomato risotto, herb oil. Roast rump of Perthshire lamb, Mediterranean vegetables, tagliatelle, rosemary jus. Trio of chocolate: chocolate ice cream, torte, white chocolate mousse.

◗ *Open all year except first 2 weeks Jan Closed Sun Mon* ✕ *Lunch except Sun Mon £–££ Dinner except Sun Mon £££* Ⓥ *Vegetarians welcome* ✸ *Children over 10 years welcome* ♿ *Facilities for disabled visitors* ✘ *No smoking throughout* ▣ *Mastercard/Eurocard, American Express, Visa, Diners Club, Switch, Delta* ▮ *Owners: Shona & Jeremy Wares*

63 Tay Street Perth PH2 8NN
Tel: 01738 441451 Fax: 01738 441461
200 yards from Perth city centre. 1 mile from main Dundee–Edinburgh road. 4 miles from Stirling to Glasgow road. [D5]

PERTH

Ballathie House Hotel

- *"A very high standard of hospitality and inspired quality cooking."*
- *Award-winning modern and classic Scottish cooking.*

BALLATHIE IS A COMFORTABLE and relaxing country house where guests enjoy exceptional lunches and dinners. Menus change daily, use local produce and offer subtle variations on classic Scottish dishes prepared by Master Chef Kevin McGillivray and his award-winning team. Winner of The Macallan Taste of Scotland Award 1994 and 1997.

Warm woodpigeon sausage served on Puy lentils with crispy shallots and balsamic syrup. Steamed fillet of salmon with a shellfish mousseline served on a vegetable and crab bisque. Chilled banana mousse with chocolate sorbet and a tartlet of caramelised bananas and sultanas.

STB ★★★★ Hotel

❍ *Open all year* 🏠 *Rooms: 43 en suite (inc. 16 Riverside rooms & suites)* 🛏 *DB&B £95–£140 B&B £70–£120* 🍴 *Special rates available* ✗ *Food available all day ££ Lunch ££ Dinner ££££* Ⓥ *Vegetarians welcome* 🧒 *Children welcome* ♿ *Facilities for disabled visitors* 🚭 *No smoking in dining rooms and no smoking lounge* 💳 *Mastercard/Eurocard, American Express, Visa, Diners Club, Switch, Delta, JCB* 🧑 *Manager: Christopher J Longden*

Kinclaven by Stanley Perthshire PH1 4QN Tel: 01250 883268 Fax: 01250 883396 E-mail: email@ballathiehousehotel.com Web: www.ballathiehousehotel.com Off A9, 2 miles north of Perth – turn off at Stanley and turn right at sign to Kinclaven. [D5]

PERTH

Exceed

- *"A city centre restaurant offering the best in local produce served by an attentive and caring team."*
- *Skilful Scottish cooking with international influence.*

EXCEED IS RUN by Willie Little who also has the excellent Cargills in Blairgowrie. This restaurant is centrally located and offers a range of culinary experiences – from traditional Scottish with a contemporary twist to an authentic Spanish Tapas menu. Everything here is cooked to the highest standard using the best Scottish produce.

Cluster of clams with white wine and garlic. Cushion of cod with organic broad beans and crisp Spanish paprika ham. Toasted marshmallow with compote of Perthshire berries.

❍ *Open all year except Christmas Day and 1, 2 Jan Closed Tue* ✗ *Lunch except Tue £–££ Dinner except Tue ££–£££* Ⓥ *Vegetarians welcome* 🧒 *Children welcome* ♿ *Facilities for disabled visitors* 🚬 *Smoking areas in restaurant* 💳 *Mastercard/Eurocard, American Express, Visa, Switch, Delta, Solo* 🧑 *Chef Proprietor: Willie Little*

65 South Methven Street Perth PH1 5NX Tel: 01738 621189 Fax: 01738 445758 E-mail: exceed@bt.connect.com Situated between South Street and High Street. [D5]

PERTH

Huntingtower Hotel

- *"Only a few minutes drive from Perth centre, offering good food and relaxation."*
- *Country house cuisine.*

HUNTINGTOWER is an Edwardian mansion standing in four acres of landscaped gardens, located in the country yet only ten minutes drive from Perth city centre. There is a choice of two restaurants – the Garden conservatory with a light informal menu; Chef David Murray displays his talents in the fine dining Oak Room.

Tartar of Tayside salmon marinated in dill and lime, accompanied with cucumber crème fraîche. Mignons of Angus fillet on fennel and celeriac rösti, with garlic, red onion and plum marmalade. Rich Blairgowrie berry pavlova with ice cream.

STB ★★★★ Hotel
Green Tourism One Leaf Bronze Award

◗ *Open all year* 🏠 *Rooms: 34 en suite* 🛏 *B&B £45–£50* 💷 *Special rates available for DB&B* ✕ *Lunch £ Dinner ££* Ⓥ *Vegetarians welcome* ✿ *Children welcome* ♿ *Facilities for disabled visitors* 💳 *Mastercard, American Express, Visa, Diners Club, Switch* ⚑ *General Manager: Michael Lee*

Crieff Road Perth PH1 3JT
Tel: 01738 583771 Fax: 01738 583777
E-mail: reservations@huntingtowerhotel.co.uk
Web: www.huntingtowerhotel.co.uk
Signposted off A85 (nr Perth Mart), 1 mile west of Perth, towards Crieff. [D5]

PERTH

Let's Eat

- *"The food, atmosphere and service all makes for a great dining experience."*
- *Modern Scottish cooking innovation.*

LET'S EAT continues to enjoy success, and deservedly so. The food is bistro-style with classic influences. Consistent popularity and high standards are maintained. Blackboard 'specials' change daily. Winner of The Macallan Taste of Scotland Award 1997 and 1998.

Seared dived Skye scallops on cucumber spaghetti with a vanilla salsa. Fillet of Turbot poached with squat lobsters and samphire in a white wine and saffron sauce. Valrhona dark chocolate tart with white chocolate sorbet.

◗ *Open all year except 2 weeks mid Jul Closed Sun Mon* ✕ *Lunch except Sun Mon ££ Dinner except Sun Mon ££* Ⓥ *Vegetarians welcome* ✿ *Children welcome* ♿ *Facilities for disabled visitors* ✎ *No smoking in restaurant area* 💳 *Mastercard/Eurocard, American Express, Visa, Switch, Delta* ⚑ *Partners: Tony Heath & Shona Drysdale*

77 Kinnoull Street Perth PH1 5EZ
Tel: 01738 643377 Fax: 01738 621464
E-mail: shona@letseatperth.co.uk
Web: www.letseatperth.co.uk
Restaurant stands on corner of Kinnoull Street and Atholl Street, close to North Inch.
3 minutes walk from High Street. [D5]

PERTH

PERTH

Let's Eat Again

- *"An excellent example of fresh Scottish produce skilfully prepared."*
- *Modern Scottish.*

THIS BISTRO-STYLE restaurant is in the heart of Perth's shopping area. Green and burnt orange decor creates a relaxed and cool atmosphere. Chef Paul Burns prepares food in classic style. The food is second to none. The great ambience and 'cool' food make this difficult to beat. Sister restaurant – 'Let's Eat', also in Perth.

Pithivier of duck confit, mushroom and spinach with a grain mustard sauce. Oven-roast cod with pesto crust, crispy salami salad. Vanilla and lemon grass crème brûlée with soft fruits.

◐ *Open all year except Christmas Day and Boxing Day, 2 weeks Jan and 2 weeks Jul Closed Sun Mon* ✕ *Lunch except Sun Mon £showto Dinner except Sun Mon ££* Ⅴ *Vegetarians welcome* ✱ *Children welcome* ✾ *No smoking in restaurant* ⊞ *Mastercard/Eurocard, American Express, Visa, Switch, Delta* Ⓝ *Partner: Shona Drysdale*

33 George Street Perth PH1 5LA
Tel: 01738 633771 Fax: 01738 621464
E-mail: shona@letseatperth.co.uk
Web: www.letseatperth.co.uk
Town centre – one-way traffic in George Street. Restaurant is halfway up on right-hand side. [D5]

Murrayshall House Hotel

- *"A golfers paradise offering relaxation, good food and friendly attentive staff."*
- *Elegant Scottish cooking.*

MURRAYSHALL has two 18-hole golf courses and a driving range and is set in the stunning Perthshire countryside. The menus in the elegant Old Masters Restaurant are based on the best of seasonally-available produce, accompanied by an extensive wine list. The country club serves informal meals and is ideal for families.

Cannelloni of salmon and monkfish with tomato and tarragon. Noisettes of lamb baked under a basil crust, served with braised white beans and pancetta. Warm cinnamon and apple charlotte served with a biscuit cup of its own ice cream.

STB ★★★★ Hotel

◐ *Open all year* 🏨 *Rooms: 41 en suite* 🛏 *DB&B £53–£80 B&B £35–£55* 🏷 *Special rates available* ✕ *Lunch (Clubhouse and Old Masters) £ Dinner (Clubhouse and Old Masters) ££* Ⅴ *Vegetarians welcome* ✱ *Children welcome* ⊞ *Mastercard/Eurocard, American Express, Visa, Diners Club, Switch* Ⓝ *Sales Development Manager: Lin Mitchell*

Scone nr Perth PH2 7PH
Tel: 01738 551171 Fax: 01738 552595
E-mail: lin.murrayshall@virgin.net
Web: www.murrayshall.com
4 miles out of Perth, 1 mile off A94. [D5]

PERTH

Parklands Hotel

- *"A Victorian town house overlooking the beautiful South Inch."*
- *Modern Scottish.*

PARKLANDS HOTEL is situated on an elevated position on the edge of Perth and most rooms have parkland views. This was once the home of the Provost of Perth and the interior reflects a refined lifestyle. The owners offer a welcoming and relaxed atmosphere with fine food and professional service.

Home-cured Scottish salmon with a tempura of native oysters. Seared loin of Perthshire venison with wild strawberries and balsamic jus. Iced Drambuie and heather honey parfait in a shortbread crust.

STB ★★★★ Small Hotel

◐ *Open all year except 26 Dec, 1 and 2 Jan* 🏠 *Rooms: 14 en suite* 🛏 *DB&B £49–£80 B&B £40–£60* 🆂 *Special rates available* ✗ *Lunch ££ Dinner ££* Ⓥ *Vegetarians welcome* ✷ *Children welcome* ♿ *Facilities for disabled visitors* ✸ *No smoking in restaurant* 🐕 *Dogs welcome* 🖭 *Mastercard/Eurocard, American Express, Visa, Diners Club, Switch, Delta, JCB* ☒ *Partner: Mr K W Mearchent*

*2 St Leonards Bank Perth PH2 8EB
Tel: 01738 622451 Fax: 01738 622046
E-mail: parklands.perth@virgin.net
Exit junction 10 from the M90 signposted Perth and Inverness. Follow Edinburgh Road past prison and through park. At end of park turn left (traffic lights). Parklands on left-hand side. [D5]*

PERTH

The Perth Theatre Restaurant, Café & The Lang Bar

- *"Whether shopping or visiting the theatre pop in for a meal."*
- *Innovative/traditional Scottish cooking.*

QUALITY LOCAL PRODUCE is the basis for Chef Martin Buchan's creative approach to the selection of dishes on offer at Perth Theatre Restaurant. Different menus are created for each major production during the season, while the Café has its own lighter day and evening menu. Restaurant, Café and Bar have been redesigned offering a welcoming atmosphere.

Smoked haddock tartlet with a hot prawn sauce. Breast of pheasant with roasted shallots in a port and black grape sauce. Lemon and almond mousse with fromage frais.

◐ *Open all year except Christmas Day and Public Holidays Closed Sun Note: Please telephone to ensure Restaurant is open in the evening* ✗ *Food available all day ££ Lunch except Sun £ Dinner except Sun – booking advised ££* Ⓥ *Vegetarians welcome* ✷ *Children welcome* ♿ *Facilities for disabled visitors* ✸ *Smoking areas in restaurant and coffee bar* 🖭 *Mastercard/Eurocard, American Express, Visa, Diners Club, Switch, Delta* ☒ *Front of House & Catering Manager: Peter Hood*

*185 High Street Perth PH1 5UW
Tel: 01738 472709 Fax: 01738 624576
E-mail: theatre@perth.org.uk
Web: www.perth.org.uk/perth/theatre
Perth city centre in pedestrian zone at middle section of High Street. [D5]*

PITLOCHRY

PITLOCHRY

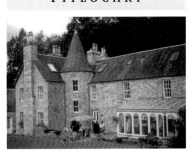

Donavourd House Hotel

- *"A most enjoyable experience in this very welcoming hotel."*
- *Innovative modern Scottish.*

DONAVOURD has an elevated position with commanding views over Strathtummel. This intimate country hotel is situated in six acres of grounds only minutes drive from Pitlochry. Warm hospitality is successfully blended with excellent cooking, where only the best locally sourced produce is used. Advance booking required.

Crispy oriental monkfish parcels with two dipping sauces. Pan-seared Perthshire lamb chops atop a spicy potato, pepper and tomato tagine. A tuile cornucopia filled with lemon mousse, seasonal berries and drizzled with a sweet tea syrup.

STB ★★★ Small Hotel

◑ *Open 15 Mar to 3 Jan Closed Christmas Day* ♨ *Rooms: 9 en suite* ⇔ *DB&B £35–£70 B&B £25–£55* ✗ *Lunch – special occasions, booking necessary Dinner ££* Ⓥ *Vegetarians welcome* ♣ *Children over 10 years welcome* ♿ *Facilities for disabled visitors* ✍ *Smoking in lounge only* 🐕*Dogs welcome* 💳 *Mastercard/ Eurocard, Visa, Switch* 🔪 *Chef/Proprietor: Nicole McKechnie*

Pitlochry PH16 5JS
Tel: 01796 472100
E-mail:
reservations@donavourdhousehotel.co.uk
Web: www.donavourdhousehotel.co.uk
Located 1½ miles south of Pitlochry. Take Pitlochry exit off A9 northbound then take immediate right under stone railway bridge, follow STB signs to hotel. [C5]

East Haugh Country House Hotel & Restaurant

- *"A wonderful 'get away from it all' offering great food."*
- *Elegant Scottish cuisine.*

EAST HAUGH is caringly owned by Neil and Lesley McGown. Guests may enjoy lunch and dinner in the Conservatory Bar and dinner only in the Restaurant. The cooking here is excellent. Traditional Sunday roast a speciality. Winner The Macallan Taste of Scotland Award 1996.

Terrine of scallops, smoked salmon and monkfish served on rocket leaves with lemon grass and cucumber dressing. Seared fillet of mountain hare with wild mushroom ragoût and brandy jus. White chocolate brûlée with ginger tuille biscuits.

STB ★★★ Small Hotel

◑ *Open all year except 20 to 26 Dec N.B. Closed Mon to Thu for lunch during Nov, Dec, Jan, Feb and Mar – unless by prior arrangement* ♨ *Rooms: 13, (11 en suite and 2 family with shared bathroom)* ⇔ *DB&B £49–£85 B&B £25–£59* 📠 *Special rates available* ✗ *Lunch ££ Dinner ££–£££* Ⓥ *Vegetarians welcome* ♣ *Children welcome* ✍ *No smoking in restaurant Smoking permitted in Conservatory Bar* 💳 *Mastercard/Eurocard, Visa* 🔪 *Proprietors: Neil & Lesley McGown*

Pitlochry Perthshire PH16 5TE
Tel: 01796 473121 Fax: 01796 472473
E-mail: easthaugh@aol.com
Web: www.easthaugh.co.uk
1½ miles south of Pitlochry on old A9 road.
[C5]

PITLOCHRY

The Green Park Hotel

- *"An extremely relaxing stay serving fine food – a great place to get away from it all!"*
- *Traditional/classical cooking.*

THE GREEN PARK HOTEL is delightful and overlooks Loch Faskally. Alistair and Diane McMenemie know their customers well and make every effort to ensure that their stay is a special one. The cooking is classical and the best use is made of local produce to ensure the flavours dominate. The dining room is tastefully decorated and overlooks the gardens.

Guinea fowl and West Coast scallop terrine studded with pistachio nuts and served with a lime mayonnaise. Roast saddle of Scottish lamb served on an aubergine confit with a basil pesto dressing. Rhubarb and rosemary brûlée with Champagne sorbet.

STB ★★★★ Hotel

◑ *Open all year* ⌂ *Rooms: 39 en suite* ➡ *DB&B £39–£64 B&B £25–£42* 🅂 *Special rates available* ✕ *Lunch £–££ Dinner £££* Ⓥ *Vegetarians welcome* ♿ *Facilities for disabled visitors* ✒ *No smoking throughout* 💳 *Mastercard/Eurocard, Visa, Switch* 🅜 *Proprietors: The McMenemie Family*

Clunie Bridge Road Pitlochry PH16 5JY Tel: 01796 473248 Fax: 01796 473520 E-mail: bookings@thegreenpark.co.uk Web: www.thegreenpark.co.uk Following Atholl Road through Pitlochry, the hotel is signposted to the left at the town limits. [C5]

PITLOCHRY

Killiecrankie Hotel

- *"A traditional hotel offering a warm welcome, situated in a scenic area near Pitlochry."*
- *Modern Scottish cooking with classic influences.*

KILLIECRANKIE's resident owners, Colin and Carole Anderson, have decorated and furnished the house very tastefully and have provided a high standard of comfort. Head Chef Mark Easton's cooking is highly professional and imaginative and his table d'hôte menus (four starters, four main courses) are well-balanced and appetising. A most attractive and well-run establishment.

Prawn and coriander risotto with pesto oil and Parmesan shavings. Pan-fried medallions of Aberdeen Angus beef with red wine sauce and chive mashed potatoes. Iced orange parfait with orange and strawberry salad.

STB ★★★★ Hotel

◑ *Open 22 Feb to 3 Jan* ⌂ *Rooms: 10 en suite* ➡ *DB&B £71–£91* 🅂 *Special rates available* ✕ *Lunch ££ Dinner 5 course menu £££* Ⓥ *Vegetarians welcome* ☈ *Children welcome* ✒ *No smoking in dining room and most bedrooms* 💳 *Mastercard/Eurocard, Visa, Switch, Delta* 🅜 *Owner/Proprietors: Colin & Carole Anderson*

Killiecrankie by Pitlochry PH16 5LG Tel: 01796 473220 Fax: 01796 472451 E-mail: enquiries@killiecrankiehotel.co.uk Web: www.killiecrankiehotel.co.uk B8079 on old A9, 3 miles north of Pitlochry. [C5]

PITLOCHRY

Knockendarroch House Hotel

- *"A relaxed family hotel offering good food."*
- *Excellent classic cooking.*

THIS ELEGANT mansion enjoys wonderful views up the Tummel Valley to the south, and of Ben Vrackie to the north. The cooking is excellent in a traditional style and hosts Tony and Jane Ross make every effort to make you feel at home – and they succeed.

Smoked breast of Barbary duck on a bed of baked rhubarb. Roast Scallops with lemon and garlic potatoes and braised fennel. Crème brûlée flavoured with saffron accompanied with honeyed pear.

STB ★★★★ Small Hotel

◗ *Open 1 Mar to Oct incl* ⊞ *Rooms: 12 en suite* ⋈ *DB&B £45–£62 B&B £35–£44* ⓢ *Special rates available* ✕ *Dinner £££ Non-residents – prior booking essential* Ⓥ *Vegetarians welcome* ⚹ *Children over 10 years welcome* ✲ *No smoking throughout* ⊞ *Mastercard/Eurocard, American Express, Visa, Switch, Delta* ⋈ *Owners: Tony & Jane Ross*

Higher Oakfield Pitlochry PH16 5HT
Tel: 01796 473473 Fax: 01796 474068
E-mail: info@knockendarroch.co.uk
Web: www.knockendarroch.co.uk
In a commanding position, 3 minutes walk from the town centre. Take Bonnethill Road and then take first right turn, into Toberargan Road and on to Higher Oakfield. [C5]

PITLOCHRY

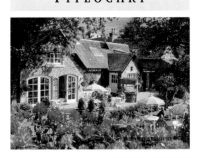

The Old Armoury

- *"Inspired cooking served within a superb restaurant."*
- *Accomplished modern Scottish.*

THIS COMFORTABLE and attractive restaurant is run by Alison McNab and her husband Angus, formerly of Skeabost House Hotel. A comprehensive wine list is available, particularly from the New World. The cooking here is fresh, skilled and innovative with good food available throughout the day. Inspected under previous owners, Alison and George Rollo.

Tempura king prawns on a bed of golden noodles enhanced with a sweet chilli sauce. Medallions of wild Perthshire venison on a caramelised onion mash with a rowanberry and claret jus. Rich chocolate cream slice surrounded by a Kahlua anglaise and raspberry coulis.

◗ *Open Mar to Dec* ✕ *Food available all day £ Lunch ££ Dinner £££* Ⓥ *Vegetarians welcome* ⚹ *Children welcome during the daytime (no children under 5 years allowed in dining room after 7pm)* ♿ *Facilities for disabled visitors* ✲ *No smoking throughout* 🐕 *Dogs welcome in the tea garden* ⊞ *Mastercard/Eurocard, Visa, Switch* ⋈ *Proprietors: Alison & Angus McNab*

Armoury Road Pitlochry Perthshire PH16 5AP
Tel: 01796 474281 Fax: 01796 474447
E-mail:
angus@theoldarmouryrestaurant.fsnet.co.uk
Situated on Armoury Road close to Loch Faskally on the way down to the Dam and Fishladder. Signposted on a brown tourist board sign at northern end of main road through town. [C5]

PITLOCHRY

The Pitlochry Festival Theatre Restaurant

- *"The theatre provides refreshments, meals and entertainment with an all-inclusive view."*
- *Modern Scottish cooking enlivened with imaginative touches.*

AT LUNCHTIME the Pitlochry Festival Theatre restaurant is buffet style with a choice of hot and cold dishes, including local fish from the 'Summer Festival Buffet'. In the evening a table d'hôte dinner is served at 6.30pm for theatregoers. New extension to the restaurant for dining area.

Trio of local smoked meats on a bed of rocket. Cushion of cod fillet with tapenade and Parmesan in herb crust on a red pepper coulis. Home-made terrine of dark and white chocolate on a Cointreau and orange sauce.

◑ *Open 17 May* ✕ *Lunch £* Ⓥ *Vegetarians welcome* ✦ *Children welcome* ♿ *Facilities for disabled visitors* ✹ *No smoking in restaurant Smoking area in Coffee Bar* 🖭 *Mastercard/ Eurocard, American Express, Visa* ⋈ *Catering Manager: John Anderson*

Port-na-Craig Pitlochry PH16 5DR
Tel: 01796 484600 Fax: 01796 484616
E-mail: admin@pitlochry.org.uk
Web: www.pitlochry.org.uk
On south bank of the River Tummel, approx ¼ mile from centre of town. Clearly signposted.
[C5]

PITLOCHRY

The Poplars

- *"Warm hospitality, good food and all the comforts of home."*
- *Scottish cooking to order, promoting traditional flavours.*

POPLARS IS A FRIENDLY and comfortable hotel with stunning panoramic vista from the hotel across the Tummel Valley. The accommodation is comfortable and pleasant. Kathleen and Ian are friendly and hospitable hosts. The hotel concentrates exclusively on the provision of a truly memorable experience to its resident guests. Service is good, courteous and attentive.

Spinach roulade with cream cheese and roast peppers drizzled with a yellow pepper sauce. Succulent Perthshire lamb chump steak on a bed of crushed potatoes and herbs accompanied by a cherry tomato and parsley dressing. Orange semolina cake with rhubarb and ginger compote.

STB ★★★ Small Hotel

◑ *Open all year* 🛏 *Rooms: 11* 🛏 *DB&B £41–£55 B&B £26–£40* 🆂🅿 *Special rates available* ✕ *Dinner ££* Ⓥ *Vegetarians welcome* ✦ *Children welcome* ✹ *No smoking in restaurant and bedrooms* 🖭 *Mastercard/ Eurocard, Visa, Switch* ⋈ *Owners: Kathleen & Ian*

27 Lower Oakfield Pitlochry PH16 5DS
Tel: 01796 472129 Fax: 01796 472554
E-mail: enquiries@poplars-hotel.co.uk
Web: www.poplars-hotel.co.uk
Between Lower Oakfield and Higher Oakfield roads. Follow sign at south end of the town.
[C5]

PITLOCHRY

Westlands of Pitlochry

- *"Friendly welcome and hearty portions of very good food using the best of local produce."*
- *Imaginative traditional cooking.*

WESTLANDS offers an interesting table d'hôte menu and an à la carte menu, both of which are reasonably priced. Meals are served in the Garden Room Restaurant. Bar meals are also available. Two of the bedrooms now have four-poster beds. Westlands is now under new ownership and was inspected under previous owners.

Ramekin of creamy West Coast prawns and wild mushrooms topped with a garlic and herb crust. Best end of lamb with a prune and rosemary stuffing served with port wine jus. Choux ring filled with elderflower frozen yoghurt and red berries.

◗ *Open all year except 25 and 26 Dec* 🏠 *Rooms: 15 en suite ⊨ DB&B £57.50–£63.50 B&B £39–£44* ⬛ *Special rates available* ✘ *Lunch £ Dinner ££* Ⓥ *Vegetarians welcome* ✶ *Children welcome* ✖ *No smoking in restaurant* 💳 *Mastercard/Eurocard, Visa* ⚑ *Partners: David & Maureen Brunton/Robert & Johan Cowan*

160 Atholl Road Pitlochry Perthshire PH16 5AR Tel: 01796 472266 Fax: 01796 473994 E-mail: info@westlandshotel.co.uk Web: www.westlandshotel.co.uk A924 into Pitlochry, Westlands at north end of town on right-hand side. [C5]

PLOCKTON

The Haven Hotel

- *"Log fires, elegant dining and skilfully prepared food – this hotel lives up to its name!"*
- *Stylish Scottish cooking.*

PLOCKTON is known as the 'jewel of the Highlands.' The Haven stands yards from the beach, looking out onto the sea. As always it continues to offer the same high standard of cuisine. Dinner menus are table d'hôte and combine fresh local produce with interesting sauces, changing daily.

Millefeuille of creamed spinach and local king scallops sautéed in lime butter, layered with filo pastry, drizzled with a balsamic reduction and concasse of tomato. Wild woodpigeon in a cracked pink pepper crust, pan-seared with a caramelised onion mash, a sloe gin residue and crispy Argyll ham. Fresh almond peachy pie with fresh cream.

STB ★★★ Hotel

◗ *Open 1 Feb to 20 Dec incl* 🏠 *Rooms: 15, 12 en suite ⊨ DB&B £55–£65 B&B £38–£41* ⬛ *Special rates available* ♟ *Restricted licence* ✘ *Lunch – 24 hours notice required ££ Dinner 5 course menu £££* Ⓥ *Vegetarians welcome* ✶ *Children over 7 years welcome* ♿ *Facilities for disabled visitors* ✖ *No smoking in restaurant* 💳 *Mastercard/Eurocard, Visa, Switch, Delta* ⚑ *Owners: Annan & Jill Dryburgh*

Plockton Ross-shire IV52 8TW Tel: 01599 544223/334 Fax: 01599 544467 Web: www.smoothhound.co.uk/hotels/thehaven.html In the village of Plockton.[B4]

PLOCKTON

The Plockton Hotel

- *"A popular waterfront location with a varied choice of dishes to suit all ages."*
- *Good quality bar food specialising in fish and shellfish.*

TOM AND DOROTHY PEARSON are charming hosts and the hotel seems to continuously bustle with folk wanting to sample some of the local dishes – and there is really something for everyone on the menu. A small garden on the shore makes this a very restful spot to reflect on your day.

Plockton Smokies: layers of smoked mackerel and herbs, cream, tomatoes and cheese, baked and topped with toasted breadcrumbs. Raspberry and Drambuie trifle: soaked sponge cake with Drambuie, layered with raspberries, topped with fresh custard and topped with fresh cream.

STB ★★★ Small Hotel

◗ *Open all year except New Year's Day* ⌂ *Rooms: 9, 1 single en suite* ⇔ *B&B from £30–£40* ▣ *Special rates available* ✖ *Food available all day* ££ *Lunch* £ *Dinner 5 course menu* ££ Ⓥ *Vegetarians welcome* ⚘ *Children welcome* ♿ *Facilities for disabled visitors* ✠ *No smoking in dining room and snug – smoking in bar* 🐕*Dogs by arrangement only* ▣ *Mastercard/ Eurocard, American Express, Visa, Switch, Delta* 🕅 *Partners: Dorothy, Tom & Alan Pearson*

Harbour Street Plockton Ross-shire IV52 8TN
Tel: 01599 544274 Fax: 01599 544475
E-mail: sales@plocktonhotel.co.uk
Web: www.plocktonhotel.co.uk
In the centre of Harbour Street, Plockton. [B4]

POOLEWE

Inverewe Garden Restaurant
The National Trust For Scotland

- *"A visit to the restaurant would complete your enjoyment of this beautiful attraction in the Highlands."*
- *Traditional Scottish home cooking.*

THE RESTAURANT at Inverewe Gardens is a light and spacious venue where visitors can enjoy home baking to full Scottish meals. Delicious and appetising Scottish food is available all day. Some of the Garden's own produce is used to enhance the dishes on offer.

Selection of home-made soups. Speciality hot dishes featuring fresh local fish and local game and meat. Vegetarian dishes available each day served with seasonal vegetables from the garden. Sandwiches and baguettes also available. Traditional Scottish puddings and homebaking.

STB ★★★★ Garden

◗ *Open 15 Mar to 31 Oct* ♇ *Licensed* ✖ *Food available all day* £ *Lunch* £ Ⓥ *Vegetarians welcome Children welcome* ♿ *Facilities for disabled visitors* ✠ *No smoking throughout* 🐕*Guide dogs only* ▣ *No credit cards* 🕅 *Catering Manager: Jackie Rich*

Poolewe Ross-shire IV22 2LG
Tel: 01445 781446 Fax: 01445 781446
E-mail: kgordon@nts.org.uk
Web: www.nts.org.uk
On A832, ¼ mile from Poolewe village. 6 miles north-east of Gairloch Ross-shire. [B3]

Poolewe

Pool House

- *"Without a doubt, Pool House is one of the finest places to eat in one of the most beautiful locations on the West Coast."*
- *Award-winning Scottish cuisine.*

POOL HOUSE HOTEL has lavishly been refurbished to a high degree of luxury. This family-run small hotel devotes its time to ensure guests are cared for. The hotel boasts its own mussel ropes, ensuring the freshest of dishes on offer from Chef John Moir. Scallops are a speciality.

Baked plum tomatoes filled with goats cheese on char-grilled asparagus salad. Roast saddle of lamb stuffed with roasted garlic, rosemary and lamb's liver on boulangere potatoes. Milk chocolate truffle terrine with white chocolate and meringue ice cream, and fresh berry compote.

STB ★★★★ Small Hotel
Green Tourism Three Leaf Gold Award

Open 1 Mar to 31 Dec Rooms: 4 luxury suites DB&B £160–£210 B&B £125–£175 Special rates available Lunch ££ Dinner ££££ Vegetarians welcome No smoking in dining room Mastercard/Eurocard, American Express, Visa, Switch, Delta, JCB General Manager: Elizabeth Miles

Poolewe by Inverewe Gardens Wester Ross IV22 2LD
Tel: 01445 781272 Fax: 01445 781403
E-mail: enquiries@poolhousehotel.com
Web: www.poolhousehotel.com
6 miles north of Gairloch on A832. The hotel is situated by the bridge, alongside the River Ewe where it meets the sea and overlooks Inverewe Gardens.[B3]

Port Appin

The Airds Hotel: Finalist The Macallan Taste of Scotland Awards 2001

- *"A little piece of heaven on earth – go and see for yourself."*
- *Fine dining.*

AIRDS HOTEL has been owned and run by the Allen family since 1978. Airds is a traditional Highland inn where guests may enjoy a consistently high standard of cooking from the kitchen which makes the very best use of the wonderful produce locally available. It is now a world-class destination placing Port Appin firmly on the map.

West Coast lobster with avocado salad and a gazpacho sauce. Fillet of turbot on a pea purée with broad beans, bacon, deep-fried prawns and a mustard velouté. Vanilla mousse with poached berries, rhubarb and a raspberry sauce

STB ★★★★ Hotel

Open 27 Dec to 6 Jan and 26 Jan to 15 Dec Rooms: 12 en suite DB&B £95–£155 Special rates available Lunch ££ Dinner ££££ Vegetarians welcome Children welcome No smoking in restaurant Dogs welcome Mastercard/Eurocard, Visa Proprietor: Graeme Allen

Port Appin Argyll PA38 4DF
Tel: 01631 730236 Fax: 01631 730535
E-mail: airds@airds-hotel.com
Web: www.airds-hotel.com
Take A828 to Appin then follow the signs for Port Appin and Lismore Ferry. [B5]

PORT OF MENTEITH

The Lake Hotel

- *"Unwind and enjoy a delicious dinner with wonderful views of the lake."*
- *Scottish cooking with French influences.*

STANDING ON THE SHORE of Scotland's only lake, The Lake Hotel with it's Art Deco style interior, continues to offer a very fine experience to its visitors. Cooking here is skilled, by an enthusiastic chef who prepares best fresh local produce and presents it with flair and excellent presentation.

Steamed West Coast mussels in a white wine, chilli and lime sauce. Aberdeen Angus fillet on a potato rösti, confit of wild mushrooms and a red wine jus. Tarte Tatin of pineapple and vanilla served with a lavender ice cream.

STB ★★★ Small Hotel

◐ *Open all year except Christmas Day, Boxing Day and first two weeks in Jan Closed Mon Tue from 1 Nov until 31 Mar* 🏠 *Rooms: 16 en suite* 🛏 *DB&B £55–£102 B&B £40–£80* 🆂🅿 *Special rates available* ✖ *lunch from £ Dinner £££* 🆅 *Vegetarians welcome* 🕈 *Children 8 years welcome in the restaurant in the evening* ♿ *Facilities for disabled visitors* 🚭 *No smoking in dining room* 🐕 *Dogs welcome* 💳 *Mastercard, American Express, Visa, Switch, Delta* 🅼 *Owners: Graeme & Ros McConnachie*

Port of Menteith Perthshire FK8 3RA
Tel: 01877 385258 Fax: 01877 385671
E-mail: enquiries@lake-of-menteith-hotel.com
Web: www.lake of-menteith-hotel.com
Turn off M9 at junction 10 onto A84, follow to A873 signposted Aberfoyle. Continue to Port of Menteith, then left down the B8034 and hotel is 250m on the right. [C5]

PORTPATRICK

Knockinaam Lodge

- *"Surely a little piece of heaven – off the beaten track!"*
- *Skilled modern British cooking.*

HERE IN THIS luxurious country house the welcome is warm and personal, your every desire met and gourmet cravings satisfied. Knockinaam has a stunning cellar and vast selection of malts. Winner of The Macallan Taste of Scotland Award 1997 and Excellence Award 1997.

Terrine of Drummore lobster with a salad of fine beans, globe artichoke and mango, with a lemon and olive dressing. Braised belly of Ayrshire pork with Puy lentils, confit garlic and a rosemary scented reduction. A large tuile basket filled with coconut ice cream and topped with Scottish summer berries.

STB ★★★★★ Small Hotel

◐ *Open all year* 🏠 *Rooms: 10 en suite* 🛏 *DB&B from £90–£170* 🆂🅿 *Special rates available* ✖ *Food available all day ££ Lunch £££ Dinner ££££* 🆅 *Vegetarians welcome* 🕈 *Children welcome* ♿ *Facilities for disabled visitors – restaurant only* 🚭 *No smoking in dining room* 💳 *Mastercard/Eurocard, American Express, Visa, Diners Club, Switch, Delta* 🅼 *Proprietors: Michael Bricker & Pauline Ashworth*

Portpatrick DG9 9AD
Tel: 01776 810471 Fax: 01776 810435
E-mail: reservations@knockinaamlodge.com
From the A77 or the A75, follow signs for Portpatrick. 2 miles west of Lochans, Knockinaam sign on right. Take first left turning, past smokehouse. Follow signs for 3 miles to lodge. [B7]

PRESTWICK

Parkstone Hotel

- *"Ideally situated on the seafront offering good food and service."*
- *Traditional Scottish cooking.*

PARKSTONE HOTEL is well run by Stewart Clarkson, Jean Taylor and Jane Clarkson who have an evident commitment to continuously upgrading and improving the hotel. The menus at Parkstone are traditional offering a good choice with all items prepared using the best local produce carefully sourced, prepared and presented.

Warm tartlet of woodland mushrooms glazed with truffle cheese. Seared loin of Ayrshire lamb, cooked pink with roasted vegetables and a red wine and juniper sauce. Whisky crème brûlée with fresh strawberries and home-made shortbread.

STB ★★★ Hotel

◑ *Open all year except New Year's Day* 🏨 *Rooms: 22 en suite* 🛏 *DB&B £52–£58 B&B £34–£38* 🈺 *Special rates available* ✖ *Lunch ££ Dinner £££* Ⓥ *Vegetarians welcome* ⚒ *Children welcome* 🚭 *No smoking in dining room* 🆔 *Mastercard/Eurocard, American Express, Visa, Switch, Delta* 🔣 *Partners: Stewart Clarkson, Jean Taylor & Jane Clarkson*

Central Esplanade Prestwick Ayrshire KA9 1QN Tel: 01292 477286 Fax: 01292 477671 E-mail: info@parkstonehotel.co.uk Web: www.parkstonehotel.co.uk From Prestwick town centre A79, follow signs to seafront (400 yards). Hotel last turning on the left before promenade, on Ardayre Road. [C6]

SELKIRK

Philipburn House Hotel

- *"A comfortable well-kept hotel offering good value for money meals."*
- *Modern Scottish.*

PHILIPBURN IS A RELAXED and informal hotel with choices of both formal and informal dining in its restaurant or bar/bistro. Menus successfully combine traditional and modern items cooked skilfully, using only the best produce. The hotel has been sensitively refurbished to a very high standard by owner Allan Deeson.

Fantail of Galia melon with smoked goose breast and citrus fruits, with an elderberry fruit coulis. Marinated escalope of Border venison seared in basil oil, with a port wine barley risotto, marmalade and cranberry sauce. Choux pastry ring centred with a crushed meringue and honeycomb syllabub cream drizzled with a warm toffee sauce.

STB ★★★★ Hotel

◑ *Open all year except 3 to 17 Jan* 🏨 *Rooms: 14 en suite* 🛏 *DB&B £55–£90 B&B £25–£70* 🈺 *Special rates available* ✖ *Lunch ££ Dinner £££* Ⓥ *Vegetarians welcome* ⚒ *Children welcome* ♿ *Facilities for disabled visitors* 🚭 *No smoking in restaurant* 🐕 *Dogs welcome in lodges and chalets – not in hotel* 🆔 *Mastercard/Eurocard, American Express, Visa, Switch, Delta* 🔣 *Proprietor: Mr Allan Deeson*

Selkirk TD7 5LS Tel: 01750 20747 Fax: 01750 21690 E-mail: info@philipburnhousehotel.co.uk Web: www.philipburnhousehotel.co.uk 1 mile from Selkirk town centre, follow signs for the A72/A707 for Peebles/Moffat. [D6]

SHIELDAIG

Tigh An Eilean

- *"Relax and enjoy the scenery and superb food and you will want to stay longer or return again soon."*
- *Scottish cuisine with French influences.*

SITTING ON THE SHORE of Loch Torridon, Tigh an Eilean commands wonderful views of the loch to the front, and the mountains to the rear. Cathryn and Christopher Field are dedicated to making the best use of local produce, especially the wealth of seafood from the area. Chef Alasdair Robertson's well-thought out menus create wonderful dishes.

Restaurant: Sauté of Hebridean scallops with fennel and pernod. Roast loin of venison with redcurrants and red wine. Caramelised rice pudding with blueberry compote and home-made iced lemon parfait. Bar: Fresh seafood stew. Fish of the day and home-made chips.

STB ★★★★ Small Hotel

◗ *Hotel open early Apr to end Oct Bar open all year except Christmas Day and New Year's Day* ▥ *Rooms: 11 en suite* ⊨ *DB&B £74–£82 B&B £49.50–£55* ▧ *Special rates available* ✗ *Soup and sandwiches available in bar all day £ Lunch – bar only £ Dinner £££* ▨ *Mastercard/ Eurocard, Visa, Switch, Delta* ▧ *Owners: Christopher & Cathryn Field*

Shieldaig Loch Torridon Ross-shire IV54 8XN Tel: 01520 755251 Fax: 01520 755321 E-mail: tighaneilanhotel@shieldaig.fsnet.co.uk The hotel and bar are located on the loch front in the middle of the small fishing village of Shieldaig, off the A896. [B4]

SKELMORLIE BY LARGS

Redcliffe House Hotel

- *"Log fires and superb food – excellent example of Scottish hospitality."*
- *Modern and traditional cuisine.*

REDCLIFFE HOUSE is surrounded by attractive gardens to the front overlooking the water. There is an atmospheric dining room which has incorporated many original features. The bedrooms are modern and well equipped. Seafood dishes are a speciality here, with both table d'hôte and à la carte menus offered.

Bradon rost served hot with white wine and parsley sauce. Seafood in puff pastry case filled with fresh fish and shellfish, cooked in lobster coulis with Cognac and cream. Pears poached in honey and saffron syrup.

STB ★★★ Small Hotel

◗ *Open all year* ▥ *Rooms: 10 en suite* ⊨ *DB&B £42.50–£47.50 B&B £35–£40* ▧ *Special rates available* ✗ *Lunch ££ Dinner £££* ▨ *Vegetarians welcome* ⚹ *Children welcome* ✄ *No smoking in dining room* ▸ *Dogs welcome by prior arrangement* ▨ *Mastercard/Eurocard, American Express, Visa, Diners Club, Switch, Delta* ▧ *Proprietors: George & Elaine Maltby*

25 Shore Road Skelmorlie Ayrshire PA17 5EH Tel: 01475 521036 Fax: 01475 521894 E-mail: elaine@redcliffehousehotel.co.uk Web: www.redcliffehousehotel.co.uk From Glasgow take M8, A8 to Greenock then A78. Skelmorlie is just south of Wemyss Bay. Hotel is on main road/seafront. [C6]

SPEAN BRIDGE

SPEAN BRIDGE

Corriegour Lodge Hotel

- *"Superb food is always available here, served in the Loch View restaurant."*
- *Excellent modern Scottish cooking.*

CORRIEGOUR is well-maintained and attractively appointed and is lovingly run and cared for by Christian Drew and her family. Her son Ian commands the kitchen which produces superb fine dining. The hotel's wine list is extensive and reasonably priced. The Loch View restaurant offers views at sunset over Loch Lochy that can seldom be beaten.

Parfait of duck livers served with toasted brioche and an orange and crab apple jelly. Medallions of venison set on mushroom pearl barley risotto with a celeriac purée, beetroot and truffle jus. Assiette of Corriegour sweets.

STB ★★★★ Small Hotel

◗ *Open 1 Feb to 30 Nov (weekends only 1 Feb to 31 Mar) and special 3/6 day breaks at New Year* 🏨 *Rooms: 9 en suite* 🛏 *DB&B £72.50– £79.50 B&B £55.50–£60.50* 💷 *Special rates available* ✘ *Lunch – by arrangement Dinner £££ Non-residents – dinner only* Ⓥ *Vegetarians welcome with prior notice* ⚘ *Children over 8 years welcome* ✍ *No smoking in restaurant* 💳 *Mastercard/Eurocard, American Express, Visa, Switch, Delta* ⚑ *Owner: Christian Drew*

Loch Lochy by Spean Bridge PH34 4EB Tel: 01397 712685 Fax: 01397 712696 E-mail: info@corriegour-lodge-hotel.com Web: www.corriegour-lodge-hotel.com Follow A82, 17 miles north of Fort William; 47 miles south of Inverness – between Spean Bridge and Invergarry. [C4]

Old Pines Restaurant with Rooms

- *"To dine and stay at the Old Pines is truly special – a food lovers' paradise."*
- *Outstanding and sophisticated cuisine.*

SUKIE IS ONE of Scotland's top chefs and her skill, enthusiasm and commitment is clearly in evidence. There is an abundance of locally sourced products with herbs and vegetables from the garden. Bill Barber is also an accomplished 'smoker' and his range of products feature in Sukie's recipes. The Macallan Taste of Scotland Award 1998.

Isle of Muck prawns and crab with home-smoked salmon and garden salad leaves. Roast John Dory and monkfish with courgettes and lime and a red onion butter sauce. Marmalade clootie dumpling with vanilla ice cream, Glayva sauce.

STB ★★★★ Restaurant with Rooms
Green Tourism Two Leaf Silver Award

◗ *Open all year except 2 weeks winter (Closed for dinner Sun [residents only] and Mon (except bank holidays)* 🏨 *Rooms: 8 en suite* 🛏 *DB&B £60–£80* 💷 *Special rates available* ✘ *Simple lunches except Mon (open Bank Holiday) ££ Dinner 5 course menu except Sun (supper to residents) and Mon £££* Ⓥ *Vegetarians welcome – prior notice appreciated* ⚘ *Children welcome* ♿ *Facilities for disabled visitors* ✍ *No smoking throughout* 💳 *Mastercard/Eurocard, Visa, Switch, Delta* ⚑ *Proprietors: Bill & Sukie Barber*

Spean Bridge by Fort William PH34 4EG Tel: 01397 712324 Fax: 01397 712433 E-mail: tos@oldpines.co.uk Web: www.oldpines.co.uk From Spean Bridge take A82 towards Inverness, left at Commando Memorial, 300m on right. [C4]

ST ANDREWS

The Old Course Hotel Golf Resort & Spa

- *"Enjoy fine food and wine overlooking the golf world's most famous view."*
- *Global influences married with fine Scottish produce.*

FOR EXQUISITE GOURMET dining in the Road Hole Grill, an informal meal or snack in Sands Restaurant, or perhaps just an afternoon tea treat – whatever your dining requirements The Old Course Hotel can oblige with excellent food and impeccable service. Mingle with visitors from all corners of the globe at this spectacular location.

Carpaccio of wild venison with the Tete de Moine cheese and soft herb salad. Roast fillet of sea bass with confit of fennel and cardamom. Pear and almond tart with candied orange cranberry ice cream.

STB ★★★★★ International Resort Hotel

◗ *Open all year* ⊞ *Rooms: 146 en suite* ⇌ *DB&B from £165 B&B from £122.50* ⓢⓟ *Special golf and spa rates available* ✖ *Food served all day £–££ Lunch from ££ Dinner from ££££* Ⓥ *Vegetarians welcome* ✻ *Children welcome* ♿ *Facilities for disabled visitors* ⊭ *Pipe and cigar smoking not permitted in restaurants* ▣ *Mastercard/Eurocard, American Express, Visa, Diners Club, Delta, JCB* ◪ *Food & Beverage Manager: Caroline-Jane Houston*

Old Station Road St Andrews Fife KY16 9SP
Tel: 01334 474371 Fax: 01334 477668
E-mail: reservations@oldcoursehotel.co.uk
Web: www.oldcoursehotel.co.uk
A91 to St Andrews on outskirts of town. [D5]

ST ANDREWS

Rufflets Country House & Garden Restaurant

- *"Experience exceptional food and wine served by some of Scotland's most charming and professional staff."*
- *Highly accomplished Scottish cooking.*

RUFFLETS OFFERS two excellent dining experiences – the informal Music Room Bar Brasserie and the award-winning Garden Restaurant. Full use is made of locally grown and caught meat, game and seafood, while much of the fruit and vegetables and all the herbs are grown in the hotel's own garden.

Duck rillette with cured fois gras, aubergine crisps, and a sweet pepper reduction. Oven-roasted noisette of venison with a parsley crust, buttered spinach, galette potato and truffle jus. Hot passion fruit soufflé with passion fruit ice cream.

STB ★★★★★ Hotel

◗ *Open all year* ⊞ *Rooms: 22 en suite* ⇌ *B&B from £190 double/twin per room* ⓢⓟ *Special rates available* ✖ *Lunch (Restaurant) Sun from ££ Dinner from ££££* Ⓥ *Vegetarians welcome* ✻ *Children welcome* ♿ *Facilities for non-residential disabled visitors* ▣ *Mastercard/Eurocard, American Express, Visa, Diners Club, Switch* ◪ *Operations Director: John Angus*

Strathkinness Low Road St Andrews Fife KY16 9TX
Tel: 01334 472594 Fax: 01334 478703
E-mail: reservations@rufflets.co.uk
Web: www.rufflets.co.uk
On B939, 1½ miles west of St Andrews. [D5]

ST ANDREWS OUTSKIRTS

The Inn At Lathones

- *"A comfortable hotel offering good local produce cooked to the highest standards."*
- *Excellent Scottish cooking.*

THE INN AT LATHONES is run by Nick and Jocelyn White, who offer traditional coaching inn hospitality. Guests feel immediately at home and this comfort is matched by a very high standard of cooking offered in the elegant, yet informal, dining room. A very special place on the outskirts of St Andrews.

Thai fish cakes with chilli crisps. Grilled lamb cutlets with lamb kidney in a Madeira sauce. Crème Catalan with pistachio ice cream.

STB ★★★★ Inn

◗ *Open all year except Christmas Day, Boxing Day and Jan* 🏠 *Rooms: 14 en suite* 🛏 *DB&B £55–£70 B&B £60–£75* 🅢🅟 *Special rates available* ✖ *Food available all day Apr to Oct ££ Lunch £ Dinner ££* Ⓥ *Vegetarians welcome* 🧒 *Children welcome* 🚭 *No smoking in restaurant* 💳 *Mastercard/Eurocard, American Express, Visa, Diners Club, Switch, Delta* 🔑 *Proprietor: Nick White*

by Largoward St Andrews Fife KY9 1JE Tel: 01334 840494 Fax: 01334 840694 E-mail: lathones@theinn.co.uk Web: www.theinn.co.uk 5 miles out of St Andrews on the A915 towards Leven. The Inn is on the main road, 1 mile before Largoward. [D5]

ST ANDREWS OUTSKIRTS

Old Manor Hotel

- *"Stunning sea views and good food with a strong local bias."*
- *Contemporary Scottish cuisine.*

OWNED AND RUN by the Clark family their Aithernie Restaurant serves both à la carte and table d'hôte dishes, imaginatively prepared and presented. The restaurant's success has been reflected by awards won in several culinary competitions for chefs Paul Steven and Roberta Drummond.

Fennel omelette, filled with fresh crab and banana served with ginger and rocket salad. Baked fillets of lemon sole with langoustine soufflé on a leek sauce garnished with black trumpet mushrooms. Baked treacle and apple tart served with spiced kumquat ice cream.

STB ★★★★ Hotel

◗ *Open all year except Boxing Day and New Year's Day* 🏠 *Rooms: 23 en suite* 🛏 *DB&B £45.50–£105 B&B £30–£90* 🅢🅟 *Special rates available* ✖ *Food available all day ££ Lunch ££ Dinner £££* Ⓥ *Vegetarians welcome* 🧒 *Children welcome* ♿ *Facilities for disabled visitors* 🚭 *No smoking in restaurant* 💳 *Mastercard/Eurocard, American Express, Visa, Diners Club, Switch, Delta, JCB* 🔑 *Owners: Clark Family*

Lundin Links Fife KY8 6AJ Tel: 01333 320368 Fax: 01333 320911 E-mail: enquiries@oldmanorhotel.co.uk Web: www.oldmanorhotel.co.uk On A915 Kirkcaldy–St Andrews, 1 mile east of Leven, on right overlooking Largo Bay. [D5]

ST ANDREWS OUTSKIRTS

The Sandford Country House Hotel

- *"Quiet country surroundings and good food."*
- *Scottish modern.*

THE SANDFORD was built in 1902 and still has many original features such as the minstrel's gallery lounge. Set in seven acres of mature gardens it is an ideal place to relax and unwind. There is a choice of dining opportunities from relaxed bar meals to the more formal occasion in the Garden Room Restaurant.

Wild mushroom risotto served with truffle oil, thyme and Islay malt whisky. Prime fillet of Angus reared beef with a Madeira reduction topped by duck pâté. Rich parfait of Glayva and Scottish heather honey.

STB ★★ Small Hotel

◐ *Open all year* 🏠 *Rooms: 16 en suite* 🛏 *DB&B £60–£80 B&B £40–£60* 🆂 *Special rates available* ✗ *Food available all day ££ Lunch ££ Dinner £££* Ⓥ *Vegetarians welcome* 🧒 *Children welcome* ♿ *Limited facilities for disabled visitors* 🚭 *No smoking in dining room* 🐕 *Dogs welcome* 💳 *Mastercard/Eurocard, American Express, Visa, Switch, Delta* 🅽 *General Manager: Fergus Buchan*

Newton Hill Wormit Fife DD6 8RG
Tel: 01382 541802 Fax: 01382 542136
E-mail: sandford.hotel@btinternet.com
Web: www.sandfordhotelfife.com
4 miles south of Dundee on A92, (formerly A914) at junction of B946 signposted Wormit. [D5]

ST BOSWELLS

Clint Lodge

- *"A totally charming and wholesome experience."*
- *Traditional Scottish cooking.*

BILL AND HEATHER Walker have carefully restored Clint Lodge, paying great attention to the finest of detail. Furnishings are carefully selected to blend into the traditional atmosphere recreated here amongst a treasure trove of family heirlooms and selected antique furniture. A real get-away-haven with excellent hospitality and superb cooking.

Gravadlax mousse with dill and mustard mayonnaise. Medallions of beef fillet with a light gravy served on a horseradish mash and fresh garden vegetables. Mint parfait with a chocolate syrup.

STB ★★★★ B&B

◐ *Open all year except Christmas, New Year and Feb* 🏠 *Rooms: 5 (4 en suite, 1 private facilities)* 🛏 *DB&B £50–£60 B&B £30–£50* 🆄 *Unlicensed – guests welcome to take own wine* ✗ *Residents only Dinner ££* Ⓥ *Vegetarians welcome* 💳 *Mastercard, Visa* 🅽 *Proprietors: Bill & Heather Walker*

St Boswells Melrose TD6 0DZ
Tel: 01835 822027 Fax: 01835 822656
E-mail: clintlodge@aol.com
At St Boswells take the B6404, continue for 2 miles across the Mertoun Bridge, turn left onto B6356 through Clint Mains village veering left. Follow this road to Clint Lodge, 1 mile on right. [D6]

ST FILLANS

The Four Seasons Hotel

* *"Stunning food in an idyllic setting."*
* *Innovative Scottish cooking.*

AT THE FOUR SEASONS you are taken in by the panoramic views of Loch Earn. Chef Campbell Cameron weaves his magic on the most beautifully presented food. Dinner is relaxed with emphasis on high quality, well-produced food. The Tarken Room is less formal but the food is of the same standard and style.

Rendezvous of West Coast seafood poached in a light tomato and tarragon consommé. Cutlet of Strathappin venison with baked pears and cinnamon infused jus. Hot chocolate and Drambuie soufflé with griottine cherries and a vanilla cream.

STB ★★★ Small Hotel

◐ *Open Mar to Jan N.B. Closed some weekdays in Nov Dec* 🏠 *Rooms: 18 en suite* 🛏 *DB&B £58–£96.50 B&B £35–£49* 🍽 *Special rates available* ✖ *Food available £££ Lunch ££ Dinner £££* Ⓥ *Vegetarians welcome* 🧒 *Children welcome* 🚭 *No smoking in restaurant* 🐕*Dogs welcome* 💳 *Mastercard/Eurocard, Visa, Switch, Delta* 🗓 *Manager: Andrew Low*

St Fillans Perthshire PH6 2NF
Tel: 01764 685 333 Fax: 01764 685 444
E-mail: info@thefourseasonshotel.co.uk
Web: www.thefourseasonshotel.co.uk
A85 – west end of village on Loch Earn. [C5]

ST MONANS

The Seafood Restaurant

* *"Relaxed atmosphere with stunning food and views."*
* *Contemporary Scottish seafood.*

THE SEAFOOD RESTAURANT sits in the harbour of St Monans in the picturesque East Neuk of Fife. Head Chef Craig Millar offers menus containing the finest local produce and Scottish seafood that is second to none. All dishes are imaginative, mouth-watering and cooked to the highest standards.

Lobster and mango salad with mizuna, basil purée and gazpacho. Seared diver scallops with sun-blushed tomatoes, lardons and tomato dressing. Prune and armagnac pudding with banana ice cream and butterscotch sauce.

◐ *Open 1 Feb to 30 Nov Closed Mon Sep to June* ✖ *Lunch ££ Dinner £££* Ⓥ *Vegetarians welcome – prior notice required* ♿ *Facilities for disabled visitors* 🚭 *No smoking in restaurant* 💳 *Mastercard/Eurocard, American Express, Visa, Switch, JCB* 🗓 *Partner: Tim Butler*

16 West End St Monans Fife KY10 2BX
Tel: 01333 730 327 Fax: 01333 730 327
E-mail: info@theseafoodrestaurant.com
Web: www. theseafoodrestaurant.com
From St Andrews drive south to Anstruther (B9131) then turn west along the A917 through Pittenweem to St Monans. Go down to the harbour and turn right. [D5]

STIRLING

Bannockburn Heritage Centre
The National Trust For Scotland

- *"A very good quality experience from start to finish."*
- *Scottish home cooking.*

L OCATED ON THIS historic site, Bannockburn's self-service restaurant offers the best of Scottish home cooking with everything from good home baking to traditional soups. It is a lovely, fresh and attractively furnished self-service restaurant with well-trained and enthusiastic staff.

Tomato, orange and basil soup served with home-made cheese scone. Scottish cheese platter served with bannocks and seasonal salad. Delicious home baking.

STB ★★★★ Visitor Attraction

◗ *Open 1 Mar to 24 Dec* ⓈⓅ *Special rates available* Ⓤ *Unlicensed* ✗ *Food available all day £ Lunch £* Ⓥ *Vegetarians welcome* ✻ *Children welcome* ♿ *Facilities for disabled visitors* ✄ *No smoking throughout* 🖃 *Mastercard/Eurocard, Visa, Switch, Delta, JCB* Ⓜ *Cafe Manager: Sally Cameron*

*Glasgow Road Stirling FK7 0LJ
Tel: 01786 812664 Fax: 01786 810892
E-mail: jfairley@nts.org.uk
Web: www.nts.org.uk
Off M80/M9 at junction 9, 2 miles south of Stirling on the A872. [C5]*

STIRLING

Olivia's Restaurant

- *"A modern restaurant in an historic setting – with skilfully cooked produce."*
- *Modern Scottish.*

O LIVIA'S is an appealing restaurant located in an historic part of Stirling centre. Decor is modern and reflects the informal style of eating here. The menus are interesting, featuring good local produce cooked with flair and imagination. It is advisable to pre-book.

Seared king scallops served with sweet chilli sauce. Pan-fried fillet of Kippin lamb on a bed of Puy lentils with a port and rosemary sauce. Pannacotta with baked rhubarb compote.

◗ *Open all year except Christmas Day, Boxing Day and 1, 2 Jan* ✗ *Lunch except Sun £ Dinner ££* Ⓥ *Vegetarians welcome* ✻ *Children welcome* ♿ *Facilities for disabled visitors* 🖃 *Mastercard/ Eurocard, Visa, Switch, Delta* Ⓜ *Manageress: Laurie Veitch*

*5 Baker Street Stirling FK8 1BJ
Tel: 01786 446277 Fax: 01786 446277
From Stirling town centre follow directions to Stirling Castle. Restaurant is approx 800 yards from castle on approach. [C5]*

STIRLING OUTSKIRTS

Glenskirlie House

- *"Relaxing atmosphere with friendly caring staff."*
- *Modern Scottish.*

GLENSKIRLIE HOUSE is owned by Linda and John Macaloney and run by their son Colin. It is a unique impressive place where everything is of the highest quality. Menus are a successful combination of traditional and contemporary – all prepared with skill both in preparation and presentation – and using the best fresh produce. A very impressive place.

Seared scallops in a potato, nutmeg and truffle oil bisque with sautéed scallions. Herb roasted loin of lamb accompanied by a gâteau of Provençal vegetables, roasted garlic and basil jus. Chocolate brûlée with passion fruit sorbet and sugar twists.

◐ *Open all year except 26, 27 Dec and 1, 2 and 3 Jan Closed Mon night ♚ Licensed ✘ Bar Lunch £ Lunch ££ Dinner except Mon £££ Ⓥ Vegetarians welcome ♣ Children welcome ♿ Facilities for disabled visitors ▦ Mastercard/ Eurocard, American Express, Visa, Diners Club, Switch, Delta ♛ General Manager: Colin Macaloney*

Kilsyth Road Banknock Stirlingshire FK4 1UF Tel: 01324 840201 Fax: 01324 841054 E-mail: macaloneys@glenskirliehouse.com Web: www.glenskirliehouse.com From Glasgow take A80 towards Stirling, take Junction 4, on A803 Kilsyth/Bonnybridge cut off. At T-junction turn right, restaurant 1 mile on right-hand side. [C5]

STIRLING OUTSKIRTS

The Topps

- *"Family-run farm guest house with a relaxed informal atmosphere."*
- *Excellent home cooking.*

THE POPULAR restaurant complements the guest house facilities. It has a small bar and comfortable dining room. Scottish owners Jennifer and Alistair Steel both cook. The menus are straightforward, usually offering a choice of four main courses. As much produce as possible comes from the farm itself.

Alistair's gravadlax – herb marinaded salmon. Lamb fillet with port sauce, fresh raspberries and wild mushrooms. Lacy crêpes filled with chocolate and Greek yoghurt sauce.

STB ★★ Guest House

◐ *Open all year ▦ Rooms: 8 en suite ▭ B&B £20–£32 ✘ Dinner ££ Ⓥ Vegetarians welcome – prior notice required ♣ Children welcome ♿ Facilities for disabled visitors ✄ No smoking throughout ▦ Mastercard/Eurocard, Visa ♛ Owners/Chefs: Jennifer & Alistair Steel*

Fintry Road Denny Stirlingshire FK6 5JF Tel: 01324 822471 Fax: 01324 823099 E-mail: 2lambs@onetel.net.uk Web: www.thetopps.com On B818 Denny – Fintry road, off M80. 4 miles from Denny. [C5]

STRACHUR

The Creggans Inn

- *"Excellent food and hospitality combined with magnificent views across Loch Fyne."*
- *Modern Scottish.*

NEW OWNERS the Robertson family provide stunning food and equally delightful hospitality. Every bedroom has a lochside view and is furnished to a high standard, whilst there is an ongoing refurbishment schedule. The cooking here is highly skilled and guests may enjoy a choice of fine dining or excellent informal bar meals.

Warm crab and Parmesan soufflé served with a smoked salmon cream. Roast rack of lamb with a rosemary and mint reduction and dauphinoise potatoes. Whisky chocolate terrine with white chocolate ice cream.

◗ *Open all year* 🏠 *Rooms: 14 en suite* 🛏 *DB&B £60–£165 B&B £45–£138* 💳 *Special rates available* ✗ *Lunch ££ Dinner £££* Ⓥ *Vegetarians welcome* 🧒 *Children welcome* ✍ *No smoking in dining room* 💳 *Mastercard/Eurocard, Visa, Switch, Delta* Ⓜ *Partners: Alex, Thomas and Onny Robertson*

Strachur Cairndow Argyll PA27 8BX
Tel: 01369 860279 Fax: 01369 860637
E-mail: info@creggans-inn.co.uk
Web: www.creggans-inn.co.uk
On A815 on the south Loch Fyne road. Creggans Inn is 8 miles from A83 Junction at Cairndow. [B5]

STRANRAER

Corsewall Lighthouse Hotel

- *"A small and quite unique hotel and restaurant."*
- *Modern Scottish cooking.*

THIS 19TH CENTURY lighthouse, now an A Listed building, has been converted with modern day comforts. A light still beams warning ships that they are approaching the mouth of Loch Ryan. Dining in the restaurant is a wonderful experience where excellent food is prepared and offered by Chef McMurtrie and his team.

Smoked 'Cree' salmon from the Marbury Smokehouse. Buccleuch Scotch beef fillet set on a horseradish mash with a red onion marmalade. Cacophony of summer fruits and berries infused in 'Galloway Pride' (whisky and heather honey).

STB ★★★★ Small Hotel

◗ *Open all year* 🏠 *Rooms: 9 (8 en suite, 1 with private facilities)* 🛏 *DB&B £55–£135 B&B £45–£125* 💳 *Special rates available* ✗ *Food available all day £ Lunch ££ Dinner £££* Ⓥ *Vegetarians welcome* 🧒 *Children welcome* ♿ *Facilities for disabled visitors* ✍ *No smoking in restaurant* 🐕*Dogs welcome – only in suites* 💳 *Mastercard/Eurocard, Visa, American Express, Diners Club, Switch, Delta* Ⓜ *Partner: Gordon Ward*

Corsewall Point Kirkcolm Stranraer DG9 0QG
Tel: 01776 853220 Fax: 01776 854231
E-mail: corsewall_lighthouse@msn.com
Web: www.corsewall-lighthousehotel.co.uk/ www.lighthousehotel.co.uk
From Stranraer take B718 to Kirkcolm (6 miles). Go straight through village then follow signs for Corsewall Lighthouse (4 miles). [B7]

STRATHPEFFER

Coul House Hotel

- *"Pavilion-style Highland country house with log fire offers comfortable and relaxed hospitality."*
- *Traditional Scottish and modern menus.*

A WARM WELCOME from owners Martyn and Ann Hill awaits guests at this elegant country house hotel, set in secluded grounds in Contin village with delightful mountain and forest views. Choose from traditional menus highlighting local specialities in the candlelit MacKenzie's Restaurant or casual imaginative fare in the cosy Tartan Bistro.

Salmon tagliatelle in a cream sauce with dill. Medallions of Scottish beef on a bed of stir-fried vegetables. Honey wafers filled with Drambuie mousse on a raspberry coulis.

STB ★★★★ Hotel

◗ *Open all year* 🏠 *3 Rooms: 20 en suite* 🛏 *DB&B £54.50–£80 B&B £39–£55* 🍽 *Special rates available* ✗ *Lunch £–££ (Restaurant – prior booking only) Dinner 5 course menu £££* Ⓥ *Vegetarians welcome* ⚘ *Children welcome* ♿ *Facilities for disabled visitors* ⚭ *No smoking in restaurant* 💳 *Mastercard/Eurocard, American Express, Visa, Diners Club, Switch, JCB* ⚑ *Proprietor: Martyn A Hill*

Contin by Strathpeffer Ross-shire IV14 9EY Tel: 01997 421487 Fax: 01997 421945 E-mail: coulhouse@bestwestern.co.uk Web: www.milford.co.uk/go/coulhouse.html North of Inverness, take A9 over Moray Firth Bridge. After 5 miles take second left at roundabout to A835. Follow road for about 12 miles until you reach the village of Contin. Hotel is ½ mile up private drive to the right. [C3]

STRATHYRE

Creagan House

- *"Their enthusiasm for good Scottish food cannot be contained, with well-informed conversation and unique surroundings."*
- *Innovative Scottish cooking.*

I N THE HEART of Rob Roy country Creagan House, originally a 17th century farmhouse, has been sympathetically and lovingly upgraded to provide baronial dining in the large hall, while more intimate surroundings may be enjoyed in the small room. Gordon is a highly skilled chef, meticulous with his preparation and presentation of all dishes.

Saffron seasoned dived scallops with angel hair spaghetti filo parcel and a white raisin and caper dressing. Breast of Gressingham duck on cassis red onion, apple and a thyme and white wine sauce. Bitter chocolate tart with a coffee bean syrup.

STB ★★★★ Restaurant with Rooms

◗ *Open all year except Feb and 1 week Oct* 🏠 *Rooms: 5 en suite* 🛏 *B&B £42.50* 🍽 *Special rates available* ✗ *Lunch parties can be arranged Dinner ££–£££ Booking essential for all meals* Ⓥ *Vegetarians welcome – with prior notice* ⚘ *Children over 10 years welcome* ⚭ *No smoking in dining hall and bedrooms* 💳 *Mastercard/Eurocard, American Express, Visa* ⚑ *Chef/Proprietor: Gordon Gunn; Co-Proprietor: Cherry Gunn*

Strathyre Callander Perthshire FK18 8ND Tel: 01877 384638 Fax: 01877 384319 E-mail: eatandstay@creaganhouse.co.uk Web: www.creaganhouse.co.uk On A84, ¼ mile north of Strathyre. [C5]

STRATHYRE

Rosebank House

- *"Fabulous food and views."*
- *Modern Scottish cooking.*

THIS TERRACED HOUSE hides such treasures within as Pete and Jill Moor have worked really hard to equip their guests with every comfort. Guests can relax in the lounge or out in the garden and take in the magnificent views of the Queen Elizabeth Forest. All meals are prepared with fresh local produce. The home baking and preserves are second to none!

Salad of home-cured gravadlax and garden fresh quails eggs. Loin steak of local pork with an apricot and garden herb crust. Rosy's brandy pudding with crème anglais.

STB ★★★★ Guest House

◑ *Open all year* 🏠 *Rooms: 4, 2 en suite* 🛏 *DB&B £36–£40 B&B £21–£25* 🆂🅿 *Special rates available* 🅻🅸 *Unlicensed – guests welcome to take own wine* ✗ *Packed lunch £ Lunch – by arrangement ££ Dinner ££ Booking essential for all meals* 🆅 *Vegetarians welcome* 🧒 *Children welcome* 🚭 *No smoking throughout* 🐕*Dogs welcome* 💳 *Mastercard/Eurocard, Visa, Delta, Switch, Solo* 🅺 *Co-Proprietors: Jill & Pete Moor*

Strathyre by Callander Perthshire FK18 8NA
Tel: 01877 384 208 Fax: 01877 384 201
E-mail: rosebank@tinyworld.co.uk
Web: www.rosebankhouse.co.uk
On the east side of the main A84 in the village of Strathyre. [C5]

STRONTIAN

Kilcamb Lodge Hotel

- *"Kilcamb continues to excel at providing wonderful food with hospitality to match."*
- *High quality Scottish cuisine.*

KILCAMB LODGE is family-owned and run by Anne and Peter Blakeway. There is a lovely blend of professional service and attention with a friendly atmosphere here. Neil Mellis cooks, presenting a highly professional table d'hôte menu which changes daily and uses the best of the produce available that day. Investor in People Award.

Grilled Loch Sunart langoustines with garlic and herb butter. Roast fillet of Angus beef with butter fondant potatoes, creamed parsley and a red wine jus. Mascarpone roulades with roast pears.

STB ★★★★ Small Hotel

◑ *Open all year except Dec, Jan and Feb N.B. Open New Year* 🏠 *Rooms: 11 en suite* 🛏 *Room only £60–£130* ✗ *Light Lunch £ Dinner 2 course menu ££ 4 course menu £££* 🆅 *Vegetarians welcome – prior notice required* 🧒 *Children welcome* ♿ *Facilities for non-residential disabled visitors* 🚭 *No smoking in restaurant* 💳 *Mastercard/Eurocard, Visa, Switch, Delta* 🅺 *Directors: Peter & Anne Blakeway*

Strontian Argyll PH36 4HY
Tel: 01967 402257 Fax: 01967 402041
E-mail: kilcamblodge@aol.com
Web: www.kilcamblodge.co.uk
On A861, 13 miles from Corran Ferry (A82, 8 miles south of Fort William). [B5]

SWINTON

The Wheatsheaf Restaurant with Rooms

- *"The Wheatsheaf are highly deserving of their numerous accolades for their food, accommodation and hospitality."*
- *Modern Scottish cooking.*

JULIE AND ALAN REID continue to offer a superb experience here. Bedrooms are prettily furnished, menus are extensive, reasonably priced and change daily. Excellent local produce is given added flavour by the chef's individuality and flair. Winner of The Macallan Taste of Scotland Award 1997.

Seared breast of woodpigeon on black pudding with bubble and squeak. Steamed fillet of halibut with langoustine tails on a wild sorrel sabayon sauce with lobster coral. Iced Drambuie and praline parfait with poached pear and hot butterscotch sauce.

STB ★★★★ Restaurant with Rooms

◗ *Open all year except 14 to 29 Jan Closed Mon* ▮ *Rooms: 7 en suite* ▰ *B&B £45–£70* ⓢ *Special rates available* ✕ *Lunch except Mon ££ Dinner £££* Ⓥ *Vegetarians welcome* ⚦ *Children welcome* ⚥ *No smoking in restaurant* ⊞ *Mastercard/Eurocard, Visa, Switch* ▮ *Proprietors: Alan & Julie Reid*

Swinton Berwickshire TD11 3JJ
Tel: 01890 860 257 Fax: 01890 860 688
E-mail: reception@wheatsheaf-swinton.co.uk
Web: www.wheatsheaf-swinton.co.uk
On B6461 Kelso-Berwick-upon-Tweed, 12 miles west of Berwick or a few miles east of A697.
[D6]

SYMINGTON AYRSHIRE

Nether Underwood

- *"A place where good food and friendliness abound – and one of the best breakfasts in Scotland!"*
- *Delicious modern Scottish cooking.*

ONLY TWO AND A HALF MILES from the busy A77 yet a world apart. Owner Felicity Thomson and her husband Austin are warm, friendly hosts and Felicity's culinary skills are most impressive. Treat yourself to innovative dinners, home-baked breads and scones from the Aga and delicious hand-made preserves and petit fours. Book now!

Courgette soup with home-made rosemary and walnut bread. Pan-fried steak of wild Scottish salmon with samphire, roasted summer vegetables, and minted Ayrshire potatoes. Rice creams with gooseberry and elderflower compote.

STB ★★★★★ Guest House

◗ *Open all year except 24 Dec to 2 Jan* ▮ *Rooms: 3 en suite (4th sometimes available)* ▰ *DB&B £70–£85 B&B £45–£55* ✕ *Residents only Dinner £££* Ⓥ *Vegetarians welcome* ⚦ *Children over 16 years welcome* ⚥ *No smoking throughout* ⊞ *Mastercard/Eurocard, Visa, Switch* ▮ *Chef/Proprietor: Felicity Thomson*

By Symington Kilmarnock KA1 5NG
Tel: 01563 830 666 Fax: 01563 830 777
E-mail: netherund@aol.com
Web: www.netherunderwood.co.uk
South of Kilmarnock on Glasgow-Ayr A77, take B730 to Tarbolton, follow brown signs to Hayes Garden Land. Pass Hayes, continue to junction marked 'Nether Underwood'. Turn right; 2½ miles from A77, turn right into tree lined lane leading to Nether Underwood. [C6]

TAIN

Mansfield House Hotel

- *"A high standard of hospitality with careful thought given to guests' needs."*
- *Confident, modern Scottish cooking.*

THIS VICTORIAN MANSION is centrally located in Tain within walking distance of shops and shoreline. Proprietors, the Lauritsen family, are excellent hosts who are highly skilled and experienced. Guests choose from the daily set menu featuring top quality local produce in skilfully executed dishes or the popular bar meals. Investor in People Award.

Roulade of monkfish, salmon and nori, with a caviar dressing. Confit of duck with armagnac cherries and a rich pan jus. Baked crème caramel with liquorice ice cream and crunchy dipped fruits.

STB ★★★★ Hotel
Green Tourism Three Leaf Gold Award

❶ *Open all year* 🏨 *Rooms: 19 en suite* 🛏 *B&B £50–£75* 🆓 *Special rates available* ✗ *Food available all day £–£££ Lunch £ Dinner £–£££* Ⓥ *Vegetarians welcome* ✹ *Children welcome* ♿ *Facilities for disabled visitors* ✍ *No smoking in restaurants* 💳 *Mastercard/Eurocard, American Express, Visa, Switch* ⚄ *Proprietors: Norman, Norma & David Lauritsen*

Scotsburn Road Tain Ross-shire IV19 1PR Tel: 01862 892052 Fax: 01862 892260 E-mail: mansfield@cali.co.uk Web: www.mansfield-house.co.uk Approaching Tain from south, ignore first entrance and continue north on A9 to second turning on right, signposted to police station and Royal Academy. [C3]

TAIN

Morangie House Hotel

- *"Popular Victorian mansion house hotel near the Dornoch Firth offering the best of traditional Highland hospitality."*
- *Good Scottish cooking.*

MORANGIE HOUSE HOTEL has very comfortable rooms with good furnishings and thoughtful extras. Under the experienced eye of John Wynne and his son Derek, well-trained staff offer cheerful hospitality. Table d'hôte and à la carte menus served in the Garden or dining rooms partner local meat and seafood specialities with old favourites.

Local fresh mussels cooked in a white wine and cream sauce. Pan-fried fillet of Ross-shire venison cooked pink and served onto a compote of red cabbage and onion surrounded by a redcurrant jus. Home-made sticky toffee pudding.

STB ★★★★ Hotel

❶ *Open all year* 🏨 *Rooms: 26 en suite* 🛏 *DB&B £55–£80 B&B £40–£60* 🆓 *Special rates available* ✗ *Food available all day £ Lunch £ Dinner ££* Ⓥ *Vegetarians welcome* ✹ *Children welcome* ♿ *Facilities for disabled visitors* ✍ *No smoking in dining room* 💳 *Mastercard/ Eurocard, American Express, Visa, Diners Club, Switch* ⚄ *Proprietor: John Wynne*

Morangie Road Tain Ross-shire IV19 1PY Tel: 01862 892281 Fax: 01862 892872 E-mail: wynne@morangiehotel.com Web: www.morangiehotel.com Just off the A9 Inverness-Wick road on northern outskirts of Tain.[C3]

TALLADALE

The Old Mill Highland Lodge

- *"An idyllic haven."*
- *Skilled home cooking.*

THIS CHARMING and elegantly furnished house is where Joanna and Chris Powell look after their guests with genuine warmth and charm. Chris is an enthusiastic cook and produces imaginative, colourful dishes utilising much locally-sourced Highland produce. Joanna uses her experience in the wine trade to complement the mouth-watering dishes with just the right wine.

Individual fresh asparagus soufflés. Salmon en croûte with a bitter orange and chive sauce. Steamed lemon sponge with lemon sauce.

STB ★★★★ Small Hotel

◑ *Open Mar to Oct* 🏠 *Rooms: 6, 5 en suite* 🛏 *DB&B £55–£70* 🅢 *Special rates available* 🍷 *Restricted hotel licence* ✗ *Dinner £££ Residents only* Ⓥ *Vegetarians – by prior arrangement* ✤ *No smoking throughout* 🚭 *No credit cards* 🅗 *Owners: Chris & Joanna Powell*

Talladale Loch Maree Ross-shire IV22 2HL
Tel: 01445 760271
On A832 at Talladale – 10 miles north of Kinlochewe and 10 miles south of Gairloch. The only establishment on the left along Loch Maree heading north. [B3]

TARBERT ARGYLL

The Anchorage Restaurant

- *"Right on the harbour – enjoy skilfully cooked seafood and other local produce."*
- *Modern Scottish.*

THE ANCHORAGE is a small restaurant with a sunny Mediterranean feel. It focuses on presenting good quality local produce in a relaxed and friendly atmosphere. Blackboard menus change daily depending on the fresh seafood available.

Smoked haddock chowder with prawns and sweetcorn. Hand-dived king scallops sautéed with pea purée and a mint vinaigrette. White chocolate brownies with a dark chocolate sauce and vanilla ice cream.

◑ *Open Feb to Dec Closed Sun Mon during winter months (please contact establishment for further details)* ✗ *Lunch please call for details Dinner except Jan £££* Ⓥ *Vegetarians welcome* 🚭 *Mastercard/Eurocard, Visa, Switch, Delta* 🅗 *Chef/Owner: Clare Johnson*

Harbour Street Tarbert Argyll PA29 6UD
Tel: 01880 820881
E-mail: mail@anchoragetarbert.co.uk
Web: www.anchoragetarbert.co.uk
The Anchorage is located beside the quay on Harbour Street, overlooking the harbour. [B6]

TARBERT ARGYLL

The Columba Hotel

- *"Excellent food, comfort, relaxation and scenic views onto East Loch Tarbert."*
- *Scottish modern cooking.*

THE COLUMBA HOTEL nestles at the quiet end of Tarbert Harbour. The bar is popular for its wholesomely different bar food. The restaurant has been elegantly restored and offers a relaxed atmosphere and a menu which makes imaginative use of the excellent local produce. The seafood on the menu is of exceptional quality.

Warm queen scallop, Tarbert smoked salmon and cucumber salad with a malt whisky and sorrel sauce. Pan-fried Inveraray venison saddle on salardaise potatoes. Raspberry and grenadine sorbet with dark chocolate and cinnamon shortbread; white chocolate and Glayva sauce.

STB ★★★ Small Hotel
Green Tourism One Leaf Bronze Award

◐ *Open all year except 25 and 26 Dec* ♨ *Rooms: 10 en suite* ⊨ *DB&B £45.95–£64.95 B&B £35.95–£43.95* ▩ *Special rates available* ✕ *Lunch £ Dinner ££* Ⓥ *Vegetarians welcome* ✻ *Children welcome* ⊬ *No smoking in restaurant* ⊞ *Mastercard/Eurocard, American Express, Visa* Ⓜ *Partners: Bob & Gina Chicken*

East Pier Road Tarbert Loch Fyne Argyll PA29 6UF
Tel: 01880 820808 Fax: 01880 820808
E-mail: columbahotel@fsbdial.co.uk
Web: www.columbahotel.com
On East Pier Road, ½ mile to the left around the harbour. Hotel on roadside. [B6]

TARBERT ARGYLL

Stonefield Castle Hotel

- *"Wonderful views and interesting walks in the spacious gardens and grounds."*
- *Modern/traditional Scottish cooking.*

STONEFIELD CASTLE is set in 60 acres of woodland gardens and is located on Loch Fyne – enjoy the breathtaking views while dining. The cooking here offers good local produce – seafood is caught locally – presented in a traditional style with modern influences and served by well-trained and friendly staff.

Grilled king prawns with oyster mushrooms, smoked Argyll ham and balsamic reduction. Potato crusted fillet of West Coast sea bass accompanied with a spring onion beurre blanc and onion confit. Warm parsnip cake with rhubarb sorbet and Drambuie anglaise.

STB ★★★★ Hotel

◐ *Open all year* ♨ *Rooms: 33 (32 en suite, 1 with private facilities)* ⊨ *DB&B £65–£90* ▩ *Special rates available* ✕ *Lunch £ Dinner £££* Ⓥ *Vegetarians welcome* ♿ *Facilities for disabled visitors* ⊬ *No smoking in restaurant* ⊞ *Mastercard/Eurocard, American Express, Visa, Diners Club, Switch, Delta*

Tarbert Loch Fyne Argyll PA29 6YJ
Tel: 01880 820836 Fax: 01880 820929
3 miles north of Tarbert on A83 to Lochgilphead. [B6]

TARBERT, ARGYLL

Victoria Hotel

- *"A busy vibrant harbourside hotel with a great atmosphere."*
- *Modern Scottish cooking.*

UNDER THE SAME OWNERSHIP for the last 14 years, the Victoria Hotel has built an enviable reputation for informal bar meals – the conservatory offers more formal dining menu. The new head chef enjoys using different local fish and shellfish. Both bar and restaurant menus offer locally-sourced produce described and presented with skill and flair.

Grilled Loch Fyne king prawns with garlic and parsley butter served with salsa verde and salad. Cod, mussel and smoked haddock fish cake topped with local scallops and beurre blanc. Passion fruit tart with an apple mint Mascarpone.

STB ★★★ Inn

◗ *Open all year except Christmas Day*
🏠 *Rooms: 5 en suite* 🛏 *DB&B £46–£48 B&B £27–£29* 💷 *Special rates available* ✗ *Lunch £ Dinner ££* Ⓥ *Vegetarians welcome* ☀ *Children welcome* ♿ *Facilities for disabled visitors* 🚭 *No smoking in restaurant* 💳 *Mastercard/Eurocard, Visa, Switch, Delta* 🔪 *General Manager: Kate Tod*

Barmore Road Tarbert Argyll PA29 6TW
Tel: 01880 820 236/431 Fax: 01880 820 638
E-mail: victoria.hotel@lineone.net
Web: www.thevictoriahotel.net
First hotel as you enter the village (on A83 from Lochgilphead) on your right-hand side. [B6]

TAYVALLICH

Tayvallich Inn

- *"A peaceful yachtsman's haven on Loch Sween offering excellent local seafood."*
- *Good Scottish cooking with some innovation.*

THE TAYVALLICH INN is beautifully situated with a spectacular outlook onto Tayvallich Bay. Andrew and Jilly's sourcing of good local produce is evident on the menus. Dishes are well-presented and offer good value for money. There is a choice of dining areas – dining room for fine dining; bistro-style or bar area for less formal.

Sound of Jura whole jumbo prawn salad with a lime mayonnaise. Tayvallich seafood platter (jumbo prawns, mussels, oyster, smoked salmon, pickled herring, hot-smoked salmon and crab claws). Home-made fruit crumbles with ice cream.

◗ *Open all year except Christmas Day and New Year's Day* ✗ *Lunch except Mon Nov to Mar £–££ Dinner except Sun to Thu Nov to Mar ££–£££ Bar suppers except Mon Nov to Mar* Ⓥ *Vegetarians welcome* ☀ *Children welcome* ♿ *Access only for disabled visitors* 💳 *Mastercard/Eurocard, Visa, Switch, Delta, JCB* 🔪 *Proprietors: Andrew & Jilly Wilson*

Tayvallich by Lochgilphead Argyll PA31 8PL
Tel: 01546 870282 Fax: 01546 870333
E-mail: tayvallich.inn@virgin.net
Web: www.tayvallich.com
2 hours from Glasgow via A82 to Tarbert. Then take A83 to Lochgilphead. Follow signs to Oban then take B841 at Cairnbaan. After 4 miles take B8052 to Tayvallich, 6 miles on single-track road. [B5]

THORNHILL DUMFRIES

Trigony House Hotel

- *"Tranquil Country house hotel popular for fishing and shooting, offering simple, elegant Scottish food."*
- *Simple, elegant Scottish cooking.*

TRIGONY, a small country house in its own gardens, became a hotel over 20 years ago. Owners Adam and Judith Moore (mother and son) have an innovative approach to menus and cooking. They continue to provide homely comfort in public and private rooms which are bright, airy and have charming views over the surrounding country.

Warm confit of duck salad with a red onion and orange dressing. Roast rack of local Dunscore lamb with roasted red pepper, aubergine and red wine gravy. Hazelnut meringue cake with fresh raspberry and a raspberry sauce.

STB ★★★★ Small Hotel

◑ *Open all year* 🛏 *Rooms: 8 en suite* 🛏 *DB&B £52.50–£62.50 B&B £35–£45* 🍴 *Special rates available* ✗ *Lunch £ Dinner ££* Ⓥ *Vegetarians welcome* ☙ *Children over 8 years welcome* ✄ *No smoking in dining room* 🐾 *Pets welcome* 💳 *Mastercard/Eurocard, Visa, Switch, Delta* ☒ *Proprietors: Judith & Adam Moore*

By Thornhill Dumfriesshire DG3 5EZ
Tel: 01848 331211 Fax: 01848 331303
E-mail: info@trigonyhotel.co.uk
Web: www.trigonyhotel.co.uk
Situated off A76, 13 miles north of Dumfries.
1 mile south of Thornhill on the Dumfries-Ayr trunk road. [C6]

THURSO

Forss Country House Hotel

- *"A very relaxing and comfortable country house hotel popular with anglers."*
- *Traditional Scottish cooking.*

SET AMONGST BEAUTIFUL mature trees four miles from Thurso, Forss House offers guests friendly, unhurried service along with good food. Run by the MacGregor family this is a well-run quite special place where excellent meals are served in the peaceful and attractive dining room. Breakfast in the conservatory gets the day off to a good start.

Gâteau of Scottish puddings with Orkney cheese sabayon. Medallions of Caithness venison with blackcurrant and liquorice jus and barley risotto. Choice of home-made desserts, local ice cream and Forss House cheeseboard.

STB ★★★★ Small Hotel

◑ *Open 5 Jan to 23 Dec* 🛏 *Rooms: 10 en suite* 🛏 *DB&B £67–£80 B&B £45–£57.50* 🍴 *Special rates available* ✗ *Food available all day ££ Lunch – residents only £–££ Dinner ££* Ⓥ *Vegetarians welcome* ☙ *Children welcome* ♿ *Facilities for disabled visitors* ✄ *No smoking in dining room* 💳 *Mastercard/Eurocard, American Express, Visa, Switch* ☒ *Proprietors: Jamie & Jackie MacGregor*

by Thurso Caithness KW14 7XY
Tel: 01847 861201 Fax: 01847 861301
E-mail: jamie@forsshouse.freeserve.co.uk
Web: www.forsscountryhouse.co.uk
4 miles from Thurso heading west on A836. [C2]

TIGHNABRUAICH

Royal Hotel

- *"Wonderful views onto the loch, freshly caught seafood and courteous, friendly service."*
- *Skilled and stylish Scottish cooking.*

AT THE ROYAL there is a stylish modern restaurant and an informal friendly bar-brasserie where local seafood (served straight from the fishermen's nets) and game is served. The food here is very popular – it is advisable to arrive early for the brasserie and booking is essential for the restaurant. Investor in People Award.

Peppered venison fillet with a Dunsyre Blue cheese and red onion salad. King scallops hand-dived in Loch Fyne with wilted spinach and herb butter. Figs, roasted and presented on sugared parfait with a fruit coulis.

STB ★★★★ Hotel

Open all year · Rooms: 11 en suite · DB&B £65–£100 B&B £37–£77 · Special rates available · Food available all day ££ Lunch £ Dinner ££–£££ · Vegetarians welcome · No smoking in dining room · Mastercard/ Eurocard, Visa, Switch, Delta · Owners: Roger & Bea McKie

Tighnabruaich Argyll PA21 2BE
Tel: 01700 811239 Fax: 01700 811300
E-mail: info@royalhotel.org.uk
Web: www.royalhotel.org.uk
Overlooking the Kyles of Bute at the end of the A8003 in Tighnabruaich. [B6]

TONGUE

Borgie Lodge Hotel

- *"Peaceful and very comfortable with a roaring log fire in the lounge."*
- *Superb home cooking with flair.*

HOME TO Jacqui and Peter MacGregor, Borgie Lodge is a small hotel in a very attractive setting which is a particular favourite with anglers. Guests will enjoy Jacqui's excellent four course daily menu which shows skilled use of the finest local produce. The hotel has its own boats and fishing rights. 'Non-fishers' welcome too!

Sautéed foie gras with peach chutney. Tranche of halibut with a herb crust and bouillabaisse sauce. Banana parfait with a toffee sauce.

STB ★★★★ Small Hotel

Open all year except 24 Dec to 3 Jan · Rooms: 7 (6 en suite, 1 private suite) · DB&B £65–£80 B&B £40–£55 · Lunch £ Dinner £££ · Vegetarians welcome · Children welcome · No smoking in dining room and bedrooms · Mastercard/Eurocard, Visa, Switch · Proprietors: Peter & Jacqui MacGregor

Skerray Tongue Sutherland KW14 7TH
Tel: 01641 521 332 Fax: 01641 521 332
E-mail: info@borgielodgehotel.co.uk
Web: www.borgielodgehotel.co.uk
Take A836 for 7 miles from Tongue, turn left at the Torrisdale Road. Borgie Lodge is ½ mile along on the right. [C2]

TONGUE

Tongue Hotel

- *"Travel to the Tongue Hotel along a road of spectacular scenery and enjoy good Scottish hospitality in charming surroundings."*
- *Modern Scottish.*

THE TONGUE HOTEL was built as a hunting lodge in the late 1800s by the Duke of Sutherland. Bedrooms are comfortable, with public rooms having character and charm. Staff are of smart appearance and provide excellent service. The surrounding area, dominated by Ben Loyal, is of great geological and ornithological interest. Investor in People Award.

Warm salad of squat lobster, avocado and seasonal leaves. Collops of Sutherland venison, new potato salad, peach chutney and summer broad beans. Slow baked baby pineapple with vanilla pod ice cream and home-made shortbread.

STB ★★★★ Small Hotel
Green Tourism One Leaf Bronze Award

◗ *Open Apr to Oct incl* 🏠 *Rooms: 16* 🛏 *DB&B £40–£75 B&B £25–£50* 🖼 *Special rates available* ✖ *Food available all day ££ Lunch £ Dinner (please phone ahead) £££*
Ⓥ *Vegetarians welcome* ⚹ *Children welcome* ✹ *No smoking during meal times*
🖃 *Mastercard, Visa, Switch, Solo* 🄽 *General Manager: Ms Karen Stoltman*

Tongue Sutherland IV27 4XD
Tel: 01847 611 206 Fax: 01847 611345
E-mail: info@tonguehotel.co.uk
Web: www.scottish-selection.co.uk
On A836 as you enter Tongue on right-hand side overlooking the Kyle of Tongue. [C2]

TROON

Cellars Restaurant & Cocktail Bar

- *"A contemporary cellar restaurant with fine Scottish menu."*
- *Modern Scottish cooking.*

CELLARS is steeped in local history of the 19th century. However, its theme throughout is impressive Art Deco, with burning candles creating a romantic and highly charged atmosphere. Dishes are conceived from locally-sourced seafoods and the best Scottish beef, fruits and vegetables. International touches are added by Robbie O'Keefe. Menu is changed monthly.

Marinated strips of sea bass, dill and onion crêpe. Layered tournedos of beef with lobster, potato galette, spring onion soufflé and port wine sauce. Poached pear, apple and armagnac tart, with fresh custard.

◗ *Open all year Closed Tue* ✖ *Lunch except Tue £–££ Dinner except Tue ££* Ⓥ *Vegetarians welcome* ⚹ *Children welcome* ♿ *Facilities for disabled visitors* ✹ *No smoking in restaurant Smoking permitted in cocktail bar*
🖃 *Mastercard/Eurocard, American Express, Visa, Switch* 🄽 *Proprietors: Malcolm & Karen Ronney*

149 Templehill Troon KA10 6BQ
Tel: 01292 317448 Fax: 01292 318508
E-mail: anchor1812@aol.com
Web: www.theanchoragehotel.com
On arriving in Troon follow directions to Troon harbour which will lead you to Templehill. The Cellars is located half a kilometre along on the left-hand side. [C6]

TROON

Piersland House Hotel

- *"Beautiful period house with lovely food, right by the golf course."*
- *International cuisine.*

PIERSLAND was built in 1899 as the home for Sir Alexander Walker, grandson of Johnnie Walker (founder of the Scotch whisky firm). The hotel has some fine Jacobean-style features. It stands in beautifully landscaped grounds that include an oriental garden. Piersland has an informal dining area – The Brasserie Restaurant which overlooks the magnificent gardens.

Sautéed button mushrooms in a cream reduction sauce flavoured by Stilton and leeks served in a crisp tortilla basket and traced by a Madeira essence. Loin of lamb with a spinach and pimento mousse, onion marmalade, served with a tarragon and tomato jus. Coconut and vanilla bavarois with passion fruit and tropical sauce.

STB ★★★★ Hotel

◗ *Open all year* 🏨 *Rooms: 28 en suite* 🛏 *DB&B £75–£90 B&B £55–£70* 🆂🅿 *Special rates available* ✕ *Lunch ££ Dinner £££* Ⓥ *Vegetarians welcome* 🧒 *Children welcome* ♿ *Facilities for disabled visitors and residents* 💳 *Mastercard/Eurocard, American Express, Visa, Diners Club, Switch* 🍴 *General Manager: Karel Kuhler*

15 Craigend Road Troon KA10 6HD
Tel: 01292 314747 Fax: 01292 315613
E-mail: reservations@piersland.co.uk
Web: www.piersland.co.uk
South corner of Troon, opposite Royal Troon Golf Club and within 3 miles of Glasgow Prestwick International Airport. Troon is the Scottish port for the Seacat crossing to Belfast. [C6]

TURNBERRY

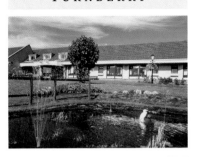

Malin Court Hotel

- *"Country hotel with spectacular views."*
- *Modern Scottish cooking.*

MALIN COURT is very professionally-run and each member of staff takes an obvious pride in their work. Chef Andrea Beach is a highly committed and competent young woman. Menus are imaginative and complemented by a short, well-priced wine list.

Slices of Parma ham with a warm potato and chive salad. King scallops and prawns pan-fried with herbs, bacon and garlic. Goats cheese flamed with brandy.

STB ★★★★ Hotel
Green Tourism Two Leaf Silver Award

◗ *Open all year* 🏨 *Rooms: 18 en suite* 🛏 *DB&B £65–£95 B&B £52–£82* 🆂🅿 *Special rates available* ✕ *Food available all day ££ Lunch from £ Dinner from ££* Ⓥ *Vegetarians welcome* 🧒 *Children welcome* ♿ *Facilities for disabled visitors* 💳 *Mastercard/Eurocard, American Express, Visa, Diners Club, Switch, Delta* 🍴 *General Manager: W R Kerr*

Turnberry Ayrshire KA26 9PB
Tel: 01655 331457 Fax: 01655 331072
E-mail: info@malincourt.co.uk
Web: www.malincourt.co.uk
On A719 Ayr–Girvan, south of Maidens, just off the A77 which leads to Turnberry then to Maidens and onwards to Culzean Castle. [C6]

TURNBERRY

The Westin Turnberry Resort

- *"Grand elegant surroundings in a hotel of international standing with grand hotel cooking offering world-class standards."*
- *Grand hotel cooking; also spa and grill-room styles.*

TURNBERRY retains many opulent Edwardian features. The main restaurant offers the best classical cooking. During the week lunch is served in the Terrace Brasserie. The Turnberry Clubhouse serves roasts, grills, fries and sandwiches. Chef Stewart Cameron, a member of the Academie Culinaire de France, was The Macallan Personality of the Year 1996.

Oak-smoked Scottish salmon with lemon and black pepper. Tournedos of Buccleuch beef with fondant potatoes herbed wild mushrooms and truffled cognac sauce. Iced cranachan parfait with raspberry compote and sweet mandarin jus.

STB ★★★★★ International Resort Hotel

◐ *Open all year except Christmas week*
🏨 *Rooms: 221 en suite* ⇔ *DB&B £125–£195 B&B £95–£145* 🆂 *Special rates available* ✘ *Food available all day ££ Lunch £££ Dinner ££££* Ⓥ *Vegetarians welcome* ✻ *Children welcome* ও *Limited facilities for disabled visitors* 🖃 *Mastercard/Eurocard, American Express, Visa, Diners Club, Switch* 🅼 *General Manager: J Stewart Selbie*

Turnberry Ayrshire KA26 9LT
Tel: 01655 331000 Fax: 01655 331706
E-mail: turnberry@westin.com
Web: www.turnberry.co.uk
A77 – 17 miles south of Ayr. 2 miles after Kirkoswald. [C6]

TURRIFF

Fyvie Castle
The National Trust For Scotland

- *"Stop off for some very good home bakes after a trip round one of Scotland's most 'lived in' castles."*
- *Home bakes and snacks.*

FYVIE CASTLE is set amidst the most wonderful grounds and, as a property of The National Trust for Scotland, everything is maintained and kept to the highest standard. It is a busy and popular property which offers good Scottish home baking – afternoon cream teas with home-made scones – cooking and light refreshments. Daily specials available.

Home-made seasonal soups with crusty roll. Local Strathdon Blue cheese with apple served in a crusty baguette. Selection of home baking.

STB ★★★ Castle

◐ *Open daily 21 Apr to 31 Aug and weekends in Oct* 🆂 *Special rates available* ✘ *Food available £ Lunch £* Ⓥ *Vegetarians welcome* ✻ *Children welcome* ও *Facilities for disabled visitors* ✲ *No smoking throughout* 🖃 *Mastercard, Visa* 🅼 *Property Manager: Robert Lovie*

Turriff Aberdeenshire AB5 8JS
Tel: 01651 891266 Fax: 01651 891107
E-mail: rlovie@nts.org.uk
Web: www.nts.org.uk
Off the A947, 8 miles south east of Turriff and 25 miles north-west of Aberdeen. [D3]

TYNDRUM

ULLAPOOL

The Green Welly Stop

- *"Enjoy the excellent choice of interesting Scottish dishes – something for everyone here! All served by a friendly team."*
- *Home cooking.*

BELINDA MUIR is proving to be a great asset to the restaurant. This family-run restaurant has become a tourist attraction in its own right and deservedly so. Here you can enjoy good home baking and cooking along with a wide variety of traditional Scottish meals and snacks. Excellent selection of goods available.

Tattie drottle. Cullen skink. Brochan buidhe. Salad selection. Strathdon Blue cheese and broccoli pasta. Haggis and Neeps. Salar smoked salmon cheesecake. Selection of desserts and Scottish cheeses.

STB ★★★ Tourist Shop

❶ *Open all year except Christmas Day, Boxing Day and New Year's Day, 8.30am-5.30pm Apr to Oct; 8.30am-5pm Nov to Mar* ✗ *Hot food available 8.30am–5pm £ Lunch £* Ⅶ *Vegetarians welcome* ✚ *Children welcome* ♿ *Facilities for disabled visitors* � *No smoking area in restaurant* 💳 *Mastercard/Eurocard, American Express, Visa, Diners Club, Switch, Delta, ATM Facility* ▨ *Partners: DD, LV & IL Wilkie; LP Gosden; FD Robertson & ES Robertson; M McIlroy*

Tyndrum Crianlarich Perthshire FK20 8RY Tel: 01838 400271 Fax: 01838 400330 E-mail: thegreenwellystop@tyndrum12.freeserve.co.uk Web: www.thegreenwellystop.co.uk On A85 to Oban and Fort William. 5 miles north of Crianlarich. [C5]

Tanglewood House

- *"Superb cuisine within a luxurious uniquely designed house."*
- *Classic cooking with Scottish ingredients.*

TANGLEWOOD HOUSE is an architecturally outstanding building situated on the shore of Loch Broom. Anne Holloway is a charming hostess who offers fine food to satisfy even the most discerning diner. The antique furnished dining room overlooks a secluded, heather covered headland with the magnificent loch and hills beyond.

Carpaccio of Aberdeen Angus beef fillet with celeriac salad. Poached Scottish-caught halibut with saffron and whisky sauce. Almond tuilles sandwiched with cream and Scottish raspberries.

❶ *Open 15 Jan to 23 Dec* ♨ *Rooms: 3 en suite* 🛏 *DB&B £70–£73 B&B £35–£38 (£17.50 single supplement)* Ⓤ *Unlicensed* ✗ *Non residents – bookings only Packed Lunch £ Dinner except Sun – negotiable £££* Ⅶ *Vegetarians welcome* ✚ *Children over 8 years welcome* ✗ *No smoking throughout* 🐕 *Dogs welcome in garden* 💳 *Mastercard/Eurocard, Visa* ▨ *Owner/Chef: Anne Holloway*

Ullapool Ross-shire IV26 2TB Tel: 01854 612059 Fax: 01854 612059 E-mail: tanglewoodhouse@msn.com Web: www.tanglewoodhouse.co.uk Approaching Ullapool from south by A835. Turn left immediately after fourth 40 mph sign, turn right over cattle grid. Take left fork down to the house. [B3]

WEST LINTON

The Old Bakehouse Restaurant: Finalist The Macallan Taste of Scotland Awards 2001

- *"The Old Bakehouse is a unique establishment, offering delicious home-cooked Scottish produce and some intriguing Danish specialities."*
- *Modern Scottish.*

IN ITS UNIQUE SETTING the Old Bakehouse Restaurant is home to many artifacts, with many touches of interest throughout this establishment. Anita and Jens are accomplished and stylish operators who have a reputation for retaining the highest of standards with great attention to detail. They have now brought their own style to the outskirts of Edinburgh.

Duck, ham and chicken terrine with honey mustard dressing. Tender loin of Lanarkshire lamb with minted red wine jus. Brown sugar meringues with strawberry Mascarpone and fresh strawberries.

◗ *Open all year except Christmas Day, Boxing Day and 1 Jan Closed Mon Tue* ♟ *Licensed* ✗ *Lunch except Mon Tue £–££ Dinner except Mon Tue ££* Ⅴ *Vegetarians welcome* ♣ *Children welcome* ♿ *Facilities for disabled visitors* ✄ *No smoking in restaurant* 🐾 *Dogs welcome* 💳 *Mastercard, Visa, Switch* ♨ *Owners: Jens & Anita Steffen*

West Linton EH46 7EA
Tel: 01968 660830
E-mail: theoldbakehouse@zetnet.co.uk
Web: www.westlinton.com/oldbakehouse/
16 miles south of Edinburgh on A702. Turn left into village at signpost – 100 yards on the left.
[D6]

WICK

The Portland Arms Hotel

- *"A very friendly hotel with a beautifully redecorated interior offering a good variety of all-day meals."*
- *Home-style and modern Scottish.*

LOCATED NEAR the Caithness coast, this welcoming inn – originally a staging post in the early 19th century – has been newly redecorated with beautiful fabrics. Guests of all ages can be assured of helpful service and very good food in Jo's Kitchen, the Bistro Bar, or the more formal Library.

Helmsdale smoked chicken with coriander and lime, bound in crème fraîche and served in a herb pancake. Roast rack of lamb on a potato and rosemary galette with an apple and apricot compote. Aga-baked meringues with a home-made raspberry sauce.

STB ★★★★ Small Hotel

◗ *Open all year* 🛏 *Rooms: 22 en suite* 🛌 *DB&B £45–£65 B&B £34–£55* 💷 *Special rates available* ✗ *Food available all day £ Lunch £ Dinner ££* Ⅴ *Vegetarians welcome* ♣ *Children welcome in Jo's Kitchen* ♿ *Facilities for disabled visitors* ✄ *No smoking in dining room and some bedrooms* 💳 *Mastercard/Eurocard, American Express, Visa, Diners Club, Switch, Delta* ♨ *General Manager: Mark Stevens*

Lybster Caithness KW3 6BS
Tel: 01593 721 721 Fax: 01593 721 722
E-mail: portland.arms@btconnect.com
Web: www.portlandarms.co.uk
On A9 at Latheron take A99 direction Wick, after 3 miles small town of Lybster, hotel on left-hand side. [D2]

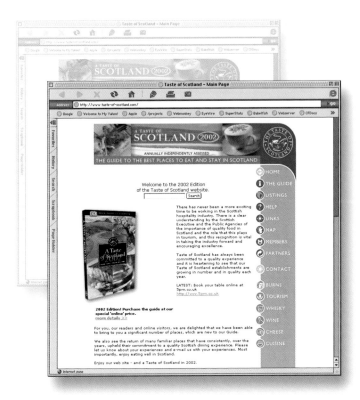

A Taste of Scotland online

Wherever you are, you can always keep in touch with what's happening on the Scottish culinary scene by logging onto The Taste of Scotland website at:

www.taste-of-scotland.com

It includes details of all the hotels, restaurants, guest houses, bed & breakfasts and visitor attractions contained in the Guide.

And that's not all – you'll find articles and features on dining and drinking, as well as great ideas for recipes and relaxation.

Subscribe to our online newsletter and keep up to date with people, places and events in the news.

www.taste-of-scotland.com also provides links to a wide range of related sites reflecting the sights, tastes, flavours – and even the sounds of Scotland!

'Water separates the
people of the world,
wine unites them.'

ANCIENT PROVERB

'Wine seems to have the power of attracting friendship, warming and fusing hearts together.' The views of the Greek writer Athenaeus still apply after nearly 2,000 years.

Alexander
Wines

IF YOU'RE READING THIS, the chances are that you're either a member of Taste of Scotland or have eaten in one (or more) of the places listed in this Guide.

If so, you may well be familiar with the name of Alexander Wines and the range of wines we supply in our role as sponsors of Taste of Scotland.

But have you ever wondered how the bottle of wine on your table – or in your cellar – actually gets there?

A PASSION FOR WINE

A successful career in wine demands three things. Curiosity is one: a constant thirst for knowledge that never tires of exploring the new and the exciting.

Realism is another: an ability to temper enthusiasm with a sound awareness of commercial imperatives.

The key, however, is passion. For wine – like music, art and food – speaks first to the senses, and only then to the mind. Without passion, wine becomes a commodity, the merchant little more than a middleman.

At Alexander Wines, we prefer the passionate approach – and so, we believe, do our customers!

Getting it right: wine with food

MATCHING WINE with food *can* be tricky, but it's not quite the minefield (some) pundits would have us believe.

As long as you choose wines with the same **body**, **texture** and **depth of flavour** as the food they're to be served with, you're unlikely to go wrong.

Remember, too, that most wines will happily partner several different types of food – and vice versa.

So, don't get stuck in the 'white wine with fish, red wine with meat' rut, useful though it is as a standby.

A little experimentation works wonders and, with practice, you will come to recognise instinctively which styles of wine are likely to do best with which types of food.

Just think, all that wine-tasting – and in such a good cause, too!

Handling the chain of events from vineyard to consumer is the job of companies like Alexander Wines.

As importers and wholesalers of fine wines, our task begins at source, visiting winegrowers in the quiet winter months to taste dozens of new vintages and new products – sometimes directly from cask in a damp, chilly cellar! – and negotiate terms of supply.

Back in the office, we re-taste to confirm our choices and select the best

WHAT MAKES A GREAT WINE REGION?

THE FAME of the world's great wine regions – Burgundy, Bordeaux, The Rheingau, Tuscany – owes nothing to chance.

Research has shown that all such regions share features which, in combination, really do seem to make the difference between 'good' and 'great' wine.

Surprisingly, grape varieties, vineyard practices and winemaking techniques are only secondary considerations.

The real keys are soil and (micro)climate, which the French refer to collectively as *terroir*.

In a nutshell, the best *terroirs* are on sheltered slopes with well-drained but not overly fertile soil, and good – but not excessive – exposure to sun.

Choose the vine varieties best suited to your *terroir* and you're set for success.

Then, and only then, does the human factor come into play.

quality and value for our portfolio before placing an order.

The job of collecting wine from the vineyard and delivering it to our Glasgow warehouse is handled by freight forwarder Anglo-Overseas.

The wine then becomes our responsibility. Storage, order processing and delivery to the customer – mainly restaurants, hotels and wine bars – make up much of the daily routine at Alexander Wines and are handled by an experienced, professional team.

But, of course, before any of that can happen, we have to place the wine. Eschewing the 'hard sell' approach, we focus on building partnerships with our clients, working with them to create exactly the right wine list for their establishment: tastings and food/wine matching are just part of the strategy, backed by ongoing training for wait staff.

At Alexander Wines, we believe in widening our customers' horizons. Passionate about wine, we want them to feel the same. The benefits, we feel, are well worth the effort!

Alexander Wines, Glasgow
Tel 0141 882 0039
Fax 0141 880 0041

'Doing the simple things and doing them well and proudly is the real magic of Speyside – the essence of the Baxter family business – past, present and future.'

Gordon Baxter

Baxters
of Speyside

AFTER MORE THAN 130 years, Baxters of Speyside take great pride in tradition, but don't be fooled into thinking they are old fashioned. A company does not succeed, in highly competitive markets, by standing still.

Confidence in the Baxters brand is a crucial factor for shoppers in more than 30 countries. Whether they buy soups, preserves, chutneys or sauces, they know they'll take home a quality product. They know to expect the flavours and textures that other prepared foods simply can't match. This involves some fairly discerning shoppers – Royal Warrants from HM Elizabeth II, HM The Queen Mother and Gustav VI, King of Sweden, are not issued lightly.

Other than the precise details of the famous recipes themselves, there is no great secret about Baxters' success. The Chairman, Audrey Baxter (above, right), puts it simply: "We are passionate at Baxters about good food which means finding the finest ingredients and creating innovative recipes which are right for today's highly discerning consumers throughout the world."

The business is run by the fourth generation of the same family in the same beautiful corner of north-east

Scotland. Their insistence on only the finest ingredients and the avoidance of artificial additives ensures consistently high quality, full of natural flavour.

The first factory opened in 1914 beside the River Spey and production facilities have been expanding ever since. As sophisticated as these have become, the Baxter family has never lost sight of the natural qualities that made their products so popular in the first place.

Between 40 and 50 new recipes are introduced each year, but only once they have proved themselves worthy of inclusion in this extraordinary portfolio of products.

New ranges to be launched by Baxters recently include Baxters and Nick Nairn Sauces, Noodle Soup in pouches and Baxters Fresh Soup.

Top Chef Nick Nairn has joined forces with Baxters to produce a range of seven delicious pan fry sauces that are easy to prepare. With exotic flavours such as Authentic Red Thai Curry and Hot and Sour Red Pepper proving to be very popular, the sauces are a true reflection of the family's ambition for the brand now and in the future. They combine the flair and enthusiasm of a

Where it all began –
George Baxter's busy store in Speyside.

top Scottish Chef with great quality ingredients and a premium contemporary presentation.

In the Summer of 2001, Baxters launched its delicious range of Fresh Soups, a logical step for a company with such a strong reputation and heritage in premium soups. Comprising of eight recipes in a homemade style, the range includes such classics as Chicken Broth, Creamy Chicken & Vegetable, Country Mushroom, Mediterranean Tomato and Minestrone as well as the more unusual Thai Chicken Noodle. The range will be updated with new seasonal varieties and is available in the chiller cabinet of most good supermarkets.

Finally, Baxters have captured the increase in consumer interest in authentic tastes and recipes from the Far East, with the launch of its innovative range of Noodle Soups in pouches. Comprising of four eastern style contemporary recipes; Thai Chicken, Indonesian Vegetable with Creamed Coconut, Cantonese Hot & Sour and Peking Shiitake Mushroom the range is innovative both in its recipes and its modern pouch packaging.

As well as being one of the great commercial successes of north-east Scotland, Baxters has its very own Highland Village which has become one of Scotland's major tourist attractions, drawing more than 200,000 visitors each year.

The centrepiece is a 19th century grocery store, complete with leather-bound ledgers and quill pens, a long mahogany counter, glass jars and bottles, and all the other shopkeeper's accounts of a bygone age. But it's much more than a reconstruction of things past – this is the actual frontage, and much of the actual contents, of the shop in which George Baxter started the whole business.

There is also a great deal more to Baxters Highland Village. Informal cookery demonstrations are held regularly and there are two restaurants serving the very best of Scottish produce. The Best of Scotland is at the forefront in the "village shops" too.

You can of course visit Baxters anytime on their extensive website at www.baxters.co.uk You can even order one of Baxters' sumptuous hampers over the internet, as well as by conventional mail.
Baxters of Speyside
Fochabers, Moray
Tel 01343 820393
Fax 01343 821696

They've become such a familiar part of our daily lives that it's all too easy to take coffee and tea for granted – but you could be missing out on a world of exotic flavours, enticing aromas and subtle blends.

Brodies
teas & coffees

COFFEE AND TEA have recently been transformed into virtual icons of style – but Brodies of Edinburgh are more concerned about the substance behind the style.

Having been in the business since 1867, Brodies are delighted with the elevated profile tea and coffee are enjoying and, indeed, the company has played its part in raising that profile.

With the public appetite for these classic beverages as intense as it has ever been, Brodies are eager to build on consumers' growing interest.

Everyone who works for Brodies shares an unshakeable commitment to quality. They know just how good tea and coffee can be – especially their own brands – and they want their customers to share in their enthusiasm and their enjoyment.

In all, they produce 20 different coffees, including the 'Dynamic Volcanic' range of rich dark gourmet coffees, specially blended and roasted for espresso and cappuccino machines.

Speaking of which, Brodies take

A great tradition
Throughout more than 130 years as coffee and tea merchants, Brodies have been importing the very finest tea leaves and coffee beans from around the world. The raw materials are shipped in from plantations and agencies, many of whom Brodies have been dealing with for generations. Samples of their crops are submitted on a regular basis, allowing Brodies to maintain levels of quality and taste throughout their extensive product ranges.

Why fresh makes the best cup of coffee

To get the very best out of coffee, freshness is essential, which is why Brodies' roasting policy is 'little and often.'

They restrict roastings to 100-kilo batches of beans at a time – no stockpiling in warehouses and no delay in getting the coffee to consumers.

You can apply the same policy – it's best to grind only the quantity of beans you need at a time.

But even if you don't want to use the grinder every time you make coffee, you can freeze the grounds and use them later, straight from the freezer, without losing that fresh taste.

tasting is believing...

over 56 luxury centres encased in bittersweet dark chocolate...

Brodies...
the Essence
of Quality

their commitment to quality into the supply of coffee-making machines and equipment to hotels, restaurants and bars.

They firmly believe that, if you have just enjoyed a meal made from the finest ingredients, then you should be able to round off that meal with coffee that's made to equally high standards.

And it should be made freshly – not left to bubble away for an hour or two before it reaches the cup!

Fast as coffee's popularity is growing, it still has a little catching up to do on tea.

Tea remains by far and away the UK's favourite drink, with 175 million cups drunk every day – that's 3½ cups for every man, woman and child.

What few of us appreciate, as we sip our way through our daily 3½ cups, is the care and attention which has been lavished on creating our favourite brand.

The end result may be very different but tea blending has much in common with production of another national favourite – Scotch whisky – where malt whiskies are artfully combined with grain spirit to produce blended whisky.

For the world of tea, the equivalent of malt whiskies are such great names as Darjeeling, Assam and Ceylon.

These are, of course, outstanding in their own right but, used in just the

Handy hints for perfect tea & coffee

RALPH LUTTON (left) is managing director of Brodies but for Ralph this isn't just a business, it's a passion – and he'd like everyone to enjoy these products as much as he does. Follow these tips, and you'll find out why his enthusiasm is catching!

right proportions, they can contribute to memorable and distinctive blended teas.

Brodies bring their own magic to these and others to create such classic blends as Scottish Breakfast, Famous Edinburgh, Earl Grey, Connoisseur and Pure China.

The same skills and expertise are brought to the creation of classic coffee blends such as High Mountain, Kenya Choice, Central American and Colombian Decaffeinated. In many cases, Brodies tailor these blends for catering customers.

The range also includes such classic single source coffees as Mocha, Old Mature Java and Pacific Costa Rica.

Recent years have seen Brodies' dedication to perfection extended to their award-winning ranges of handmade chocolates, again using only the finest natural ingredients.

So, Brodies have proved once again that, when it comes to matters of taste, taste matters.

If you'd like to know more, visit our website at:

www.brodiemelrose.co.uk

■ Warm the cafetière or teapot first to ensure you're working at the optimum temperature. The water should have just reached boiling point. Allow 2-3 minutes to infuse teabags properly, 3-5 minutes for leaf tea. 'That way you are drinking tea as opposed to coloured water,' says Ralph.

■ Different teas and coffees can taste differently at different times of the day. Experiment to find out what suits you.

■ Try to make your tea and coffee in Scotland! Scottish water is ideally suited for both – it's good, fresh and soft and really brings out the colour and flavour in tea and coffee.

■ If you're keeping an eye on your caffeine intake, buy better coffee. The higher the quality, the lower the caffeine content.

■ Some quality teas, such as Assam and Darjeeling, are not particularly suited to use in teabags. Generally, these teas taste better made from leaves.

Skara Brae … one of the best preserved groups of Stone Age houses in western Europe.

Scotland's wealth of historic buildings from the
Highlands and Islands to the Borders provide a taste of
our country's past and rich heritage. Historic Scotland are
committed to bringing that heritage vividly to life.

Historic
Scotland

SYMBOLISING THE SPIRIT of the
country, Scotland's historic
buildings form a precious national
resource offering Scots and visitors
alike a wonderful insight into the
history and traditions which colour and
flavour Scottish culture.

More than 300 splendid properties
and sites – from prehistoric dwellings
to stone circles, abbeys to cathedrals,
and castles to palaces – are in the
direct care of Historic Scotland. It
protects them for current and future
generations and presents them for the
enjoyment of visitors.

Proceeds from admissions to the
properties and from purchases made at
their visitor centres and shops support
Historic Scotland in its vital
preservation work and care of the
natural environment around its sites.

The best known and most visited of
Historic Scotland's properties is
Edinburgh Castle. This imposing
landmark has dominated Scotland's
history, providing a stronghold and
residence to many kings and queens of
the past. It houses the Scottish Crown

Caerlaverock Castle

For visitors of all ages, Historic
Scotland's superb collection of
properties promises a great day
out. Throughout the year, a full
programme of events offering a
diverse range of activities ensures
that there is something for
everyone to enjoy in spectacular
surroundings.

Many of the entertainments
give visitors a chance to step back
into the past to experience living
history presentations and watch
battle re-enactments, jousting
tournaments, falconry and fencing,
music recitals and drama
productions.

A unique choice

Representing more than 5000 years of Scottish history and embodying the essence of Scots architecture, art and design, the wide and diverse range of Historic Scotland properties includes a unique choice of attractions, many of which are situated in the country's most breathtaking scenery.

Each, like Stirling Castle (above), has its own distinctive character and a vivid tapestry of tales to tell.

Here, we can only give you a flavour of some of them and the varied and fascinating treasures they offer.

Jewels and the Stone of Destiny.

Stirling Castle, where Mary Queen of Scots was crowned, is one of Scotland's grandest castles. Perched on a volcanic crag, this impressive building with its restored medieval Great Hall overlooks some of Scotland's most important battle sites, including Bannockburn.

The moated ruin of **Caerlaverock Castle** (pictured on page 231) near Dumfries, which stands guard over the Solway Firth, was the scene of two famous sieges and today has an exhibition on siege warfare and a siege-theme adventure park.

Built following the Battle of Culloden, **Fort George**, near Inverness, is one of the most outstanding artillery fortifications in Europe. Virtually unchanged, it presents a complete view of an 18th century fort.

Iona Abbey (above) and the impressive skyline of Edinburgh Castle (below).

Become a Friend of Historic Scotland

By becoming a Friend of Historic Scotland, you can help to safeguard the rich heritage of Scotland and preserve the country's wealth of outstanding historic properties, such as Linlithgow Palace (left). Friends of Historic Scotland can take advantage of a range of benefits including:

Inchmahome Priory, set on the largest of three islands in the Lake of Menteith and founded in the 13th century for a small community of Augustinian canons, is among the most attractive of Scotland's medieval religious houses.

Linlithgow Palace, set in its own park beside a loch, was a favoured residence of the Stewart kings and queens and its beautiful ruins still show why it was a favourite with royals for hundreds of years.

Founded by St Columba in 563, **Iona Abbey** has a special spiritual significance and atmosphere. The restored abbey and monastic buildings house one of the most comprehensive collections of Christian carved stones in Scotland.

Skara Brae on Orkney, hidden under sand dunes for hundreds of years, was uncovered by a storm in 1850 and is one of the best preserved groups of Stone Age houses in western Europe, presenting a remarkable picture of life in Neolithic times.

- Free entry to all of the properties in the care of Historic Scotland.
- Discounted entry to English Heritage, Welsh Cadw and Manx National Heritage properties.
- A quarterly colour membership magazine.
- Exclusive membership events and holidays.

Friends' Memberships, which are available on an annual or lifetime basis, are available at all staffed Historic Scotland properties. Alternatively, you can call 0131 668 8999 – and take advantage of a £5 discount on a new annual membership by quoting Taste of Scotland.

To find out more about Historic Scotland, you can log onto our extensive website at:

www.historic-scotland.gov.uk

Fort George

MATURED IN SHERRY WOOD
DISTILLED IN **1979** AT MACALLAN

EST.D · 1824

MACALLAN · SCOTLAND

The

MACALLAN

GRAN RESERVA

Single Highland Malt

Scotch Whisky

18

EIGHTEEN YEARS OLD

DISTILLED AND BOTTLED BY

'About the most delicious malt ever... if you see it, grab it!' So said novelist Sir Kingsley Amis, who knew a thing or two about whisky, when describing The Macallan. But just what does it take to make a 'great' single malt?

The Macallan
The Malt

WHEN YOU TAKE A SIP of malt whisky you are actually experiencing a taste of Scotland's heritage.

Scotch whisky – the very name signals its unique relationship with the country that has created it.

It's all too easy, though, in the romantic Scotch mists which tend to swirl around the subject, to lose sight of what a remarkable product it is.

Romance, of course, has its place but the qualities of Scotch – and Scotch malt whisky in particular – need little embellishment.

To earn the name of Scotch, a whisky must be matured in oak casks in Scotland for at least three years. Whisky and oak have a unique rapport and, the more time the two spend in each other's company, the more interesting the result is likely to be.

The Macallan, for instance, is available at various ages, from 10 years old up to more than 50 years old and, as you might expect, becomes more complex and intriguing with each passing year.

Malt whisky has been legally

Visit Easter Elchies, home of The Macallan

Everyone who works at The Macallan knows what an extraordinary product they have and they're all too keen to share their enthusiasm.

The spring of 2001 saw the opening of a brand new Visitor Centre at the home of The Macallan, the Easter Elchies estate in the heart of Speyside. Using the latest interactive technology to tell The Macallan story, the centre also hosts tours and tutored tastings, although it's probably best to call in advance (01340 872 280).

And, of course, you can find out all about The Macallan at any time on our website at:
www.themacallan.com

The ultimate collector's item

The Macallan has its devotees all over the world but none has proved quite as devoted as Norman Shelley (above) whose dedication has won him a place in the record books.

He spent around £200,000 on a unique 76-bottle collection of The Macallan, some of which dated back more than 150 years. Not only has Norman been inaugurated into The Macallan 'Hall of Fame,' he has won a place in the Guinness World Records for the most expensive single purchase of whisky ever. The collection is being kept at Easter Elchies House, the traditional home of The Macallan, and is on display at the new Visitor Centre there.

● Shopping for The Macallan isn't always like that, of course! The Macallan is widely available in all major retail outlets as well as specialist off licences and quality On Trade establishments throughout the UK.

distilled in Scotland since around the time Christopher Columbus brought back some interesting news from the west.

The Macallan maintains a great tradition of distilling in the Spey Valley. Its own origins date back to medieval times when drovers would rest on their journey at Craigellachie, a fording point on the River Spey.

The Macallan keeps the spirit of tradition alive in many ways. It's not that they are reluctant to embrace new technologies, for instance, but should these do anything to alter the spirit,

then the old technology will do very nicely, thank you.

As Master Distiller David Robertson comments: 'We are committed to tradition, but not for tradition's sake.'

He and his colleagues like to be sure that, no matter where or when it is consumed, a glass of The Macallan is instantly recognisable, from its uniquely darker colour to its richer taste.

David sums up The Macallan approach: 'At every stage of the production process, we take an economic hit in the name of quality. No compromise in our production methods is allowed.

'Visitors to our distillery are sometimes surprised that we have to ask them to move aside so that a barrel can be moved or an aspect of the distillation monitored closely – but this is very much a working distillery, not a Scottish theme park!'

And as to the future? 'Because we work so far in advance,' says David, 'we know today that for at least the next 25 years, The Macallan drinker can be guaranteed the quality for which The Macallan is renowned, and we are continually working to secure that quality for ever more.'

Nosing and Tasting

A full appreciation of malt whisky can be a sensory delight, involving smell, taste and sight. The golden glow from a dram of single malt is certainly a sight for sore eyes, but this is where the palate and – even more so – the nose really come into their own. Calling on his vast knowledge and experience of making whisky, David Robertson, The Macallan's Master Distiller, has designed spider charts to help enthusiasts get the most out of their malt.

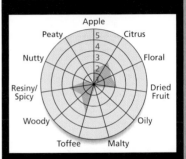

Here's David's view on The Macallan 10 Years Old, for instance:

Colour: Mahogany.

Nose: Slightly toffee sweet with hints of dried fruit, cloves and sherry.

Palate: Deliciously smooth and well-rounded dried fruit flavour with a touch of sherry sweetness and wood.

Finish: Medium long.

Now you try!

It's the ultimate feel-good food. Rounding off a meal, cooling down on a hot day, or just as a little reward – everyone has their own favourite ice cream moments. And for a growing number of us, Mackie's is the ice cream of choice for those special moments.

Mackie's
Ice Cream

HAPPINESS IS TUB-SHAPED – and you only have to dip a spoon into some Mackie's Ice Cream to appreciate the fundamental truth of that statement.

There are a number of very good reasons why Mackie's are Scotland's leading brand of luxury ice cream, and are fast gaining ground south of the border, too.

The main one is quality and that's something upon which the Mackie family have very strong views. Another is freshness, at every stage of production and distribution.

But, throughout all their activities, the Mackies never lose sight of one essential factor – ice cream is a fun product.

And yet, less than 20 years ago, the Mackie brand name did not exist, other than as a prominent dairy farming family in Aberdeenshire, where they have been farming around 1500 acres of land at Westertown for four generations.

It was around the mid 1980's that, with public showing a growing liking

Mackie's – designed for flavour

Aberdeenshire sun and rain help grow:

- designer crops like lupins with high protein
- designed to feed designer cows – 460 jerseys
- designed to produce designer milk, the creamiest per litre
- designed to make designer ice cream, the smooth and creamy experience of Mackie's
- designed to please designer taste – ice cream lovers like you.

Ice cream cyberworld

MACKIE'S
of Scotland

If you want to know more about Mackie's, their products – and how to win 'free ice cream for a year' – check out their interactive website at:

www.mackies.co.uk

Like Mackie's Ice Cream, it's colourful and it's fun! It also has a new Tub Shop offering serious portable refrigeration such as motorised cool boxes and portable freezers along with fun Mackiefied merchandise such as tub-shaped cufflinks.

The site also provides a home for the growing number of Friends of Mackie's, several competitions, information on ice cream, the Mackie's range, recipes and the chance to send a 'moocard' to friends!

for skimmed and semi-skimmed milk, Maitland Mackie decided to use the surplus cream to make luxury dairy ice cream.

But this was not simply a business expedient. If the Mackies were going to make ice cream, they would make the very best ice cream they could.

Which explains why their concept of 'affordable luxury' has become so popular and why their products – and their service – keep winning awards.

Mackie's are very particular about what goes into their ice cream. Their farming team is dedicated to the production of feed for their herd of 460 Jersey cows, the largest of its kind in the UK.

The dairy herd has gradually changed from Friesian cattle because Jerseys produce the creamiest milk – the 'designer' milk required to make Mackie's ice cream. (And this change is reflected in the redesign of the company's logo to show a Jersey rather than the black and white Friesian they started out with.)

Using state-of-the-art technology, the dairy currently produces more than four million litres of ice cream a year and has the capacity for much more.

A computer-controlled system ensures the right quantities of milk and

Morag

New Products

The range of Mackie's ice creams has been growing steadily over the past 15 years but any new addition to the fold has to pass some pretty stringent quality tests before it's given the Mackie stamp of approval. The Mackie's Taste Panel, drawn from the company's 57 employees, has a busy schedule of quality checks – taste, textures, flavours – to make sure existing products are meeting the usual high standards.

The current range includes: Traditional, Honeycomb Harvest, Strawberry & Cream, Raspberry Shortcake, Peaches & Cream, Rum & Raisin, Caramel Choc Mint, Absolutely Chocolate, vanilla in a soft scooping Cream of Scottish, Strawberry Organic and a popular Organic version of Traditional.

But the Panel's highly tuned tasting skills are also called upon to put new products through the same rigorous regime. The key tasks of Mackie's new product development kitchen are to work towards the continual improvement of existing products, develop new flavours and new ice cream products and 'blue sky' experimentation – looking for true innovation! These new ideas may have been prompted from within – Mackie's have a highly trained and enthusiastic workforce – or suggested by their customers and consumers out in the marketplace.

cream are delivered to the mixing vessel. The dry ingredients are then added and the mixture is pasteurised.

A spiral freezer helps freeze the ice cream quickly to ensure a satisfyingly smooth texture.

Rigorous quality controls are carried out throughout the process and before it goes out to shops.

The whole production process takes less than 24 hours from fresh milk from the farm to ice cream in the tub – giving Mackie's its fresh and creamy taste.

Karin, Mac and Kirstin (left) make sure the Mackie family traditions are upheld.

A. McLELLAND & SON

SINCE 1850

CHEESE MARKET

A.McLelland & Son A. McLellan

CHEESE MERCHANTS

cheese - milk's leap toward immortalit

Cheese – available in every supermarket, delicatessen, grocery outlet and restaurant in Scotland. But where does it come from? A tour around Scotland's cheese-making regions provides some mouth-watering answers.

McLelland Cheeses

IF YOU WANT A FLAVOUR of a nation's character, you can learn a surprising amount from its cheeses – it's certainly the case in Scotland.

Most of our cheddar-type cheeses are produced by A McLelland & Son Ltd at creameries throughout Scotland. The cheeses produced can say a lot about an area and its people.

In the south-west, surrounded by the lush, rolling Galloway countryside, the Caledonian Cheese Company in Stranraer is one of the most modern creameries in Europe. It makes the popular Galloway Medium, McLelland Mature and Seriously Strong cheddars, as well as 'own label' products for many leading retailers.

Beeswing, along the road near Dumfries, provides a fascinating contrast with the Loch Arthur Creamery, a charity-based organic cheesemaker, where Criffel, Crannog and Farmhouse Cheese are produced.

Further up the west coast, the Clyde islands have a beguiling appeal, set amid stunning land and seascapes. And the islands' creameries produce cheeses which are equally stunning.

The ferry leaves from Ardrossan for the Isle of Arran where Arran Dunlop cheese is produced by the Torrylinn Creamery.

Back to the mainland and a few miles north is Wemyss Bay, the ferry terminal for the Isle of Bute, and Rothesay Creamery, home of Bute and Rothesay Cheddars.

Torrylinn and Rothesay, both part of the McLelland portfolio, welcome visitors and have shops on site.

Back on the mainland and further

McLelland Cheese and Spinach Souffle

INGREDIENTS
50g Scottish butter
50g plain flour
350ml milk
100g Seriously Strong Cheddar, grated
100g Galloway Cheddar, grated
75g baby leaf spinach, chopped
6 eggs, separated + 2 egg whites
25g pistachio nuts, chopped
Freshly ground salt and pepper

METHOD
◼ Pre-heat oven to 190°C (gas mark 5)
◼ Melt butter and add flour to form a roux. Gradually stir in milk and bring to the boil, creating a smooth thick sauce.
◼ Allow to cool slightly, then beat in egg yolks.
◼ Mix the two cheeses and reserve 50g to mix with the chopped pistachio nuts for the topping.
◼ Stir in 150g of the mixed cheeses and chopped baby leaf spinach.
◼ Season.
◼ Scatter with reserved cheese mix and pistachio.
◼ Bake for approx. 15–20 minutes until well risen and set with a light golden colour and attractive crust.
◼ Serve with a light salad and fresh locally made bread.

With thanks to John and Jean Bowman at Ards House, Connell (see page 170) for testing and trying out the recipe on their guests.

west lies the rugged Kintyre peninsula. There is spectacular scenery on almost every turn of the road south to Campbeltown. As manager of the Campbeltown Creamery, George MacSporran oversees production of Mull of Kintyre and Campbeltown cheddars.

Campbeltown is also the home of the Inverloch Cheese Company, an independent cheesemaker responsible for Gigha Fruits and Taste of Gigha truckles, and also goats milk cheese.

Further north again, Oban is the ferry port for Mull where the colourful little town of Tobermory has its romantic legend of lost treasure from the Spanish Armada.

One very real treasure is the Isle of Mull Cheese Company, run by Jeff and Chris Reade, producers of traditional handmade Isle of Mull Cheddar and Tobermory Flavells with added flavours.

Right up on the northern coast, the port of Scrabster is point of departure for the ferry to Stromness in the Orkney Isles. A short drive takes you to Kirkwall and the award-winning Orkney Cheese Company and Orkney Island Cheddar.

Orkney also has a handful of small cheesemakers whose products are, in the main, only available on the Orkney Isles.

Return to the mainland and follow the route south-east to Tain where Highland Fine Cheeses is owned by the Stone family, descendents of The Macdonald, Lord of the Isles. Here they specialise in old recipe cheese such as Caboc, Galic and a recently introduced cows milk cheese – Strathdon Blue.

South again to Kinfauns, north of Perth, where the privately-owned Howgate Dairy Foods make a number of soft cheeses such as Scottish Brie and St Andrews.

South of Glasgow, in the small Ayrshire town of Mauchline, once a favourite haunt of national bard Robert Burns, the Scottish Cheese Packing Centre packs most of the cheddar cheese carrying the McLelland brand, along with major supermarket 'own label' cheeses.

Even if you are only able to take in parts of our 'grand cheese tour' you'll see how the diversity of Scotland's cheeses matches the diversity of its landscape – and its people.

If you want to know more about Scotland's cheeses, and the McLelland brands in particular, visit our website.

1 Stranraer	6 Tobermory
2 Beeswing	7 Orkney
3 Arran	8 Tain
4 Rothesay	9 Kinfauns
5 Campbeltown	10 Mauchline

A family tradition

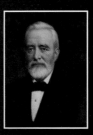

FOR MORE than a century and a half, the McLelland family have been involved in the dairy industry – they are now the third largest cheddar manufacturer in Britain.

Despite its rapid growth, particularly in recent years, it is still very much a family business – five generations and counting, from founder Archibald McLelland (above) to today's chairman Hugh Irvine (right). The company is involved with five of Scotland's six main creameries and acts as distributor for many of the country's smaller cheesemakers.

A. McLelland & Son Ltd,
New Cheese Market
Townhead
Glasgow G4 0EF

Visit our website at
www.mclelland.co.uk

The National Trust
for Scotland

Nobody can doubt the extraordinary variety and richness of Scotland's heritage and nowhere is it better shown than in the properties owned and cared for by The National Trust for Scotland.

A taste
of Scotland's heritage

THE SHEER DIVERSITY of the Trust means that it offers something for everyone – days out for the family, events and guided walks, holiday cottages in stunning locations, practical conservation work for volunteers and, of course, the chance to enjoy fine food.

The Trust's restaurants, cafes and tearooms all have their own style and are furnished to complement their surroundings but share the common aim of bringing the finest tastes of Scotland to your table, from traditional specialities to inspired contemporary cuisine.

Looking around the choice of properties to visit, and many of them are listed in this book, it can be difficult to know just where to begin! Culzean Castle, offers a fantastic day out for everyone, with its combination of Robert Adam designed castle, colourful gardens and the surrounding country park with woodlands and seashore to explore.

Similarly, Brodick Castle, on the

Guarding Scotland's treasures

Founded in 1931, The National Trust for Scotland was established to act as a guardian of Scotland's magnificent heritage of architectural, historic and scenic treasures and to encourage public access to them. It now cares for some 120 properties and benefits from the support of over 230,000 members, making it Scotland's leading conservation charity.

The richness and purity of Scotland

We are fortunate enough in Scotland to have on our doorsteps a wonderful array of fresh produce, which we concentrate on sourcing locally for all our menus. Menus aim to reflect the richness and purity of Scotland and are created using wholesome, natural food. Our catering managers skilfully prepare dishes which not only reflect the property and its history but also reflect Scottish regional dishes.

On menus this year you will see items such as Tattie Drottle, Musselburgh Pie and Border Tart. We are also fortunate enough in some of our larger sites to be able to use produce from our friendly Head Gardeners. In Culzean, for instance, visitors can sample some of the fresh fruits available over the summer months from the Castle Garden; or some of the seasonal salads on offer at Inverewe, picked from the magnificent Walled Garden.

Isle of Arran, enjoys a spectacular setting and has an excellent restaurant with full meals or light snacks available.

The National Trust for Scotland is Scotland's largest garden owner. As the seasons turn, the gardens change in colour and texture and those changes are often reflected in the varied dishes on offer.

Threave Garden, in the south west and Inverewe Garden in the north west will satisfy both the eye and the appetite!

In Aberdeenshire, the Trust owns some of the area's finest castles and stately homes and, today, the kitchens are still put to good use.

Fyvie Castle, Crathes Castle and Haddo House should be on any itinerary for exploring the north east's rich heritage. Brodie Castle, near Nairn, is another not to be missed.

In Edinburgh, the Restaurant at No 27 Charlotte Square has become established as one of the city's quality establishments with a full evening menu available.

The Coffee House, meanwhile, is open every day and is the perfect venue for morning coffee, light lunch or afternoon tea in style.

Pollok House, in Glasgow, has long

TAKEN ON TRUST

 As a charity, The National Trust for Scotland depends for its support on the subscriptions of its members, donations and legacies, which can be specified for particular properties or can be used to support the Trust's vital conservation work nationwide. Membership brings the benefit of free access to properties for twelve months and the added advantage of free entry to properties of the National Trust in England, Wales and Northern Ireland.

Wherever you are in Scotland, look out for the Trust and you will be assured a warm welcome and a visit to remember for years ahead. Further information from:

The National Trust for Scotland
Wemyss House
28 Charlotte Square
Edinburgh EH2 4ET
0131 243 9300
or from the web site at
www.nts.org.uk

had an enviable reputation for its home baking and now has a delicious lunch menu.

Some of Scotland's most notable historic sites are in the care of The National Trust for Scotland. Bannockburn, Culloden and Glenfinnan Monument all reflect turbulent periods in the country's history – and their visitor centres offer excellent home cooking.

A number of the properties are licensed, especially where functions and evening meals are provided, with selections of Scottish beers and fine wines available.

Facilities can be hired for receptions, product launches or other social events including weddings and parties. Full details are available from our Head Office.

Pictured l-r

Food from the land

Crathes Castle, Grampian

Home baking

Glenfinnan Monument, Highlands

Next time you're shopping, look for Tartan Quality Mark salmon … and you can be confident the salmon are from the cool, clean waters of Scotland's Highlands and Islands.

Salmon
the king of fish

BECAUSE SALMON CAN ONLY thrive in a good, clean environment, salmon farms are mainly located in these remote rural areas where the water is clean and sheltered by the rugged coastline.

Tartan Quality Mark salmon is produced in Scotland by members of Scottish Quality Salmon (SQS), the organisation dedicated to improving the quality and sustainability of salmon farming in Scotland.

Membership represents around 65% of the tonnage produced by the Scottish salmon farming industry and SQS operates within an integrated, independently certified and quality assured chain from loch to larder.

Smoked salmon and guacamole salad

Before cooking a whole salmon, wash it under cold running water to remove any stray scales or bones. Pat it dry with kitchen paper, both inside and out. Never wash salmon portions as you'll lose the juices; instead, pat them all over with a piece of damp kitchen paper. Bake salmon in foil in its own juices to preserve its flavour and goodness; and to keep salmon portions moist during grilling, go for thicker cuts – thin ones dry out quicker. Two minutes before grilling sprinkle over some salt to draw out the natural juices. Before cutting cooked salmon, refrigerate it for several hours or freeze it for a short time as this will help the flesh to hold its shape.

The salmon that looks right – cooks right

Spicy salmon, coconut and coriander broth

Whether you're after fresh or smoked salmon, make sure it bears the Tartan Quality Mark, which you'll find as a label on prepacked salmon portions or as a gill tag on whole fish.

To ensure its freshness, check the salmon is silvery in colour, with bright eyes; the gills are pale pink; there's a seafresh smell; the flesh is cold and firm. The flesh should be orangey-red in colour and have a moist appearance. The packaging should be hygienic and sealed. When you buy raw, unprepared salmon for cooking as a main course: 275-300g (9-10oz) per person; 1.8kg (4lb) for 6 people; 2.3kg (5lb) for 8; 4kg (9lb) for 16 people. Once prepared and cooked, 50g (2oz) per person is sufficient if you're serving salmon as a starter and 125-175g (4-6oz) will feed each person as a main course dish. Don't forget that if a recipe requires flaked salmon a 175g (6oz) cooked salmon steak will produce about 100g (3oz) of fish once you've discarded skin and bones; and if you need chopped or strips of smoked salmon look out for smoked salmon pieces.

The Scottish salmon farming industry itself contributed £150 million to Scottish food exports in 1999, representing nearly 40% of total Scottish food exports. The biggest export market is France where the salmon produced by members of Scottish Quality Salmon was the first non-French product to be awarded the prestigious Label Rouge accolade.

Scottish Quality Salmon is really healthy – highly nutritious, containing protein, vitamins (B, C, D and E) and minerals (sodium, potassium, calcium, magnesium, phosphorus, iron, copper, zinc, manganese and selenium). Salmon contains the essential Omega-3 fatty acids – vital ingredients in a healthy diet. Studies have shown that Omega-3 fatty acids can help to reduce the risk of heart disease, improve brain development in young children and help alleviate the symptoms of rheumatoid arthritis.

For mothers-to-be there is increasing evidence to demonstrate the importance of Omega-3 fatty acids in the development of the child in the womb – particularly in the last three months of pregnancy, a baby's brain cell and retina development can benefit if mothers eat oil-rich fish.

Both the Food Standards Agency and the World Health Organisation reinforce the importance of high quality oil-rich fish like salmon – they recommend eating one portion of oil rich fish per week to ensure a healthy balanced diet.

If you are on line, log on to: www.scottishsalmon.co.uk for more information – it's the definitive web guide to Scottish Quality Salmon … the King of Fish, fresh from the loch.

Far left: seared salmon with black bean sauce and noodles.

Centre: salmon koulibiac.

Near left: chilli salmon patties with lime dressing.

Details of these and other recipes are available on our website at: www.scottishsalmon.co.uk/recipes

Peppered Salmon & Fusilli Pasta Salad with Basil Oil

Serves 4. Preparation/cooking time: 25 minutes

Ingredients
340g (¾lb) Scottish Quality Salmon fillet
Freshly ground black pepper
450g (1lb) dried weight fusilli pasta (cooked)
450g (1lb) tomatoes (chopped)
110g (4oz) green beans (cooked)
1 packet fresh basil (chopped)
¼ pint olive oil
Parmesan, shavings to garnish
Spring parsley for garnish
Handful of black olives

1. Season the salmon with freshly ground black pepper
2. Place under a hot grill for 5-10 minutes until cooked
3. When cool, flake the salmon and mix with the cooked fusilli
4. Add the chopped tomatoes, green beans and lots of chopped basil
5. Season and drizzle with olive oil, mix thoroughly
6. Garnish with shavings of parmesan, spring parsley and black olives

Nutrition
Fat content: 43.1g
Carbohydrate (energy): 25.3g
Kilocalorie: 571
Fibre: 3g

All values are for one serving using listed ingredients.

Packed into a relatively small corner of Scotland are some of the most spectacular land and seascapes in Europe. The fact that Skye and Lochalsh is also home to some equally spectacular eating places simply adds to its allure.

Skye & Lochalsh

N OW CONSIDER HOW CREATIVE these eating places are with the abundance of fine produce and ingredients harvested from the land and sea around them, and you have a vivid illustration of how a food cycle really ought to work.

And in Skye & Lochalsh, it does work – splendidly!

The road to the isles – and there's more than one, incidentally – leads through scenes of outstanding beauty and communities where warm hospitality is second nature.

Not that there's anything new about that. Recounting his journey to the Western Isles of Scotland in 1773, Samuel Johnson wrote: 'Their suppers are, like their dinners, various and plentiful.'

The good doctor added: 'At the tables where a stranger is received, neither plenty nor delicacy is wanting.'

He also rated the Scottish breakfast as a world-beater and this was a man who knew a thing or two about such matters.

Proving once again how produce from Skye & Lochalsh can be combined to spectacular effect – loin of Isle of Skye Lamb from Isle of Skye Lamb Producers, with golden oregano and ginger mint from Glendale salads.

A 'renaissance of food culture'

A local food and drink initiative in Skye and Lochalsh has encouraged a resurgence of self–confidence amongst producers of fresh, simple food grown in a sustainable way.

Robert Muir *(above)*, Chief Executive of Skye and Lochalsh Enterprise, explains: 'Local producers have begun a renaissance of food culture that reflects both the area's strong crofting tradition and its clean, green and natural environment. They harvest some of the finest quality food in the world – heather reared lamb, traditional highland beef, prawns and lobsters straight from the creel, hand made cheeses, fresh fragrant herbs, delicious locally grown vegetables and organic salad leaves, to name but a few.

'The challenge now is to engage consumers, to think about where their food comes from and to consider the positive effects on a local economy of 'buying local first', as has been demonstrated so ably here in Skye and Lochalsh. The festival provides us with that opportunity to promote and share not only a taste of Scotland, but a distinctive flavour of Skye and Lochalsh.'

As there was no tourist industry to speak of in the eighteenth century – Dr Johnson was probably Scotland's first real tourist – most of the local produce went south, and much prized it was.

Now, a great deal more of that produce graces the tables of the area's growing number of high quality eating establishments, several of whom have the awards to prove it.

If catering for visitors to the area is a comparatively recent occupation, the more traditional industries of fishing and crofting go back many hundreds of years.

On Skye, for instance, where you are never more than five miles from the sea, the piers and jetties yield up a superb and diverse range of fish and shellfish.

A FESTIVAL OF FOOD

The range, diversity, freshness and quality of eating and drinking in Skye & Lochalsh is so impressive that, in September each year, it takes four extremely busy days to celebrate the fact.

The Talisker Skye & Lochalsh Food & Drink Festival is now firmly established in the calendar and draws growing numbers of visitors eager to dig a little deeper into the area's culinary delights.

While the festival does, indeed, provide ample opportunity for indulgence, a visit to Skye and Lochalsh at any time is a superb opportunity to savour an exceptional food and drink experience, celebrating fresh local produce in a friendly and harmonious atmosphere, within a spectacular natural environment.

And the extensive range of local produce includes the liquid kind, too. Talisker, the only single malt whisky produced on Skye, has been sponsoring the festival for several years.

Once described by Robert Louis Stevenson as the 'king o' drinks' Talisker is produced at Loch Harport where the distillery has its own visitor centre.

The Isle of Skye Brewery, set up in the northern port of Uig in1995, produces a popular range of cask and bottled beers, several of which have won awards.The brewery's many fans can now buy its beers far and wide around the country.

While a fair proportion of what is caught is bound for export to other parts of the UK and further afield, the local restaurants and shops make the most of the daily catch to provide their customers with the freshest of dishes.

There is also a strong crofting tradition in Skye and Lochalsh and the beef, lamb and venison is of the highest quality.

As with seafood, more and more restaurants are now able to obtain locally reared meat.

It is entirely possible – and indeed advisable – to enjoy an entire meal made from local produce.

From herbs to vegetables to fruit, breads and baking – the diversity of flavours is as rich as you're likely to find anywhere.

www.sale.hie.co.uk

The road bridge to Skye (above left)

Some examples (left) of the wealth of fresh food offered up by the land and seas around Skye & Lochalsh.

Walkers' products are instantly recognisable, boldly and unashamedly packaged in traditional tartan that reflects the company's pride in producing some of the great tastes of Scotland.

Walkers
of Aberlour

FEW COMPANIES wear their Scottishness quite so proudly on their sleeves as Walkers but then few companies can match their success.

The fact that their shortbread and biscuits have earned a unique place in Scottish culture is down to one basic fact – they're very, very good.

You'll find Walkers' products on the shelves of your local shop and, if your local shop happens to be Harrods or Fortnum & Mason, you'll find them there, too. In fact, they are now sold in more than 60 countries around the world.

Overseas sales have been so successful that Walkers have received the Queen's Award for Export Achievement no less than three times, making them the only Scottish food company to gain such a distinction.

This all seems a very long way from its humble beginnings when, in 1898, Joseph Walker had to borrow enough money to buy some flour and rent a small baker's shop in the beautiful Speyside village on Aberlour.

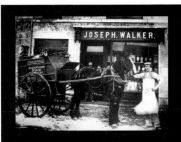

Joseph Walker was just 21 when, with the help of a £50 loan he opened his first bakery in 1898. His heart was set on creating the world's finest shortbread and he spent his first year in business perfecting his recipe. It wasn't long before word started to spread and shooting parties from local estates were making detours to Joseph's bakery. Demand increased rapidly, prompting a move to a larger shop and the purchase of a horse and cart to make deliveries further afield. And the rest, as they say, is history!

Proud as they are of their past, Walkers take an innovative and creative approach to new products and markets. The new fairy tale chocolate chip shortbread is a prime example. A splendid gold biscuit barrel, decorated with scenes from seven well-loved European fairy tales, it's packed with mini chocolate shortbreads lavished with dark and white chocolate chips. Packaging for luxury Scottish Biscuits has been given a smart new look. The range includes Sultana, a classic favourite with a crisp, light texture, two rich Chocolate Chunk varieties (with or without roasted hazelnuts), the zesty taste of Fruit & Lemon, the spicy exotic tang of Stem Ginger or the irresistible combination of Toffee & Pecan, which manages to be chewy and crunchy at the same time!

More than a century on, the company is still based in this Highland village and is still owned and managed by his three grandchildren, with a fourth generation of the Walker family now involved.

Almost 800 people are employed over the three factories in Aberlour and a fourth in Elgin and, for many of them, working with Walkers has become a family tradition, too.

All of the shortbreads and biscuits are made to the famous Walker recipe which has remained unchanged for the last 100 years. Only natural ingredients are used and none of the products contain additives, colourings or flavourings.

Each Walker product is certified kosher (OUD) and, because no animal

Walkers Shortbread
Aberlour, Speyside

Tel 01340 871 555
Fax 01340 871 355

E-mail:
enquiries@walkers-shortbread.co.uk
Web www.walkersshortbread.com

fats are used, they are suitable for vegetarians.

The company's first organic range was recently introduced, baked to the traditional recipe but using only organic flour, butter and sugar. This range also includes organic wheat'n'oat biscuits, an ideal accompaniment to cheese. Both products are certified by the Soil Association.

Walkers also produce a range of organic products for Duchy Originals. Duchy Originals was established by HRH The Prince of Wales to help foster sustainable farming methods, natural food products – and to raise funds for The Prince of Wales charitable foundation. The range is baked using organic wheat and oats harvested from the Prince's Highgrove estate.

The Walkers product portfolio also includes traditional biscuits, cakes, oatcakes and meringues, as well as shortbread.

Glenfiddich Cake is crammed with fruit, deliciously rich and moist, with a generous measure of malt whisky. It is produced in co-operation with the famous distillery, which lies near Walkers in the Spey Valley, an area known as Quality Corner because of the many family companies producing goods which have become world famous as outstanding examples of what Scotland has to offer.

Shortbread Dessert

INGREDIENTS

1 packet Walkers Shortbread, coarsely crumbled
200g (8oz) raspberries
200g (8oz) canned peach slices, finely chopped
5ml (1 teaspoon) sherry
1 x 450g Greek style yoghurt

METHOD

- Prepare this dessert about two hours before serving.

- Mix the prepared fruit with the sherry.

- In four sundae dishes, arrange in alternate layers with shortbread crumbs.

- Chill.

- Serve each with a generous topping of yoghurt and raspberries.

Serves four.

Farmers'
Markets

FARMERS' MARKETS have become a regular feature in towns and cities throughout Scotland since the first market was run in Perth in the late 1990s. Farmers' markets sell fresh, locally grown produce directly to the public in an informal, convenient location, which enhances the shopping experience for the consumer. The defining characteristics of all farmers' markets are:

- the products are produced within a defined local area
- the food producer runs the stall
- only products he or she produces are allowed to be sold.

Farmers' markets give consumers the opportunity to meet the producer, ask questions about the produce, and purchase fresh quality product at a competitive price. Customers can also be assured of the provenance of the produce as market rules lay down stringent standards, which must be met before a producer is allowed to sell at the market.

Producers also benefit from farmers' markets. They get the opportunity to receive full value for their product by selling directly to the consumer. Selling direct is concerned with shortening the food supply chain, cutting out the middleman and making more from the end price.

There are other direct routes to market for the producer such as farm gate sales, box schemes (usually organic), farm shops, mail order, telesales, E-commerce – but farmers' markets offer an immediate 'shop window' to a receptive audience keen to purchase locally produced quality food perceived to be natural and straight from the farm.

Most farmers' markets are held in town centre locations and whilst there was some initial concern amongst shop keepers, studies in several towns have shown that 'foot fall' and spending in the shops actually goes up on market days. Councils and town centre managers have not been slow in recognising this economic benefit and have been very supportive in the development of farmers' markets across Scotland.

Farmers' markets also hold wider economic and environmental benefits in terms of savings in 'food miles'. Some food sold in supermarkets

Lloyds TSB

can travel thousands of miles compared with food at farmers markets, which is generally produced within a thirty-mile radius of the market.

As farmers' markets expand and progress to become an integral part of food retail sector, they require direction, common high standards and a marketing strategy. To address these issues, the

Scottish Agricultural Organisation Society Ltd, a leading rural industry development organisation (full details available on **www.saos.co.uk**), has been instrumental in helping to establish the Scottish Association of Farmers' Markets (SAFM) in partnership with farmers' markets throughout Scotland.

SAFM – owned and managed by the member farmers' markets – has a number of key functions to perform including the promotion of the concept of farmers' markets in Scotland; providing advice in establishing new markets; developing existing markets; representing farmers' markets to Government and other agencies, and providing model rules and regulations on health and safety, environmental and other regulatory considerations.

Full details of the Scottish Association of Farmers' Markets and information on forthcoming markets throughout Scotland are available on **www.scottishfarmersmarkets.co.uk** or by phoning 01738 449430

WHERE FARMERS MARKETS ARE HELD ON A REGULAR BASIS

- **Aberdeen**
- **Angus**
- **Ardrishaig**
- **Ayr**
- **Banff**
- **Cambuslang**
- **Campbeltown**
- **Dalkeith**
- **Dornoch**
- **Dundee**
- **East Dunbartonshire**
- **Edinburgh**
- **Elgin**
- **Forfar**
- **Fort William**
- **Freeport**
- **Galashiels**
- **Glasgow**
  - Byres Road • Barras
  - Candleriggs • St Enoch Sq.
- **Haddington**
- **Hamilton**
- **Inverness**
- **Irvine**
- **Kelso**
- **Kilmarnock**
- **Kirkcaldy**
- **Largs**
- **Lochwinnoch**
- **Nairn**
- **Orkney**
- **Paisley**
- **Peebles**
- **Perth**
- **Rothesay**
- **Skye & Lochalsh**
- **Stirling**
- **Stornoway**
- **Tain**
- **Uist**
- **Benbecula**
- **Wick**

A true taste of

IF YOU'RE A LOVER of food looking for a true taste of Scotland, then our Food Festivals are the perfect way to sample the very best of local produce.

Both locals alike and visitors to Scotland have long recognised the quality of eating and drinking that Scotland offers, and the Food Festivals held throughout the country each year are a great opportunity to enjoy the best that each region has to offer. Stock up your larder with tasty produce as used by Taste of Scotland member establishments, and learn first hand what are the regional specialities of your chosen destination.

Each Food Festival also offers a great experience for all the family with lots to see and do. For example, while visiting the Talisker Skye and Lochalsh Food and Drink festival, why not take a tour of the Talisker Distillery and sample a wee dram? Perhaps you might choose to go whale watching after a walk to the northernmost point of Skye, taking a delicious picnic of local goodies to keep your energy levels up!

And, of course, you won't be short of places to dine on the finest food while in the area: use your Taste of Scotland Guide to ensure that you experience the best local eateries throughout your stay.

So, for added culinary delights, why

Virgin **trains**

not time your visit to coincide with a Food Festival near you? The pick of the crop are listed opposite:

To find out more about the dates and locations of these festivals and others, contact Taste of Scotland on 0131 220 1900 or visit our website at www.taste-of-scotland.com for more information.

Alternatively, you can contact VisitScotland on 0131 332 2433 or visit the website at www.visitscotland.com

SCOTLAND'S FOOD FESTIVALS

- Aberdeen Food and Drink Festival
- Arbroath Food Festival
- Ayrshire and Arran Food Festival
- Celtic Food and Drink Festival – Scottish Crannog Centre, Loch Tay, Perthshire
- Galloway Fine Food Event
- Taste of Grampian
- Highland Food & Drink Festival
- Johnshaven Fish Festival
- Festival of Food – Museum of Scottish Country Life, East Kilbride
- Tarbert Sea Food Festival – contact the Oban Sea Food Festival for details
- Oban Sea Food Festival
- Orkney Food Festival
- Perth Food Festival
- Taste of Moray
- Taste of Royal Deeside Food Week

Tower Restaurant

Edinburgh & Lothians

NOWHERE IS QUITE like Edinburgh, a cosmopolitan capital with world status. There's a sense of history and tradition, yet this is no backward-looking city. It's the home of the new Scottish Parliament and the setting for the world's largest arts celebration, the Edinburgh Festival.

Cafes, bars and restaurants reflect Edinburgh's unique ambience – from traditional pubs with Scots-brewed beer to upbeat contemporary eating places with international flavour. Traditional Scottish ceilidhs, frenetic night life, alternative clubs, plus an all year programme of popular theatre and concerts all add to the range of entertainments.

A short bus-ride to the city edge will let you escape into the breezy slopes of the Pentlands. To the west of the city, there is a choice of stately homes to visit, including Hopetoun House, House of the Binns and Dalmeny House, their sumptuous surroundings contrasting with the ruined splendour of Linlithgow Palace, birthplace of Mary, Queen of Scots. The Lothians surround the city as a relaxing and inviting alternative to bustle and city pace.

AULD REEKIE TOURS

Scotland's scariest tour company (as featured on television). Takes you on an underground journey into eerie caverns, working witches temples and a legendary haunted vault steeped in paranormal occurrences. All tours leave from the Tron Church on the Royal Mile.

Tel/Fax 0131 557 4700

Website www.auldreekietours.co.uk

auldreekietours@blueyonder.co.uk

BRODIE, MELROSE, DRYSDALE & CO.

Since 1867, we have brought the best coffees and teas from all around the world, back to Edinburgh to be expertly blended and roasted. Espresso, cappuccino – a coffee to suit every palette . . . and every tea we blend has a quality that is Tea Council Approved.

Brodies Melrose Drysdale & Co Ltd.

Tel 0131 554 6331

BURNSIDE FARMS

We specialise in supplying fresh poultry, free range and organic poultry, game and exotic products to hotels and restaurants. Game from our own and surrounding estates is processed on site, ensuring traceability. Imported poultry direct from farms in Normandy is also available. We bone, stuff and vacpac products on site, depending on customers' requirements.

Rutherford Lodge, Kelso TD5 8WW

Tel 01835 822418

CAKES FOR SPECIAL PEOPLE

A huge range of home-made cakes that really taste as you would want them to if you had made them yourself. Cakes, shortbread, tablet, flapjacks, preserves, all sold at Farmers Markets held in Kirkcaldy (last Saturday of each month) and Glasgow, off Byres Road (2nd & 4th Saturday of each month). Probably the best cake stall in Scotland. Wedding cakes also a speciality.

19 Clark Avenue, Edinburgh EH5 3AX Tel 0131 552 2079

CARBERRY CANDLE COTTAGE

Carberry Candles are made on site at our craft cottage where you can choose from a huge selection of perfumed candles. There is also a permanent Christmas Shoppe, a demonstration unit, a factory production video, a coffee shop and a bargain corner.

Musselburgh EH21 8PZ Tel 0131 665 5656

CARMICHAEL ESTATE FARM MEATS

If you value single Estate wine from French vineyards or coffee from a single Estate plantation in Brazil, you should taste the farmed venison, beef and lamb of Scotland's oldest family run single Estate business (est. 1292). Available at Carmichael Farm Shop, A73 Biggar-Lanark, farmers markets or on-line.

Tel 01899 308336

Website www.carmichael.co.uk/venison

EDINBURGH ZOO

Scotland's most popular wildlife attraction! Encounter over 1000 animals – furry, feathery and scaly – from all over the world. And enjoy a wide range of culinary experiences, from snacks to fine dining, under new management. Open every day from 9.00am.

Corstorphine Road, Edinburgh EH12 6TS
Tel 0131 334 9171 Website www.edinburghzoo.org.uk

GEOFFREY (TAILOR) HIGHLAND CRAFTS LTD

Probably the best Highland Outfitters in the world, Geoffrey (Tailor) Kiltmakers, a family run business in their 30th year in 2001, now incorporates the exclusive and exciting new range 21st Century Kilts. Offering the most comprehensive and widest choices available in the kilt world today. Open 7 days all year round.

57-59 High Street, Royal Mile, Edinburgh EH1 1SR
(next to John Knox House)
Telephone 0131 557 0256
Email enquiries@geoffreykilts.co.uk
Website www.geoffreykilts.co.uk
USA & Canada Toll Free 1 800 566 1467

EDINBURGH CASTLE

The best known and most visited of Historic Scotland's properties is Edinburgh Castle. An imposing landmark which has dominated Scotland's history and provided a stronghold and residence to many kings and queens of the past, it houses the Scottish Crown Jewels and the Stone of Destiny.

A MCLELLAND & SON LTD

Cheese is not produced in the Edinburgh area on a commercial scale but Scottish cheddars are available in all the major retail outlets. In addition, Ian Mellis, a specialist cheesemonger, has a shop in Edinburgh selling Scottish cheeses not normally sold in supermarkets.
Valvona and Crolla, a high-class delicatessen, sells cheeses from all over the world at their Elm Row shop.

New Cheese Market, Black Street, Townhead,
Glasgow G4 0EF Tel 0141 552 2962

MERCAT WALKING TOURS

Edinburgh's original ghost and history walks. Historically accurate, atmospheric and truly terrifying tours in the Old Town. Visit sinister, hidden Vaults and the legendary Mary King's Close – the underground street devastated by plague in 1645. Scotland's scariest ghost tours and premier history walks start at the Mercat Cross, Royal Mile.

Tel/Fax 0131 557 6464
Website www.MercatTours.com

THE ROYAL YACHT BRITANNIA

See what life was like for the Royal Family and crew on board *Britannia*. Take an audio tour of the most famous ship in the world and follow in the footsteps of the rich and famous.

Ocean Drive, Leith, Edinburgh EH6 6JJ
Tel 0131 555 5566
Website www.royalyachtbritannia.co.uk

SCOTTISH SEABIRD CENTRE

Discover the fascinating world of seabirds using remote controlled cameras at the Scottish Seabird Centre, North Berwick Harbour. See puffins and gannets and sometimes dolphins. And don't miss close-up live images of seal pups all winter. Observation deck with sweeping offshore views; visit our auditorium, shop and cafe. Fully licensed.

The Harbour, North Berwick EH39 4SS
Tel 01620 890202 Website www.seabird.org

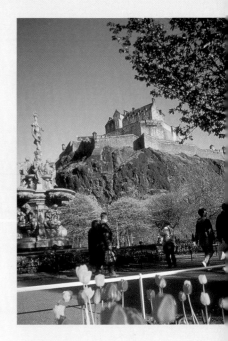

Establishments in this area

A Room In The Town	Edinburgh	Howies Restaurant	Edinburgh
Atrium	Edinburgh	Howies Stockbridge	Edinburgh
Balmoral Hotel	Edinburgh	Igg's Restaurant	Edinburgh
blue bar cafe	Edinburgh	Keepers Restaurant	Edinburgh
Bouzy Rouge	Edinburgh	La Garrigue	Edinburgh
Bruntsfield Hotel - The		Lafayette	Edinburgh
Potting Shed	Edinburgh	Le Café Saint-Honoré	Edinburgh
Caerketton Restaurant	Edinburgh	Livingston's Restaurant	Linlithgow
Outskirts		Marynka Restaurant	Linlithgow
Cafe Hub	Edinburgh	No 27 Charlotte Square	Edinburgh
Caledonian Hilton Hotel	Edinburgh	No 3 Royal Terrace	Edinburgh
Castle Venlaw Hotel	Peebles	Old Bakehouse	
Channings Restaurant	Edinburgh	Restaurant	West Linton
Cringletie House Hotel	Peebles	Open Arms Hotel	Dirleton
Dalhousie Castle and		Restaurant At The	
Spa	Edinburgh	Bonham	Edinburgh
Outskirts		Scotch Whisky Heritage	
Daniel's Bistro	Edinburgh	Centre	Edinburgh
Dubh Prais Restaurant	Edinburgh	Sheraton Grand Hotel	Edinburgh
Duck's at Le Marché		Skerries Seafood	
Noir	Edinburgh	Restaurant	Edinburgh
Grain Store Restaurant	Edinburgh	Stac Polly	Edinburgh
Greywalls	Gullane	Stockbridge Restaurant	Edinburgh
Haldanes Restaurant	Edinburgh	Sunflower Restaurant	Peebles
Henderson's Salad Table	Edinburgh	Tower Restaurant and	
Houstoun House Hotel	Edinburgh	Terrace	Edinburgh
Outskirts		Witchery by the Castle	Edinburgh
Howgate Restaurant	Edinburgh		
Outskirts			

Stonehaven Harbour

Grampian Highlands, Aberdeen & the North East Coast

RICH IN HISTORIC CASTLES, royal connections and whisky distilleries this unique corner of Scotland has hills tumbling down to a dramatic coast with its fishing villages and beaches. It has more than a hundred miles of unspoilt seacoast and more mountain tops over 4000 ft than anywhere else in Scotland. For those looking for a more action packed break, the north east offers everything from hillwalking to mountain biking and horse riding to mention a few.

Some say that because this corner of Scotland was bypassed by some of the main events in Scotland's stormy history, many of its castles survived. Whatever the truth, the many castles built to the west and north of Aberdeen – represent the finest of Scotland's castle building tradition and the very best of those lie on a signposted castle trail.

Speyside is home to more than half of Scotland's distilleries! A signposted trail takes you round distilleries open for visitors to take a tour (and, usually a sample dram).

ABERDEEN SCOTCH MEAT

One of the UK's leading suppliers to the catering industry. Aberdeen Scotch Meat, owned and managed by Mathers (Inverurie) Ltd Group, offer a complete range of Scotch beef, lamb, pork and poultry products. The company also procure and process wild Scottish game, including venison and various game birds.
Braikley Park, Tarves AB41 7NJ Tel 01651 852000

BALMORAL ESTATES

Balmoral Castle holds a unique place in history, many aspects of which – art, heraldry, fine arts, transport – feature in the exhibitions and displays in the Castle Ballroom and around the estate. Gardens, walks and pony trekking complement the attractions for a great day out.
The Estates Office, Balmoral Estates, Ballater, Aberdeenshire AB35 5TB
Tel 013397 42334 Fax 013397 42034
Email info@balmoralcastle.com
Website www.balmoralcastle.com

BENROMACH DISTILLERY

Benromach Distillery warmly welcomes visitors all year round. Located in Forres, this family-owned and managed distillery is now part of the Malt Whisky Trail. Tour the distillery – an STB FourStar Visitor Attraction – and enjoy an award-winning dram in The Malt Whisky Centre, once the old drier house.
Invererne Road, Forres, Moray IV36 3EB
Tel 01309 675968 Website www.benromach.com

BURNSIDE FARMS

We specialise in supplying fresh poultry, free range and organic poultry, game and exotic products to hotels and restaurants. Game from our own and surrounding estates is processed on site, ensuring traceability. Imported poultry direct from farms in Normandy is also available. We bone, stuff and vacpac products on site, depending on customers' requirements.
Rutherford Lodge, Kelso TD5 8WW
Tel 01835 822418

THE GLENLIVET DISTILLERY

In this enchanted Speyside glen, the raw elements of life itself are transformed into the pure golden essence of The Glenlivet, the very heart and soul of Scotland's finest whisky region. Distillery located on B9008, 10 miles north of Tomintoul.
Tel 01542 783220
Website www.theglenlivet.com

DALLAS DHU HISTORIC DISTILLERY

Just South of Forres, this charming distillery is preserved as a Victorian time capsule. No production is carried out on site but there is a small quantity of whisky maturing which keeps the taste alive. Part of the Malt Whisky Trail, visitors can follow the old–style processes from start to finish.

JOHNSTONS CASHMERE CENTRE

One of the most beautiful in the country and the only Scottish mill to transform cashmere from fibre to garment. Take a guided tour of the mill, view the audio-visual presentation and browse through the shop. To complete the experience, enjoy home bakes and refreshments in the relaxing atmosphere of our coffee shop. Open all year – free admission.

Newmill, Elgin, Moray
Tel 01343 554099

A MCLELLAND & SON LTD

Highland Fine Cheese in Tain produce Caboc, Galic and Crowdie from recipes dating back to the 16th Century. In 2000 they re-introduced a blue cows milk cheese, Strathdon Blue, and won Best Scottish Cheese at the British Cheese Awards in 2000. All cheeses are available through the supermarket chains and selected delicatessens. A. McLelland & Son Ltd assist in marketing their products.

New Cheese Market, Black Street, Townhead, Glasgow G4 0EF Tel 0141 552 2962

MORAY FIRTH WILDLIFE CENTRE

The mouth of the River Spey provides a rich feeding ground for dolphins, otters, osprey and other varied birdlife. Visitors to the Wildlife Centre can also experience a fine selection of food, where snack and light lunches are made using the finest local ingredients, many of which contain organic produce.

Spey Bay, Fochabers, Moray IV32 7PJ
Tel 01343 820339 E-mail enquiries@mfwc.co.uk
Website www.mfwc.co.uk

SUTHERLANDS OF PORTSOY

Gourmet's Choice Scottish Smoked Salmon – the finest quality fresh fish, selected from the pure waters off the islands of Scotland. A family run business, steeped in the tradition of fish smoking since the turn of the century.

Harbourhead, Shore Street, Portsoy, Banff AB45 2RX
Tel 01261 843255 Email sales@gourmetschoice.net
Website www.gourmetschoice.net

WATMOUGH'S

Holders of 2 Royal Warrants, Watmough's carry a complete range of sea fish and shellfish and many exotic species, such as Red Snapper, Mullet Tuna and Sea Bass. Traditionally cured specialities include kippers, Finnans, smoked mackerel, smoked haddocks and smoked salmon.

29 Thistle Street, Aberdeen
Tel 01224 640321 Fax 01224 315983

Establishments in this area

A Taste of Speyside Restaurant	Dufftown	Horsemill Restaurant	Banchory
Allan	Aberdeen	Lairhillock Inn & Crynoch	
Ardoe House Hotel	Aberdeen	Restaurant	Aberdeen
Atholl Hotel	Aberdeen	Macdonald Thainstone House	
Auld Kirk Hotel	Ballater	Hotel	Inverurie
Balgonie Country House Hotel	Ballater	Marcliffe at Pitfodels	Aberdeen
Banff Springs Hotel	Banff	Meldrum House Hotel	Oldmeldrum
Castle Hotel	Huntly	Minmore House	Glenlivet
Craigellachie Hotel	Craigellachie	Norwood Hall Hotel	Aberdeen
Craiglynn Hotel	Aberdeen	Old Monastery Restaurant	Buckie
Darroch Learg Hotel	Ballater	Old West Manse	Banchory
Deeside Hotel	Ballater	Raemoir House Hotel	Banchory
Fyvie Castle	Turriff	Simpson's Hotel Bar/Brasserie	Aberdeen
Glen Lui Hotel	Ballater	Station Restaurant	Ballater
Green Inn Restaurant	Ballater	Udny Arms Hotel	Newburgh
Haddo House	Ellon	Victoria Restaurant	Aberdeen

Glasgow & River Clyde

Greater Glasgow & the Clyde Valley

SCOTLAND'S LARGEST CITY, Glasgow has built a reputation over more than a decade as a place of renaissance and renewal. With its traditional heavy industries only recalled now in heritage centres, Glasgow has taken the down to earth friendliness of its own citizens as a foundation for a new culture.

One of Europe's great cultural destinations, Glasgow has over twenty museums and galleries housing magnificent collections of arts and artefacts.

Anyone who loves shopping will love Glasgow. The city has the largest retail centre in the UK outside London, with all the trading high street and designer names on offer.

Leaving behind the bustle of the city the Tourist Route winds through the Clyde Valley. With dramatic ruined castles, industrial heritage, country parks and historic towns and villages there are plenty of surprises to be found.

BRODIE, MELROSE, DRYSDALE & CO

Renowned for our expertise in Teas & Coffees, we also produce a luxury range of handmade chocolates. Using only the finest natural ingredients, we create chocolates with distinction. Made by a dedicated team of chocolatiers, our range has won 'Scottish Food Awards' for taste, quality and innovation.
Tel 0131 554 6331

THE BURRELL COLLECTION

Accumulated by wealthy Glasgow shipowner, Sir William Burrell, and gifted to the city in 1944, the Burrell Collection includes exceptional examples of medieval tapestries, stained glass, fine art and oriental artefacts.
Open Monday-Saturday 10am-5pm Sunday 11am-5pm.
2060 Pollokshaws Road, Glasgow G41 1AT
Tel 0141 287 2550

CAKES FOR SPECIAL PEOPLE

A huge range of home-made cakes that really taste as you would want them to if you had made them yourself. Cakes, shortbread, tablet, flapjacks, preserves, all sold at Farmers Markets held in Kircaldy (last Saturday of each month) and Glasgow, off Byres Road (2nd & 4th Saturday of each month). Probably the best cake stall in Scotland. Wedding cakes also a speciality.
19 Clark Avenue, Edinburgh EH5 3AX
Tel 0131 552 2079

CARMICHAEL ESTATE FARM MEATS

If you value single Estate wine from French vineyards or coffee from a single Estate plantation in Brazil, you should taste the farmed venison, beef and lamb of Scotland's oldest family run single Estate business (est. 1292). Available at Carmichael Farm Shop, A73 Biggar-Lanark, farmers markets or on-line.
Tel 01899 308336
Website www.carmichael.co.uk/venison

CHATELHERAULT

Hunting Lodge designed by William Adam set in a country park with ten miles of woodland and river walks. Other attractions – Visitor centre, café, shop, adventure playground, garden centre, Cadzow Castle, ancient oaks and white Cadzow cattle. Open daily, admission free, car and coach parking, disabled access.
Tel 01698 426213 Fax 01698 421532

GARDINERS OF SCOTLAND

A family company manufacturing high quality, hand-made confectionery ranging from speciality Malt Whisky fudges to assorted fudges in attractive tartan tins and cartons. Also a Millennium range featuring coffee, rum & raisin, chocolate, Malt Whisky vanilla and assorted fudges.
Turfholm, Lesmahagow ML11 0ED
Tel 01555 894155

BOTHWELL CASTLE

In a beautiful setting overlooking the River Clyde, this fine 13th century castle was much fought over during the wars of Independence. In the most famous siege in 1301, 7000 English troops were deployed against this mighty castle. Remarkably, part of the original keep survives.

LAGOON LEISURE CENTRE

The Lagoon is a modern facility with a free form leisure pool consisting of water features, flume and wave machine. Sauna, jacuzzi and steamroom facilities. Fitness Suite with state of the art equipment. Aerobics/dance studio. Olympic size ice rink. Excellent bar and catering facilities. Ample parking and disabled access.

Mill Street, Paisley
Tel 0141 889 4000 Fax 0141 848 0078

MACCALLUMS OF TROON

Dedicated to supplying the serious cook with the best fresh produce available, we source from all corners of the world. With Scotland having one of the finest natural larders to be found in the world, it makes our job a little easier!

944 Argyle Street, Glasgow G3 8YJ
Tel 0141 204 4456

A MCLELLAND & SON LTD

A. McLelland & Son Ltd., Scotland's largest and oldest cheese factor, have their administration and distribution departments based at The New Cheese Market in Glasgow. They have an output of approx. 20,000 cases per week creating an annual turnover of £100 million. Cheese is distributed from their modern premises to supermarkets throughout the British Isles and Northern Europe on a daily basis.

New Cheese Market, Black Street, Townhead,
Glasgow G4 0EF Tel 0141 552 2962

NATIONAL TRUST

Enjoy the variety of Glasgow's vibrant culture, from a typical tenement flat of 1892 to the stunning Edwardian interior of Pollok House in Pollok Country Park. A new exhibition at Hutchesons' Hall, in the city centre, celebrates the 'new' Glasgow style and examples by Alexander 'Greek' Thomson and Charles Rennie Mackintosh put it into context.

THE TALL SHIP AT GLASGOW HARBOUR

The Tall Ship at Glasgow Harbour is open all year and offers the chance to explore one of the last remaining Clydebuilt sailing ships, the s.v. Glenlee. Exhibitions, activities and events for children, a fully licensed riverside cafe bar and nautical souvenir shop are all on offer.

100 Stobcross Road, Glasgow G3 8QQ
Tel 0141 339 0631 Website www.thetallship.com

Establishments in this area

Artà	Glasgow	La Bonne Auberge	
Babbity Bowster	Glasgow	(Holiday Inn Hotel)	Glasgow
Beardmore Hotel		Lodge on Loch Lomond	
Outskirts		Hotel and Restaurant	Loch Lomond
Bouzy Rouge	Glasgow	Lux	Glasgow
Buttery	Glasgow	Makerston House	Paisley
Cameron House Hotel and		Nairns	Glasgow
Country Estate	Loch Lomond	Pollok House	Glasgow
Carlton George Hotel,		Puppet Theatre	Glasgow
Windows Restaurant	Glasgow	Restaurant Rococo	Glasgow
City Merchant Restaurant	Glasgow	Shieldhill Castle	Biggar
Coach House Coffee		Skirling House	Biggar
Shop	Loch Lomond	Stravaigin	Glasgow
Corinthian	Glasgow	Stravaigin 2	Glasgow
Gavins Mill Restaurant	Glasgow	Ubiquitous Chip	Glasgow
Outskirts		Uplawmoor Hotel &	
Gingerhill	Glasgow	Restaurant	Glasgow
Outskirts		Outskirts	
Hill House	Helensburgh	Westerwood Hotel,	
Hilton Glasgow		Golf & Country Club	Cumbernauld
(Camerons Restaurant)	Glasgow	YES Restaurant,	
Inn On The Green	Glasgow	Bar & Café	Glasgow
Kirkton House	Helensburgh		

Loch Bad a' Ghaill

Highlands & Skye

THIS IS ONE of the last wildernesses in Europe. No single image can capture the scale and diversity of these northlands. This is an area which appeals directly to the heart. However the Highlands & Skye are not just about landscape. There are interesting towns and villages to discover as well as great beaches, golf courses and numerous walking trails amongst lots of other things to see and do.

From the Highland capital of Inverness, roads run out like wheel-spokes to the western seaboard. Skye beckons with its saw-toothed Cuillin ridges, along with other points of scenic spectacle.

An almost indefinable but calm quality of light is a characteristic of northern excursions. The northlands are certainly peaceful and appeal to visitors who want to recharge. Yet no mater how remote, there are always places to stay and to find refreshments.

Some of Scotland's finest scenery can be seen without leaving the road but should you wish to get to grips with the wilderness then the options are endless. Though the Highlands offer all kinds of active pursuits, they can offer almost spiritual experience – or, at the very least a chance to pause, drink in the air heavy with the scent of heath, and re-charge. One thing is guaranteed: you will return home refreshed.

ATTADALE GARDENS

Old rhododendron and woodland garden with views of sea and Skye, surrounding one of the prettiest houses on the West Coast. Outstanding ponds and waterfall garden, planted with primula, iris, meconopsis and giant gunnera. Restored Victorian kitchen and herb garden. Sunken formal garden. PLANTS FOR SALE. Open April-October, 10am-5.30pm, Monday-Saturday.

Strathcarron, Wester Ross IV54 8YX
Tel 01520 722217 Fax 01520 722546
E-mail info@attadale.com Website www.attadale.com

BAXTERS OF SPEYSIDE

Set on the banks of the River Spey, Baxters Highland Village is one of Scotland's top tourist attractions, with over 200,000 visitors annually. Open throughout the year with ample free parking for cars & coaches. Browse the Old Shop Museum, visit our speciality retail shops or enjoy a meal or snack in our Restaurant.

Fochabers, Moray
Tel 01343 820393 Fax 01343 821696

BELLA JANE BOAT TRIPS

Taking you to Loch Coruisk and the seals in the heart of the Skye Cuillin mountains. Voted 'Most Enjoyable Visitor Attraction in Skye' and holds an STB 4–star grading. Telephone bookings essential between 7.30am–10.00am.

Elgol, Isle of Skye IV49 9BJ
Tel 0800 7313089 Website www.bellajane.co.uk

BEN NEVIS DISTILLERY

Why not come along to the Legend of the Dew Ben Nevis Visitor Centre and learn how we take pure mountain water from Britain's highest mountain and distill it along with only two other natural ingredients to produce our fine West Highland Malt Whisky and taste a sample of our blend.

Lochy Bridge, Fort William PH33 6TJ
Tel 01397 702476

BRIGHTWATER CENTRE

Set amid stunning scenery, this inspiring interpretative Centre vividly illustrates the cultural and natural history of the area. Exclusive boat trips operate to the island haven on Eilean Ban featuring a Stevenson Lighthouse, wildlife hide and Gavin Maxwell's Long Room.

The Pier, Kyleakin, Skye IV41 8PL
Tel 01599 530087 Website www.eileanban.com

DUNDONNEL SMOKED SALMON

Premier quality smoked Scottish salmon sent First Class mail (almost next day) throughout the UK, Small Packet/Airmail to Europe under 2 kilos, over 2 kilos via DHL. Our customers tell us 'it is the best!' and have been coming back for more – since 1983.

Sea View, Dundonnell IV23 2QZ
Tel 01854 633317
Website www.smokedsalmon.uk.com

HIGHLAND TRUFFLE CO.

In the historic town of Elgin – the Malt Whisky Capital of the World – is a small workshop where sumptuous chocolates, truffles and petit fours are made by a small team of talented young confectioners. Indulge yourself, or choose a stylish gift from our exclusive range. Order online at www.highlandtruffles.com
16 Pinefield Parade, Pinefield Industrial Estate, Elgin IV30 3AG
Tel 01343 552200

FORT GEORGE

Built following the Battle of Culloden, Fort George took 21 years to complete at a cost that today would be around £1 billion. It remains an active army barracks but has never seen a shot fired in anger. Reconstructed barrack rooms depict soldiers' lives in the 18th and 19th centuries.

THE HYDROPONICUM

Set amid spectacular scenery, guided tours of The Hydroponicum show a magnificent array of flowers, fruits, herbs and vegetables growing in different climatic zones without either soil or pesticides. Enjoy the relaxing atmosphere of the Lilypond Cafe and indulge in good home cooking, the freshest of salads and hydroponic produce.
Achiltibuie, Ullapool, Ross-shire IV26 2YB
Tel 01854 622202 Website www.thehydroponicum.com

MACBETHS BUTCHERS

To castles or cottages, hotels and restaurants or to you in your own home, Macbeth's will supply the finest beef born and reared on our own farms, as well as local pork, lamb, poultry, venison and game Wholesale and mail order price list available with overnight delivery throughout mainland UK.
11 Tolbooth Street, Forres, Moray IV36 2RW
Tel 01309 672254.
Website www.scottish-beef.com

TODS OF ORKNEY

Manufacturers of the Stockan & Gardens brand of oatcakes, shortbread and biscuits – once tasted, never forgotten! Our oatcakes come in a range of shapes and flavours and, along with shortbread, are available in new gift boxes. We also operate a mail order service.
18 Bridge Street, Kirkwall, Orkney KW15 1HR
Tel 01856 873165
Website www. stockan-and-gardens.co.uk

Establishments in this area

Albannach	Lochinver
Ardvasar Hotel	Isle of Skye
Atholl House Hotel	Isle of Skye
Baxters Highland Village	Fochabers
Bosville Hotel	Isle of Skye
Brodie Castle	Forres
Bunchrew House Hotel	Inverness
Cafe 1	Inverness
Cawdor Tavern	Nairn
Coul House Hotel	Strathpeffer
Creag Mor Hotel	Gairloch
Cuillin Hills Hotel	Isle of Skye
Culloden House Hotel	Inverness
Culloden Moor Visitor Centre Restaurant	Inverness
Duich House	Glenshiel
Dunain Park Hotel	Inverness
Dunorin House Hotel	Isle of Skye
Glendruidh House Hotel	Inverness
Glenmorangie - The Highland Home at Cadboll	Fearn by Tain
Golf View Hotel & Leisure Club	Nairn
Haven Hotel	Plockton
Hotel Eilean Iarmain	Isle of Skye
Inver Lodge Hotel	Lochinver
Inverewe Garden Restaurant	Poolewe
Kinkell House	Dingwall
Kinloch Lodge	Isle of Skye
Knockomie Hotel	Forres
Lodge at Daviot Mains	Daviot
Lovat Arms Hotel	Beauly
Made In Scotland	Beauly
Mallin House Hotel	Dornoch

Mansefield House Hotel	Elgin
Mansfield House Hotel	Tain
Morangie House Hotel	Tain
Myrtle Bank Hotel	Gairloch
Newton Hotel & Highland Conference Centre	Nairn
Old Mill Highland Lodge	Talladale
Old Smiddy Guest House	Laide
Ord House Hotel	Muir of Ord
Plockton Hotel	Plockton
Pool House	Poolewe
Ramnee Hotel	Forres
Ristorante La Riviera	Inverness
Rockvilla Hotel & Restaurant	Lochcarron
Rosedale Hotel	Isle of Skye
Roskhill House	Isle of Skye
Rowan Cottage	Isle of Skye
Royal Golf Hotel	Dornoch
Seafields Restaurant and Grill at The Taste of Moray	Inverness
Seafood Restaurant	Kyle of Lochalsh
Shore House	Kishorn
Skeabost House Hotel	Isle of Skye
Summer Isles Hotel	Achiltibuie
Sunny Brae Hotel	Nairn
Tanglewood House	Ullapool
Three Chimneys Restaurant And The House Over-By	Isle of Skye
Tigh An Eilean	Shieldaig
Tongue Hotel	Tongue
Viewfield House	Isle of Skye
Visitor Centre - Storehouse of Foulis	Evanton
Woodwards Restaurant	Inverness

Old Man of Hoy

Outer Islands

THE OUTER ISLES appeal to visitors looking for the experience of somewhere different and especially to those who love the sea. A white and dazzling beach all to yourself as far as the eye can see in possible in the Western Isles, or close encounters with seabird colonies are an everyday occurrence on Orkney and Shetland. All three island groupings are distinctive and different from each other.

The Western Isles lie at the very edge of Europe, where these peaceful islands have a natural, rugged beauty, with dazzling beaches, plentiful wildlife and a unique culture and tradition.

On the vivid green islands of Orkney, standing stones and ancient mounds are an everyday part of the landscape – ever present reminders of these ancient northlands. However, Orkney is not entirely rural. Kirkwall, its main town is busy with visitors and offers an excellent choice of local craftware.

Shetland is special. Over 100 islands and skerries make up the archipelago of Shetland. Only 15 of the islands are continuously inhabited and most have excellent sea and air services.

BAXTERS OF SPEYSIDE

After more than 130 years in business, Baxters of Speyside satisfy traditional and contemporary tastes with an extraordinary range of soups, jams and preserves. An unrivalled reputation for quality and flavour puts their products at the top of shopping lists around the world.

Fochabers, Moray
Tel 01343 820393 Fax 01343 821696

BELLA JANE BOAT TRIPS

Taking you to Loch Coruisk and the seals in the heart of the Skye Cuillin mountains. Voted 'Most Enjoyable Visitor Attraction in Skye' and holds an STB 4–star grading. Telephone bookings essential between 7.30am–10.00am.

Elgol, Isle of Skye IV49 9BJ
Tel 0800 7313089 Website www.bellajane.co.uk

SKARA BRAE

In 1850, a storm uncovered the ruins of the best preserved prehistoric village in Europe. Skara Brae dates from around 3000BC, inhabited before the Egyptian pyramids were built. The surviving houses are remarkably complete, containing stone furniture and hearths, presenting a remarkable picture of life in Neolithic times.

A MCLELLAND & SON LTD

The Orkney Cheese Company in Kirkwall (part of the McLelland portfolio) produce Orkney Island Cheddar, a regular winner at The Royal Highland Show. This medium, mature and vintage cheddar is available at all major retail outlets and direct to the public at the creamery. A new purpose-built Creamery will be opened early in 2002.

New Cheese Market, Black Street, Townhead, Glasgow G4 0EF Tel 0141 552 2962

ORKNEY CREAMERY

Deliciously creamy ice cream that tastes the way ice cream used to. Made with naturally good milk and cream produced from Orkney's fabled pastures. Orkney Ice Cream is available in a wide range of tempting flavours and pack sizes to suit any occasion. Winner of the Food from Scotland Excellence Award 2001.

Crantit Farm, St Ola, Orkney KW15 1RZ
Tel 01856 872542
Email graham@orkneyicecream.com
Website www.orkneyicecream.com

ORKNEY HERRING CO. LTD.

A delicious range of high quality sweet cured herring and salmon products. Available in retail and catering packs through wholesale distributors. Contact us for further information and recipe leaflets.

Garson Industrial Estate, Stromness, Orkney, KW16 3JU
Tel 01856 850514 Email sales@orkneyherring.com
Website www.orkneyherring.com

SALAR FLAKY
SMOKED SALMON

Award-winning Salar Flaky
Smoked Salmon is extremely
tasty and utterly delicious! It
is ready to serve, is perfect
with salad and it makes a
seriously good sandwich. It
can also be flaked and used in cooked dishes
– just add your own creative and imaginative
skills in its serving!

The Pier, Lochcarnan, Isle of South Uist, Outer
Hebrides HS8 5PD Tel 01870 610324 Fax 01870 610369
E-mail info @salar.co.uk Website www.salar.co.uk

TODS OF ORKNEY

Manufacturers of the Stockan
& Gardens brand of oatcakes,
shortbread and biscuits –
once tasted, never forgotten!
Our oatcakes come in a range
of shapes and flavours and,
along with shortbread, are available in new
gift boxes. We also operate a mail order
service.

18 Bridge Street, Kirkwall, Orkney KW15 1HR
Tel 01856 873165
Website www. stockan-and-gardens.co.uk

WILDABOUT (HISTORY)
ORKNEY TOURS

Wildabout History Tours will
take you on an imaginative
journey into over 5000 years
of the rich historic tapestry
that awaits you here in
Orkney. Walk through
Neolithic, Pictish, Viking and Scottish history,
taking time at each location. Wildabout is
Fun, Flexible and Educational. It's an
UNUSUAL TOUR!

5 Clouston Corner, Stenness, Orkney KW16 3LB
Tel 01856 851011 E-mail wildabout@orkney.com
Website www.orknet.co.uk/wildabout

Establishments in this area

Almara	Isles of Shetland	Monty's Bistro	Isles of Shetland
Borgie Lodge Hotel	Tongue	Orasay Inn	Isle of South Uist
Busta House Hotel	Isles of Shetland	Orkney Hotel	Isles of Orkney
Cleaton House Hotel	Isles of Orkney	Park Guest House &	
Creel Restaurant & Rooms	Isles of Orkney	Restaurant	Isle of Lewis
Forss Country House Hotel	Thurso	Portland Arms Hotel	Wick
Foveran Hotel &		Royal Marine Hotel	Brora
Restaurant	Isles of Orkney	Scarista House	Isle of Harris
Langass Lodge	Isle of North Uist	Stepping Stone Restaurant	Isle of Benbecula
Leachin House	Isle of Harris	Woodwick House	Isles of Orkney

Blair Castle

Perthshire, Angus & Dundee and the Kingdom of Fife

Delve into history, discover castles and glens, glorious gardens and quiet market towns.

ANGUS & DUNDEE – With scattered woods, neat farms and meandering back roads, the long vale known as Strathmore divides Angus, with the coastline of golf courses, fishing towns, red cliffs and golden beaches on the one hand, and the long line of the Highland edge, the hills of the Grampians, on the other. Dundee offers a journey of discovery, not just at the Dundee Science Centre and Dundee Contemporary Arts, but also literally at RRS Discovery with its tales of polar exploration. Great museum and art gallery as well.

KINGDOM OF FIFE – Defined by two Firths to north and south, Fife was an independent kingdom. This gentle, rural land has many attractive inland villages to explore. The coastal villages, whose story is bound up with the sea, are highly appealing. On the shoulder of north-east Fife lies St Andrews. Once the ecclesiastical capital of Scotland, it's now world renowned as the home of golf, and also has Scotland's oldest university – as well as excellent shopping!

PERTHSHIRE – In the heart of Scotland, you'll find a holiday that's as varied as the scenery. The old county of Perth has many faces – the upbeat, county town of Perth, the hinterland of prosperous farmlands, then the grand hills with plenty to enjoy for walker and botanist. A string of holiday towns mark the Highland edge – Aberfeldy, Dunkeld, Pitlochry.

BAXTERS OF SPEYSIDE

Set on the banks of the River Spey, Baxters Highland Village is one of Scotland's top tourist attractions, with over 200,000 visitors annually. Open throughout the year with ample free parking for cars & coaches. Browse the Old Shop Museum, visit our speciality retail shops or enjoy a meal or snack in our Restaurant.

Fochabers, Moray
Tel 01343 820393 Fax 01343 821696

BLAIR CASTLE

Set in spectacular Highland scenery, Blair Castle is the traditional home to the Earls and Dukes of Atholl. There can be few more comprehensive collections of arms, furniture, paintings and other memorabilia in Great Britain.

Blair Castle, by Pitlochry, Perthshire PH18 5TL
Tel 01796 481207 Website www.blair-castle.co.uk

DRUMMOND CASTLE GARDENS

A mile-long, beech-lined avenue leads to a formidable ridge-top tower house. Enter through the woven iron yett to the terraces and suddenly revealed is a magnificent Italianate parterre. These are Scotland's largest and most important formal gardens and amongst the finest in Europe. Open 1st May to 31st October, daily 2pm-6pm (last entry 5pm).

Tel 01764 681 257/433 Fax 01764 681 550
Email thegardens@drummondcastle.sol.co.uk

DRUMMOND TROUT FARM

Feed the fish, see the salmon ladder and our underwater camera. Enjoy the views, spy on the wildlife or catch your tea! Young or old, the choice is yours at Drummond Trout Farm and Fishery. 1 mile west of Comrie – just off the A85. See us at Farmers' Markets for the best of our produce.

Comrie, Perthshire PH6 2LD Tel 01764 670500
Website www.drummondtrout farm.co.uk

GARDINERS OF SCOTLAND

A family company manufacturing high quality, hand-made confectionery ranging from speciality Malt Whisky fudges to assorted fudges in attractive tartan tins and cartons. Also a Millennium range featuring coffee, rum & raisin, chocolate, Malt Whisky vanilla and assorted fudges.

Turfholm, Lesmahagow ML11 0ED
Tel 01555 894155

ST ANDREWS CASTLE

The castle of the Archbishops of St Andrews sits alongside what was once the largest cathedral in Scotland. Today, visitors can enter the mine and counter–mine built during the great siege of 1546–47 and look down into the bottle dungeon from which death was the only release.

MACKAYS

Award winning preserves and confectionery. Our preserves, marmalades and curds are all made in traditional open pans using 100% natural fruit. This combination creates that special home made flavour. Food From Scotland Excellence (Export) Award for our Luxury Preserves.

21 Thistle Street, Carnoustie, Angus DD7 7PR
Tel 01241 853109

A MCLELLAND & SON LTD

Howgate Dairy Foods Ltd, established in 1966 and now based at Kinfauns near Perth on a site with a history of cheesemaking going back 200 years, produce Scottish Brie, St Andrews and other similar cheeses. They currently hold a Royal Warrant of Appointment to HM Queen Elizabeth II.

New Cheese Market, Black Street, Townhead, Glasgow G4 0EF Tel 0141 552 2962

NATIONAL TRUST

A rich heritage reflects this area's important role in the country's past. Historic Killiecrankie was the scene of the first shots fired in the Jacobite cause and many of the buildings in the picturesque town of Dunkeld date from the Battle of Dunkeld in 1689. In Kirriemuir, visitors can even visit Never Never Land at the birthplace of Peter Pan author JM Barrie!

PERTH LEISURE POOL

One of Scotland's top visitor attractions, Perth Leisure Pool is a tropical wonderland "where summer never ends!" With 2 flumes, wild water, whirlpools and bubble beds, training and teaching pools, children's lagoon, kiddies interactive pool and even an outdoor pool, this is the perfect family destination. Open 7 days, 10am-10pm.

Tel 01738 492410 Website www.perthleisurepool.co.uk

Establishments in this area

11 Park Avenue	Carnoustie
63 Tay Street Restaurant	Perth
Allt-nan-Ros Hotel	Onich by Fort William
An Crann B&B and Restaurant	Fort William
Ardconnel House	G'town/Spey
Auchendean Lodge Hotel	Dulnain Bridge
Auchterarder House	Auchterarder
Balbirnie House Hotel	Glenrothes
Ballachulish House	Ballachulish
Ballathie House Hotel	Perth
Bank Restaurant	Crieff
Boat	Boat of Garten
Bunrannoch House	Kinloch Rannoch
Butterchurn	Kelty
Cargills Restaurant & Bistro	Blairgowrie
Carlin Maggie's	Kinross
Carnoustie Hotel, Golf Resort & Spa	Carnoustie
Corriegour Lodge Hotel	Spean Bridge
Corrour House Hotel	Aviemore
Crannog Seafood Restaurant	Fort William
Crieff Hydro	Crieff
Cross	Kingussie
Cuilcheanna House	Onich by Fort William
Culdearn House Hotel	G'town/Spey
Dalilea House	Ardnamurchan
Dalmunzie House Hotel	Glenshee
Davaar House Hotel and Restaurant	Dunfermline
Denfield House	Auchterarder
Donavourd House Hotel	Pitlochry
Dormy Clubhouse	Auchterarder
Doune	Knoydart
Drumnacree House Hotel and The Oven Bistro	Alyth
Dunnikier House Hotel	Kirkcaldy
Eagle View Guest House	Newtonmore
East Haugh Country House	

Hotel & Restaurant	Pitlochry	Murrayshall House Hotel	Perth
East Mains House & The		No 4 Cameron Square	Fort William
Music Room Restaurant	Auchterhouse	Old Armoury	Pitlochry
Exceed	Perth	Old Bridge Inn	Aviemore
Feorag House	Ardnamurchan	Old Course Hotel Golf	
Fernie Castle Hotel	Letham, nr Cupar	Resort & Spa	St Andrews
Fish Market	Mallaig	Old Forge	Knoydart
Four Seasons Bistro & Bar	Onich by Fort	Old Library Lodge &	
William		Restaurant	Arisaig
Four Seasons Hotel	St Fillans	Old Manor Hotel	St Andrews
Garvock House Hotel	Dunfermline	Outskirts	
Glen Loy Lodge Hotel	Banavie	Old Pines Restaurant	
Glenfinnan Monument	Glenfinnan	with Rooms	Spean Bridge
Glenturret Distillery	Crieff	Onich Hotel	Onich by Fort
Gordon's Restaurant		William	
with Rooms	Inverkeilor	Osprey Hotel	Kingussie
Green Park Hotel	Pitlochry	Ostlers Close Restaurant	Cupar
Grouse & Claret Restaurant	Kinross	Parklands Hotel	Perth
House of Bruar	Blair Atholl	Peat Inn	Peat Inn
Huntingtower Hotel	Perth	Pend	Dunkeld
Inn At Lathones	St Andrews	Perth Theatre Restaurant,	
Outskirts		Café & The Lang Bar	Perth
Kenmore Hotel	Kenmore	Perthshire Visitor Centre	Bankfoot
Kilcamb Lodge Hotel	Strontian	Pier House	Knoydart
Killiecrankie Hotel	Pitlochry	Pines	G'town/Spey
Kind Kyttock's	Falkland	Pitlochry Festival Theatre	
Kinloch House	Blairgowrie	Restaurant	Pitlochry
Knockendarroch House		Poplars	Pitlochry
Hotel	Pitlochry	Rosemount Golf Hotel Ltd	Blairgowrie
Let's Eat	Perth	Royal Dunkeld Hotel	Dunkeld
Let's Eat Again	Perth	Royal Hotel	Comrie
Lochside Lodge &		Rufflets Country House &	
Roundhouse Restaurant	Kirriemuir	Garden Restaurant	St Andrews
Lodge On The Loch Hotel	Onich by Fort	Sandford Country	
William		House Hotel	St Andrews
Loft Restaurant	Blair Atholl	Outskirts	
March House	Kincraig	Seafood Restaurant	St Monans
Moorings Hotel	Fort William	Strathardle Inn	Kirkmichael
Mountview Hotel	Nethy Bridge	Water's Edge	Ardnamurchan
Muckrach Lodge Hotel		Westlands of Pitlochry	Pitlochry
& Restaurant	G'town/Spey		

Isle of Arran

South of Scotland

are walks to suit all abilities. Eating out is a pleasure too with a choice of hotels, inns and restaurants to suit all tastes and pockets.

DUMFRIES & GALLOWAY – Rugged hills, craggy coastlines, dark forests, rivers and lochs, this is truly undiscovered Scotland. You'll be amazed by the vast open spaces and the variety of breathtaking views. Due to the warm Gulf Stream crossing the coast it provides an environment for plants which you might not expect to find in Scotland. With over 200 miles of coastline this region offers some of the best sea angling in Britain. With great walking, over 30 golf clubs, an excellent choice of cycle routes both on and off road, there's always lots to do.

AYRSHIRE & ARRAN – Ayrshire abounds with deep history and industrial heritage. The birthplace of Robert Burns, Scotland's most famous poet, Ayrshire boasts over 30 golf courses as well as a wide range of attractions and activities. Off this coast, the profile of Goat Fell marks the highest point of the island of Arran. For generations, this holiday isle has attracted walkers, climbers and outdoor lovers.

THE SCOTTISH BORDERS – A landscape of gently rolling hills, unspoilt moorland, river valleys and rugged coastline, the Scottish Borders will surprise you with its diversity and charm. A turbulent history has left a legacy of castles and abbeys just waiting to be explored, along with friendly towns and charming villages. Should you feel more energetic, there

AYRSHIRE FARMERS' MARKET CO-OPERATIVE

Markets in Ayr ,Irvine, Kilmarnock,Largs, Paisley held throughout most months on Saturday mornings come and enjoy fresh local seasonal food direct from the producers ....indeed fall in love with local food!

Howard Wilkinson, Market Organisor
Tel 01560 484861

BURNSIDE FARMS

We specialise in supplying fresh poultry, free range and organic poultry, game and exotic products to hotels and restaurants. Game from our own and surrounding estates is processed on site, ensuring traceability. Imported poultry direct from farms in Normandy is also available. We bone, stuff and vacpac products on site, depending on customers' requirements.

Rutherford Lodge, Kelso TD5 8WW
Tel 01835 822418

CARMICHAEL ESTATE FARM MEATS

If you value single Estate wine from French vineyards or coffee from a single Estate plantation in Brazil, you should taste the farmed venison, beef and lamb of Scotland's oldest family run single Estate business (est. 1292). Available at Carmichael Farm Shop, A73 Biggar-Lanark, farmers markets or on-line.

Tel 01899 308336
Website www.carmichael.co.uk/venison

CREAM OF GALLOWAY DAIRY CO.

We have over 30 delicious ice creams made only with ingredients you'd be proud to use in your own kitchen, including favourites Sticky Toffee, Caramel Shortbread and Malt Whisky. There are also 4 organic ice creams and 4 organic frozen yogurt flavours including Elderflower and Honey & Ginger.

Rainton, Castle Douglas DG7 2DR
Tel 01557 814040

DOON VALLEY HERITAGE CENTRE

Dunaskin is unique. Europe's best preserved Victorian Ironworks situated in the heart of beautiful Ayrshire countryside on the A713, Dunaskin is rated Four Star by the Scottish Tourist Board. Gift shop, restaurant, audio-visual presentations and guided tours.

Waterside, Patna, Ayrshire KA6 7JF
Tel 01292 531144 E-mail Dunaskin@btconnect.com
Website www.dunsakin.org.uk

GALLOWAY SMOKEHOUSE

Award-winning smoked foods using the best in raw materials, oak sawdust and a hint of syrup and dark rum. Fish, meat, cheese and shellfish all smoked on-site. Shop and mail order service.

Carsluith, Newton Stewart DG8 7DN
Tel 01671 820354 Fax 01671 820545
E-mail allan@gallowaysmokehouse.co.uk
Website www.gallowaysmokehouse.co.uk

MELROSE ABBEY

Once the richest abbey in Scotland, the ruins at Melrose retain a unique elegance with a fine collection of medieval carvings including gargoyles of demons, hobgoblins and even a pig playing the bagpipes. A medieval casket containing an embalmed heart – believed to be that of Robert the Bruce – is buried in the grounds.

A MCLELLAND & SON LTD

Although the Caledonian Cheese Company in Stranraer is the most modern cheese making plant in Europe, there has been a creamery on the site for over 100 years. They produce Scotland's best-selling cheddar cheeses (Galloway, McLelland Mature and Seriously Strong). All cheese produced is marketed by A. McLelland & Son Ltd., Glasgow, and packed by the Scottish Cheese Packing Centre in Mauchline, near Kilmarnock.
New Cheese Market, Black Street, Townhead, Glasgow G4 0EF Tel 0141 552 2962

MACALLUMS OF TROON

Dedicated to supplying the serious cook with the best fresh produce available, we source from all corners of the world. With Scotland having one of the finest natural larders to be found in the world, it makes our job a little easier!
944 Argyle Street, Glasgow G3 8YJ
Tel 0141 204 4456

Establishments in this area

Apple Lodge	Isle of Arran	Kinloch Hotel	Isle of Arran
Argentine House Hotel	Isle of Arran	Kirroughtree House	Newton Stewart
Auchrannie Country		Knockinaam Lodge	Portpatrick
House Hotel	Isle of Arran	Lodge at Carfraemill	Lauder
Balcary Bay Hotel	Auchencairn	Longacre Manor	Castle Douglas
Black Sheep Inn	Newton Stewart	Malin Court Hotel	Turnberry
Braidwoods	Dalry	Mansfield House Hotel	Hawick
Brodick Castle Restaurant	Isle of Arran	Montgreenan Mansion	
Burts Hotel	Melrose	House Hotel	Irvine
Cavens	Kirkbean	Moorings Hotel	Largs
Cellars Restaurant &		Nether Underwood	Symington
Cocktail Bar	Troon	Parkstone Hotel	Prestwick
Chirnside Hall Country		Philipburn House Hotel	Selkirk
House Hotel	Chirnside	Piersland House Hotel	Troon
Churches Hotel	Eyemouth	Pirates Cove Restaurant	
Clint Lodge	St Boswells	& Guest House	Isle of Arran
Corsemalzie House Hotel	Newton Stewart	Roxburghe Hotel, Golf Course	
Corsewall Lighthouse Hotel	Stranraer	and Fairways Brasserie	Kelso
Cosses Country House	Ballantrae	Scott's At The Crown	Lockerbie
Craigadam	Castle Douglas	Selkirk Arms Hotel	Kirkcudbright
Distillery Restaurant	Isle of Arran	Somerton House Hotel	Lockerbie
Dryburgh Abbey Hotel	Melrose	Threave Garden	Castle Douglas
Dryfesdale Hotel	Lockerbie	Trigony House Hotel	Thornhill
Ednam House Hotel	Kelso	Visitor Centre Restaurant,	
Enterkine House	Ayr	Culzean Castle & Country	
Fins Seafood Restaurant	Fairlie	Park	Ayr
Fouters Bistro	Ayr	Well View Hotel	Moffat
Horizon Hotel	Ayr	Westin Turnberry Resort	Turnberry
Ivy House	Ayr	Wheatsheaf Restaurant	
Jedforest Hotel	Jedburgh	with Rooms	Swinton
Kilmichael Country			
House Hotel	Isle of Arran		

Duart Castle

West Highlands & Islands, Loch Lomond, Stirling & Trossachs

FROM THE ROMANTIC highland landscapes of Argyll to the gentler hills of the lowland edge, there's plenty to attract visitors. The islands add a special dimension to any visit here. This beautiful area takes in Highland and Lowland, mainland and island, lochs both landlocked and salty. In fact it has just about everything!

With the high hills ranged along the northern horizon, the town of Stirling has for centuries been a gateway. In olden days the castle, dominating the Lowland edge from its high rock, was the guardian of routes to the north, as well as the chief residence of the Stewart monarchs of Scotland.

To the north, Crianlarich is ringed by mountains, enjoyed by walkers, climbers and wildlife enthusiasts. Westward lies one of the most scenic areas of Scotland, where long fjord-like sea-loch run far inland, and mild south-westerlies bring a sparkling greenness and vivid colouring to the landscapes.

Oban is the gateway to the islands with good ferry links. Discovering the West Coast islands and the Firth of Clyde by ferry is a pleasure.

ATTADALE GARDENS

Old rhododendron and woodland garden with views of sea and Skye, surrounding one of the prettiest houses on the West Coast. Outstanding ponds and waterfall garden, planted with primula, iris, meconopsis and giant gunnera. Restored Victorian kitchen and herb garden. Sunken formal garden. PLANTS FOR SALE. Open April-October, 10am-5.30pm, Monday-Saturday.

Strathcarron, Wester Ross IV54 8YX
Tel 01520 722217 Fax 01520 722546
E-mail info@attadale.com Website www.attadale.com

CALLANDER HOUSE

Experience the atmosphere of a Georgian working kitchen, sample a taste of the daily prepared dishes. The drawing room and morning room have been restored, providing a grand setting for conference and marriage ceremonies. Along with the tea shop at the stables, they offer a selection of food which reflects the culinary heritage of the great kitchen at Callander House.

Callander Park, Falkirk FK1 1YR Tel 01324 503787
Website www.falkirkmuseums.demon.co.uk

GREAT GLEN FINE FOODS

We have the largest selection of Scottish speciality foods in the world. Visit our Confectionery Factory Visitor Centre and see our confectionery being made. Free admission and free tasting of tablet! Adjacent to Ballachulish bridge on A82.

Old Ferry Road, North Ballachulish,
Fort William, Inverness–shire PH33 6RZ
Tel 01855 821277
Email greatglenfinefoods@talk21.com

STIRLING CASTLE

Possibly the grandest of all Scotland's castles, Stirling overlooks two of the most famous battlefields in Scottish history – Stirling Bridge and Bannockburn. Inside, its architecture is outstanding with the recently restored Great Hall of James IV, the Renaissance Palace of James V and the Chapel Royal of James VI.

INVERAWE SMOKEHOUSES

Continuing the traditional methods of smoking, so rarely found these days. Our delicious range of smoked fish, game. pates and meats is a must for all gourmets. Order direct from our mail order catalogue or our shop.

Taynuilt, Argyll PA35 1HU Tel 01866 822446
Email info@inverawe.co.uk
Website www.smokedsalmon.co.uk

A MCLELLAND & SON LTD

The cheese produced in Rothesay, Arran and Campbeltown Creameries are all part of the range offered by McLelland's Cheese Market in Glasgow. Each produces high quality cheese, available through the major supermarkets, by mail-order and direct from the Creamery shops. In Campbeltown there is also a specialist cheesemaker producing 'Gigha Fruits' (flavoured cheese, shaped as fruits and waxed).

New Cheese Market, Black Street, Townhead, Glasgow G4 0EF Tel 0141 552 2962

P & C MORRIS

The finest handcrafted terrines and stocks, all produced in-house by our team of dedicated chefs. A range of fine Scottish foods sourced from individual and small-scale producers, mixed with a selection of speciality fruit and vegetables.

M8 Foodpark, 1 Keppochill Place, Port Dundas, Glasgow Tel 0141 332 4474

NATIONAL TRUST

The stunning scenery and turbulent history of the Highlands and Islands is represented by The National Trust for Scotland through the properties in its care. Glorious gardens, historic houses, magnificent mountains, remote islands and the scene of the last major battle fought on mainland Britain reflect the cultural and natural heritage of the north of Scotland.

TASTE OF ARGYLL

Visit a traditional fishmonger and game dealer and see the range of fresh, locally caught fish and shellfish. Selection changes daily; smoked fish products, salmon, trout, kippers etc – all selected for their superb quality and value. Mail order available.

8 Stevenson Street, Oban PA34 5NA
Tel 01631 564787

Establishments in this area

Airds Hotel	Port Appin	Green Welly Stop	Tyndrum
Anchorage Restaurant	Tarbert, Argyll	Highland Cottage	Isle of Mull
Ardanaiseig Hotel	Kilchrenan	Holly Tree Hotel, Seafood	
Ardeonaig Hotel and		& Steak Restaurant	Glencoe
Restaurant	Killin	Killin Hotel	Killin
Ards House	Oban	Kilmeny Country Guest	
Ardsheal House	Kentallen	House	Isle of Islay
Balinakill Country House		La Bonne Auberge Brasserie	Falkirk
Hotel	Clachan	Lake Hotel	Port of Menteith
Bannockburn Heritage		Loch Fyne Oyster Bar	Cairndow
Centre	Stirling	Loch Melfort Hotel and	
Barcaldine House	Oban	Restaurant	Oban
Blarcreen Farm Guest		Lochnagar	Bridge of Weir
House	Oban	Macdonald Inchyra Hotel	Falkirk
Bowfield Hotel & Country		Makerston House	Paisley
Club	Howwood	Manor House	Oban
Bridge House Hotel	Ardrishaig	Monachyle Mhor	Balquhidder
Bridge of Orchy Hotel	Bridge of Orchy	Old Byre Heritage Centre	Isle of Mull
Cairnbaan Hotel	Cairnbaan	Olivia's Restaurant	Stirling
Calgary Hotel	Isle of Mull	Radisson SAS Airth	
Chatters Restaurant	Dunoon	Castle Hotel	Airth by Falkirk
Columba Hotel	Tarbert	Redcliffe House Hotel	Skelmorlie
Creagan House	Strathyre		by Largs
Creggans Inn	Strachur	Roineabhal Country House	
Crinan Hotel	Crinan	Bed and Breakfast	Kilchrenan
Croft Kitchen	Isle of Islay	Rokeby House	Dunblane
Cromlix House	Dunblane	Roman Camp Country	
Druimard Country House	Isle of Mull	House Hotel	Callander
Druimnacroish Hotel	Isle of Mull	Rosebank House	Strathyre
Dunvalanree	Carradale	Royal Hotel	Tighnabruaich
East Lochhead Country		Stonefield Castle Hotel	Tarbert, Argyll
House & Cottages	Glasgow	Taychreggan Hotel Ltd	Kilchrenan
Outskirts		Tayvallich Inn	Tayvallich
Enmore Hotel	Dunoon	Tiroran House	Isle of Mull
Fascadale House	Lochgilphead	Topps	Stirling Outskirts
Gathering Restaurant and		Tormaukin Hotel and	
O'Donnells Irish Bar	Oban	Restaurant	Glendevon
Gleddoch House Hotel &		Unicorn Inn	Kincardine-
Country Estate	Glasgow		on-Forth
Outskirts		Victoria Hotel	Tarbert
Glenmachrie Country		Waterfront Restaurant	Oban
Guest House	Isle of Islay	Western Isles Hotel	Isle of Mull
Glenskirlie House	Stirling Outskirts	Willowburn Hotel	Oban
Grange Manor Hotel	Grangemouth	Yacht Corryvreckan	Oban

Feedback

TASTE OF SCOTLAND FEEDBACK

As visitors to Taste of Scotland member establishments, your views are vital in our continuing quest to present the very best of Scottish cuisine and hospitality. Send your comments on meals in places listed in this Guide to:
Taste of Scotland, 33 Melville Street, Edinburgh EH3 7JF

Establishment visited ....

Date of visit ....   Meal taken ....

Comments ....

....

Name ....

Address ....

....

Tel No... Fax No ....

E-mail...

- -

Establishment visited ....

Date of visit ....   Meal taken ....

Comments ....

....

Name ....

Address ....

....

Tel No... Fax No ....

E-mail...

THE MACALLAN TASTE OF SCOTLAND AWARDS 2002

Send to: Taste of Scotland, 33 Melville Street, Edinburgh EH3 7JF

I nominate .... (Establishment)
for a Macallan Taste of Scotland Award

Date of visit ....   Meal taken ....

Comments ....

....

Name ....

Address ....

....

Tel No... Fax No ....

E-mail..

THE MACALLAN TASTE OF SCOTLAND AWARDS 2002

Send to: Taste of Scotland, 33 Melville Street, Edinburgh EH3 7JF

I nominate .... (Establishment)
for a Macallan Taste of Scotland Award

Date of visit ....   Meal taken ....

Comments ....

....

Name ....

Address ....

....

Tel No... Fax No ....

E-mail..

TASTE OF SCOTLAND FEEDBACK

As visitors to Taste of Scotland member establishments, your views are vital in our continuing quest to present the very best of Scottish cuisine and hospitality. Send your comments on meals in places listed in this Guide to:
Taste of Scotland, 33 Melville Street, Edinburgh EH3 7JF

Establishment visited ....

Date of visit ....   Meal taken ....

Comments ....

....

Name ....

Address ....

....

Tel No.. Fax No ....

E-mail..

Establishment visited ....

Date of visit ....   Meal taken ....

Comments ....

....

Name ....

Address ....

....

Tel No.. Fax No ....

E-mail..

THE MACALLAN TASTE OF SCOTLAND AWARDS 2002

Send to: Taste of Scotland, 33 Melville Street, Edinburgh EH3 7JF

I nominate .... (Establishment)
for a Macallan Taste of Scotland Award

Date of visit ....   Meal taken ....

Comments ....

....

Name ....

Address ....

....

Tel No... Fax No ....

E-mail..

THE MACALLAN TASTE OF SCOTLAND AWARDS 2002

Send to: Taste of Scotland, 33 Melville Street, Edinburgh EH3 7JF

I nominate .... (Establishment)
for a Macallan Taste of Scotland Award

Date of visit ....   Meal taken ....

Comments ....

....

Name ....

Address ....

....

Tel No... Fax No ....

E-mail..

Establishment Index

INDEX

** = New Member for 2002   NTS = National Trust for Scotland property

D

E

EYEWITNESS *TRAVEL GUIDES*

USER-FRIENDLY and sophisticated, DK's award-winning *Eyewitness Travel Guides* are bursting with stunning photographs, floor plans to key sights and cutaway illustrations. Detailed 3D street maps ensure that you find your way around with confidence. Practical sections give travellers inside information on local customs, transport, language, food, festivals, bars, hotels, museums, restaurants, galleries, and shopping.

Every Page is a New Adventure

EYEWITNESS *TRAVEL GUIDES*

Every Page is a New Adventure

Notes